THE
TWENTY-FIVE
YEAR CENTURY

*A South Vietnamese General
Remembers the Indochina War
to the Fall of Saigon*

Lam Quang Thi

University of North Texas Press
Denton, TX

10 9 8 7 6 5 4 3 2 1

Permissions:
University of North Texas Press
P.O. Box 311336
Denton, TX 76203-1336

The paper used in this book meets the minimum requirements of the American National Standard for Permanence of Paper for Printed Library Materials, z39.48.1984. Binding materials have been chosen for durability.

Library of Congress Cataloging-in-Publication Data
Lâm, Quang Thi, 1932–
    The twenty-five year century : a South Vietnamese general
    remembers the Indochina war to the fall of Saigon / Lam Quang Thi.
        p.   cm.
    Includes bibliographical references and index.
    ISBN 1-57441-143-8 (cloth : alk. paper)
        1. Lâm, Quang Thi, 1932– 2. Indochinese War, 1946–1954—
    Personal narratives, Vietnamese. 3. Vietnamese conflict, 1961–
    1975—Personal narratives, Vietnamese. 4. Generals—Vietnam
    (Republic)—Biography. I. Title: 25 year century. II. Title.

DS556.93.L36 A3 2002
959.704—dc21
                                                        2001052828

Design by Angela Schmitt
Cover photo courtesy of Lam Quang Thi

To my grandchildren: Amy, Eric and Brandon,
so they can understand their heritage.

To my wife whose support and encouragement
have made this endeavor possible.

To my comrades-in-arms and allied soldiers
who had fought and died for a just cause.

CONTENTS

Illustrations

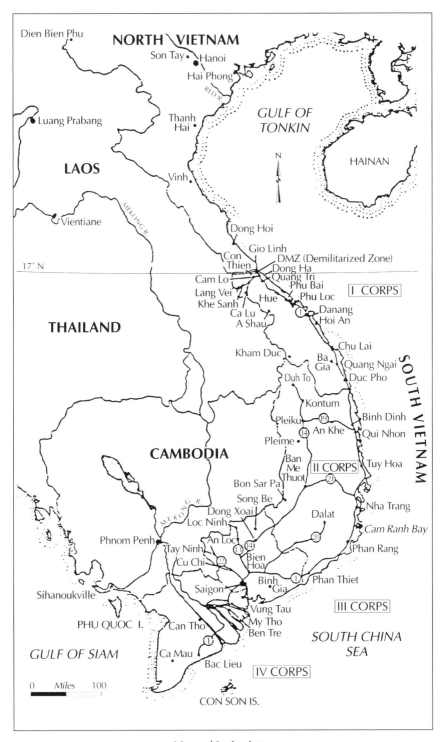

Map of Indochina

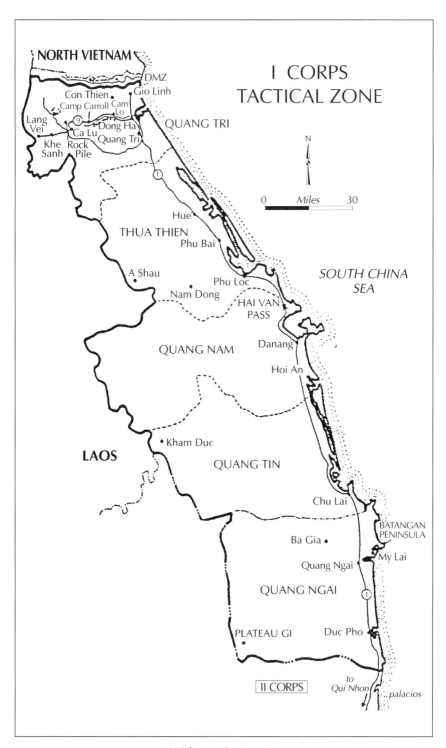

I CORPS
TACTICAL ZONE

NORTH VIETNAM

DMZ
Con Thien · Gio Linh
Camp Carroll Cam
Lo
Lang
Vei
9 Dong Ha QUANG TRI
Ca Lu Quang Tri
Khe Rock
Sanh Pile

N

0   Miles   30

Hue

THUA THIEN
Phu Bai

A Shau
Phu Loc   SOUTH CHINA
SEA
Nam Dong
HAI VAN
PASS

QUANG NAM   Danang

Hoi An

LAOS
· Kham Duc

QUANG TIN

Chu Lai

BATANGAN
PENINSULA
Ba Gia ·
My Lai
Quang Ngai

QUANG NGAI

PLATEAU GI   Duc Pho

to
II CORPS   Qui Nhon   palacios

Military Region I

II CORPS
TACTICAL ZONE

I CORPS

LAOS

Dak Sut

Tou Morong

to Quang Ngai

Dak To

DOXA

KONTUM

Ben Het

AN LAO VALLEY

Hoai Nhon

Kontum

BINH DINH

(14)

MANG YANG PASS

BINH KHE PASS

Pleiku

Edap Emang

An Khe

(19)

Duc Co

PLEIKU

LA DRANG VALLEY

Qui Nhon

Pleime

SOUTH CHINA SEA

CAMBODIA

CHU PONG MOUNTAIN

PHU BON

PHU YEN

Tuy Hoa

Ban Don

DARLAC

Ban Me Thuot

(21)

KHANH HOA

Bon Sar Pa

Nha Trang

QUANG DUC

TUYEN DUC

Dalat

NINH THUAN

Cam Ranh Bay

(14)

LAM DONG

(20)

Phan Rang

Di Linh

BINH THUAN

III CORPS

N

(1)

Phan Thiet

to Saigon

0   *Miles*   50

palacios

Military Region II

III CORPS
TACTICAL ZONE

to Ban Me Thuot

MILITARY
REGION
10

CAMBODIA

Bu Gia
Map

Dak Son

Loc Ninh

FISH
HOOK

BINH
LONG

Song Be

PHUOC LONG

II CORPS

An Loc

Dong Xoai

to Dalat

22 TAY NINH
WAR ZONE
C

MUI BA
DEN

WAR ZONE
D

LONG
KHANH

20

Tay
Ninh

13

BINH DUONG

BINH TUY

BOI LOI
WOODS Bon Suc

IRON
TRIANGLE

PARROT'S
BEAK

1

Cu Chi

HAU
NGHAI

HO BO
WOODS

Bien Hoa

Hoc
Mon

Xuan Loc

to
Phan Thiet

Long Binh

Gia Dinh

BIEN HOA

1

Saigon

15

Bear Cat

LONG AN

4

BIEN HOA

Binh Gia

IV CORPS

GIA DINH

PHUOC TUY

RUNG
SAT

to My Tho

Vung Tau

SOUTH
CHINA SEA

N

0   Miles   30

Military Region III

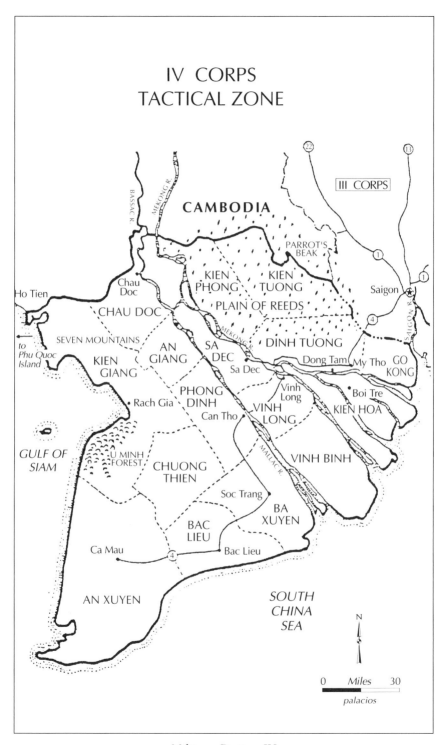

IV CORPS
TACTICAL ZONE

Military Region IV

INTRODUCTION

A FEW YEARS AGO, I was invited to deliver a speech about the former Army of the Republic of Viet Nam at a general convention of the Vietnamese communities overseas in Dallas, Texas. I began my address with a quotation from Victor Hugo:"*Ce siecle avait deux ans!*"(This century had two years!). For the French poet, a great admirer of Napoleon, the nineteenth century indeed could only be remembered by its first two years when two important treaties were signed: the Treaty of Luneville (1801) with Austria, which restored France's rights to its natural frontiers and the Treaty of Amiens (1802) with Great Britain which reestablished peace in Europe and confirmed France's supremacy on the European continent. "As for me," I went on, "if I could borrow from the great French poet, I would say that, for a great number of young men of my generation, this twentieth century had only twenty-five years. In fact, in a period of exactly one-quarter of a century, from 1950 to 1975, which covered our entire military careers, we participated in the birth of the Vietnamese National Army in 1950; we grew up and fought with this army that achieved some of the greatest military feats in contemporary history, during the Viet Cong Tet Offensive in 1968 and during North Vietnam's multi-division Great Offensive in 1972. Our careers abruptly ended with its tragic demise in 1975."

Thus, when my son, Andrew Lam, a journalist and writer, suggested I write my memoirs to describe my life as a soldier in the former Army of the Republic of Viet Nam (ARVN) during those turbulent years and also to give my account of both the Indochina and the Viet Nam Wars, *The Twenty-Five Year Century* appeared to be an appropriate title for my book.

I must admit that, at first, I was reluctant to write a book about myself because I agree with the French proverb that "*le moi est haissable*" (the "me" is detestable). This was why, when I wrote my first book, *Autopsy: The Death of South Viet Nam,* in 1985 to try to explain the main causes of the fall of South Viet Nam in 1975, I made a point of excluding personal details of my life. However, after taking a hard look at my son's suggestion, I changed my mind.

First, I recognized that since the fall of South Viet Nam, many books on Viet Nam had been written by American soldiers, journalists, historians, and public officials. Robert McNamara, secretary of defense under both Presidents Kennedy and Johnson, broke his long silence and wrote *In Retrospect: Tragedy and Lessons of Viet Nam* (1995) to admit his own errors during the war. The book was intended as *mea culpa* for his mistakes, which cost almost 60,000 American lives. It stirred a lot of controversy; it caused anger among Vietnamese communities as well as U.S.Viet veterans, but added nothing new to the already vast library of the Viet Nam War. I find it interesting that Mr. McNamara put his mistakes in writing. Written confessions can be, after all, a lucrative way of easing one's conscience.

Even the Vietnamese Communists had written quite a few books (which were eagerly translated into English) to brag about their military and political achievements after the war. Among them, North Viet Nam's Gen. Van Tien Dung's *The Great Spring Victory* (1975) had been widely circulated in the West and closely scrutinized by Pentagon officials. Not to be outdone, Truong Nhu Tang, a former cabinet minister in the Viet Cong's Provisional Revolutionary Government (PRG) wrote *Memoir of a Viet Cong* (1985) to tell the story of his life and his frustrations with the heavy-handed tactics of his comrades to the North.

On the other hand, I was sad to notice that only a handful of books had been written in English by journalists, public officials, and soldiers from the former Republic of Viet Nam. To my knowledge, only three former ARVN generals had published their memoirs in English, with the help of American ghostwriters, who may or may not have accurately reflected the authors' thoughts.

A second reason for me to write my memoir was that most of the books on Viet Nam were written right after the war when emotions were high and when only limited information and data had been collected. I thought that, after twenty-five years, emotions have somewhat subsided, and the dust, hopefully, has finally settled on the controversial Viet Nam War and that this necessary *recul historique* would allow me, an active participating actor in the drama, to think more clearly, to verify, analyze, and group events and to put them in a clear historical perspective.

More importantly, with the collapse of Communism in Europe, especially in the former Soviet Union, the economic and, to a lesser extent, political opening of China and the predicted demise of the remaining Marxist regimes in developing countries, including Viet Nam, one crucial question arose: "Did the Indochina and the Viet Nam Wars, which killed an estimated one and a half million soldiers on both sides and two million civilians, effectively contribute to the final collapse of international communism or were they, after all, mere, and very costly, exercises in futility?" "The fatal dilemma of the communist system," said Dr. Zbigniew Brzezinski in *The Grand Failure: The Birth and Death of Communism in the Twentieth Century* (New York: Scribner's,1989), "is that economic success can only be purchased at the cost of political stability, while political stability can only be sustained at the cost of economic failure" (102). If Marxist-Leninism is bound to crack under the pressures of its internal contradictions, then does it mean that the Indochina and Viet Nam Wars had no impact on the course of human history?

Rather than trying to provide an answer to the above questions, I believe a parallel could be drawn with the American Civil War. If we assume that democracy and human rights are the irreversible trends of history, then does it mean that the costly American Civil War to abolish slavery was an unnecessary undertaking? Whatever the answers to these questions, we can take solace in the belief that, as depicted in the Myth of Sisyphus, even in their most futile undertakings, human sufferings have their intrinsic grandeur and, from time to time in the course of human history, the citizens of certain nations, *les peuples martyrs*, have been called upon to bear the burden and to suffer for the advancement of the human race. My concern, however, is that in war, that moral grandeur could only be achieved at too high a price in terms of human lives.

It is this writer's conviction that the American Civil War accelerated the process of emancipation of oppressed people and that the Indochina and Viet Nam Wars bought time for the Free World to regroup, marshal its energy, and to finally win the Cold War. If this were not true, then these memoirs are a sad illustration of the extent of the devastation and human tragedy caused by two unnecessary wars.

1

EARLY YEARS

SOUTH VIET NAM HAD ALWAYS been the richest region of the country. Its delta, traversed by the Mekong River, which forks into the Mekong in the North and the Bassac in the South as it enters South Viet Nam from Cambodia, had always served as the nation's rice basket. South Viet Nam originally was part of the Khmer empire. The Vietnamese conquered it during their long and sometimes bloody southern expansion in which they annexed the Cham kingdom in Central Viet Nam and the lowlands of the Khmer empire in the South.

Bac Lieu, my natal province, was the richest province of South Viet Nam. Located at the southern tip of the Indochinese Peninsula, it consisted of vast stretches of fertile rice fields, which could be covered only, as the local saying goes, by "herons flying with extended wings" (*co bay thang canh*). These rich lands were owned by just a few people who made up the Southern elite. These wealthy landowners were often called the "playboys of Bac Lieu" (*cong-tu Bac Lieu*) because they indiscriminately spent their money to maintain a lavish lifestyle. As legend tells it, one day a Bac Lieu playboy burned a one hundred piasters (*dong*) bill to look for a one-*dong* theater ticket lost by his ladyfriend. (Recently, one female Vietnamese journalist, learning that I had come from Bac Lieu, wondered out loud how on earth a native of that notorious province could have risen to the rank of general in the army.)

Despite its wealth and the extravagant lifestyle of its playboys, Bac Lieu remained a backward place. Hence, this couplet of folk verse:

Bac Lieu is a backward country.
Its rivers swarm with chot fishes[1] and its banks with
   Chinese.

Bac Lieu, in fact, boasted one of the biggest Chinese conglomerations in Viet Nam. My maternal grandfather was of Chinese descent. In the early 1900s, he was the richest landowner in Bac Lieu. According to my mother, my grandfather escaped to Bac Lieu from Phnom Penh, Cambodia, where he had beaten up a royal prince during a brawl at a fashionable French *lycée,* which was attended by the princes and princesses of the royal family and by the children of wealthy residents. In Bac Lieu, he amassed a huge fortune in land deals and, along with a few influential members of the Southern elite, he was awarded French citizenship by the French colonial administration. As a result, my mother was a French citizen in her own right. I remember that every time there was a French presidential election, she would consult with us regarding the merits of each candidate and then she would make her own decision. General De Gaulle appeared to be her favorite politician at the time. However, I was not automatically awarded French citizenship since my father was not a French citizen. French laws did allow me to opt for French status when I reached the age of twenty-one, on condition that I would have to serve for two years in the French Army under the French mandatory military service system.

Just before World War I, my grandfather went to France to undergo treatment for diabetes, taking with him his two oldest sons. He later died during the war in Montpellier where he was later buried. My oldest uncle, true to the tradition of a *cong-tu* Bac Lieu, preferred the playboy's *dolce vita* to the strenuous life of a foreign student in Paris. He loved to frequent the dancing halls of Montparnasse rather than the classrooms of the Sorbonne and proved a disappointment to the family for having failed to pursue the academic goals set forth for him by my grandfather. When the war broke out, he was drafted into the French Army and took part in the battle for the defense of Verdun.

While my grandfather and his two oldest sons were in France, the family fortune was entrusted into the hands of his oldest daughter, whom we called *Di Hai* (or Maternal Aunt Number Two). In South Vietnam, for some superstitious reason or possibly out of modesty, the oldest child is automatically assigned the number two rank. Di Hai had a free rein in managing the family affairs since my grandmother was in poor health and my mother and her younger sister had both been sent off to study at a Catholic convent in Soc Trang, about thirty kilometers north of Bac Lieu. There was one problem: Di Hai loved to gamble, and in the course of her addictive gambling, she sold off most of the family's land holdings. By the time my uncles returned from France, the family retained ownership of only two strips of farm lands located along the muddy and tortuous Co Co (or Heron's Neck) River, near the My Thanh estuary which empties into the South China Sea.

After my grandmother's death, my mother was sent to Saigon to attend another Catholic school and it was during that time that she converted to Catholicism. She spent most of her weekends at the residence of her *marraine* (or godmother), Mrs. Nguyen Huu Hao, who was to become Emperor Bao Dai's mother-in-law.

At twenty, my mother married my father, who was the oldest son of a wealthy family in Vinh Trach Hamlet, located about five kilometers southeast of Bac Lieu. Although my father was not a Catholic, the church allowed the marriage because shortly before that the Vatican had approved the wedding of Princess Nam Phuong, the Catholic daughter of my mother's *marraine,* to Emperor Bao Dai, a Buddhist.

Like my two uncles and sons of well-to-do families in the South, my father was sent to study in France at an early age. He attended a lycée in Paris where he obtained a baccalaureate degree in philosophy. He then enrolled at the Faculty of Law in Bordeaux, but before completing requirements for his law degree, he decided to go back to Viet Nam to manage the family affairs. His father owned not only large acreages of farmland in Bac Lieu but also an important rubber plantation in Tay Ninh, near the Cambodian border.

My paternal grandfather was one of the founders of the Cao Dai religious sect, which worshipped, not only Jesus Christ and the Buddha, but also Confucius and, strangely enough, Victor Hugo. At that time, my grandfather, involved in an underground movement against colonial rule, was being pursued by the French authorities. To avoid arrest, he had fled to Thailand (known then as Siam). Later he died in exile and his body was secretly brought back to Viet Nam for burial. One day, Tho, my older brother, and I were escorted to Tay Ninh by our aunt (my father's younger sister) to attend his funeral.

From Saigon we took a bus to Tay Ninh where we arrived at nightfall. My aunt rented a small horse-drawn carriage which brought us from Tay Ninh to the rubber plantation where my grandfather was to be buried. We traveled at night to avoid the notice of French authorities. It was, for me, a very frightening experience since the carriage owner told us that we would have to follow a small village road infested with tigers. As I clung to the corner of the seat, listening to the singsong of the small bells that danced under the horse's neck and watching the dim light of the small petroleum lamp that swung under the roof eve of the carriage, I panicked at the thought of some tiger suddenly surging from a roadside bush. (Thirty years later, when Tho's infantry division operated in the Tay Ninh area, he and I, then both generals, revisited our grandfather's grave.) Right after his marriage, my father was appointed to the coveted position of Chief of the Agriculture Department of Bac Lieu. After Tho and I were born, the family moved to Saigon where my father worked for a French brewing company. According to my mother, Tho was a beautiful baby while I was rather dark-skinned and dull. That prompted my father to predict a good future for Tho and a more modest one for me. Tho would likely become a doctor or an engineer while I would make a good auto mechanic.

However, my parents' marriage, which had been arranged through a matchmaker, did not last: in 1937, after the birth of her fourth son, my mother, who was only twenty-seven, decided to leave my father. She brought the four of us back to the family's farmland in Tam Vu. The property was located on the right bank of the Co Co River within the limits of Soc Trang Province and was managed at the time by Uncle Number Nine.

Uncle Nine was unmarried. He had a giant shepherd dog named Caesar that followed him everywhere he went. An educated man (too young to accompany my grandfather to France, he instead attended Lycée Chasseloup Laubat in Saigon), Uncle Nine spent his spare time teaching us the rudiments of the complex structure of French grammar. He also introduced us to the joys of French history and civilization.

Every day, after breakfast, I would accompany him on his routine trips to the field, during which he discussed and solved all the problems related to rice-growing. He often carried a double-barrel shotgun which he used for hunting the *colliers bleus* or blue-collared wild ducks during the rainy season and sparrows or other small birds which fed on paddy at harvest time. Caesar would dash forward right after he heard the detonations and would bring back the dead birds, which I carried home. With the *colliers bleus* my mother would prepare a succulent *vit tiem* dish (steamed duck with spices and mushrooms). Sparrows and *becassins* (small marsh birds with long beaks) roasted with salted butter, were delicious and prized by my brothers and me.

My mother adapted remarkably well to her new life. Iron-willed, she would now devote the remainder of her days to raising her four sons. This was the reason she never remarried. According to a folk belief in Viet Nam, a family of four sons was blessed with *Tu Quy* or the Four Worthies, while a family of five sons was cursed with *Ngu Quy* or the Five Devils. I don't think that my mother subscribed to such theories: every time she was angry at us and punished us collectively for bad conduct, she used to call us the Four Devils. In retrospect, however, the concept of *Tu Quy* may have some merit after all: Tho and I turned out to be the only two brothers who rose to the rank of general in the modern history of South Vietnam.

In any event, my mother firmly believed that education was the key to success, and she worked hard to ensure that we all received an adequate education. This was relatively easy before World War II, when my mother was able to collect rent from our tenant- farmers in the form of rice that she and Uncle Nine would sell to the Chinese merchants who came to our property at harvest time to buy at cheap prices. They would store their rice at their huge warehouses in Cho Lon where they would resell later at much higher prices. Life proved rather easy for the four of us who spent our days racing on water buffaloes like the cowboys of Texas. We also enjoyed cockfighting, mostly during the Tet festivities which followed a good harvest. On these occasions, all our uncles and cousins would gather at our farm to pay respects to the ancestors. My mother would see to it that enough pigs were butchered and roasted, rice cakes in prodigious amounts were prepared, and that we were properly dressed for the festivities. The children received *li-xi* (or New Year's "lucky bills" inside small red envelopes) that we spent on firecrackers and fresh watermelons.

At the end of World War II, the French came back to Indochina to reestablish their control over their old colonies. After the war broke out between the Communist Viet Minh and the French Expeditionary Corps, most of the countryside became unsafe. My mother and the four of us left our Tam Vu farmhouse and moved to Bac Lieu with Uncle Four. Uncle Four had no children. According to my mother, right after he came back from World War I, Uncle Four was recommended for the position of treasurer in Bac Lieu; but he had no money to bribe the French province chief, so the job went to a Frenchman. Now, after World War II, he managed a rice alcohol distilling plant for an absentee owner who lived in Paris. As security deteriorated in the rural areas, my mother could no longer collect the rent from the farmers. She and one of her nieces decided to rent a kiosk in the Bac Lieu market to sell fabrics and other wares. In that period, she endured many hardships in order to achieve her goal of providing an adequate education for her children. In retrospect, my mother was, without question, the woman I admired most in my life. Recently, one of my cousins and a daughter of Aunt Di Hai, who lived in France and whom I had not seen for years, told me that she had always revered my mother almost as a saint. Compared to her mother who loved to gamble and who, in the process, sold off most of the family's land holdings, my mother, with her unswerving devotion to her religion and to her children, was obviously almost a saint. This was why, objectively, what my cousin said may have been an overstatement. But, somehow, at the bottom of my heart, I tended to agree.

After we completed our elementary education, Tho and I were sent to Can Tho, an important provincial capital about one hundred kilometers north of Bac Lieu, to pursue our secondary education. The education system imposed by France upon her colonies was very stringent and selective. Small provincial towns, such as Bac Lieu, had only five-year elementary schools. In order to go on to the secondary level, young Vietnamese who lived in the Mekong Delta had to compete in tough entrance examinations for admission to four-year secondary schools in either Can Tho or My Tho, the latter being located about thirty kilometers south of Saigon. I was admitted to Can Tho's College Phan Thanh Gian (named after a hero who committed suicide after he failed to defend the Citadel of Vinh Long against the French in the nineteenth century). Tho failed the entrance examination and had to attend a private secondary school, also in Can Tho.

Our Aunt Di Hai, who married a wealthy landowner in Can Tho and who lived in a comfortable villa on a large acreage planted with all kinds of fruit trees on the outskirts of the city, was kind enough to take us in during our first school year. For us, the *nha que* (peasants) from a small city with only two small elementary schools (one for boys and one for girls), College Phan Thanh Gian with its complex of well designed two-story brick buildings, including a dormitory for the *élèves internes*, and surrounded by a two-meter high brick wall, looked like a military fort or a citadel and was both impressive and intimidating. The headmaster of the school was Truong Vinh Khanh, a son of the illustrious scholar Petrus Truong Vinh Ky, a linguist credited with introducing the *quoc ngu* or romanized script into Vietnamese literature and journalism. Mr. Khanh had studied in France and earned both a French *license es lettres* (theoretically the equivalent of an American Bachelor of Arts degree in literature) and a law degree. All the professors were Vietnamese and quite a few had graduated from French universities. One of them, Nguyen Van Kiet, also a *licensie es lettres* from the Sorbonne, taught French literature for the senior class. He would later join the Viet Cong and become a minister of education in their Provisional Revolutionary Government. Most of the professors, however, had graduated from the *École Pedagogique* in Hanoi where they trained for two years after they had won their *Diplome d'Études Primaires Superieures* for the four-year secondary curriculum and passed the stringent entrance examination.

All the classes were taught in French, although every week we did have one hour of Vietnamese (called *Annamite* at that time). I had been an above average student in Bac Lieu but at College Phan Thanh Gian, I was unable to hold my own and during my freshman year, I ranked among the bottom third of my class.

Toward the end of our academic year, one extraordinary event was about to disrupt our lives and start a chain of events which would profoundly affect not only our future but the future of the nation. On the morning of March 9, 1945, when I arrived at school, I saw Japanese soldiers mounting guard at the gates. Afterwards, the headmaster told the students that, as a result of a *coup d'état* staged by the Japanese forces, the pro-Vichy regime of the French Administration in Indochina had been overthrown, that our campus had been seized by a Japanese unit, and that the school would be closed for the rest of the academic year. I later learned that French citizens had been arrested all over the country and sent to concentration camps. I also learned that the Japanese were in the process of forming a new government in Hue under Tran Trong Kim as prime minister. These events confused me greatly and gave me mixed feelings. Although I did not particularly like the Japanese and viewed their theme of "The Greater East Asia Co-prosperity Sphere" with skepticism, I did admire their military skills and discipline. I was also proud that an Asian country, which had soundly defeated the Imperial Russian Baltic Fleet in 1905 at the historic Battle of Tsushima, had again succeeded in overthrowing an important colonialist power like France. At any rate, Tho and I wasted no time packing and bidding farewell to our aunt and cousins. We took the first bus back to Bac Lieu.

During that time, I witnessed the first act of war near our farm in Tam Vu. One day, American fighter planes strafed a wedding procession on the Co Co River with machine guns. The American planes apparently mistook the boats—which were required to carry Japanese flags—as part of a Japanese river convoy. The bride and a few other people were killed instantly, and many guests were wounded. The wounded were brought to our farm for emergency care. This was my first taste of war and I did not know that I would to later witness more senseless slaughter in my adult life.

The Japanese occupation of Indochina was short-lived. On August 10, 1945, Japan surrendered after two atomic bombs were dropped on Hiroshima and Nagasaki. The Japanese defeat unleashed a chain of political events whose consequences for the future of our country were impossible to predict. On September 2, the Viet Minh took over and at once formed a coalition government in Hanoi. Emperor Bao Dai abdicated with a historic declaration: "I would rather be a citizen of a free country than the king of an oppressed one." The newly installed Viet Minh government had to cope with a pressing problem: the return of the French to Indochina. As a matter of fact, on September 11, 1945, nine days after the establishment of the Hanoi government, the French Expeditionary Corps landed in South Viet Nam with British forces under the command of General Gracey. (According to an international agreement signed by the victorious powers of World War II, the British received the mandate to disarm the Japanese south of the sixteenth parallel while Nationalist China assumed the same responsibility north of the sixteenth parallel.) The French quickly occupied Saigon and within six months controlled all the territories south of the sixteenth parallel. On January 1, 1946, the British effectively transferred their responsibilities to the French. Implementing their traditional strategy of "divide and conquer," the French created the autonomous "Republic of Cochinchina" on June 1, 1946.

On March 6, 1946, Gen. Jacques-Phillipe Leclerc (a French World War II hero whose armored columns were the first to liberate Paris) landed at Hai Phong with his Corps Expeditionnaire. On March 18, he moved his troops to Hanoi and met with little resistance. After a series of unsuccessful negotiations with Ho Chi Minh and his cabinet in Hanoi, Halong Bay, Dalat, and Fontainebleau, the French troops occupied Hai Phong on October 20. On December 12, 1946, the Viet Minh declared a general war against the French.

Even long before their war declaration, around the end of 1945, the Viet Minh had brutally cracked down on French sympathizers, calling them *Viet Gian* or "Vietnamese traitors." One of my father's cousins, who studied law in Hanoi, was arrested and executed by the Viet Minh during his trip back to Bac Lieu in early 1946 for having worn a pair of socks with blue, white, and red, the colors of the French flag.

I remember that, one day, Viet Minh officials from the local district, without warning, came and quickly surrounded Uncle Four's farmhouse. Then they proceeded to search every corner of the house for weapons: in colonial days French citizens were allowed to buy arms for their own protection. When the Viet Minh took over the government, they ordered that all weapons should be surrendered to the authorities. Uncle Four had surrendered his pistol and one shotgun, but he had completely forgotten about the second shotgun that was hidden behind a wood chest in the living room. Somehow, the Viet Minh failed to uncover the hidden shotgun during their search; otherwise, Uncle Four would have been executed for noncompliance with government orders.

That night, after the Viet Minh left, Uncle Nine and I wrapped the shotgun in an old piece of clothing, and under cover of darkness, we paddled a small sampan to the middle of the Co Co River and threw the shotgun into its raging waters. Nonetheless, the Viet Minh later threw both Uncle Four and Uncle Nine in jail for alleged pro-French sentiments: but for the intervention of Mr. Sau, a friend of the family who served as a Viet Minh battalion commander, they could have been executed by a popular tribunal. Mr. Sau had taught at the Bac Lieu elementary school and he was a reserve NCO in the French Army. Since the Viet Minh needed people with some military background, they gave him the command of a newly formed battalion, although he was not a member of the Communist Party.

During the months of turmoil and confusion following the French return to Indochina, my family and the families of our uncles were constantly on the move to avoid both the Viet Minh paramilitary units and the Cambodian bandits, who were armed by the French to fight against the Viet Minh. First, all of our uncles and their families rendezvoused at our Tam Vu farmhouse and one night, under cover of darkness, we sneaked out of our farm to escape our Cambodian tenant-farmers whom we believed were about to rise up and slaughter our families. Then, we marched across the rice fields in the thick of the night to a neighboring farm where we boarded three waiting barges. Tho and I took turns paddling the barge which transported and housed Uncle Four's family and our own.

As mentioned earlier, South Viet Nam used to be a part of the Khmer empire that was annexed to Viet Nam during its southward expansion. The Cambodians had never forgotten that fact and, although they normally lived peacefully amid the Vietnamese, they could become very brutal and even bloody when they were incited and urged to rise up against their historic enemy. Consequently, after they were armed by the French, they went on a rampage and massacred entire Vietnamese villages and raped Vietnamese women.

At last, after months of terror during which we constantly moved from village to village, mostly at night, we all returned safely to Bac Lieu as soon as the French regained firm control of all major urban areas. Shortly after that, College Phan Thanh Gian was reopened. However, since the old campus was now occupied by a unit of the French Corps Expeditionnaire, the College had to move to an adjoining elementary school campus which consisted of one nondescript two-story brick building with a large recreation yard. Since many former students failed to report after these turbulent months, the College agreed to admit new students through a more lenient entrance examination. As a result, my brother Tho and my two cousins (sons of Uncle Seven, the other son who went to France with my grandfather) were also admitted to College Phan Thanh Gian.

We all lived, again, with Aunt Di Hai during that school year in Can Tho. However, since we had left Can Tho in 1945, Aunt Di Hai had suffered a double tragedy in her family. Her oldest son, a master-sergeant in the French Army, was killed during a military operation in Bien Hoa, north of Saigon, and her husband was slain by the Viet Minh a few months later, when he went to Camau, about one hundred kilometers southwest of Bac Lieu, to collect rent from the farmers for one of his absentee landlord friends. During our third school year, Aunt Di Hai moved to Bac Lieu to live with her oldest daughter. As a result, Tho, Thoi (our younger brother who was a freshman) and I had to move to different *pensions* in the city that accommodated students from the provinces, and this created one more financial burden for our mother.

One unexpected result of these tragic events was that my academic performance took a turn for the better. Since some of the brightest former students had failed to report for the new academic year and since I had practically devoured French magazines and novels during the time the school was closed, my French had improved remarkably. Although I was not very good at math, I studied very hard and achieved top scores in French literature, history, and geography, and at the end of the second year, I ranked among the top ten of my class.

There were some noticeable changes in the teaching staff when the school reopened in 1946. Truong Vinh Khanh, who had been appointed Minister of Education in the new Government of Cochinchina established by the French, was replaced by Nguyen Van Cuong, also a *licencie es lettres* from the Sorbonne. A few former professors, killed by the Viet Minh, were replaced by new recruits who were not graduates of the École Pedagogique, but, instead, had a full baccalaureate degree. The short reign of terror under the Viet Minh had a visible effect on the campus and profoundly altered the professor-student relationship; it politicized the academic environment beyond recognition. Since most professors were trained by the French and tended to be more or less conservative, they regarded the younger generation with suspicion. Their own experiences with the Viet Minh the previous year compounded the problem. One of the professors, Nguyen Van Trong, who taught science, was a French citizen. He had been arrested by the Viet Minh local administrative committee that included some of his former students. Along with other *Viet Gian,* he had his hands tied behind his back. A long bamboo stalk was inserted between the hands and the back of the *Viet Gian*, who would then be thrown in groups into the river to drown. He was saved *in extremis* the night before the mass drowning by one of his former students. One day, I heard noisy cries in the hallway, then I saw Mr. Trong brandish a revolver and run after a student while yelling in French: "*Toi, sacre Viet Minh! Je vais te tuer!*" ("You dammed Viet Minh, I am going to kill you!") Later, I was told that Mr. Trong was angry because the student had failed to do his homework. So the teacher beat him up, called him a Viet Minh and chased him down the hallway with his revolver.

Toward the end of 1946, a new tragedy occurred in the family: Uncle Seven, who had been appointed Under-Secretary for Information in the Government of Cochinchina a few months earlier, was killed in an ambush near My Tho with Truong Vinh Khanh, minister of education and son of the famous scholar Truong Vinh Ky. By that time, the French controlled only the major urban centers, while most of the countryside was under the control of the Viet Minh. The main arteries which linked the provinces with Saigon were so unsafe that the French had to organize military convoys escorted by armored cars to move supplies and equipment from one city to another. Since there were no airlines to connect Saigon with the provinces, the only means of transportation was by road and the section of Route Nationale 4 (RN4) from My Tho to Soc Trang was considered the most dangerous in the whole Delta.

Consequently, Tho and I had to accompany French military convoys to return to Bac Lieu to spend our summer vacations in July every year. To do that, we had to submit our requests to the French military authorities in Can Tho and check with them every day because they would not disclose the time or date of departure until the last minute, afraid that any early disclosure would be leaked to the Viet Minh.These trips were fraught with danger because of possible ambushes by Viet Minh regular units.The irony was that the most famous, and most feared, Viet Minh commander at the time was a distant cousin of mine. His name was Lam Quang Phong and he commanded a Viet Minh regiment in the notorious U.Minh Forest in Rach Gia Province.

Sometimes, due to the lack of *convois routiers*, we had to follow the French *convois fluviaux* (or "river convoys") which escorted civilian commercial and passenger barges. These convoys had to make a detour through the South China Sea along the lower Bassac, and then follow the river linking the small town of Bay Sau in Soc Trang Province to the city of Bac Lieu. Because of this long detour it was not unusual to take three days for us to reach our final destination. Neither was it unusual to be awakened in the middle of the night by the fire fights between the Viet Minh dug in along the river banks and the French naval escort vessels.

In any event, after the death of Uncle Seven, his children were awarded scholarships to attend the French Lycées Chasseloup Laubat and Marie Curie in Saigon. The French government also gave Uncle Seven's wife a life pension in recognition of her husband being *"mort pour la France."* According to my mother, shortly after his return from France, Uncle Seven caused a sensation in Bac Lieu by beating up an arrogant Frenchman during an argument. Since Uncle Seven was also a French citizen, nothing happened to him. Under the French colonial administration, beating a Frenchman was unheard of and because he did it and got away with it, Uncle Seven became an instant hero. Since we all held him in great esteem, his death was a shock to all of us and caused profound sadness in the family.

During that time, politicians from the three regions of Viet Nam went to Hong Kong to meet with Emperor Bao Dai, who lived in exile there after he surrendered power to the Viet Minh, to invite him to go home and head a National Front against the Communists and to negotiate with the French for national independence. In May 1948, Gen. Nguyen Van Xuan, an officer in the French Army and a graduate of the elite École Polytechnique, formed the Provisional Central Government to replace the Government of Cochinchina. The new government pledged allegiance to Emperor Bao Dai.

I paid scant attention to these important political developments because I was focused on my academic pursuits. For the remaining years at the school, I continued to work hard and make progress in all disciplines; by the time I graduated in June 1949, I was awarded the *prix d'excellence* for scholastic achievement. The annual awards ceremony took place at the downtown theater in the presence of high French civilian and military officials. As the *prix d'excellence* was the highest price, it was donated by the highest military official in Can Tho. Tran Van Soai was his name. Soai, a man of limited education, commanded the paramilitary forces of the Hoa Hao religious sect. After he rallied to the French authorities, the French gave him the honorary rank of "one-star" general, although there was no such a rank in the French Army. (A French brigadier general wore two stars.) Possibly to compensate for his lack of formal education, he donated the prize of a sizable collection of leather-bound novels by Honoré de Balzac, Alphonse Daudet, and Gustave Flaubert, all famous nineteenth century French writers.

At the end of the school year, but before the final exam for the *diplome d'études superieures*, Tho and I went to Saigon to take the exam for its French equivalent, the *Brevet Elementaire*. Of the three hundred or so candidates, only thirty successfully passed and, fortunately, I was one of them.

I subsequently passed the *diplome d'études superieures* exam with *mention assez bien*. Armed with two precious and hard-won diplomas, I returned to Bac Lieu and started a tutoring class to teach French and math to the lower classes' students while waiting to pursue higher studies in Saigon. During that summer vacation, twice a month at my mother's request, I escorted the "pig convoys" from Bac Lieu to Saigon. My mission was to negotiate with the French soldiers, who manned numerous small outposts along RN4, for the speedy passage of our trucks loaded with live pigs. My mother, in partnership with some Chinese merchants, had purchased them in Bac Lieu to be resold to the Chinese slaughterhouses in Cho Lon at substantial profits.

In the meantime, Uncle Four wrote to his friend, Le Van Kim, headmaster at the Lycée Petrus Ky in Saigon, who agreed to admit Tho and myself to the freshman class at his institution. (Mr. Kim and my uncle had served in the same unit in the French Army Reserve.) Lycée Petrus Ky was named after the nineteenth century distinguished linguist and scholar Truong Vinh Ky.

In many developing countries, institutions of higher learning were mostly located only in major urban centers, beyond the reach of the peasantry. The situation was probably worse in Viet Nam where the education system was a replica of the French system, which was one of the most inflexible and selective in the world. In France where the majority of high positions in the government and private businesses were reserved for a small elite, possession of the famous *Baccalaureat* and graduation from the *Grandes Écoles* were a necessary condition for a successful career. In Viet Nam, a baccalaureate degree or *tu-tai* proved a sine qua non if one were to obtain a good position in the government or in the army. Vietnamese youngsters from the age of twelve had to go through four years of what was called Secondary Education, First Level. If they passed the tough final examination and obtained the *Diplome d'Etudes*

Superieures, they had to spend two more years to obtain the *tu-tai 1*, and one more year to for the *tu-tai 2*, majoring in liberal arts, experimental sciences, or mathematics. The last three years constituted the Secondary Education, Level Two. Lycée Petrus Ky was the only institution in South Viet Nam (beside the French Lycée Chasseloup attended by a few privileged Vietnamese boys) that provided Vietnamese youngsters the opportunity to obtain the full baccalaureate degree. Tho and I were fortunate enough to be admitted to that prestigious institution.

However, the political situation in Saigon in 1949 was very worrisome. Frequent antigovernment demonstrations and arrests created an environment of insecurity that hindered any serious academic pursuit. Tho and I participated in some of these demonstrations, which were instigated by the Viet Minh, because we believed them to be a truly patriotic movement. We even volunteered to post their leaflets on the city's walls at the risk of being caught and tortured by the French secret police.

Because many young Vietnamese mistook the Viet Minh for genuine nationalists whose only goal was to get rid of French colonialism, many followed them and joined the *maquis* to fight the French. The fascinating story of Lam Quang Phong, my distant cousin, was a case in point. Phong descended from a wealthy family of landowners in Rach Gia Province on the Gulf of Siam. His great-grandfather, Lam Quang Ky, had fought against the French under Nguyen Trung Truc, a national hero. Lam Quang Ky, arrested and executed by the French, was mourned as a martyr in Rach Gia where a street had been named after him.

After completing his French baccalaureate degree at Lycée Petrus Ky, Phong pursued advanced studies at Hanoi University. When the Viet Minh declared war against the French in 1945, he returned to the South and joined the *maquis*. His legendary exploits provoked much admiration among young Vietnamese. He successfully ambushed French military convoys and overran their outposts; he quickly rose to the rank of regiment commander. He was feared by the French, who had even put a price on his head. However, since he descended from a *bourgeois* family and refused to become a member of the Communist Party, and because his fame as a military commander was viewed as a threat to the party hierarchy, the Viet Minh decided to get rid of him.

As Phong later told me, one night he led one of his battalions in the attack of a French outpost on RN4 between Bac Lieu and Soc Trang. He succeeded in capturing the outer perimeters of the outpost, but the French offered strong resistance from the central tower, causing heavy casualties to his unit. He gave the order to withdraw to avoid pursuit and destruction by the French at daylight. On his way to his secret base, he fell into an ambush and was seriously wounded. He told me that he knew the ambush was the work of a Viet Minh special security unit, because only high-ranking Viet Minh military officials knew of his planned route of withdrawal. Back at the base, he formally requested to be allowed to go to Rach Gia to treat his wounds because the Viet Minh did not have antibiotics in the maquis. He also requested that his wife, who was gravely sick with untreated malaria, be permitted to accompany him. The Viet Minh agreed to this, hoping to use the French to get rid of him. According to Phong, the Viet Minh reasoned that the French would arrest and try him in a military tribunal and would send him to a firing squad. They did not want to execute Phong themselves because it would create dissension in his regiment where his men still remained loyal to him.

After he arrived at Rach Gia with his wife in a sampan, the police agent to whom he reported could not believe his eyes. Phong handed his pistol to him and asked that he be taken to the province chief who was a friend of the family. The province chief made the necessary arrangements for Phong and his wife to go to Saigon and report to an influential member of the Government of Cochinchina, who was also a relative of Phong's. After Phong was treated for his wounds, his relative made arrangements for him to see the commander of the French Forces in Cochinchina, Gen. De la Tour du Moulin.

When Phong in civilian clothes and wearing a pair of Viet Minh sandals, was ushered into General du Moulin's office, he saw the French general sitting behind a large desk and a French captain standing at his side, his hands hidden in his pockets. Phong knew that the captain was pointing a gun at him. Phong saluted the French general who remained imperturbable.The French general did not invite Phong to sit down. Following was the conversation as related by Phong:

"Are you Lam Quang Phong?" asked the general.

"Yes, I am Lam Quang Phong."

"I understand you hold a full French *baccalaureate* degree."

"Correct."

"I understand you are in the *rebellion.*"

"No, General, I am in the *resistance.*"

Visibly angry, the French general paused for a moment, then, knocking his desk with his pencil, said:

"All right, in the resistance. If you rally to the government, I will make you a major."

Seeing Phong's hesitation, the French general added:

"Major in the French Army."

After another pause to judge Phong's reaction, the general went on:

"I will send you to Saint-Cyr to attend an advanced course. After that, you will serve as a major in the French regular army."

Phong politely declined the offer. He said he preferred to go back to the *maquis* and fight in the resistance. He then saluted and requested permission to leave. The French general let Phong go, knowing full well that the Viet Minh would get rid of him when he returned.

As the French general had correctly predicted, Phong was tried for treason and sentenced to death by a Viet Minh popular tribunal. He was saved from execution by the mothers of the men in his regiment who staged a demonstration in front of the headquarters of the Administrative Committee of the Resistance. These women threatened to pull their sons out of the regiment if Phong were executed. Later, Phong was liberated by the French during an operation in the Viet Minh U Minh Forest secret base, that also served as a detention camp for French prisoners of war. One French lieutenant who was detained with Phong was also rescued during the operation. In 1954, after the Geneva agreements, Phong rallied to the Vietnamese National Army. He attended the United States Command and General Staff College and eventually rose to the rank of colonel in ARVN's Special Forces.

It should be noted that, not only a good segment of the student population harbored pro-Viet Minh and antigovernment sentiments, but also some officers who were trained by the French and who served in their auxiliary units, also joined the *maquis* or were sympathetic to the Viet Minh cause.

Tran Thien Khiem, who would later rise to full general and become a prime minister, was a case in point. After he graduated from the French "School of Inter-Arms for Far-East Asia," Khiem joined the Viet Minh. Distrusted by the latter, Khiem came back to the government side. In 1947, after Phong conducted a daring raid on the city of Bac Lieu that he occupied for one whole night (that was the first time a Viet Minh force had ever occupied a city since the French return to Indochina), Khiem, then an aspirant (a rank equivalent to warrant officer in the US Army) and a platoon leader in a *Garde Republicaine* company in Bac Lieu, was arrested and tortured by the French Director of Security for suspected connivance with the Viet Minh. He was released only on the personal intervention of Uncle Four, who was at the time a member of the *Conseil de Cochinchine*, a rubber-stamp organization appointed by the French to oversee the government.

Because many young Vietnamese believed the Viet Minh to be a genuine patriotic movement and volunteered to work for them, Lycée Petrus Ky became a hotbed of antigovernment and even terrorist activities. One day, in 1949, six strangers came to the school and summarily executed one student for alleged spying activities for the government. On September 1, 1949, Tran Van On, a student in my class, was killed by the police during a demonstration near the Gia Long Palace, which served as the residence of the Prime Minister. More demonstrations followed On's funeral and the students finally walked out of classes and demanded the unconditional release of the students who had been arrested by the police. Tho and I once again headed back to Bac Lieu to an uncertain future.

In Bac Lieu, I continued my tutoring class and helped my mother with the pig business. I also decided to prepare the *tu-tai 1* on my own by devouring all the textbooks dealing with the curriculum of the first two years of the Secondary Education, Level Two. In June 1949, I passed the *tu-tai 1* with a *mention passable*. My mother was elated. Overnight, I became a celebrity in Bac Lieu. One wealthy family offered to send me to France for further schooling on the condition that I would marry their daughter. I politely declined to my mother's chagrin. Uncle Four, who had no children, also offered to finance my studies in France, but I again declined because I knew he was not rich and I did not want to become a further burden to someone who had already helped us so generously during these difficult times.

In the meantime, a treaty was signed on March 8, 1949, between French President Vincent Auriol and Emperor Bao Dai recognizing "an independent and united Viet Nam" within the framework of the French Union. Bao Dai returned to Viet Nam on April 28, 1949, and on July 2, he formed a new cabinet in which he was both Head of State and Prime Minister. The treaty also provided for the creation of a national army, which would incorporate all paramilitary units and armed religious factions in existence at the time.

After the French pacified most of the territories south of the sixteenth parallel, they established in June 1946 a puppet government which was called the autonomous *Republique de Cochinchine*. To accelerate their pacification program and release French units from their static defense responsibilities, the French also created company-size units called *Les Gardes Republicaines* and other local auxiliary forces. In January and March 1947, some armed units of the Cao Dai and Hoa Hao religious sects rallied to the French and were integrated into the *Gardes Republicaines*, but in practice they remained quasi-independent and retained full control of the specific territories that the French assigned to them. In Ben Tre Province, the French armed various Catholic groups and organized these into commando units called *Unites Mobiles pour la Defense de la Chretiente* (or U.M.D.C.). These units were under the command of a controversial figure, Colonel Le Roy, a French officer whose father was a former soldier of the French Corps Expeditionnaire and whose mother was a Vietnamese woman from Go Cong Province. Colonel Le Roy was also appointed province chief of Ben Tre. Resorting often to assassination and bloody reprisals, he was temporarily able to pacify the Viet Minh-infested Ben Tre Province. In the meantime, the Binh-Xuyen forces which used to be an armed gang under Le Van Vien, rallied to the government and were put in control of the cities of Saigon and Cho Lon where it operated the lucrative prostitution and gambling business, reportedly with the tacit agreement of Emperor Bao Dai himself.

In Central Viet Nam, the first paramilitary units were created in Hue. These units were called *Viet Binh Doan* and were under the control of the Council of the Regency of Central Viet Nam.

In North Viet Nam, after the French had pacified most of the provinces in the Red River Delta, a Vietnamese administration was established, first under a Council of Security, then under the Governor of North Viet Nam; in July 1948, a Regional Force was created under the name of *Bao Chinh Doan*.

In theory, the above disparate paramilitary forces and armed religious sects would be integrated into the newly created National Army; however, in reality, these forces remained under the tactical control of the French military authorities. It was not until the establishment of the First Republic under President Ngo Dinh Diem that Viet Nam was able to integrate these different factions into a truly coherent and disciplined army.

To train the cadres for the new army, a military school named *l'École Inter-Armes* was created in Dalat in 1950. Tho and I wanted to enroll at the school for many reasons. The new school was created to train career officers for the national army of a newly independent country, so Tho and I were excited at the prospect of being able to command a unit of a truly national and unified army.

By that time, we also realized that Ho Chi Minh was not a true nationalist but was a loyal member of the international Communist movement directed by Moscow and that the Viet Minh, with its terror tactics, its popular tribunals, and summary executions, was not a viable alternative to the French colonial administration or its puppet *Gouvernement de Cochinchine*. Tho and I predicted that the French government, which started to receive increasingly important American military aid for its troops in Indochina, would be forced to bend to American pressure to grant full independence to the three states of Indochina and to speed up the creation of their national armies. In fact, at a graduation ceremony at Lycée

Chasseloup Laubat, Gen. Jean de Lattre de Tassigny, French high commissioner and commander in chief of French forces in Indochina, openly called for the active participation of young Vietnamese in the war efforts, without which, in his opinion, the war could not be won. De Lattre expressed his confidence in the ability and willingness of Vietnamese youth to defend their country in these inspiring words: "Be men. This means that if you are communists, join the Viet Minh. There, there are people who fought well for a bad cause. But if you are patriots, fight for your country, because this war is yours. . . . In the dawn of independence, we need more sweat and blood to raise a crop of free men. I believe that Viet Nam will be saved by you. . .!" Commenting on de Lattre's electrifying speech, Saigon newspapers predicted that mandatory military service was only a question of time. That was another reason for us to enroll at *l'École Inter-Armes* without further delay.

For me, de Lattre's speech made sense. So far, young Vietnamese had remained passive and even hostile to the war, because they considered it merely a French effort to reestablish its hegemony over the states of Indochina. Now, however, France had taken steps to give independence to its former colonies. In the face of the Viet Minh's recent successes in North Viet Nam and the danger of collapse of the Red River Delta, young Vietnamese could no longer stay on the sidelines. If they supported the Viet Minh, they should join their ranks and, like them, try to "fight well for a bad cause." On the other hand, if they were against the Communists, they should serve in the new National Army and fight to defend their country. There were no other alternatives.

It should be noted that Viet Nam was not the only Asian country at war. Since the end of World War II, it seemed that there was no end to military conflicts in Asia triggered by Communist expansionism. Young men were fighting and dying on both sides of the ideological divide in Malaysia and the Philippines. After the debacle of the Chinese Nationalist Army, which opened the China-Viet Nam border to the flow of supply of equipment and ammunition to the Viet Minh, there were now indications that the North Korean Army, supported and supplied by the Soviet Union and China, may have been preparing to invade the South. In the midst of this echo of war which reverberated throughout Asia, I saw no alternative to a military career, despite the fact that, since I was a child, I had hoped to attend a law school in France and become a lawyer.

On the other hand, we were fully aware that, in an underdeveloped country such as Viet Nam, which was facing an internal communist insurrection, the Army would play a crucial role in the affairs of the country and would open many opportunities for hard-working, ambitious young men. Further, Lycée Petrus Ky was still closed due to the boycott of protesting students. Also in the same year, our two younger brothers, Thoi and Than, were attending College Phan Thanh Gian in Can Tho and we did not wish to be a burden for our mother anymore. For Tho and me, the Army was our hope and it appeared to be the way of our future.

2

MILITARY APPRENTICESHIP

CANDIDATES TO THE FIRST CLASS of the School of Inter-Arms were required to have an equivalent of a secondary education, Level One. Tho and I were qualified to take the entrance examination, which was administered in Saigon and which we passed without difficulty. We also passed the physical examination and toward the end of June 1950, we were ordered to accompany a French military convoy to Dalat. This was the first time I had been out of the lowlands of the Western Region of South Viet Nam. I was struck by the diversity of the landscape of our country as our convoy, after leaving the lush, green rice paddy fields of Bien Hoa, passed the huge French-owned rubber and tea plantations and slowly threaded its way between dense tropical forests and gently rolling hills. Occasionally, we could see small Montagnards villages with thatch-roofed houses built on wooden stilts.

I was amazed at the majesty of the chain of small mountains which formed what was called the *Hauts Plateaux* of Viet Nam. We saw these as our convoy passed the Lien Khang waterfalls and started to climb the steep and winding Prenn Pass, which led to the beautiful city of Dalat. Once we emerged from the pass to approach the southern suburb of the city, we felt invigorated by the pine-scented air of the Hauts Plateaux. From a distance, Dalat looked like a postcard of a French small mountain town with red-roofed gothic churches, stone-walled villas hidden behind tall pine trees, green valleys and romantic lakes.

Further west, overlooking the city was the 2,167-meter-high, twin-peaked mountain of Lang-Bian. According to Montagnard mythology, in the La Ngu Thuong area where Mount Lang-Bian was located, lived two powerful tribes: Lat and Sre. The Lat tribe had a young chief named Lang. Lang fell in love with Bian, a daughter of the Sre tribe, but was prevented from marrying her because of the hostility between the two tribes. One day, Lang and Bian decided to climb to the top of the mountain and to sit there until they died. After their deaths, the members of both tribes decided to bury the two lovers at the site. To show their affection, the tribesmen brought stones to improve their tombs, which kept growing each passing day until they became the two peaks of Mount Lang-Bian.

In 1916, the first hotel in Dalat was constructed near the central lake and was appropriately named Lang-Bian Palace Hotel. It was a wood structure built on piers with large verandas to conform to the local Montagnard style. When Dalat entered a new phase of development in 1922, the French architects who designed the expansion plan, in an effort to preserve the natural beauty of the city, ruled that no buildings could be constructed which would block the view of Mount Lang-Bian.

Due to its breathtaking beauty and moderate climate, its variety of exotic flowers, an abundance of vegetables and fruits normally found only in European countries, Dalat quickly became an ideal resort city for the French and also for wealthy Vietnamese. If Saigon was called "the jewel of Asia," Dalat, in the words of a French architect who participated in the original design of the city, was described as "a corner of France on the Asian Alps."

Dalat was also an important cultural center. In addition to the Lycée Yersin built in 1935, the Catholic order of Notre Dame created a lycée for girls, which it named *Notre Dame de Lang-Bian*. Later, the school changed its name to "*Couvent des Oiseaux*"; it was a prestigious school reserved for girls from wealthy French and Vietnamese families. These two schools also received students from Cambodia and Laos.

The School of Inter-Arms was located on a small hill approximately five kilometers north of the city center, near the village of Chi Lang. It was bordered to the east by the Farraut Farm (the farm was owned by a Frenchman, Mr. Farraut, one of the first residents of Dalat) and a small lake with the romantic name of *Lac des Soupirs* (Lake of Laments). Immediately to the south was *Hôpital Catroux* (named after a French governor), a military hospital which tended mostly to French convalescing servicemen. To the north and north-west of the school were rolling hills partially covered with pine trees. This area was used as firing ranges and also for field exercises.

The school itself consisted of a complex of newly built wooden barracks which served as the dormitory for the cadets, a cadet mess hall, a gymnasium, a recreation center, and an office building that housed the staff and faculty. The school would be expanded later under President Diem and succeeding governments into a modern military academy complete with a state-of-the-art engineering labo-ratory and library. However in 1950, it was an unpretentious mili-tary facility designed to train commanders for small units of the newly created National Army. The surrounding beautiful hills, pine forests, lakes, and green valleys, however, more than compensated for the austerity of the campus.

The school was commanded by Lieutenant Colonel Gribius, a highly decorated French officer. (Gribius would later rise to the rank of lieutenant general and command a French army corps in Ger-many.) Most of the staff and instructors were also French. The first class at the School of Inter-Arms consisted of 139 cadets. Approxi-mately one-quarter of the class was composed of cadets who had previously served as noncommissioned officers in the French Army. Most had combat experience; some had been awarded the presti-gious French *Croix de Guerre* and other distinguished medals.

The corps of cadets was divided into six brigades. Originally, all brigade commanders were French officers. However, during the school year two Vietnamese officers were put in charge of the bri-gades. The six brigades constituted the division. The division com-mander was a captain by the name of de Buissonniere, an armor officer from a noble family. (It was a tradition in the French Army that most of the officers coming from the French nobility chose to serve in the Armor or *Arme Blindée*, not unlike their ancestors who distinguished themselves in the old French *cavalerie*.)

By coincidence, Tho and I were assigned to the 2nd Brigade. Lieutenant Bonneau, our brigade commander, was a typical prod-

uct of the French Military School of Saint-Cyr, which trained career officers for the French Army. Very athletic, with a flattop hair
cut, Lieutenant Bonneau was very strict on discipline and physical
presentation. He used to tell us that an army officer must be physically and morally elegant. For us, he exemplified the ideal image of
an army officer. Since Bonneau played basketball at Saint-Cyr, he
was appointed coach for the school basketball team where Tho and
I belonged. We often played against the teams of the French Lycée
Yersin and the *École des Enfants de Troupes* which trained the
sons of French veterans to become NCOs in the French Army.
Bonneau requested to be assigned to a combat unit and was killed
in North Viet Nam, while defending an outpost in the Red River
Delta. The Indochina War was a graveyard of the elite of the French
officer corps. It was estimated that the French lost the equivalent of
one full class of Saint-Cyr every year during that war.

Replacing Lieutenant Bonneau as commandant of the 2nd Brigade was 2d Lt. Nguyen Van Bich, who had served as a noncommissioned officer in a French airborne unit in North Viet Nam.

At the School of Inter-Arms, all of the classes were conducted
in French and teaching materials came directly from Saint-Cyr. In
addition to daily physical exercises and drill, we learned military
discipline, weapons, tactics for small units, topography, and communication. We received lectures on the employment of different
arms on the battlefield. As in other military schools, we were initiated into military discipline through a period of physical and men-
tal trial where we were hazed at every occasion to test our ability to
sustain heavy pressure under combat conditions. West Point cadets named this period "Beasts Barrack." We called this first month
of the life of a military cadet the period of "Metamorphosis," in
which we were transformed overnight into disciplined soldiers who
must, according to the French military code of conduct, "obey without hesitation nor murmur."

After we survived this initiation, we were allowed to spend our
weekends in downtown Dalat. We took advantage of this newly found
freedom to explore the beauty and elegance of this unique resort
station and to enjoy the exquisite French food or simply to chase
beautiful, rose-cheeked girls from the exclusive *Couvent des*

Oiseaux Catholic School. I spent most of my weekends at a wooden lodge owned by the sister of one of my roommates. Her husband was an army doctor and the lodge served as their retreat and hunting camp. It was located about ten miles south of Dalat in the middle of a pine forest. We would go there Saturday afternoon after the weekly inspection, and would return late Sunday, tanned, relaxed, and ready for another tough week ahead.

During that time, one event stood out in my memory. On a Sunday afternoon, two cadets were badly mauled by French Senegalese soldiers on a bus which brought them back to the campus. I happened to be the *Sergent de Semaine* (or Duty Sergeant for the Week) that historic day. The *sergent de semaine* was responsible for the internal discipline of the corps of cadets and reported directly to the *officier de semaine* of any security or discipline violations which happened during the week. As the sergent de semaine, I called an urgent meeting with the representatives of the six Brigades to discuss our course of action.

After some emotional debate, we unanimously decided that the entire division would go the Imperial Cabinet of Bao Dai to file our protest. Consequently, I ordered the division to be assembled in *tenue de sortie* (city uniform) and, in columns of four and under my command, the cadets marched the five kilometers to Emperor Bao Dai's civil cabinet headquarters. I and the representatives of the six Brigades were received by Nguyen De, Bao Dai's chief of cabinet. Nguyen De promised to request the French authorities that Senegalese soldiers involved in the reported incident be punished and that in the future all Senegalese soldiers be banned from convalescing in Dalat. Satisfied, I ordered the division back to the barracks.

Sure enough, Colonel Gribius and Captain de Buissonniere were waiting for us at the school; I was ordered to report to the school commandant without delay. I accepted full responsibility for the division's action. Very angrily, Colonel Gribius decided that I be punished with fifteen days of *arrêt de rigueur* and put in solitary confinement. That meant that I would be confined to a small cell at the end of every working day for fifteen days and that the punishment would be on my official record and would affect my final grade.

Soon after that incident, the school instructed each brigade to elect a representative who would act as its official spokesman. I was unanimously elected Representative for the 2nd Brigade and later for the whole division. Again, by coincidence, Tho was selected to replace me as the representative for the 2nd Brigade. Shortly after these elections, Colonel Gribius invited the representatives of the division and brigades for dinner at his residence. He was very gracious and made a point of not mentioning the last incident.

In the middle of the school year, we were allowed a one-week vacation to spend the Tet with our families. Tho and I decided to return to Bac Lieu for our first military leave. A few weeks before the vacation, the school organized a solemn ceremony in which we were given the epaulettes bearing the Greek letter *alpha* meaning that we were officially recognized as "officer-candidates" or "*aspirant*" to become officers. My mother was very proud of us, and Uncle Four, who was at the time a member of the Council of Representatives (the equivalent of a National Assembly but appointed by the government) invited us to the Tet reception given by the province chief.

The last period of our school year was devoted mostly to field exercises (ambush, *coup-de-main*, attack, and defense). Sometimes, we would spend whole weeks maneuvering in the field or participating in field trips to become acquainted with different arms and services.

As graduation approached, we learned that the Viet Minh had received increased military aid directly from the new Chinese Communist regime. Since Chang Kai-shek's Nationalist Army had been defeated by Communist forces under Mao Tse-tung and evacuated to the island of Formosa two years earlier, there was no longer a controlled border between China and Viet Nam. Intelligence reports indicated that the Chinese had transferred to the Viet Minh modern, U.S.-supplied weaponry captured from the Nationalist Army, including artillery guns. With increased military aid from the Communist bloc, the Viet Minh was able to form regular divisions and in early 1951, these divisions were ready to participate in limited offensive operations. At the same time, the French, under heavy pressure, were in the process of withdrawing from the Cao

Bang- Lang Son border area to concentrate their forces on the defense of the rich and populated Red River Delta. As a result, it was expected that the war would intensify and would draw closer to Hanoi and urban centers. The number of casualties, civilian and military, would substantially increase in a not too distant future. It was also about that time that the United States, determined to contain Communism in Asia, started to give money and military aid to the French Corps Expeditionnaire in Indochina.

At the same time, the military situation in Korea was far from encouraging. After war broke out in mid-June the previous year, Allied Forces incurred serious setbacks and withdrew to the enclave of Pusan in the southeastern tip of the Korean peninsula. Although General Douglas MacArthur's daring landing in Inchon in September 1950 allowed the United Nations troops to recapture Seoul and to inflict damaging losses to the North Korean Army, it incited the Chinese Army to cross the Korean border in January 1951 and to launch massive attacks on the United Nations Forces, which had to retreat on all fronts. In March, the new commander of United Nations Forces in Korea, Lt. Gen. Matthew Ridgway, again liberated Seoul, but three months before we graduated, in April 1951, General MacArthur was relieved of his command by President Truman and the situation became a stalemate.

Since the end of World War II, international Communism had spread like an unstoppable wildfire throughout Southeast Asia. I was too young to understand the complexities of geopolitics. However, it was obvious that French military setbacks at the Viet Nam-China border regions, the growing insurgency movements in Malaysia and the Philippines, and the Communist invasion of South Korea, which came on the heels of the conquest of the mainland of China by Mao Tse-tung's peasant army, seemed to confirm the success of Moscow-supported wars of liberation in Third World countries. These events also seemed to substantiate the new domino theory. In any event, it was a particularly disturbing period for an officer-to-be in a developing country facing an armed Communist insurgency within its own border. It did not take a genius to foresee a grim future for our country and tougher times for its young army.

A week before graduation, we were allowed to select the branch of the armed forces in which we wanted to serve, based on our final grade. Despite fifteen days of *arrêt de rigueur* for having led the unauthorized march and also despite my poor grade in marksmanship, I ranked twelfth at graduation. I decided to choose the artillery because it was a new arm in the Vietnamese Army and would offer more opportunities for advancement. In the French Army, armor was considered an *arme noble* and artillery was considered an *arme savante*; and the majority of the graduates of the French elite École Polytechnique chose to become *artilleurs*. After all, Napoleon was himself an *artilleur* and became one of the greatest captains of history. Tho, without hesitation, chose the *arme noble;* he had longed to become a *cavalier* even before he entered the School of Inter-Arms.

We graduated in July 1951.The ceremony was presided over by Emperor Bao Dai himself. After the usual speech in which he instructed us to serve the country with honor, he pinned the epaulettes of second lieutenant on Bui Dzinh, valedictorian of the graduating class. The remaining class received their new rank insignia from the school instructors. I was nineteen and proud of my achievement. I decided to forget about the war and to enjoy, for a moment, my new status as an officer in the National Army.

After the ceremony, we celebrated in the city, wearing our shining uniforms and our hard-won officer epaulettes. Then we all headed back to our families to spend a month leave before reporting to our assigned units. Because I chose to become *artilleur*, I was required to undergo a six-month artillery course before reporting for combat duty.

Tho took advantage of his vacation to marry his fiancée in Saigon. After I attended his wedding, I returned to Bac Lieu to spend the vacation with my mother, because I suspected that I might be sent to the North after the completion of my artillery course. Given the deteriorating situation in the Red River Delta, I might not be able to come back to see her again. My mother, who was a fervent Catholic, told me that she would pray for me every night. She kept her promise and, who knows, her prayers might have been instrumental in my safe return from the Indochina War and particularly from the hell of the North Viet Nam campaign.

In August 1951, I reported to the French Artillery Training Center at Phu Loi, near the city of Thu Dau Mot, approximately thirty kilometers northwest of Saigon, to be trained as an artilleryman. The Phu Loi center was created by the French to train artillery NCOs for the French Corps Expeditionnaire. The school organized a special six-month course to train the three of us, who had just graduated from Dalat and had chosen to serve in the soon-to-be-created Vietnamese Artillery. The center itself was rather primitive and consisted of old wooden barracks surrounded by barbed wire fencing. The firing range was so insecure that one day the French instructor and the three of us received sniper fire as we approached our observation post. We had to resort to infantry tactics, combining fire and movement, to attack in the direction of enemy fire to dislodge Viet Minh snipers from the dirt mound that served as the observation post.

The curriculum at the center consisted of materials, survey, gunnery, and artillery tactics and techniques. Artillery gunnery and survey required advanced knowledge in math. Around that time, General de Lattre de Tassigny, commander in chief and French high commissioner in Indochina, realizing that the war could not be won without active participation of young Vietnamese, persuaded Emperor Bao Dai to decree a general mobilization. Thus, the first Reserve Officers School was created in Thu Duc in July 1951 to train the reserve cadres for the National Army. Subsequently, the reserve officers who opted for the artillery branch were also sent to Phu Loi for training.

After completing the basic artillery course at Phu Loi, I was assigned to a French artillery battery in Bien Hoa, north of Saigon, for further training. The battery was located in a French rubber plantation. The owner of the plantation also owned a large lumber company called *Bien Hoa Industries Forestieres* (or BIF). He lived in a huge mansion complete with swimming pool, tennis court, and Cambodian servants. He often invited the officers of the battery to his house for a tennis match.

This was the first time I had witnessed the luxurious life of the French *colons*; it reminded me of the lives of American plantation owners in the South depicted in the movie *Gone with the Wind*. I spent most of my weekends, however, in Saigon. The French battery commander was kind enough to provide me with a jeep and a driver. I would stop at the villa of Uncle Seven's wife and change to civilian clothes, then I would stroll the popular Rue Catinat with one of my cousins. We would eat lunch at one of the fashionable French restaurants in the commercial district and watch the most recent movie in town. I wanted to take advantage of my short stay in South Viet Nam and enjoy the good life as long as I could, because, as I had earlier predicted, I had already received an order to report to the newly created Vietnamese 3rd Artillery Battery in North Viet Nam at the end of my current temporary assignment.

Before I left for North Viet Nam, the Battery was ordered to participate in an operation in the famed "Iron Triangle," near the Cambodian border. This area, consisting of dense forests and abandoned French rubber plantations, served as one of the most important Viet Minh secret bases in South Viet Nam. A French lieutenant and I were appointed to a *Detachement de Liaison et d'Observation (DLO)* attached to a French infantry battalion. The first night, as we bivouacked in a rubber plantation, we were harassed by enemy mortars. The French officer and I took turns adjusting artillery fire on the suspected enemy mortar location. I realized how difficult it was to adjust artillery at night when you could not see the impacts and when you could not ascertain your own location. In these situations, you had to throw away your books and act according to instinct and common sense.

Also, it was during that operation that we learned that General de Lattre had died in France where he had been undergoing cancer treatment. It was a shock for the entire French Corps Expeditionnaire as de Lattre was considered one of the best French generals. For Mrs. de Lattre, her husband's death had all the features of a Greek tragedy, since their only son, Lt. Bernard de Lattre de Tassigny, had died the year before, when his commando unit was overrun while defending a hillside outpost in Ninh Binh Province in North Viet Nam. True to the French concept of *noblesse oblige*, General de Lattre had refused to keep his son behind a desk in Saigon or Hanoi. He insisted, instead, that his son command one of the French elite commando units which were trained in operations behind enemy lines, although Bernard, descending from a French noble family, was himself an armor officer. After Bernard's death, de Lattre wrote his wife a moving letter requesting her forgiveness for failing to keep their son alive.

At last, my three-month temporary assignment ended. I bade farewell to the officers of the French battery and, taking advantage of an unexpected vacation given me by the French battery commander, I returned again to Bac Lieu to see my mother before heading to an uncertain future in the tough battlefields of North Viet Nam.

3

NORTH VIET NAM

IN FEBRUARY 1952, I BOARDED an Air France flight to Hanoi. At that time, Air France provided daily passenger service between Saigon and Hanoi and also between other capitals of what was called *les États d'Indochine*. When I landed in Gia Lam Airport on the outskirts of Hanoi, the city was shrouded under a light but persistent rain, called *cachin*, that was characteristic of North and Central Viet Nam. The *cachin* could last for days in the winter. It caused streets to be submerged under ankle-deep mud in certain commercial districts. Pedestrians wore rubber boots to navigate between the potholes and mud ponds. Everywhere I went, I noticed a sense of urgency as battles raged closer to the city. At night, rumblings of artillery fire could be heard in the distance.

General de Lattre had died only a few months earlier. Mao Tse-tung had consolidated his power over the entire Chinese mainland. The French outposts near the Chinese borders had been abandoned and the French were fighting against Viet Minh regular divisions around the chain of forts that de Lattre had built in the *Trung-Du* (Middle Region) to protect the Red River Delta. Decisive battles were expected in a few months when the rain stopped and everywhere I went, I felt an air of resignation and pessimism characteristic of residents of a city under siege.

Hanoi was a much smaller city than Saigon. It looked like a provincial town. Despite the fast-approaching war, Hanoi, however, retained the charm and pride of a city famous for its culture, tradition, and its numerous historical landmarks. As soon as I arrived in the city, I immediately reported to the Vietnamese Third Military Region Headquarters, which was located at the center of the city, near Ho Hoan Kiem Lake (Lake of the Restored Sword). As legend tells it, in the fifteenth century when King Le Loi arrived at the shores of the lake, a giant tortoise rose from the waters and gave him a sacred sword with which he defeated the Chinese invaders. Later King Le Loi returned the sword to the tortoise and he ordered a temple to be built in the middle of the lake in its honor.

With the creation of a National Army, there were also created four Military Regions (MRs) whose mission was to provide administrative and logistical support to the newly formed infantry battalions and other combat support units. The tactical control of these units was still retained by the French military authorities. The Military Regions were under the control of a general staff in Saigon. The Chief of the General Staff, Lt. Gen. Nguyen Van Hinh, was an officer in the French Air Force, and had distinguished himself during World War II.

The day after my arrival, I paid a visit to an old friend of the family, Lam Ngoc Huan, who was chief of cabinet to the governor of North Viet Nam. Mr. Huan invited me to his residence located on a quiet street abutting the left bank of the Red River. This house had been occupied by Gen. Vo Nguyen Giap when the Viet Minh took over the government in 1945. It was a beautiful two-story French villa with a red tile roof and stucco exterior walls and a large front yard covered with bougainvillea trees. I would later come back to see him and his family whenever I had the occasion to return to Hanoi to relax and spend a few days away from the killing fields of the Red River Delta.

At the Third Military Region, I met two old friends from the School of Inter-Arms. They took me on a tour of the city, which included the Old Citadel with some of the busiest commercial streets in town. They also showed me the two lakes located within Hanoi proper and the famous *Chua Mot Cot* (or Single-Column Pagoda) famous for its unique architecture.

I was surprised to see that, although located near China, the North, unlike South Viet Nam, had not been influenced by Chinese culinary art and had been able to preserve its traditional cuisine. I particularly liked the popular *pho* (beef noodle soup) and *bun than* (chicken soup with vermicelli). However, I had never been able, to this day, to eat dog meat or even the *tiet canh vit* (duck prepared with raw blood); both of these dishes were prized by the Northerners and considered two of their most cherished delicacies.

One week after I arrived in North Viet Nam, I reported to the 3rd Artillery Battery in Bac Ninh, approximately fifty kilometers east of Hanoi. According to the official Table of Organization and Equipment (TOE), each battery had approximately one hundred men and was equipped with four guns. The 3rd Artillery Battery was stationed inside the Bac Ninh Citadel, which was used as a training center for new draftees under the general mobilization decree signed by Emperor Bao Dai. The battery personnel lived in tents under which we would shriver to death during the cold winter nights. When it rained, our boots were washed away by storm water. The battery was commanded by a French officer, Lieutenant Sormani. There were also two other French lieutenants acting respectively as battery assistant and *officier de tir* (or gunnery officer). 2d. Lt. Nguyen Xuan Thinh, my classmate at the School of Inter-Arms, and I were the only Vietnamese officers assigned to the battery. Most of the battery NCOs were French and the gunners were mostly new draftees.

I was startled to see that the battery was equipped, not with artillery guns, but instead with four French-made 120-mm mortars with a practical range of only five kilometers. The first month, Thinh and I had to familiarize ourselves with this new weapon. We were also charged with training the Vietnamese NCOs and new recruits on gunnery practice and procedures. Once a week, we would participate in firing practice in the nearby rice fields. We would warn the farmers and buffalo boys not to venture into our improvised firing ranges. At the end of the day, we would stop at a local bar to have a beer before heading back to our tents.

Bac Ninh was a very small town and its streets were even dirtier than some of Hanoi's worst streets. Bac Ninh was known, however, for having some of the most beautiful girls in North Viet Nam; I later learned that most girls from well-to-do families had emigrated to Hanoi because of the war and the insecurity in small towns.

The sanitary situation within the Citadel worsened with the winter rains. Plumbing was nonexistent. The streets were unpaved and as there was no storm drain, we had to walk sometimes in knee-deep mud in certain heavily trafficked areas. I had not lived in such primitive conditions before and was surprised that the French officers appeared very comfortable with their life in the training camp. The only time I could find some relaxation was at the Officers Mess where we gathered at the end of the day. Since there were both French and Vietnamese instructors at the training center, the Officers Mess prepared separate French and Vietnamese menus. The center was under the command of a French major and his assistant was a Vietnamese captain by the name of Ha Thuc Sanh, who came from the Viet Binh Doan paramilitary organization in Hue. Captain Sanh would preside over the Vietnamese section of the Officers Mess and I had a great time conversing and exchanging opinions with other fellow officers regarding the current political and military situation in Viet Nam.

In Bac Ninh, I became acquainted with Dr. Nguyen Ngoc Thang, the medical officer at the camp. Dr. Thang graduated from a medical school in France and was drafted into the army under the decree of general mobilization. His family lived in Hanoi and sometimes I would give him a ride when I drove to Hanoi on a weekend pass. Dr. Thang's family lived in an apartment on the second floor of a building located near Ho Hoan Kiem Lake. Often, he would invite me to eat seafood in the commercial district or to go window shopping in the French quarter, just a few blocks from his home. Dr. Thang had a younger sister, Khanh, who was a student at the famous Trung Vuong High School (named after the national heroines, the two Sisters Trung, who defeated the Chinese in the first century AD and who committed suicide by throwing themselves into the Hac Giang River after they were in turn defeated by the enemy). Khanh was a very charming and reserved girl. She would accompany us during our promenades or excursions in the city. In these occasions, Dr. Thang would lend me his civilian suits, which were too short for me. Strolling with Khanh behind Dr. Thang and his wife along the tree-lined streets of the French quarters I often felt very embarrassed, not only because of my uncomfortable civilian attire, but also because I had difficulties communicating with her and understanding her singing Northern accent and different vocabulary. Not unlike Parisians or Bostonians who generally speak a better and purer French and English than, for example, the *Marseillais* or Texans, the residents of Hanoi tended to speak a more academic and more correct Vietnamese than the Southerners whose language had been somewhat corrupted and influenced by Chinese, Cambodian, and even French.

In this regard, I experienced a linguistic shock the day I arrived in Hanoi. Since there was no military transportation available, I had to use a *cyclo-pousse* (or pedicab) to get to the Bachelor Officers Quarters. When we arrived at the quarters, the cyclo-pousse man asked me if I wanted him to carry my wooden trunk to my room. In the North, the word for "trunk" is *"hom,"* which means "coffin" in the South. So, I was stunned when he offered to carry my own coffin to my room. I had not yet started my military career and here someone had already offered to dispose of my coffin. That obviously did not bode well for a young officer about to see combat.

On many occasions, Dr. Thang implied that he would be glad to have me as a member of his family despite the fact that he knew I came from Bac Lieu, the land of the *cong-tu*; but I was so young and, with the war going on, my future seemed precarious to say the least. There was a Vietnamese saying: "No university (degrees), no marriage,"[2] which accurately described the fact that, traditionally, girls from good families preferred to marry well-educated men. However, as young male Vietnamese had to serve in the army one time or another since the 1950 general mobilization, the girls were resigned to look at the army for prospective husbands. By the way, that was exactly what a very old popular folk verse had long ago advised:

> *Wise men look for their wives at the crowded markets.*
> *Wise girls look for their husbands amid the military camps.*[3]

My friendship with Dr. Thang was short-lived however, for our battery received order to move to an outpost near Son Dong, northeast of Hanoi, after three months of training in Bac Ninh. Son Dong was a small village located in the *Trung Du* or Middle Region of North Viet Nam where General de Lattre had built a chain of strong points to defend against enemy infiltration into the lowlands. At our new position, we spent entire days drawing panoramic sketches of the chain of mountains in front of us with the coordinates, directions, and distances of the most important features. From our position, we could also see, in a distance, the imposing Mount Ba Vi, one of the highest mountains of the Trung Du Region. Occasionally, we would adjust mortar fire on possible enemy routes of approach to our positions; we recorded the fire data that could be instantly used in case of enemy attacks.

Fortunately, in 1952, the situation was relatively quiet around Son Dong. One weekend every month, I would go to Hanoi to buy food and liquor for the battery Officers Mess. According to French military tradition, the youngest officer in the unit was responsible for the Officer Mess and since I was the youngest officer in the battery, one of my assignments was to see to it that the officers were adequately fed and that we had an ample supply of wine and assorted *aperitifs* and liquor. Although all Frenchmen loved to drink, it was common knowledge in the French Army that the French *artilleurs* drank more than the officers of other arms. I had no problem with that; however, when they were drunk, the French started to sing obscene songs and I was very disturbed just to sit there and to listen to their profanities. One of their favorite songs, entitled "L'artilleur de Metz," was so outrageous that I often walked away when they started to sing.

I often took advantage of my "resupply" missions in Hanoi to stop by Dr. Thang's apartment and to invite Khanh and her younger brother to have *pho* with me. I would let them choose the best *pho* restaurant in town. Then we would drive around Hanoi in my jeep and Khanh would explain the history of each landmark or points of interest that we visited. However, as the war intensified and our battery received combat missions in the Delta, I rarely had occasion to come back to Hanoi; as a result, I gradually lost contact with Dr.Thang and his family.

A few months after we moved to Son Dong, our battery received American 105-mm HM-3 howitzers, which could fire up to seven or

eight kilometers. Around August 1952, we received an order to move
to the city of Nam Dinh, approximately one hundred kilometers
southeast of Hanoi, to support the combat missions in the area.
The battery took up position in an old Catholic seminary and organized two Detachments of Liaison and Observation (DLO) whose
mission was to accompany and provide fire support to combat units.
Second Lieutenant Thinh and I were appointed team leaders and
were instructed to be ready, at a moment's notice, to participate in
combat operations within the Nam Dinh Sector.

To facilitate the coordination and implementation of the pacification program and what the French called the *Defense en Surface*,
each MR was subdivided into military sectors whose boundaries
usually coincided with the political boundaries of the provinces involved. Each sector was subdivided into subsectors whose boundaries, again, typically coincided with the political boundaries of the
different administrative districts which constituted the province.
Typically, a subsector was under the tactical responsibility of the
infantry battalion commander whose units operated in the area. As
Nam Dinh was the third largest city of North Viet Nam (after Hanoi
and Hai Phong), Nam Dinh Sector was one of the largest and most
important military sectors in the North.

To be able to provide continuous and effective fire support to
the combat units involved in military operations within the sector
limits, we were provided with up-to-date information (name of unit,
radio code, type of materials, and radio frequencies, for instance)
of all French artillery units located within the sector so we could
contact them at any time to request artillery fire. Occasionally, we
were ordered to accompany the French Navy convoys in order to
provide close support in case of attack or harassment by Viet Minh
elements dug in along the river banks. These were difficult missions because a slightly short or long artillery fire could hit the ship
and cause heavy damage. However, I especially loved to escort these
convois fluviaux because the Navy always took good care of its
guests. The service was impeccable, the china shining and the food
was always good and, more importantly, it was free.

One day, I was instructed to act as liaison officer with the sector's
staff, which controlled a regiment-size operation along the Phu Ly

River, north of Nam Dinh. We took up position on a small hill over-looking the river and watched the attack conducted by a Vietnam-ese infantry battalion on a heavily defended village located on the opposite bank of the river below. The first wave failed to get a hold on the edge of the village and had to retreat with heavy casualties. At the battalion commander's request, I ordered a concentration of artillery fire on the village. When we lifted the artillery, the battal-ion commander committed his reserve company, which succeeded in capturing a corner of the village from which the battalion was able to expand and capture the assigned objective. The comman-dant of the reserve company was wounded during the assault and was brought to the sector's headquarters for medical aid before be-ing evacuated to Nam Dinh. I was surprised to recognize the wounded officer as one of my classmates at the School of Inter-Arms in Dalat. In fact, many of my friends who served in the infantry, had been wounded or killed in action during their first year after graduation.

During that time, the battery received six reserve officers who had just completed their training at Phu Loi. They were to receive additional field training before being assigned to the two to-be-formed batteries which would make up the 3rd Vietnamese Artil-lery Battalion. They were rotated to my DLO team as team assistant.

At Nam Dinh, I met two Vietnamese captains from the South who graduated from the French Armor School of Saumur. One of them, Capt. Huynh Ba Xuan, was also a resident of Bac Lieu and was two classes ahead of me at College Phan Thanh Gian in Can Tho. His father, a rich landowner, was killed by the Viet Minh and he volunteered to attend the first officer course organized by the French to form cadres for their auxiliary forces. He had previously served as an aide-de-camp to General de Lattre. These two officers were assigned to a newly formed Vietnamese armored squadron in Nam Dinh. They had their wives with them and rented an apart-ment in downtown Nam Dinh. Often, I would have dinner with them at their apartment where they graciously served southern dishes that I cherished.

Around October 1952, the battery received four 105-mm M-2 guns which were quite an improvement, because the new guns could fire up to twelve kilometers and were the American standard field artillery guns in World War II. With the new equipment, the battery's mission was to participate in mobile operations throughout the Delta. Our first mobile operation was in the Catholic fiefdom of Phat Diem. The battery was transported from Nam Dinh to Phat Diem by a *convoi fluvial*. Phat Diem's diocese was under the strong leadership of Archbishop Le Huu Tu, who had been a high school classmate of Ho Chi Minh. With the aid of the French, Monsignor Tu had armed and trained a strong Catholic paramilitary organization to protect the Catholic population of Phat Diem. He was feared and respected by both the Viet Minh and the French.

In October, the French launched an operation to clear the area northeast of Phat Diem to destroy the enemy within that area. I was assigned as a DLO with a Vietnamese infantry battalion whose mission was to clear the road that linked Phat Diem to Nhac Quan (about ten kilometers northeast of Phat Diem), and to occupy the strategic Nhac Quan Catholic seminary. As we left the northern outskirts of Phat Diem, the front company was pinned down by automatic rifle fire from Viet Minh elements dug in behind an earth barricade in the middle of the road. I went to the front to meet with the company commander. After I determined the coordinates of the enemy machine gun's location, I ordered my assistant, Aspirant Phat, to request smoke fire on the enemy position. I then made a small adjustment and ordered an artillery salvo. The first round hit the enemy on target. Three enemy soldiers were killed and two weapons captured including an automatic rifle. After a few more skirmishes, we reached Nhac Quan late that night. I immediately installed an observation post on the roof of the multi-story seminary and put Phat in charge of the observation post. The next day, we adjusted artillery fire around the seminary as a precaution against possible enemy attacks. When we rejoined our battery at the end of the operation, Lieutenant Sormani congratulated me for my action. He informed me that he would recommend me for a combat citation. He wanted to know if I would like to be awarded the French *Croix de Guerre* or the Vietnamese *Croix de Vaillance* (Gallantry Cross). I opted for the latter which I thought was more appropriate for a Vietnamese officer serving with a unit of its National Army and fighting for his own country.

After a few days of rest in Nam Dinh, our battery was ordered to participate in a multi-battalion operation in the area approximately thirty kilometers southwest of Nam Dinh. The battery took up position in a small hill located midway on the national road linking Nam Dinh to the city of Ninh Binh. The battery was to provide direct support to a French Moroccan infantry battalion whose mission was to attack the heavily defended village of Luong Kiet located two kilometers from the road and approximately five kilometers from our battery position. Lieutenant Sormani asked me to join his DLO team, which was to march with the battalion's headquarters.

The first elements of the Moroccan battalion were repulsed by violent counterattacks right after they reached the edge of the village. Previously, the Viet Minh's tactics consisted of digging in behind the bamboo hedges that typically surrounded the Vietnamese villages in the Red River Delta and destroying the attacking forces in the open with machine-gun fire before they got a foothold in the village. To counter this tactic, the French usually concentrated heavy artillery preparations on the edge of the village before launching the attack. As a consequence, the Viet Minh moved their main defense line twenty-five to fifty meters behind the exterior bamboo hedges. From there they launched their surprise counterattacks to repulse and destroy the enemy the moment it got a hold on the edge of the village.

To coordinate the attack on Luong Kiet after the first setback, the commander of the Moroccan battalion installed his command post in a small cemetery approximately 500 meters from the village. Lieutenant Sormani and I were required to mass all available artillery fire on the located enemy positions behind the edge of the village, including the fire from a French 155-mm howitzer battalion. The battle raged all day and Luong Kiet was finally captured by day's end, but in the meantime the cemetery was filled with dead or wounded Moroccan soldiers. Some had had their head or limbs shot up. One soldier lying near me had had his left eye taken by a bullet but somehow managed to survive. I had never in my life seen so many dead and wounded people. Somehow, it seemed to me that these young Moroccans were fighting for a bad cause and should not have died in a strange land for a France that wanted, not so much to stop Communist expansionism in Asia, but to re-impose her hegemony on her former colony and to continue her unfinished (and unwanted) *mission civilisatrice.*

In other instances, however, I had no sympathy for foreign soldiers fighting in the French Corps Expeditionnaire. I recall one day where I accompanied a battalion of Senegalese *tirailleurs* during a *ratissage* (mopping-up) operation in Hung Yen Sector. Since I was the only Vietnamese in the battalion, one woman in a village where the battalion camped for the night came to see me. She was in tears and told me that one Senegalese soldier had raped her and had taken one of her chickens. Very upset, I took the woman to the French battalion commander and insisted that he investigate the incident and take necessary disciplinary actions. The French major promised he would do that; however I did not hear from him again regarding this incident.

It was clear that these kinds of incidents were very harmful to the nationalist cause in its fight against Communism. These incidents, of course, were adroitly exploited by the Viet Minh who posed as champions of the struggle for national independence against colonialist oppression. As for me as well as my fellow officers, we were caught in a painful dilemma. Personally, I tried to reconcile the fact that I had to temporarily fight alongside the French Army to defeat the Communist Viet Minh with my belief that, in the end, France would give in to international pressures and accord true independence to our country as well the countries which formed the *États d'Indochine.*

This was, at least, what I explained to the NCOs and enlisted men of the battery when I was appointed *officier d'action morale* under a new directive from the Vietnamese General Staff. The problem was that I did not receive any guide from the Military Region regarding how to plan and implement a moral action program within the unit. So, I designed my own program; it consisted of lecturing our men on the history of our nation (including our past victories against the Chinese invaders, our successful southward expansion, and the final unification of our country in the nineteenth century), and the reasons why we had to temporarily ally ourselves with the

French in the fight against the Viet Minh, which was supported by China, our historic enemy. I took special care not to offend the French officers by omitting from my lecture the story of our fight against French colonialism in the late nineteenth century and early twentieth century because I was fully aware that we needed the French in our struggle to eliminate the Communist insurgency.

Shortly after the Ninh Binh operation, our battery received orders to move to the Hung Yen Sector in the heart of the Red River Delta. The new battery's mission consisted of providing close support to the Vietnamese infantry units involved in static defense throughout Hung Yen Sector, which was one of the first sectors to be transferred to the Vietnamese military authorities. Occasionally, we also received a mission to support the French *Unites d'Intervention* operating in the area. Often, as a DLO, I accompanied these units throughout Hung Yen Province. Most of the time, we did not meet any of the enemy, but sometimes we had to fight all night long to dislodge and destroy, one by one, small Viet Minh pockets of resistance well entrenched in different parts of the village; often hungry and exhausted, I slept under a haystack to avoid the bitter winter cold of North Viet Nam. I remember one day, after one of these *ratissage* operations, a Viet Minh prisoner was brought to the battalion commander for interrogation. The prisoner trembled violently as his thin black pajamas did not provide adequate protection against the winter rain. The French major turned to me and said:

"Please, Lieutenant, tell him that a soldier never trembles."

I did not make the translation because I thought the statement was somewhat irrelevant. Besides, I was not sure the man was a Viet Minh soldier. He might have been simply a poor rice farmer caught in the middle of a war he did not comprehend.

Later as a battery commander, during the winter operations, I liked to smoke a pipe, which gave me a feeling of warmth and at the same time was not easily detected by the enemy at night. I calibrated my pipe to coincide with a certain number of *milliems*, which was used in the army as a unit of measurement of an angle. Rather than be burdened with cumbersome binoculars, I would adjust the fire by measuring the angle between the impacts and the target in terms of my pipe and making necessary adjustments based on the respective ratios of my distance and the battery's distance to the target. When, for example, I ordered my gunnery officer to fire "two pipes" to the right, he would know that he should move the guns forty milliems to the right. I believed at the time that artillery, after all, was not an absolute *arme savante* and that the *artilleur* sometimes could also improvise. However, I was to learn later that a good officer has, first, to master the techniques of warfare before he can improvise. In other words, you can not be an artist without being first a technician and it took me many years to learn that simple truth.

At last, after a short period of consolidation at the small village of Van Tri, the battery detached one artillery platoon consisting of two 105-mm howitzers to Cho Noi outpost, approximately twenty kilometers northeast of the city of Hung Yen. The mission of the platoon was to provide support to small outposts manned by auxiliary forces and located within the 105-mm howitzers'range. Second Lieutenant Thinh and I rotated to Cho Noi as platoon leader. Cho Noi was manned by a regular company under the command of 2d. Lt. Tran Van Cuong, one of my classmates at Dalat. Cuong told me that Cho Noi was located on an important enemy communication route and had been attacked in the past by elements of the Viet Minh's famous 42nd Regiment that operated in the Hung Yen area.

One of the targets of the Viet Minh in the area was the Catholic village of Cao Xa located approximately seven kilometers east of Cho Noi. Cao Xa was defended by Catholic militia units under the command of the local priest. As a new platoon leader, my first visit, understandably, was with the priest of Cao Xa. The latter proudly showed me his defense plan complete with bunkers, fences, and an artillery fire support plan. He also discussed communication procedures in case of enemy attack on the village. After I adjusted a few rounds of smoke ammunition to verify and update the predetermined protective fire in his defense plan, the priest invited me to have lunch with him and before I left, he presented me with a bottle of Mass wine. Cuong later told me that the Cao Xa priest was very aggressive, and often he personally led ambush teams outside of the perimeter of defense of his village to intercept and kill enemy reconnaissance elements.

About two weeks after I arrived in Cho Noi, the Viet Minh overran Phu My outpost located approximately eight kilometers east of Cho Noi. One Vietnamese regular infantry company under the command of a French lieutenant was sent to Phu My to rebuild and occupy the outpost. As the artillery platoon commander, I went to Phu My and stayed there for two weeks to provide fire support to the company during the initial phase of occupancy. A month after I left Phu My to return to Van Tri, the outpost was again overrun by the Viet Minh. Many soldiers were killed during the attack, including the French company commander.

During that time, Capt. Huynh Ba Xuan, whom I met at Nam Dinh, assumed the command of the one infantry battalion in Hung Yen. One morning, during an inspection of one of the outposts in his subsector, Xuan was captured by the Viet Minh who, unknown to him, had taken the outpost the previous night. When Xuan arrived at the outpost, a detachment of Viet Minh in National Army fatigue uniforms rendered the honor. After the usual ceremony, the Viet Minh overpowered Xuan and his escort. Hung Yen Sector requested artillery fire on the outpost, but it was too late: The Viet Minh had already fled with their prized prisoner.[4]

In late December 1952, the Viet Minh closed in on Cho Noi. Every day, we received mortar and machine gun fire from nearby villages while Cao Xa was under constant harassment. Some nights, the Viet Minh sent reconnaissance teams to cut the barbed wire around the outpost and to make probing attacks; I had to set the timing of the artillery shells to explode one second after they were fired to blast away enemy reconnaissance elements. One night, the enemy launched a heavy attack on Cao Xa while harassing my artillery platoon with intense mortar preparation. One of my gun crews was decimated by an enemy 82-mm mortar round but we kept firing with the remaining gun to provide needed support for Cao Xa. We were trapped in Cho Noi for two months. To bury my gunmen killed by enemy mortar attack, I asked Cuong to send a night patrol into a nearby village to confiscate some coffins. Due to direct enemy machine-gun fire, we had to bury our dead at night in the vacant lot just outside the outpost. Because we ran out of food and ammunition after one month under siege, the above items had to be dropped by parachute. Throughout the siege of Cho Noi, Cuong and I slept during the day and stayed awake at night to prepare for a possible enemy attack. During these long watches, we reminisced about our happier times at l'Ecole Inter-Armes. Finally, one morning we were glad to welcome the French paratroopers who fought their way to our rescue. I was surprised to see marching among the paratroopers, Gen. Rene Cogny, who commanded the French *Deuxieme Division de Marche* and who had tactical responsibility for Hung Yen Sector. Brigadier General Cogny was a product of the prestigious French École Polytechnique, which was founded by Napoleon to provide officers for the artillery and engineer branches of the French Army. A tall, handsome man, Cogny played rugby at the École Polytechnique and was a former artillery officer. He would later rise to the rank of major general in charge of all French Forces in North Viet Nam. His reputation, however, was tarnished somewhat by the controversy which followed the French defeat at Dien Bien Phu in 1954.

As General Cogny walked to the front gates of the outpost with his paratroopers, the enemy fired machine guns at us from the nearby village. I saw the French general talk to his aide-de-camp and minutes later, two U.S.-made Bearcat fighters dove from the sky and the village was engulfed in flames under the impact of napalm bombs. After the enemy machine gun was silenced, Cogny turned and asked me to stand at attention. Then he congratulated me for my actions and pinned on my fatigue uniform the *Croix de Vaillance* with palm, which was the highest Vietnamese decoration for valor in combat.

That same day, my platoon was relieved by a platoon under 2d. Lt. Nguyen Duc Thang, a reserve officer from the first class of Thu Duc Reserve Officers School. As my trucks towing the damaged 105-mm guns rolled past the outpost gates, I looked back at the new graves of my gun crew killed by enemy mortar fire and, completely exhausted, physically and morally, after two months of encirclement, I suddenly started to cry in silence.

In February 1953, Thinh, Thang, and I were promoted to the rank of lieutenant. Normally, a second lieutenant was required to serve two years before being promoted. However, we became lieutenants six months ahead of our contemporaries because each of us was slated to assume the command of a battery. For Thang, it was a very early promotion because he graduated from the Thu Duc Reserve Officers School almost six months after Thinh and I graduated from Dalat. I was, however, not at all surprised at Thang's promotion. Thang came from a well-to-do family in Hanoi. He attended the French Lycée Albert Sarraut and obtained the French baccalaureate degree in Math with *mention bien*. He was a hardworking officer and spent his spare time devising new methods of applying his advanced knowledge in math to artillery gunnery techniques. He was liked and admired by the French officers who wanted to push him ahead. (Like Thinh and myself, Thang was to rise to the rank of lieutenant general. In 1967, he was to serve briefly as minister of rural development under Gen. Nguyen Cao Ky, his classmate at the Reserve Officers School.)

Soon after my promotion, I assumed the command of the 2nd Battery located in Bac Nao, also in Hung Yen Sector. At twenty, I was excited and proud to be trusted with the command of an artillery battery in combat. Bac Nao was a strong and well-defended outpost manned by a regular infantry company. The battery was split into two platoons. One platoon, under the command of 2d. Lt. Duong Thai Dong, was stationed at the Tho Truong outpost, five kilometers north of Bac Nao. Tho Truong was defended by an infantry company under the command of 2d. Lt. Dao Mong Xuan, just out of the School of Inter-Arms of Dalat. Shortly after I arrived in Bac Nao, the Viet Minh launched a coordinated attack on Tho Truong. Although the first attack was repulsed, the enemy kept heavy pressure on the outpost with renewed small probing attacks and mortar fire.

The road to Tho Truong was cut in many areas and ammunition and other supplies had to be air dropped. The morale of the troops in Tho Truong was dangerously low and it was expected that the outpost would fall at any moment. Taking advantage of a lull in the enemy attack, I ordered artillery protective fire along the road from

Bac Nao to Tho Truong and drove my jeep to the besieged outpost. My arrival raised the morale of the garrison. As the highest-ranking officer, I took over the defense of the outpost. My first task was to pinpoint enemy mortar and automatic weapons positions and to destroy them with artillery fire from my artillery platoon at Bac Nao. I directed Second Lieutenant Xuan, the outpost commander, to send out night ambushes to detect enemy movements which I harassed with artillery fire. Finally, after three days, the Viet Minh decided they had enough and lifted the siege.

Around May 1953, my battery moved to Van Tri to rotate with Thinh's 1st Battery.Van Tri was a small village of approximately four kilometers in perimeter. It had been occupied as a military base for many years and its residents had long ago evacuated it and emigrated to nearby villages. My battery occupied the southern portion of the village while the northern portion was defended by an infantry company. A small creek crossed the village in a northerly direction. The village was surrounded by barbed wire fencing and mines were installed inside the barbed wire to provide additional protection. Every night, the infantry company would send ambush teams outside the perimeter of defense to provide early warning in case of enemy attack.

In June, one month after my battery moved to Van Tri, the Viet Minh's crack 42nd Regiment attacked the village. Around 2:00 A.M., under cover of darkness, enemy sappers infiltrated along the creek and opened the way for the main assault. At the same time, Van Tri was bombarded with heavy 82-mm mortar fire. As soon as I heard the first explosions, I rushed to the battery position, but it was already occupied by the enemy. We exchanged small arms fire around the gun pits when one mortar round landed a few meters from me. One piece of shrapnel hit my left leg as I tried to rally my men. Under heavy pressure, the battery personnel withdrew to the northern part of the village still defended by the infantry company. Around 5:00 A.M., the subsector commander sent one company to our rescue. By that time, however, the enemy had already started to withdraw. I rushed back to our battery and ordered my crews to shoot point blank at the retreating enemy with the two guns that were still usable. A patrol that was sent out to pursue the enemy reported a dozen Viet Minh killed by artillery shells. The battery had two killed; a few soldiers were wounded. Two howitzers were damaged, one machine gun and a few individual arms were lost.

Looking back at the defense of Van Tri, I think that our biggest mistake was the lack of coordination between the infantry company and the artillery battery. The coordination was more difficult as these units were constantly rotated and the defense plan was not updated to take into consideration the new friendly as well as enemy situation. One other problem was the limited ability of artillery units to defend themselves against enemy ground attack. The mission of artillery units was essentially to provide fire support to combat units, so they were not provided with enough personnel for their own defense. In Van Tri, our battery had to defend a sector almost one kilometer long and well-trained enemy sappers could penetrate any weak points in our defense perimeter. Once inside, the enemy could spread out and cause chaos among friendly ranks because there were no alternate rings of defense. Later, during the Viet Nam War, the Viet Cong were successful in developing a similar tactic dubbed "The Blossoming Flower," which consisted of concentrating on a weak point in the enemy defense, normally the boundary between two adjacent units, quickly attacking the central command and control post and then spreading outward to attack the remaining defensive areas from behind. Furthermore, I was very inexperienced at the time and did not master the principle of defense in depth, which I was to learn later at the U.S. Command & General Staff College. However, as a commander I was responsible for the losses incurred by my unit and, although an investigation committee from the Third Military Region cleared me of any wrongdoing, to this day, Van Tri remains a very bad memory.

Shortly after that incident, I was struck with a severe bout of malaria and had to be hospitalized at the military hospital of Vo Tanh in Hanoi. When I got out of the hospital, I was granted a two-week leave. I decided to return to the South to visit my mother. As my mother opened the door and saw me standing there, she almost fainted. She thought that I had returned from the grave. Rumor had it that I was already killed during a Viet Minh attack on my position, and since she had not received any news from me for some time, she believed I was really dead. I was very moved when she told me that, as promised, she had prayed for me every night and that her prayers had now been answered. I realized then how forgetful I was. Since I had assumed the command of 2nd Battery in Hung Yen, I was so burdened with my new responsibilities and I was so tired and sick after the attack on Van Tri that I had completely forgotten to write to my mother.

Back in Saigon, I went to the General Staff Headquarters and asked to see Lt. Col. Tran Van Don, the armed forces chief of staff. Although my visit was unscheduled, Colonel Don received me immediately. Wasting no time, I requested to be transferred to an artillery unit in the First Military Region in the South. Colonel Don promised that he would recommend approval of my request. I was happy to see that things appeared to be looking up for me and that I would be able soon to come home again and to serve in my native Mekong Delta.

After two days in Saigon, I flew to Hai Phong to rejoin my unit, which had moved to the 3rd Artillery Battalion's *Base Arrière* (Rear Base), located twenty kilometers west of Hai Phong, in a small town named Vat Cach Thuong. That night, as I was leaving a Chinese restaurant in Hai Phong Chinatown, a jeep stopped in front of me. The driver was 2d. Lt. Duong Thai Dong, my deputy battery commander. He was elated to see me back. He informed me that the battery was undergoing a two-month training and reorganization period. It had received new howitzers to replace the ones that were damaged during the Van Tri attack.

Dong drove me to Vat Cach Thuong. This was the first time I visited my battery's rear base. It consisted of one prefabricated building that served at the same time as office, sleeping quarters, and warehouse. This was also the second time I met with the battalion commander, Major De Vries, a skinny and humorless officer. The only thing I liked about Major De Vries was that he was very polite and did not sing obscene songs at dinners.

It was also during that period that I first tried a Moroccan food that was to become one of my favorite dishes. On a Moroccan holiday, the officers of our battalion were invited to have lunch with a Moroccan artillery regiment also located at Vat Cach Thuong. The

Moroccan *artilleurs* prepared their national dish called *couscous*, which consisted of lamb served with wild rice, onion, potatoes, raisins, and a specially prepared sauce. I loved it so much that later, every time I had occasion to spend a few days in Hanoi or Saigon, I would make it a point to go to a Corsican or Greek restaurant to eat the famous Moroccan *couscous*.

Around August 1953, my battery was declared operational again. We moved to Bui Chu to support a Vietnamese infantry battalion in its mission to capture the important Catholic seminary of Quan Son Ha located about thirty kilometers south of the city of Bui Chu. Since we expected to meet strong enemy resistance, I went with the battalion. However, we reached the seminary at day's end without incident. Two weeks after our battery left Bui Chu, the Viet Minh attacked the seminary and inflicted heavy losses to the infantry battalion that defended it.

Shortly after the Bui Chu operation, my battery was attached to a French artillery battalion and participated in a multi-regiment amphibious operation named "Operation Mouette." Mouette was launched to search for and destroy Viet Minh forces and supplies in the Thanh Hoa area. The city of Thanh Hoa, located approximately 200 kilometers south of Hanoi, near the border with Central Viet Nam, had always been under the control of the Viet Minh. The operation consisted of landing an amphibious force to capture the old Sam Son Beach and moving a column by RN1 from Ninh Binh to link up with the amphibious force. The operation met with little resistance as the Viet Minh had been able to escape the pincer movement. My battery moved along the deteriorated *Route Nationale* with the French artillery battalion and took up positions in rolling hills covered with tall elephant grass. We were told that the Ninh Binh-Thanh Hoa area was infested with tigers. Consequently, during the entire operation we were more concerned about tigers than about a possible Viet Minh attack.

In November 1953, shortly after our battery returned to Vat Cach Thuong following Operation Mouette, I received my transfer order, directing me to report to the 1st Vietnamese Artillery Battalion in Can Tho, South Viet Nam. I was happy that my request finally had been granted, but I was saddened by the thought that I had to leave the men who had fought under my command and whom I had grown to love as my own family. With a heavy heart, I bid farewell. Then Lieutenant Dong, the new battery commander, drove me to Hai Phong Airport where I boarded an Air France flight to Saigon. This was to be my last flight out of North Viet Nam; I would never return to that troubled but beautiful land again.

4

LAOS AND
HAUTS PLATEAUX

AFTER A FEW DAYS OF relaxation in Bac Lieu, I headed back to Can Tho and reported to the headquarters of the 1st Artillery Battalion located in Binh Thuy, five kilometers west of the city. Things were looking up. I finally was able to serve in my native Mekong River Delta. Can Tho had changed very much since the days I was a student at College Phan Thanh Gian. New construction had sprung up downtown, businesses were booming, and the people appeared more prosperous.

Can Tho Sector had been transferred to the Vietnamese authorities and the Sector Commandant was Lt. Col. Nguyen Khanh, a young and energetic officer. The military situation was relatively quiet with occasional skirmishes with small Viet Minh units. The 1st Artillery Battalion Headquarters and the Headquarters Battery were housed in three villas located on the western bank of the Binh Thuy River. The biggest villa was used as the office for the battalion commander, a French major, and also as Officers Quarters.

I was temporarily assigned as Operations Officer for the battalion. In that capacity, I accompanied the battalion commander during his field inspections. One week after I reported for duty, I accompanied a DLO team attached to a Hoa Hao auxiliary unit operating in its area of responsibility north of the Bassac River. In contrast to operations in North Viet Nam where the DLO teams had to march with the infantry units they were supporting, in the Mekong Delta, we rode comfortably in a sampan along the multiple rivers and canals which crisscrossed the countryside while the infantry progressed on both sides of the canal. If contact with the enemy was made, we would stop our sampan, disembark and, most difficult at all, try to determine the enemy location hidden behind thick coconut trees in front of us. Unlike a village in North Viet Nam, which was typically well delineated by a surrounding line of uninterrupted bamboo hedges, the village in the Mekong Delta could stretch for many miles along a main canal with no readily identifiable borders. I believed that the difference in physical settings between the Northern village and its Southern counterpart showed the differences in mentality and social attitudes; the villages in the North constituted close-knit social structures with their own rules and traditions,[5] while the Southern villages were more open, more flexible, and less structured.

I loved every minute of my stay at the 1st Artillery Battalion. As an Operation Officer, I had no command responsibilities. My duties consisted of revising training materials for the batteries, accompanying the battalion commander in field inspections, preparing reports, and updating tactical maps of the military operations in progress.

My happiness was short-lived, however. In early December 1953, the battalion received orders to move to Laos to support military operations around the strategic area of Seno-Savannakhet in Central Laos. The Viet Minh had taken the city of Thakhek, north of Savannakhet, and the French had moved their reserve units to reinforce the defense of the important Seno Airport. The Viet Minh offensive in Central Laos helped divert French troops from Dien Bien Phu, its main objective. As our battalion was making preparations for the long trip to Laos, it received a new commander. Major Goussault was a reserve officer with no combat experience. A Vietnamese officer, Maj. Bui Huu Nhon, was also assigned to the battalion. Major Nhon graduated from the first Officers Class organized by the French in Dalat and had attended the French Artillery School. However, Major Nhon had no official function in the battalion because the French were not ready to transfer the battalion to Vietnamese officers.

In any event, soon after Major Goussault arrived, he ordered me to report to the 3rd Battery in Vinh Long and to be prepared to take over the unit that was still under the command of a French officer. I sometimes asked myself whether I would be better off staying in North Viet Nam and fighting my familiar war in the Red River Delta or to participate in a foreign adventure and fight in a strange and far-away land.

Just before Christmas 1953, the entire battalion moved to Laos via Cambodia. The trip took about five days. Surprisingly, we were neither harassed nor attacked by the Viet Minh during our movement. However, a regrettable incident with the Cambodian Army took place in the city of Kratie, located on the Mekong River, where we bivouacked for the night. Some Cambodian officers, learning that we were a Vietnamese artillery unit, wanted to encircle and attack our battery. They brought machine guns and put them in position in front of our battery. Obviously, they were upset that a unit of the Vietnamese Army, their historic enemy, had entered their country without authorization, and, for them, this was equivalent to an act of war. The French military officials in Kratie had to intervene before the Cambodians lifted the siege and let us depart without further incident.

I took over the command of the 3rd Battery at Pakse in South Laos. The 3rd Battery was originally a French unit and most of the NCOs and enlisted men were of Cambodian descent; they had served many years under contract with the French. These Cambodian soldiers understood and spoke a broken French but their Vietnamese was very limited. Because they still remained loyal to the French, they were not sympathetic to the fact that a Vietnamese officer would assume the command of the battery. Further, deep in their hearts, the Cambodians considered the Vietnamese invaders who took their lands and killed their ancestors. However, despite the inherent hostility they had toward the Vietnamese, they had to honor their contract and to serve reluctantly under the new Vietnamese leadership.

I was aware of acute racial tension that was developing within the battery and knew that this tension, if not resolved immediately, would destroy the combat effectiveness of the unit. Therefore, I asked for the Cambodian Master-Sergeant who was the spokesman for the Cambodian soldiers. I told him that we were going to fight in a foreign land and that we needed to be united and to love each other as members of the same family if we were to survive this war together and return to our homes. I also told him that my maternal grandfather came from Cambodia and that in all probability, I, myself, might have Cambodian blood in my veins, and as a result, I considered all Cambodians my friends. The Cambodian Master-Sergeant was visibly moved. He promised me that the Cambodian soldiers would loyally serve under my command until the expiration of their contract in approximately five months. I hoped that by the time their contract expired, they would change their mind and re-enlist. Otherwise, my battery would cease to function unless trained replacements were provided.

At this time, there were two French NCOs who stayed on to handle the supply and maintenance operations for the battery. They were helpful in obtaining supplies and spare parts for vehicles. These last items had become critical after a long trip which took us through two different countries. I was amazed to see that in the most difficult circumstances, they always managed to have in reserve an ample supply of *vin d'intendance* (quartermasters wine), a very condensed, strong burgundy red wine. Thus, I was glad when they told me they volunteered to stay in the battery until the end of the current campaign.

As soon as we arrived in Seno, our battalion took up position within the perimeter of defense of the airport to provide support to the French airborne units recently dispatched from their new *camp retranche* of Dien Bien Phu. During one of the staff meetings that took place after our arrival, I met Major Bigeard who commanded the famed 6th B.C.P (*Bataillon Colonial Parachutiste*). His battalion had just come from Dien Bien Phu to boost the defense of the strategic Seno Base. Major Bigeard was a legendary figure in the French Corps Expeditionnaire. He had participated in many daring rescue operations in North Viet Nam. His unit was especially instrumental in the successful withdrawal of French forces from the Cao Bang-Lang Son border area.

With regard to the situation in Dien Bien Phu, Major Bigeard was certain the French would ultimately prevail. "*Dien Bien Phu est imprenable*"[6] said Bigeard with confidence. Four months later,

Major Bigeard was taken prisoner at Dien Bien Phu when the *camp retranche* surrendered to the Viet Minh after fifty-five days of savage fighting. (After the war, Bigeard rose to the rank of lieutenant general and served as sub-minister for defense under General De Gaulle.) History has proven that overestimating one's fire power and underestimating the enemy's ingenuity and tenacity was very costly to the French in 1954, and to the Americans two decades later.

On January 5, Bigeard's 6th B.C.P was heavily engaged with elements of the Viet Minh 320th Division around Ban Hine Siu, a small village about twenty kilometers north of Seno. On January 6, the 3rd Vietnamese Parachutist Battalion (3rd V.P.B.), that recently came from Cat Bi, near Hai Phong, North Viet Nam, was ordered to move to Ban Hine Siu to reinforce the 6th B.C.P. On January 9, at 5:00 AM., the Viet Minh launched a coordinated attack on 3rd V.P.B. at Ban Hine Siu. The Vietnamese parachutists were evicted from their defensive positions, but counterattacked at 6:30 AM. and reoccupied their positions at 9:30 AM. Friendly losses: fifty-one killed, eighty-four wounded, 101 missing. Enemy: 200 killed, many weapons captured.

About two weeks after we arrived in Seno, the Viet Minh overran the strategic Laotian base of Tchepone near the border with Viet Nam. Tchepone was located on RN9, which linked Savannakhet with the Vietnamese coastal city of Quang Tri. Situated near the famous Ho Chi Minh trail, Tchepone constituted an obstacle to the free flow of ammunition and supplies for the Viet Minh units operating in Laos and South Viet Nam and, thus, was the primary target for the Viet Minh before they launched their offensive in Laos.

The French decided to send one infantry battalion from the Cambodian Army to make a reconnaissance in force in the direction of Tchepone. My battery was selected to accompany the Cambodian battalion in this mission. The task force, transported by trucks, progressed in two echelons along RN9: the first echelon was composed of the battalion staff and three infantry companies. The first echelon was followed by a convoy of about thirty vehicles that carried supplies for the Tchepone base. My battery marched with one infantry company about three kilometers behind the first echelon. I detached to the battalion one DLO team under 2d. Lt. Duong Van Dan. Since the maps of Laos were of very small scale (1/1,000,000 or one mm. on the map represented one km. on the terrain), they could not be relied upon to determine our positions within an acceptable accuracy range. As a result, I requested that the 1st Artillery Battalion send me a survey officer who would sit on my jeep and who would regularly identify approximately our battery position on the map based on the mileage as shown on my jeep's odometer.

Around 2:00 PM., Lieutenant Dan reported that his column had received sniper fires and that the battalion commander had ordered the troops to disembark and to deploy on both sides of the road. Looking at the map, I realized that the battalion had just entered an area of dense forests and could fall into an ambush at any moment. I ordered the battery to take up position on a small jungle clearing near the road. My men had to use machetes to cut small trees and underbrush and my gunnery officer had to rely on compasses to set direction for the guns. This was not usual artillery field procedure, but under imminent attack we had no time to use more sophisticated survey equipment. Soon, Lieutenant Dan reported that his column had fallen into an ambush and was under strong attack by the enemy. He requested immediate close support on a small road junction just in front of the column. Not sure of the accuracy of my battery position, I first fired two rounds of smoke ammunition.

"On target! Fire for effect! Fire for effect!" yelled Lieutenant Dan on his radio.

Then his radio felt silent. I continued to fire as fast as I could to save the Cambodian battalion and, hopefully, to protect its retreat. Soon the first elements which had survived the first onslaught fell back to my position and reported that they were being pursued. I called my battalion headquarters in Seno and requested that reinforcements be sent immediately to my position to help defend my battery and to gather and reorganize the surviving elements of the Cambodian battalion.

About one hour later, a French parachutist company arrived and took up position in front of my battery to prevent a possible Viet Minh attack. By nightfall, my battalion commander informed me that Lieutenant Dan and the French infantry battalion commander had safely arrived in Seno. Later Lieutenant Dan told me that the first artillery salvos hit the Viet Minh as they got out of their foxholes to launch their assault, which prompted the French battalion commander to yell: "The artillery has arrived! We are saved!" However, despite heavy casualties inflicted by artillery fire, the Viet Minh continued their assault and, under heavy pressure, the battalion retreated in chaos. The French major asked Dan to take him directly to Seno through the jungles by bypassing my position that he thought must have already been overrun by the enemy. Most of the vehicles that accompanied the reconnaissance column were reported to have been burned by the Viet Minh.

After the Viet Minh's bloody ambush on RN9, and just a few days before the 1954 Tet (Vietnamese New Year), my battery was instructed to move to the city of Savanakhet to provide fire support to the French garrison defending the city. Savannakhet was a charming and sleepy little town located on the east bank of the Mekong River. From the vantage of my position on the southwestern outskirts of the city, I could see the Thai villages and their inhabitants on the opposite side of the river. The French military officials of Savannakhet Sector, understandably, instructed me not to fire into the Thai side under any circumstances. I spent the first week in Savannakhet adjusting artillery protective fire around various supplies and ammunition depots.

Fortunately, the situation around Savannakhet was relatively quiet. 2d. Lt. Duong Van Dan happened to have a relative who ran a small business in Savannakhet. He invited us to his home to celebrate the Tet with his family. To my surprise, there was an important Vietnamese community in the city. The Vietnamese mostly worked as mid-level civil servants in the Laotian government. They were proud to see that a Vietnamese artillery unit had come to help defend a Laotian town. Some of the sons of Vietnamese immigrants also served as officers in the Laotian Army and I was pleasantly surprised to see that the majority of Laotian officers spoke fluent Vietnamese. My men enjoyed their stay in this peaceful and hospitable city. Further, the Vietnamese New Year was also celebrated by the cosmopolitan population in Laos and gambling, although not legal, was generally accepted as a necessary part of the Tet festivities. My Cambodian soldiers, who loved to gamble, had a very good time.They somehow managed to beat the more innocent Laotians in these illicit activities and indulged themselves in food and luxury goods.

My happiness was again short-lived. About two weeks after our arrival in Savannakhet, the 1st Artillery Battalion was instructed to move to the Hauts Plateaux (Highlands) Region. It was to be attached to the newly formed Vietnamese Groupement Mobile (G.M.) No.11.The Vietnamese General Staff, at the instigation of the French High Command, had agreed in early 1954 to create sixty-six light infantry battalions to protect populated areas and to relieve the French forces from their static defense. Six G.M.s were also created to fight against regular Viet Minh units. Each G.M. consisted of three regular infantry battalions and one artillery battalion. G.M 11 was under the command of Lt. Col. Nguyen Khanh, the former commander of Can Tho Sector. Khanh graduated from the first Officer Course organized by the French. He subsequently attended the French Parachutist School at Pau in France. Khanh commanded the first Vietnamese parachutist company and was considered at the time one of the most promising young officers in our army. (He would later rise to the rank of full general and served a short time as a controversial chief of state in 1964.)

On March 1954, the 1st Artillery Battalion left Seno and moved to Ban Me Thuot via an abandoned dirt road which linked the Cambodian city of Kratie with the Vietnamese Hauts Plateaux. From Ban Me Thuot, we were directed to Pleiku to join G.M 11 whose mission was to secure RN19 which connected Pleiku to the coastal city of Qui Nhon. To carry out its mission, G.M.11 decided to occupy the strategic Mang Yang and Deo Mang hills which controlled the eastern section of RN19. Each of these positions would be occupied by one infantry battalion and one artillery battery. The G.M.11 and the 1st Artillery Battalion Headquarters would occupy An Khe, a small city located fifty kilometers east of Pleiku. The third infantry battalion was held in reserve in An Khe.

My battery provided direct support to the 1st Infantry Battalion, which had the mission of defending Mang Yang Pass about thirty kilometers east of Pleiku. Maj. Tran Hoang Quan, commander of the 1st Infantry Battalion, was an experienced officer from the Cao Dai religious sect. The Cao Dai sect was a strong supporter of the Japanese before 1945 and its officers had been trained by Japanese officers to fight against the French. Like many officers from different paramilitary organizations, the officers from the Cao Dai sect were integrated into the National Army in 1950 to provide cadres for the newly created infantry battalions.

As soon as we had completed our defensive preparations on Mang Yang, we were harassed by the enemy's repeated probing attacks; soon we were surrounded by elements of a regular Viet Minh regiment. Since we ran out of food, one night Major Quan sent out a patrol to steal a pig from a nearby Montagnard village. Unlike the corpulent and well fed pigs in the Mekong Delta, Montagnard pigs were small and skinny. However, after almost one month on rations, Major Quan's roasted pig was one of the best meals I had ever eaten.

By that time, the enemy controlled the portion of RN19 between Pleiku and Mang Yang. As I had run out of artillery ammunition, I requested to be resupplied by parachutes. I asked the French sergeants who were still in my battery to send the requisition and to coordinate the air drop with French pilots involved in the resupply mission. Air drop had almost become a routine for me since my days at Cho Noi in Hung Yen Province. The first crate fell near my tent. I rushed out and ordered the men to open the crate to retrieve the 105-mm shells from the containers. Surprisingly, the crate did not contain artillery ammunition but a well-preserved barrel of good *vin d'intendance*. I asked for the French Master-Sergeant. He saluted, smiling:

"*Mon Lieutenant*, I hope you would agree with me that *le vin d'intendance* is as necessary to the *artilleurs* as artillery ammunition."

I went to see Major Quan and presented him with a bottle of the wine. I also suggested that *le vin d'intendance* would go a long way with Montagnard pigs. He readily agreed.

In June 1954, the infantry battalion and the artillery battery at Deo Mang Pass, east of An Khe, were overrun by the Viet Minh's 803rd Regiment. The battalion commander, Maj. Nguyen Van Bich, my former instructor at the School of Inter-Arms, had been able to escape, but Lt. Dao Duy An, the battery commander, was taken prisoner. The Viet Minh towed all four 105-mm howitzers to their secret base in the coastal area of Binh Dinh. To prevent fire support to the Deo Mang position, the Viet Minh also fired mortars at the G.M.11 Headquarters and the artillery battery located at An Khe. There were no reported casualties at the G.M.'s staff but the battery commander was wounded. The defeat of Deo Mang was a heavy blow to the still untested G.M.11.

In June, the French Command in the Hauts Plateaux decided to relieve G.M.11 with the French G.M.100 which had just returned from its campaign in Korea.(The Armistice which ended the Korean War was signed the previous year and some of the French units fighting in Korea were directed to Indochina to reinforce the embattled French Corps Expeditionnaire.) So, on June 14, 1954, the 1st Infantry Battalion was ordered to open and secure RN19 west of Mang Yang for the safe passage of G.M.100 on its way to An Khe. 2d. Lt. Tran Van Phan, my deputy, acted as DLO with the battalion. Around noon, the 1st Battalion secured the assigned portion of RN19 without incident. As usual, the battalion was able to check only the area immediately adjacent to the road. Unknown to it, a Viet Minh regiment was waiting in the jungle a few hundred meters from both sides of the road. As the head echelons of G.M.100's convoy started to climb the first elevations of Mang Yang Pass about ten kilometers west of Mang Yang, the Viet Minh went into action. They first destroyed the lead vehicles with recoilless rifle fire and pinned down the column with heavy machine-gun fire from the hills located on the north side of the road. At the same time, assault elements broke through 1st Infantry Battalion's securing forces and destroyed in close combat G.M.100's units trapped on RN 19. Those who escaped to the small jungle clearings south of the road were also eliminated by waiting Viet Minh elements. The situation was so confused that I could only execute harassing fire a few hundred meters from both sides of the road to slow the attack and to prevent Viet Minh reinforcement.

By the time the fire had ceased, G.M.100 was no more. The Colonel who commanded G.M.100 and the commander of its artil-

lery battalion were both killed by the first recoilless rifle fire. The
payroll officer for the G.M. was probably also killed because Lieutenant Phan and his DLO team, who were the first elements to reach
the scene, saw Vietnamese money bills scattered all over the place.
Although they reported that they did not have time to amass any
money, I noticed that they had new shoes and new transistor radios
after we finally returned to Pleiku. All artillery guns as well as most
of the transportation vehicles were destroyed during the ambush.
Of a total of about 2,000 men, only a few hundred survived the
onslaught. There was no doubt in my mind that the annihilation of
G.M.100 on the infamous RN19 marked a turning point in the
Indochina War. The fall of Dien Bien Phu three weeks later was the
final blow to French efforts in Indochina and the beginning of its
decline as a colonialist power.

G.M.11 withdrew to Pleiku without incident the day its counterpart was destroyed on RN19. I remember that day. As my battery moved to a new position approximately fifteen kilometers east
of Pleiku to provide close support to the withdrawal of G.M.11 from
An Khe, I received many French soldiers who had survived the
bloody ambush. They stopped at my battery position and asked for
water. A young French lieutenant shook his head in disbelief and
told me: "*Il n'est ni beau ni fort!*" (He is neither handsome nor
strong") referring to General de Beaufort, the French general who
was in charge of the operations in the Hauts Plateaux. ("*Beau*" means
handsome and "*fort*" means strong in French.) Colonel Khanh, the
G.M.11 commander, directed me to conduct harassment fire
throughout the night to help the retreating units. For all practical
purposes, An Khe and RN19 were under the control of the Viet Minh,
who now were free to move their troops and supplies to the Hauts
Plateaux from their secret bases in the coastal area. By then the
French High Command knew that the strategic Binh Dinh-Qui Nhon
coastal area had to be recaptured if the Hauts Plateaux were to be
saved.

Thus, after three weeks of reorganization in Pleiku where G.M.11
received new replacements for its losses on Deo Mang, the unit was
ordered toward the coastal region north of Nha Trang to take part
in Operation "Atlante" aimed at recapturing the Viet Minh-controlled

Binh Dinh area. As we stopped for the night in Ban Me Thout, the Cambodian Master-Sergeant came to see me in my tent.

"Lieutenant," he said, "our contract expires today and we ask that we be allowed to return to our homeland in the Mekong Delta. Effective today, we will not participate in any combat operations."

For these Cambodian peasant-soldiers, Ban Me Thuot, Pleiku, and An Khe belonged to another world in which they had no interest. They had fought with great courage during the last six months because they were men of their word and they had honored their contract. But now the contract had expired and they felt they had no obligation to continue to fight, especially in this faraway land. After a day of tough negotiations and friendly persuasion, they agreed to extend their contract and to participate in other operations from which some of them never returned.

The next day, we proceeded toward the coastal area. I still recall the night we arrived in Nha Trang on May 7, 1954. It was my twenty-second birthday. As my battery camped for the night on a soccer field on the southern outskirts of the city, I received word that the battalion commander wanted to see me. When I arrived at the tent which served as the Officer Mess for the battalion staff, I was surprised to see that the French officers were openly weeping.

"Thi, Dien Bien Phu *vient de tomber*" (Dien Bien Phu has just fallen), said Major Goussault, wiping his tears, as I entered the tent.

General de Castries,[7] I was informed, had surrendered with the garrison. He was taken prisoner along with the survivors of the onslaught. Major Bigeard, the Indochina War hero, was also taken prisoner. Bigeard, along with the other *officiers parachutistes*, had in fact proposed to de Castries to wage a last battle, a *baroud d'honneur*, to break out of the encirclement. De Castries refused on the ground that it would be a hopeless and costly undertaking.

Although the fall of Dien Bien Phu had been anticipated, I was shocked and saddened by the news.

Gen. Henri Navarre, who had replaced General de Lattre as commander in chief in Indochina, had decided to move into Dien Bien Phu, an important opium producing area, reportedly to deny this important money generating resource to the Viet Minh, to induce them to fight, and to destroy them in a projected *bataille rangee* where the French would have superiority in fire power. The French established their *camp retranche* in a large valley surrounded by high mountains. Dien Bien Phu, with a perimeter of defense measuring sixteen kilometers by nine kilometers, consisted of a series of reinforced outposts surrounding a runway which could accommodate most of the French transport aircraft available at that time. The garrison was defended by 15,000 men including some of the best French troops (paratroopers and legionnaires).

Navarre, however, did not realize that the Viet Minh would be able to bring in their artillery and that the camp would be subject to deadly direct artillery fire from enemy batteries well bunkered in the surrounding hills. The French colonel who commanded all artillery units in Dien Bien Phu, frustrated and ashamed at being unable to return fire, committed suicide a few days earlier. A few months before the fall of Dien Bien Phu, President Eisenhower had seriously considered American intervention by providing air support—including the use of tactical nuclear weapons—for the besieged garrison under two conditions: the French would have to give genuine independence to the countries of Indochina and the British would have to join the Americans in their proposed intervention. However, the British were reluctant and, as a result, Dien Bien Phu was left to its tragic fate.

I offered condolences to the French officers and returned to my tent. I knew that the fall of Dien Bien Phu was the beginning of the end of the French presence in Indochina. It was also to be the beginning of the dismantlement of the French colonial empire in Africa.

I hoped that the Americans would step in to stop Communist expansion in Asia in accordance with the U.S. policy of "containment" advocated by John Foster Dulles, secretary of state under President Eisenhower. Further, the French departure would mean true independence for our country. With the help of the Americans, we would have a good cause to fight for.

The next day, our battalion received the order to move to Chi Thanh, approximately forty kilometers north of Nha Trang to participate in Operation Atlante. G.M.11 was part of a multi-battalion column which would move from Nha Trang and destroy the enemy forces in the Chi Thanh-Ninh Hoa area. The main attack was

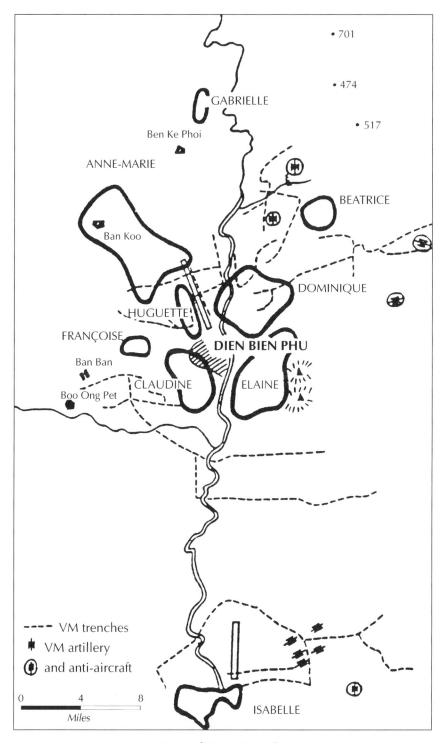

- - - VM trenches
⚔ VM artillery
⊛ and anti-aircraft

701
474
517

GABRIELLE

Ben Ke Phoi

ANNE-MARIE

Ban Koo

BEATRICE

DOMINIQUE

HUGUETTE

FRANÇOISE

Ban Ban

Boo Ong Pet

CLAUDINE

DIEN BIEN PHU

ELAINE

0   4   8
Miles

ISABELLE

Siege of Dien Bien Phu

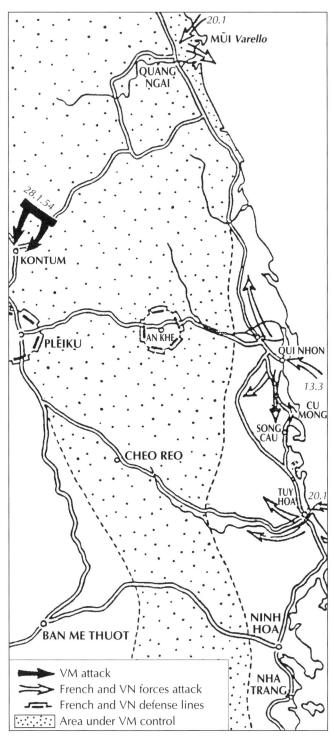

Operation Atlante (March 1954–July 1954)

assigned to a French amphibious task force which would land further north to capture an area south of Qui Nhon. As RN1 was heavily damaged in the Viet Minh-controlled area north of Nha Trang, the battalion travelled on an old railroad track at a tortoise's speed. We arrived at Chi Thanh by day's end without incident. Chi Thanh was in a small valley surrounded by high mountains. The G.M.'s headquarters as well as the three artillery batteries and one infantry battalion occupied the valley floor while elements of the other two infantry battalions were ordered to hold the important surrounding high ground.

During the first week, the battalion patrols reported contact and skirmishes with small Viet Minh units. Soon these skirmishes increased in intensity. At the same time, the railroad tract which represented our unique line of communication with Nha Trang was cut off and for all practical purposes, G.M.11 was trapped in the small valley of Chi Thanh.

As we were preparing for a long and bloody siege, I received an order to attend an advanced artillery course in France. Major Goussault refused to let me go because, according to him, he had an acute need for experienced battery commanders. Although what he said was absolutely true (one battery commander was taken prisoner and another wounded), I thought that this course was an important stepping stone for my military career and it was only fair that I be allowed to attend. So, I went to see Colonel Khanh, the G.M. commander, and explained to him that as much I would love to stay and fight, this advance course would be crucial for my career and professional advancement. He agreed, somewhat reluctantly. I then went back to the 1st Artillery Battalion commander and politely asked him if he had anything he wanted me to take to his wife in Paris. Major Goussault was not amused. He called Colonel Khanh and asked him to reconsider, but Khanh was a man of his word. He told the French major to let me go and to appoint a new battery commander. The next day, I transferred the command of my battery to 2d. Lt. Le Tri Tin, a staff officer at battalion headquarters. I felt sad and somewhat guilty for abandoning my men in these difficult times, but I was so eager to visit France and to advance in my military career, that nothing would stop me. Soon, a

Cessna piloted by Lt. Vo Dinh, one of my classmates at Dalat, landed on the small dirt air strip of Chi Thanh and took me to the safe haven of the lovely resort city of Nha Trang. After one day of rest and relaxation on the beach, I boarded a French military transport aircraft for Saigon.

When I reported to the General Staff for processing procedures, I was informed that I had been promoted to the rank of captain. Maj. Bui Huu Nhon and three other captains were also slated to attend the same advanced artillery course in France.

5

BETWEEN TWO WARS

WHEN I WAS A CHILD and attended the elementary school in Bac Lieu, I was taught that France was *la mere patrie*. I also learned through history books that *"nos ancêtres sont des Gaulois"* (our ancestors are the Gauls). Later at College Phan Thanh Gian, I was captivated by the French Revolution which began with *la Prise de la Bastille*, continued with Robespierre's *Terreur* and ended with Napoleon's *Premier Empire*. Like Victor Hugo, I admired Napoleon's military exploits. I followed with passion his skillful tactical maneuvers at Iena and Austerlitz, which Hugo immortalized in his epics. I memorized Hugo's famous phonetic verse describing Napoleon's heavy artillery moving to the front:

"Et ces lourds canons roulant vers Austerlitz."[8]

At College Phan Thanh Gian, we were also initiated to the rationalist philosophers of the eighteenth century. We admired the immortal works of the French poets of the *l'École Classique* of the seventeenth century. Most of all, however, we adored the lyric poems of Lamartine, Victor Hugo, Alfred de Musset, and Chateaubriand, who represented the nineteenth century's *École Romantique*.

Imbued with French culture and civilization, I dreamed of being able to visit, not the "mother country" or "the country of our ancestors, the Gauls," not the *"puissance colonilisatrice"* that conquered an important empire under the pretext of a noble *mission civilisatrice*, but the country of Voltaire and Rousseau, the country that produced some of the greatest philosophers and writers in the world. Thus, it was with trepidation and excitement that I landed at Orly Airport outside of Paris in late May 1954.

I was aware that there were two Frances: the France represented by their administrators and businessmen in her colonies and the Metropolitan France, which extolled the ideals of *"Liberté, Fraternité et Égalité."* It was a known fact that the first France, the colonial France, attracted mostly applicants from the less educated southern regions of France including the island of Corsica. These people went to the colonies to find fortune and social status and tended to form, from generation to generation, an entrenched social and political structure of their own, which had little connection to the *Metropole*.

Thus, when I arrived in France in May 1954, it was the second France, the France of thinkers, artists, and poets, the France that pioneered the ideals of liberty and equality that I wanted to visit and explore. To immerse myself in the academic world I missed, I rented a room in a hotel in the Quartier Latin, near La Sorbonne. Since I had almost two weeks before reporting to the French Artillery School at Chalons-sur-Marnes, I had ample time to explore Paris. The Quartier Latin was the academic center of France and contained many of its *Grandes Écoles*; it also contained an impressive community of Vietnamese students. A good portion of those students were influenced by Communist propaganda and had participated in pro-Communist activities in France. I had no problems with people expressing their views, but I despised the students who claimed to be Communist but did not have the stomach to go home and to fight for the cause they professed to believe in. Many of them, lured by well-paying jobs in the metropole, would remain in France after graduation. We scornfully called them *"les communistes de salon."* It struck me, however, that France was fighting a deadly war against the Communists in Indochina and would not hesitate to crack down on any pro-Communist activities in Viet Nam, but at the same time it tolerated Communist subversive activities on its soil. I thought France should be given credit for having demonstrated her willingness to uphold fundamental democratic principles, at least in the metropole. One decade later, the United States would face a similar problem with its students. However, there was a big difference in that the demonstrations in American universities in the 1960s were organized by American, not Vietnamese students; although a few of these students may have been sympathetic to the Viet Cong, most of them just wanted to express their antiwar sentiments.

My first visit in Paris was to the *Jardin de Luxembourg* which was located two blocks from my hotel. When I was young, I was mesmerized by the beauty of Anatole France's prose, especially the immortal passage *"La Rentrée des Classes"* (Back to School) in which he described le Jardin de Luxembourg that he crossed on his way to school in the autumn and where *"les feuilles qui jaunissent dans les arbres qui frissonned....tombent une a une sur les epaules des statues."* [9] I also attended lectures given by philosophy professors at La Sorbonne across from my hotel. During my spare time, after daily excursions by Metro to visit the usual tourist attractions, I liked to sit for hours in one of these numerous sidewalk cafes on the Boulevard Saint Michel in the Quartier Latin where I felt relaxed and far away from the bloody battlefields of Indochina.

Finally, after two weeks of exploration and discovery in Paris, we took a train to report to the Artillery School at Chalons-sur-Marne. Chalons was a sleepy little town located in the middle of the French champagne country, about 150 kilometers east of Paris. This was one of the poorest regions of France; except for the production of champagne, there were no other noticeable industries which could provide employment to the local residents. I was not surprised that Chalons was chosen as the site for the French artillery school, because, typically artillery schools are located in the most desolate areas of the country where land is not very productive, and can be used as artillery firing ranges.

Since Chalons was situated on the invasion route for the Germans, it had witnessed many battles during two World Wars. During World War I, for example, after occupying the eastern part of France, the German Army, for unknown reasons, decided to bypass Paris and move southward; in the process it exposed its right flank to a successful French counterattack in the Marne River region. This counterattack was later known as the *Bataille de la Marne* and the taxis used to transport the troops to the front were called *les taxis de la Marne*. The austerity of the champagne region, its inclement climate and the fact that it was the site of many past battles had an impact on its residents who appeared more reserved and not as open and outgoing as *les gens du Midi* in France's southern regions.

The one-month advanced course was designed for artillery field-grade officers slated for positions as artillery battalion commanders or staff officers in Great Units such as divisions and army corps. In our class, there were many foreign officers including officers from Israel and from various Arab countries. They all got along quite well. We learned artillery tactics, artillery employment, and organization in Great Units, including the techniques of counter-battery at army corps level. The highest units we had in Viet Nam were the newly created Groupements Mobiles; these were simply an equivalent of a regimental task force and we had difficulties visualizing the organization at Corps level. Nevertheless, this advanced class opened new horizons and showed us that there were more possibilities beyond the command of a battery or battalion if South Viet Nam was to expand her army. During this course, we participated in field maneuvers at Corps level in the area known as the Champagne Pouilleuse, east of Chalons. I enjoyed these field exercises where I had opportunities to see the French countryside, talk to the farmers, and to see their way of life.

Every day, when we were not in the field, a bus would take us to the Officers Club in downtown Chalons for lunch and dinner. True to the French artillery tradition, even for lunches, we were served aperitifs which included *pernod*, a strong anise-based alcohol that the French relished, a three-course affair including soup, fish, meat, salad (which the French ate after the main course) and dessert. Of course, white wine was served with fish and the *piece de resistance* was *arose* with an abundance of red wine. After dessert, we were served coffee, then liquor (that the French appropriately called "*digestif*"). After these "typical" luncheons, I could hardly stay awake for afternoon classes. Since we were in the country of champagne, dinners typically ended with a good bottle of champagne from the nearby *caves d'Epernay*.

A month earlier, Mr. Mendès France had become the new prime minister; he promised the French people that he would conclude a peace agreement with the Viet Minh. When I was at Chalons, the French and Viet Minh delegations were meeting at Geneva with representatives of the United States, Great Britain, the Soviet Union, and Communist China to work out the terms of the new peace agreement. After Dien Bien Phu and the anticipated French disengagement from Indochina, Algeria was to be the next trouble spot and the French generals were determined to keep it at all costs. (Later, the French generals in Algeria rebelled against General De Gaulle who wanted to grant independence to Algeria. The rebellious generals even threatened to send parachutist units to Paris to overthrow the French Third Republic.)

At that time, the French were actively recruiting Indochina veterans to fight in Algeria. I was tempted to take a commission in the French army, but the images of young Moroccan soldiers dying in the village of Luong Kiet, far from their home, flashed in my memory and I thought it made no sense for me to fight and die for a bad cause. Also, I was eager to return to Viet Nam to serve my country at this critical juncture of its history. Further, my mother and two young brothers needed me at home; how could I desert them at this critical time?

When I landed at Tan Son Nhut Airport in mid-July 1954, the Geneva Accords had been already signed. Viet Nam was partitioned at the seventeenth parallel. The agreement provided for a general election to be held in two years, in 1956. Mr. Ngo Dinh Diem, back from exile in the United States, was appointed prime minister of the post-war government in the South. Mr. Diem had served as a *Thuong-Thu* (the equivalent of a prime minister) in the Imperial Court of Hue before 1945. He was a Catholic and a protégé of Cardinal Spellman.While in the United States, he met Senator John F. Kennedy, who supported his nomination as prime minister of South Viet Nam.

Looking back to the Indochina War, I think the main causes of the failure of French policy in Indochina were the opposition of the French government to progressive and orderly development of South Viet Nam toward independence under a genuine nationalist gov-

ernment and, more importantly, not allowing the early creation of
a strong Vietnamese Army.

In 1950, for example, the Vietnamese Army had only thirteen
combat battalions. At the peak of the Indochina War in 1953, when
the Viet Minh had six fully manned and equipped infantry divisions
with a total strength of 425,000 men (including their popular and
guerrilla forces), the Vietnamese Army had only forty-five combat
battalions and a general effective force of 198,000 men.

However, when Diem returned to Viet Nam in July 1954, the army
was not his immediate concern, for he had to handle a heavy flow of
refugees from North Viet Nam. To his credit, his government succeeded
in relocating one million Northerners in the South. A good portion of
these refugees were Catholics who preferred to abandon their property and the graves of their ancestors rather than live under a Communist regime. These Catholic groups would constitute a powerful
political force that would play an important role in the shaping of the
political landscape of South Viet Nam in years to come.

After I returned from Chalons-sur-Marne, I was appointed commanding officer of the 4th Artillery Battalion stationed at Pleiku in
the Hauts Plateaux. I spent most of my time supervising the training of the battalion and tried to remedy the shortcomings in the
employment of artillery based upon my personal experiences of the
last war. I also focused my attention on proper maintenance of all
motor vehicles and artillery equipment in order to put the battalion
in a permanent state of readiness should hostilities resume.

Most of the officers and men of the battalion had participated in
the campaign of the Hauts Plateaux. One of the most distinguished
officers of the battalion was 2d. Lt. Nguyen Tien Ich. A gunnery
officer with the full baccalaureate degree in mathematics, Ich later
joined the Navy and was sent to the French Naval School at Brest
where he graduated at the top of his class. He subsequently attended
the Massachusetts Institute of Technology (MIT) to become a math
instructor at the Vietnamese Military Academy; he would later become the first Vietnamese with a doctoral degree from that prestigious institution.

The most difficult problem for me in this new command, however, was communication within the battalion; most of the soldiers

were Montagnards from the Rhade tribe who could speak a broken French but not Vietnamese. The Montagnards had no written language and each tribe had its own dialect. In the past, French missionaries, in order to preach and to convert them to Christianity, tried to create a codified written language for all tribes, but their success appeared limited. The Rhade tribe was the most advanced among the Montagnards of the Hauts Plateaux. Many members of the Rhade tribe served in the French Army and a few of them rose to the rank of officer. As the French were withdrawing from Indochina, they secretly encouraged the Montagnards to rebel against the new Vietnamese government. As a result, the Montagnards formed a new political front called the *Front Unifie Pour La Liberation Des Races Opprimees* (FULRO). It is interesting that more than two decades later, the American were to use the same organization as leverage against hostile South Vietnamese government officials.

One regrettable incident happened during my command of the 4th Artillery Battalion. One day, the French Command of the 4th Military Region organized a soccer tournament for all units in the Hauts Plateaux. Thanks to my assistant, Lt. Ho Van Phuoc, who had played soccer for the Lycée Petrus Ky and who had extensively trained my battalion team, we eliminated three competing teams and reached the final. We played against the team of a French transportation unit in Ban Me Thuot. The French scored 1-0 during the first halftime. My team came back and scored toward the end of the match, but my *avant-centre* accidentally hit a French player in the abdomen during the melee. The Frenchman later died in Ban Me Thuot military hospital. Colonel Sockel, commanding the Ban Me Thuot Sector, declared that my team's score was void and gave the trophy to the French team. He also announced on the loudspeakers that he wanted to see me at once after the game. Visibly angry, he scolded me and threatened to punish me for using violent tactics. I told him I was sorry for the death of the French soldier, but assured him that it was not intentional and that, unfortunately, accidents do happen in sports. He let me go without the *arrets de rigueur* he had originally threatened me with; he was well aware that any punishment at that time would inflame the anti-French sentiments within the Vietnamese units in the Hauts Plateaux.

The garrison life of a young officer in this remote Montagnard village of Pleiku was rather dull. To kill time, I subscribed to a correspondence course for the preparation of the French baccalaureate in philosophy. Every night, I devoured a multitude of textbooks on psychology, logic, and metaphysics.

Even in this lost Montagnard town, we were not spared from new political developments in Saigon. The transitional period between a complete French withdrawal from Indochina and the consolidation of the new U.S.-backed government of Ngo Dinh Diem, in fact, had given rise to a new conflict between the pro-French and pro-government factions within the Army. The pro-French faction was led by Gen. Nguyen Van Hinh, the chief of the General Staff. A former officer in the French Air Force who had seen combat in World War II, General Hinh harbored political ambitions of his own. A petition was circulated within the units requesting support for General Hinh. Although I did not sign the petition, I believed that we needed a strong government in this crucial post-war period to cope with anticipated Communist subversion activities and even a possible renewal of hostilities. I also believed that only an army officer could provide the leadership required. On the other hand, I had not previously heard of Ngo Dinh Diem and was concerned that his long exile in Europe and in the United States would cause him to be out of touch with the political and military realities of the country.

To my surprise, Ngo Dinh Diem had an important group of loyal supporters among Catholic officers and also among officers from Central Viet Nam. Maj. Huynh Van Cao, a Catholic from Hue and commander of an infantry battalion in Phan Thiet, openly defied General Hinh by proclaiming support for Diem. More importantly, U.S. Col. Edward Lansdale, who had successfully groomed and supported President Magsaysay in his efforts to crush the Huk Communist insurgency in the Philippines, had recently come to Viet Nam to advise and support Diem in his efforts to consolidate power. To provide military backbone to the new regime, Colonel Lansdale recruited Gen. Trinh Minh The, a Cao Dai officer, who agreed to put his forces at the disposal of the new government. At last, under pressure from the United States, the French gave in and agreed to the departure of General Hinh. Emperor Bao Dai, who was still chief of state but who lived in France most of the time, appointed Gen. Nguyen Van Vy, also a former officer in the French Army, as the new chief of the General Staff, but the appointment was strongly opposed by the Cao Dai officers under Gen. Trinh Minh The. Finally, the position was given to Gen. Le Van Ty, also a former officer in the French Army. However, General Ty, a fatherly figure with no political ambitions, was considered more malleable and more suitable for the job.

Around February 1955, I was assigned to the new artillery school at Phu Loi which had been recently transferred to the Vietnamese Army by the French. The artillery school was put under the control of the commander of the Thu Duc Inter-Schools System. The new school commandant was Lt. Col. Bui Huu Nhon, who had been my classmate at Chalons-sur-Marne. Colonel Nhon, without my knowledge, had requested my transfer to the school as director of instruction in charge of training.

The French had one advisory team of two officers and one NCO remaining at Phu Loi. One month after my arrival at the artillery school, Major Lucas, a cigar-chewing American officer, joined the advisory team, which he finally took over around April 1955. By that time, as a result of an agreement between the United States and France, all military aid to the countries of Indochina was handed directly to these countries and the training of the Vietnamese Army was officially transferred by the French to the Americans. Consequently, an organization called "Training Relations Instruction Mission" (TRIM) was created in Saigon. Major Lucas and his new American advisory team reported to the TRIM at Thu Duc Inter-Schools Command. A new organization named U.S. Military Assistance and Advisory Group, Viet Nam (or MAAG-V) was soon created to take over the training of the South Vietnamese Army.

The American training program provided for sending Vietnamese officers to the United States to be trained at various service schools. Thus, in September 1955, the first Vietnamese officers were sent to Fort Benning, Georgia, to attend the basic infantry course.

Subsequently, artillery officers were also sent to attend the basic artillery and survey courses at Fort Sill, Oklahoma. Major Lucas informed me that I was slated to attend the Artillery Advanced Course at Fort Sill, possibly within one year. To prepare me for this, he volunteered to spend one to two hours every night giving me practical lessons in English.

Around July, 1955, Colonel Nhon became the commander of the artillery branch of the army. I succeeded him as commander of the Artillery School and was promoted to major. At twenty-three, I was one of the youngest majors in the Vietnamese Army. In the same month, the artillery school, along with the engineer school, moved to an old French armored regiment's barracks in downtown Thu Dau Mot. The *5ème Regiment Cuirassie,* consisting mostly of Moroccan soldiers, was one of the French elite units. It was one of the first units to withdraw from Indochina after the Geneva Accords, possibly to be sent to Algeria to crack down on the new Algerian rebellion.

The new school complex was an impressive fort located on a small hill surrounded by a two-meter-high brick wall. It consisted of two three-story metal buildings which were used as classrooms and sleeping quarters for the students and one two-story office building. On both sides of the tree-lined street leading to the school, there were large masonry villas which were used as residences for the faculty and staff.

This was one of the happiest periods of my military career. As a relatively young officer, I was given the responsibility of training new artillery officers and NCOs, and also of inculcating a new tradition and shaping a doctrine for the infant Vietnamese Artillery. Since Thu Dau Mot was only about thirty kilometers from Saigon, I spent most of my weekends at the Lido Officers Club at Gia Dinh, at the northern outskirts of Saigon, where I played tennis and swam in its Olympic-size swimming pool.

During that time, Diem undertook the difficult task of unifying the army and consolidating his leadership. First, he ordered the airborne units and the troops of Gen. Trinh Minh The to attack the armed gangs of Binh Xuyen and to evict them from the Cho Lon area where for years, they had controlled organized gambling and prostitution with the tacit support of Emperor Bao Dai.

While the murderous street combats between the Binh Xuyen and the government forces took place around a bridge in Cho Lon named the "Y" Bridge, some of the Cao Dai leaders arrested Gen. Nguyen Van Vy. Vy had previously received orders from Bao Dai to replace Gen. Nguyen Van Hinh as chief of the General Staff. Lt. Col. Do Cao Tri, commander of the airborne brigade, called Diem and threatened to attack the Independence Palace if the Cao Dai did not release General Vy, who was an airborne officer in the French Army. (There was a strong camaraderie among parachutists.) General Vy was released and left for France, but Gen. Trinh Minh The was killed near the "Y" Bridge in Cho Lon while directing the attack on the Binh Xuyen stronghold. Defeated in Cho Lon, the Binh Xuyen withdrew to their Rung Sat secret base, a marshy area near Vung Tau, where they were annihilated by the troops under Col. Duong Van Minh, a rising star in the South Vietnamese Army.

After this first success, Diem elevated Colonel Minh to brigadier general. He also ordered him to organize a large-scale operation to pacify the Mekong Delta and to destroy the dissident Hoa Hao forces in the region. The Hoa Hao were essentially Buddhist but they followed a Buddhism that had been transformed and adapted to the mores and customs of the peasants of the Mekong Delta. The Hoa Hao were a staunch anti-Communist religious sect. They considered the Viet Minh their sworn enemy because the Viet Minh had assassinated their leader, Huynh Phu So. However, the Hoa Hao were independent people and they did not want to relinquish the economic and political control of their traditional fiefdom in Long Xuyen and Chau Doc. The pacification operation under the command of General Minh lasted one year, from May 1955 to May 1956. It resulted in the surrender of Gen. Tran Van Soai and his troops and the capture and execution of Ba Cut, the fiercest of all Hoa Hao dissident leaders.

On October 23, 1955, Diem, having consolidated his political power, organized a national referendum, which resulted in the overthrow of Bao Dai and the formation of the First Republic on October 26, 1955. He was its first President. On that date, the Vietnamese National Army became the Army of the Republic of Viet Nam (ARVN). By that time, I strongly supported Mr. Diem in his efforts to unify the National Army because I was increasingly impressed by his successes. I also acclaimed the results of the referendum because Bao Dai, who preferred to live in France rather than provide leadership at home, was, in my opinion, unfit to govern the country.

I believed at that time that Diem was the man of the hour. He had rescued South Viet Nam from the edge of bankruptcy after the 1954 Geneva Accords. He had created a unified national army by defeating the armed religious sects and assimilating various semi-independent paramilitary forces left by the French. He had succesfully resettled one million refugees from the North. From the ashes of the 1945-1954 war, he had created a strong, properous, and internationally recognized Republic.

Within the army, a new reorganization plan called for the creation of the following units:
   • Four Field Infantry Divisions
   • Six Light Infantry Divisions
   • One Airborne Brigade
   • Four Armored Regiments
   • Eleven Artillery Battalions
   • Thirteen Regional Regiments
   • Six Religious Sect Infantry Regiments
The light infantry divisions and the religious sect regiments were later deactivated and replaced by regular infantry divisions.

In May 1956, I was instructed to attend the Advanced Artillery Course in the United States. While I took my physical examination at the military Cong Hoa General Hospital in Saigon for the trip to the United States, I met my future wife. Ngoc Bich was a librarian at the hospital. Born in Thai Binh, North Viet Nam, she attended Lycée Trung Vuong in Hanoi and enrolled in an Army social work course in Saigon in 1953. During the evacuation of North Viet Nam right after the Geneva Accords, she flew to Hanoi every day in French military transport aircraft, under all weather conditions, to pick up Northern refugees. She was awarded the Vietnamese gallantry cross for her action.

In July 1956, I boarded a flight for the United States. The trip took almost a week because we had to stop at Clark Air Force Base in the Philippines, at Guam, and at Honolulu; at these stops, we had to wait for days for the next available flight. Three Vietnamese captains also traveled with me.

After five days of sightseeing in San Francisco, we took a train to Fort Sill, Oklahoma. Like the French artillery school at Chalons-sur-Marne, Fort Sill was located in a desolate area. Fort Sill was a U.S. Army reservation at Lawton, Oklahoma, seventy-five miles southwest of Oklahoma City. The school originally had been established in 1869 as a cavalry base for operations against the Indians. Nicknamed the "University of the Artillery," the school offered basic to advanced artillery courses and was responsible for the testing of new artillery weapons and the preparation of doctrine and procedures for artillery employment within the U.S. Army.

When we arrived at Fort Sill in the summer of 1956, it was very hot and the thermometer often exceeded 100 degrees. At that time, the Bachelor Officers Quarters (BOQ) were not equipped with air conditioning. Some nights, it was so hot that we had to sleep on the floor with a fan working ceaselessly. One day, an American officer asked me whether it was customary for Vietnamese to sleep on the floor.

The Advanced Artillery Course was designed for battery and battalion commanders, so most of the students were field grade officers. We spent most of our time in the field performing surveys to determine the coordinates of the battery position and observation posts or to adjust artillery fire under the scorching Oklahoma sun. We would come back to our BOQ at the end of the day, dirty and exhausted. Because our English was limited and we could understand only about fifty percent of what the instructors said in class, we had to spend more time to do the required reading and to complete our home work. Our efforts paid off. One day the instructor discussed the results of the first exam on gunnery, which was the most difficult subject of the course. As he explained the answer to each test question, one student impatiently asked:

"Tell me! Are there any 'max' (maximum score) on this test?"

The instructor pointed in my direction and answered calmly, "Yes, Major Thi from Viet Nam."

I was surprised and I grew more confident in my belief that I could overcome my English deficiency with hard work. A week later, a Vietnamese captain from my group achieved the highest score in survey.

Our social life at Fort Sill was rather limited as there was little recreation besides the rodeo and Indian dances that our fellow American student officers took us to see during our first month at the school. The nearest town, Lawton, had no Chinese restaurant and offered no recreation. The first time we went to Lawton to eat Mexican food, I was amazed to see that one black major in our class, who was in civilian clothes, dutifully went to sit on the rear seat of our bus like other black civilians. In the restaurant, there were restrooms reserved for colored people. One captain from our group, not knowing in what category yellow people were classified, asked the restaurant manager whether he should go the colored people's restroom. The manager told him that it was OK for him to go to the restrooms reserved for whites.

To my pleasant surprise, I discovered that Fort Sill was a city by itself, complete with cinemas, post exchanges (PX), officers clubs, tennis, and swimming pools. We spent our weekends playing tennis and shopping at the PX; in the evening we would relax and eat a good T-bone steak at the Officers Open Mess. This was a welcome departure from the buffalo meat that was typically served at the Field Officers Mess.

Toward the middle of the course, the school organized a trip to Oklahoma City for the Allied students to watch an airshow. Some of the kids at the airport asked us whether we were from Indonesia. When we told them we were from Viet Nam, they shook their head; but when we explained that Viet Nam was one of the countries of Indochina, they understood. Apparently, Viet Nam was still unknown in 1956. However, this was going to change because Americans began to become increasingly involved in this faraway Indochinese Peninsula.

At last, the Advanced Artillery Course came to an end and since we had one week to report back to Fort Mason in San Francisco, we decided to travel by Greyhound bus through Texas and Southern California to see the country.

When I reported to the Artillery Command after my return to Saigon in late November 1956, I was informed that no decision had been made regarding my new assignment. I took advantage of this unanticipated break to go out with Ngoc Bich. We decided that we would marry early the following year. My mother did not like the idea that I was marrying a Northerner, but she was not opposed. On January 4, 1957, our wedding took place in Cho Lon. Three days later, we drove to Bac Lieu for our honeymoon. Capt. Nguyen Van Be, Chief of Bac Lieu District, a classmate of mine at College Phan Thanh Gian, lent me a jeep and a carbine rifle. My wife and I drove around the countryside and to the beach. I also played tennis and occasionally I would spend a day hunting wild ducks with Dr. Ha. I was twenty-four, a major in the artillery. I had been awarded three gallantry crosses, graduated from the French and U.S. artillery schools, and I had a wonderful wife. The country was at peace. For me, "*c'etait la vie en rose!*" and I looked forward to my new assignment.

In February 1957, after the Tet festivities, I reported to the Command & General Staff College in Saigon as artillery instructor. This was not an enviable assignment because most of the teachers and students were politically undesirable officers. In fact, the first coup d'etat against President Diem was organized by disaffected officers from that school.

However, for a newly married officer, a Saigon job was welcome news. Like other instructors at the Command & General Staff College, I was allocated one studio unit on Tran Hung Dao Boulevard in downtown Cho Lon. At night, my wife and I frequently ate Chinese noodles or *com ga* (rice and steamed chicken) at a nearby restaurant and during the weekends, we loved to watch cowboy films at a Chinese theater located on the same block.

Gen. Tran Van Minh, the school commandant, was an ardent tennis player. He invited me and another instructor, Maj. Vinh Loc, a distant cousin of Emperor Bao Dai, to play tennis with him at Lido Officers Club in Gia Dinh almost every Saturday night. Gen. Tran Van Minh was nicknamed "Little Minh" as opposed to General Duong Van Minh, nicknamed "Big Minh" by the American press. Gen. Duong Van Minh was an excellent tennis player and always played opposite General Tran Van Minh. Maj. Vinh Loc and I would take turns playing as double partners to the two Minhs and some

Saturday nights the generals would not release us before two or three o'clock in the morning. My marriage was almost ruined by these nocturnal tennis matches between two Southern generals who had fallen into disgrace with the new regime.

By that time, my original excitement and hope in Mr. Diem had vanished. After he overthrew Emperor Bao Dai, President Diem created a Republic, but the problem was, he acted like an emperor. He tolerated no organized opposition; his critics were harrassed or arrested. His decrees became laws. He gradually transformed South Viet Nam into a quasi-police state where the security apparatus was rigidly controlled by his brother Ngo Dinh Nhu, the intellectual of the family. Mr. Nhu had graduated from the French *École de Chartres* that trained librarians and archivists. He had worked as an archivist in Hanoi where he met his wife, the daughter of Tran Van Chuong, a well-known lawyer. To help his brother consolidate power, Nhu organized a security network which reported any dissident activities in the Army and in the government. To crack down on Communist subversion, Nhu also launched a large-scale anti-Communist denunciation campaign (*To Cong*) throughout the country. It was estimated that from 50,000 to 100,000 people were sent to detention camps; many were not Communist activists.

To provide a political and philosophical basis for his authoritarian regime, Diem created the only authorized political party, the semi-secret Can Lao Party and organized a large scale political indoctrination program for administration officials and army officers. The program was run by another brother, Monsignor Ngo Dinh Thuc, Archbishop of Vinh Long. The Can Lao Party was built on a newly created philosophical doctrine of "Personalism" or "*Nhan Vi,*" a curious amalgam of Confucianism, Christianity, and a school of thought founded by French philosopher Emanuel Mounier. A Catholic thinker, Mounier, in reaction to the Communist promises of a classless society, advocated authoritarian social organizations where masses of alienated people could find unity and satisfaction through active participation in society. Mounier predicted the emergence of strong and moralistic leaders. It was no wonder that such a philosophy was viewed favorably by Diem, who considered himself a moralistic leader.

Armed with a philosophical and moralistic mandate, Mr. Diem undertook the task of reforming Vietnamese society. To exercise control over the villages, which for many centuries formed the basic social and political structures of Viet Nam, he abolished the elected village councils and replaced them with appointed Catholic Northerners.

A Can Lao Party apparatus, similar to the Communist model, was also established within the Army; one Can Lao-affiliated officer at each unit was responsible for insuring the "political correctness" of the unit and for reporting any "deviations" or "suspicious activities" of the unit commander. Needless to say that many unit commanders at regiment level and above were also members of the Can Lao Party. It was a well-known fact that to advance under Diem's regime, one had to be a member of the Can Lao Party, a Catholic, and a resident of Central Viet Nam. Since I had none of these qualifications, I was automatically eliminated from possible consideration for promotions or for important positions within the Army.

In December 1957, I was appointed artillery commander for I Corps in Danang, Central Viet Nam. My wife could not accompany me because she was expecting our first child. After Tuan, our son, was born in February 1958, my wife joined me in Danang with my mother, who helped my wife take care of our child during the first few months. At that time, I Corps had two regular infantry divisions and one light infantry division. Each regular division had one organic 105-mm artillery battalion and the light infantry division had no artillery. There was also one 155-mm howitzer battalion under the tactical control of I Corps Headquarters.

As Corps Artillery Commander, I was responsible for supervising the training of all artillery units under Corps and divisions' control. To prepare for a possible renewal of hostilities, our staff surveyed all usable battery positions throughout MRI. We established a file for each position including nature of terrain, access, camouflage, and coordinates. Once a year, we would participate in a Corps field maneuver. Gen. Duong Van Minh, commander of the Field Command, and his staff would act as referee. The maneuver typically began with an enemy coordinated offensive along the DMZ followed by the withdrawal of friendly forces, a defense along a line of contact deep into our territory and concluded with a successful friendly counter-offensive to recapture lost ground. Although we always won in the maneuvers, the heated final critique sessions often created unnecessary tensions between the staff of I Corps and Field Command.

Around September 1958, I accompanied a Vietnamese military delegation to visit Korean units and military installations in Korea. Five years after the armistice had been signed, Seoul still bore scars of the war. I was struck by the resignation of the Korean people and their determination to rebuild the country. I was also impressed by the discipline and motivation of the Republic of Korea (ROK) Army units we visited. During our free time, the Vietnamese assistant military attaché in Seoul drove us downtown to buy Korean ginseng; I bought a few pounds of precious *nhan sam* (human-shaped ginseng) for my wife who was pregnant with our second child.

My stay in the MRI was relatively uneventful, except for the political situation which had become increasingly unbearable. Although Central Viet Nam, theoretically, was under the administrative responsibility of a government-appointed governor, all important decisions had to be approved by Ngo Dinh Can, President Diem's youngest brother. After President Diem's father, Ngo Dinh Khai, a mandarin in the Imperial Court and the first director of the famed Quoc Hoc (National) School in Hue, and Diem's oldest brother, Ngo Dinh Khoi, were killed by the Viet Minh in 1945, Can volunteered to stay home to take care of his mother. A man of limited education and intelligence, Can had become increasingly powerful and arrogant after his brother became president. By the time I joined I Corps in Danang, he had become a *de facto* Viceroy of Central Viet Nam and his instructions automatically became law.

It was customary for me, at every Tet and also at the birthday of President Diem's mother, to accompany the I Corps' field grade officers delegation headed by Gen. Tran Van Don, the corps commander, to present our respects to the President and his mother. Very old and feeble, she lay on a couch in the middle of the reception room. Ministers and province chiefs courting favor and army generals itching for promotion, would dutifully stay in line to pay respects and to present expensive gifts to the family. Sometimes,

President Diem would meet with the generals and field grade officers in the evening; on those occasions, he would launch himself into never-ending discourses on national politics and the philosophy of *Nhan Vi*. During these sessions, we were not allowed to ask questions.

Col. Lam Quang Phong, my distant cousin from Kien Giang, later recounted his curious meeting with Ngo Dinh Can. At the time of the meeting, Phong was a major serving in the Regional Forces Headquarters in Saigon. One day, he was instructed to fly to Hue to see Can, but no reasons were given. He became nervous after waiting two days in a hotel in Hue. Phong suspected that Can knew he was a former Viet Minh regiment commander and since both Can's father and older brother were killed by the Viet Minh, Can might have lured him to Hue simply to assassinate him. Finally, at around 2:00 AM. the third day, he was awakened and was ordered to report to Can at once. When he arrived at the Ngo family's residence, he was ushered immediately into Can's study. Phong was startled to see two generals sleeping in the ante-room waiting to be seen. One of them was none other than General Don, the I Corps Commander.

Can asked Phong to sit down and told him he had heard that Phong was an expert on Vietnamese traditional martial arts. He wanted Phong to teach martial arts to his Self-Defense forces in Hue. He then asked Phong to make a brief presentation of some of the moves. He seemed appreciative, asked a few questions, and when Phong asked permission to leave, Can told him he would like to see him at Thuan An Beach the next day.

It was raining when Phong reported to Can's small thatch-roofed hut at the beach. Inside the hut were two beds in the middle of the main room. One bed was a little higher than the other. Mr.Can was resting on the higher bed and invited Phong to lie down on the lower one. Then Mr.Can started to discuss martial arts and politics. In the middle of the discussion, the servant whispered something in Can's ears and Phong heard him reply:

"Let him wait."

Looking outside, Phong saw a tall man standing motionless in the rain. Guessing Phong's curiosity, Can simply said:

"He is the president of the National Assembly."

In May 1959, my wife gave birth to our daughter Bich Ngoc. In December, I was assigned as deputy artillery commander at the Joint General Staff (JGS). In this capacity, I was allocated a small house located in the military complex of Hanh Thong Tay on the northern suburb of Gia Dinh. It was a two-bedroom, wood frame detached unit with a corrugated fiber-cement roof. The house was part of an officer quarter of a nearby artillery battalion. The residential complex, surrounded by a brick wall, had banana and papaya trees that transformed the complex into a sort of oasis in the middle of a busy military installation. Although our house was of rather modest quality, typical of military installations, my wife and I immensely enjoyed our new life at Hanh Thong Tay, away from the traffic and noise of downtown Saigon, and, mostly, away from the suffocating political atmosphere of Central Viet Nam.

Two months after my new assignment, I headed an artillery delegation to visit artillery units in the United States. Our tour included stops at Fort Lewis, Washington; Fort Carlson, Colorado; and Fort Hood, Texas. Our most important visit was understandably the Artillery School at Fort Sill, Oklahoma. As soon as we arrived at the school, we were invited to attend a workshop where we discussed the employment of artillery in a counter-insurgency environment with the school staff and faculty. In 1960, the United States was preparing for a possible military involvement in Viet Nam; the U.S. military was understandably eager to learn from our experiences from the Indochina War. The U.S. artillery school was also interested in the use of artillery in guerrilla warfare.

Drawing from my experiences as a battery commander in North Viet Nam, Laos, and the Hauts Plateaux during the Indochina War, I told the faculty that in a guerrilla warfare environment, the artillery should be able to defend itself against enemy raids. To do so, it was of the utmost importance that artillerymen be trained to set the proper timing so that artillery shells could explode in mid-air in front of the battery to stop enemy human wave assaults. Artillery units should also be able to fire in all directions; artillery unit commanders should develop tactics to use in support of friendly units involved in static or area defense. One other problem encountered in counter-insurgency operations in developing countries was the lack of accurate, up-to-date maps, and artillery officers sometimes had to be creative and even to do away with textbook regulations. I recounted my experiences in Laos where I had to use a compass to orient my guns and the mileage on my jeep to determine my battery positions.

The second day of our visit, we were given a tour of the school facilities. Fort Sill had changed so much since my days as a student back in 1956. The un air-conditioned old barracks which had served as our BOQ had been replaced by new buildings equipped with modern air conditioning. I was impressed with the introduction of high technology into gunnery and survey techniques which, as a result, were faster and more accurate.

I took advantage of my assignment at the Artillery Command to further my academic studies. So, in August 1960, I enrolled at a night philosophy class at the Catholic *Institut Tabert* to prepare for my French baccalaureate degree in philosophy. My goal was to ultimately obtain the *licence* in philosophy. I knew I may not have enough time to complete all my studies because the Viet Cong (VC) had recently stepped up their activities. While the situation in South Viet Nam was quiet from 1954 to 1956, the VC had started a political struggle combined with terrorist activities in the rural areas in 1957 after Diem rejected countrywide elections which were to be held in 1956 under the Geneva Accords. While there were a total of 193 political assassinations in 1958, for example, for the last four months of 1959 alone, 119 assassinations had been recorded. In 1959, the VC, following directions from Hanoi, began their armed struggles against the government of South Viet Nam. On September 26, 1959, two companies of ARVN's 23rd Division were ambushed north of Saigon. Twelve soldiers were killed and most of the weapons were lost.

In November 11, 1960, a coup d'état worsened the already precarious political and military situation in the country and constituted a major setback for Diem's regime. By 1960 it was apparent to everyone that President Diem's one-man rule, the excess and corruption of his entourage, and the growing power of a centralized oligarchy had caused dissatisfaction and resentment in the population and in the Army. A Pentagon study cited by Neil Sheehan in

The Pentagon Papers fittingly described Mr. Diem's background. Being "the product of a family that was both zealously Roman Catholic and a member of the traditional Mandarin ruling class, Mr. Diem was authoritarian, moralistic, inflexible, bureaucratic and suspicious."[10]

The only surprise was that the coup leader, Col. Nguyen Chanh Thi, was a protégé of President Diem. Thi, who commanded the Airborne Brigade, was born in Hue from a peasant family and had served as an NCO in a French paratroops unit. President Diem incorporated him into the National Army with the rank of major and elevated him to the powerful and trusted position of Commander of the Airborne Brigade. President Diem agreed to negotiate with the coup leaders and stalled for time while waiting for his loyal troops to come to his rescue. When it was apparent that the coup had failed, Colonel Thi and some of the coup leaders fled to Cambodia for political asylum.

At the time of the coup, Col. Nguyen Xuan Trang, the Artillery Commander, was visiting the United States and I was appointed Acting Commandant of the Artillery. On the morning of November 11, hearing on the radio that a coup was taking place, I rushed to my office. I was appalled to see that one artillery battalion had taken up position in front of the JGS Headquarters building and was ready to fire on the Presidential Palace. Gen. Le Van Ty, Chairman of JGS, was begging the battalion commander not to fire because indiscriminate artillery fire in the capital would cause heavy casualties to civilians. Due to lack of clear instructions, the battalion commander hesitated but finally agreed to hold fire until further notice from the coup leaders. By noon, it was apparent that the coup had failed. The battalion commander hurried to the airport and flew to Cambodia with Colonel Thi and his followers. If the coup leaders had ordered artillery fire, I was certain the presidential guard unit would have capitulated, President Diem would have been captured, and South Viet Nam's military and political future, for better or for worse, would have taken a dramatically different turn.

Around 3:00 AM. on November 11, 1960, my younger brother, Lt. Lam Quang Thoi, ordered his company of parachutists to attack the Presidential Guard Brigade Headquarters on Thong Nhut Bou-

levard. The Guard Brigade offered little resistance and the headquarters was captured around 5:00 AM. Thoi's company, in conjunction with other airborne units, was ordered to encircle and be
prepared to assault the heavily defended Presidential Palace, in the
event of the failure of pending negotiations between the coup leaders and the President. In the meantime, my oldest brother, Maj.
Lam Quang Tho, who commanded an armored regiment in My Tho,
had received an order to move his regiment to the capital to rescue
the president along with elements of the 7th Infantry Division. When
he arrived at the gates of the Presidential Palace, the coup, for all
practical purposes, had been aborted. Tho took his younger brother
inside the Palace under his protection. That same night, a representative of the Military Security Agency came to see me in my
office and questioned me on my activities during the day. I was
certain that Thoi and I would have been arrested after the coup,
had Tho not come to the rescue of President Diem with Gen. Tran
Thien Khiem, the IV Corps Commander. President Diem later appointed Tho to the post of My Tho Province Chief as a gesture of
appreciation for his action.

Meanwhile, I continued to make progress in my academic pursuits. I ranked at the top of my class at the Institut Tabert. In April
1961, I passed the French baccalaureate in philosophy. I subsequently enrolled at the Faculty of Letters to prepare for the *licence*
in philosophy.

In November 1961, I was promoted to lieutenant colonel and
was assigned to the vacant position of artillery commander in Field
Command Headquarters under Lt. Gen. Duong Van Minh, the hero
of Rung Sat. By 1961, however, General Minh, like many other generals from the South, had fallen into disgrace with the Diem regime. The Field Command was theoretically created to provide
tactical control of all military operations in the country, but in practice, these operations were under the direct supervision of the corps
commanders. As a consequence, the Field Command had little to
do and General Minh spent most of his afternoons playing tennis at
the Lido Officers Club in Gia Dinh.

At the Field Command, in addition to advising the Field Command staff of the employment of artillery in the Military Regions, I

was assigned the mission of working with American officers from the U. S. Army Chemical Corps to test the efficacy of the defoliation program, using the now famous Agent Orange. I prepared operation orders for General Minh's signature, directing Military Regions to provide ground security for the defoliation operations. I would often accompany the spraying teams on a C-123 transport aircraft equipped with spraying equipment, flying at tree-top level over the dense jungles, which were used as Viet Cong secret bases in Military Regions III and IV. From my own experiences, the defoliation program was a huge failure; at first, the leaves turned yellow and fell off after a few weeks, but when we returned a few months later to assess the lasting effects of the defoliant, we noticed that the trees appeared to have grown more vigorous and the leaves thicker than before the spraying.

With regard to the cancer-causing effect of Agent Orange, I don't believe studies have been conclusive. No ARVN soldiers, to my knowledge, reported any cancer or any deformities of their children. After the war, the VC claimed that Agent Orange was the source of medical problems afflicting the Vietnamese population; in my opinion, this was part of their overall propaganda scheme.

Adm. Elmo Zumwalt, who, as commander of the in-country U.S. Naval forces in Viet Nam, ordered the defoliation operations along the main rivers in the Mekong Delta, also believed that Agent Orange caused cancer. Admiral Zumwalt, in fact, believed that his son, a naval officer who had served in the Mekong Delta as commander of a PBR (Patrol Boat, River, also known as swift boat), had died of cancer due to exposure to Agent Orange. It is significant to note, however, that no other members of Lieutenant Zumwalt's PBR crew—who theoretically had been exposed to the same amount of the defoliant as their commander—had died of cancer, at least at the time of Lieutenant Zumwalt's death. Further, a subsequent study on the effects of Agent Orange showed that the rate of cancer among Air Force crews who flew the defoliation missions during the Viet Nam War was not higher than that of U.S. servicemen who had not been exposed to the defoliant.

Although President Diem was able to crush the 1960 coup, he became increasingly suspicious of army officers who hadn't demonstrated loyalty to his regime. An entrenched system of cronyism within the Armed Forces, combined with increasing political repression, caused further frustration and resentment among the officer corps. On January 26, 1962, two fighter pilots dropped bombs and strafed the Presidential Palace in an effort to kill President Diem. One bomb landed fifty meters from Diem but he was unhurt. Lt. Nguyen Van Cu escaped to Cambodia where he was granted political asylum. Lt. Pham Phu Quoc had to crash land on the Bien Hoa River because his plane was hit by anti-aircraft fire. Lieutenant Quoc was imprisoned by the Diem regime but was released after the 1963 coup d'état. He was later killed during an air raid over North Viet Nam.

In the meantime, the fighting intensified in the Mekong Delta and the U.S. started to become militarily involved. On February 7, 1962, two U.S. Army air support companies of 300 men arrived in Saigon, increasing the number of U.S. military personnel in South Viet Nam to 4,000. On February 8, the U.S. recognized its South Viet Nam military command and established the "U.S. Military Assistance Command, Viet Nam" (MAC-V) under Gen. Paul D. Harkins.

On January 2, 1963, the VC scored a psychological victory in Dinh Tuong Province. On that day, the 7th Division launched an operation to capture a suspected VC radio transmitter station, which had been located in the village of Ap Bac, approximately ten kilometers southwest of the city of My Tho. For the first time, one VC battalion stood up and fought against regular ARVN units. In the first few minutes of the fighting, three U.S. helicopters that lifted one battalion of the 7th Division into the landing zone, were downed by enemy fire. The 7th M113 Mechanized Company, due to heavy fire and also due to difficulties in crossing three canals southwest of Ap Bac, was only able to link up with the first heliborne elements near the landing zone around 4:30 PM. Brig. Gen. Ly Tong Ba, a brave officer decorated with the U.S. Silver Star and the French Croix de Guerre, who, as a captain, commanded the 7th Mechanized Company at Ap Bac, reported that his U.S. advisor panicked during the firefight and was unable to provide assistance.[11] At 6:00 PM., one battalion of parachutists was dropped west of Ap Bac, but it was too late for the parachutists to assemble and launch the assault on the village. Col. John Paul Vann, the outspoken advisor to the

7th Division, blamed ARVN officers for failure to capture Ap Bac. In reality, it was a case of bad luck and inexperience, but American reporters, based on extravagant remarks made by U.S. advisors, some of whom saw combat for the first time, jumped on the Ap Bac "debacle" to paint a bleak picture of the war progress in Viet Nam.

Some military analysts believed that the Ap Bac Battle was a milestone in the evolution of the Communist insurgency from guerrilla warfare into the new stage of conventional warfare. In reality, the VC battalion was caught in Ap Bac by surprise and since they could not disperse and escape during daytime, they had no choice but to stay and fight. The first attempt at conventional warfare, in my opinion, happened in 1968 with the Tet Offensive in which the VC staged surprise coordinated attacks on most of South Viet Nam's cities. Although the VC scored an undeniable psychological victory and the Tet Offensive was a turning point in the Viet Nam War, the enemy suffered the loss of an estimated one-half of their war-making potential and returned to their traditional guerrilla warfare tactics. I believe the true stage of conventional warfare did not start until 1972 when Hanoi launched their multi-divisional offensives supported by armored regiments and orchestrated by Corps Headquarters. In the end, the collapse of South Viet Nam in 1975 was not caused by a victorious guerrilla warfare conducted in the South. Repeated North Vietnamese Army (NVA) multi-divisional assaults supported by heavy artillery and armored regiments and directed by regular Corps and Army Commands finally overwhelmed South Viet Nam.

At any rate, the battle of Ap Bac, in conjunction with the VC's increased activities in the Delta, confirmed my fear that time was running out for me in my academic pursuit. I tried not to be distracted by the deteriorating military and political situation. When I was not busy with the defoliation project, I often left my office in the afternoon to attend lectures at the Faculty of Letters. When I was busy and could not attend, my wife would go to the Faculty of Letters and buy copies of the lectures or lessons which were sold by the Faculty's staff. Finally, in April 1962, I passed my certificate of French literature and the next year, I obtained my certificate in Psychology and Ethics.

Shortly after the battle of Ap Bac, I was assigned as G-3 (Operations and Training) to the Army Command under Gen. Tran Van Don, the former I Corps commander. Like the Field Command, the powerless Army Command was created by the Diem government to get rid of generals who had become political liabilities. Unlike the Air Force or Navy Commands, which had tactical and administrative control of their subordinate units, the Army Command had only an advisory role. As the Army commander, General Don visited all Military Regions to assess the military situation and the effectiveness of the pacification program. He made a report to the President and to the Chief of JGS. As his G-3, I accompanied him on these trips and it was my duty to draft these reports for his approval. Like Gen. Duong Van Minh, another Southerner who had become politically unreliable and was relegated to an unimportant function in Saigon, General Don had a lot of free time between his inspection tours around the country; unlike Gen. Duong Van Minh, who was an ardent tennis player, General Don preferred the company of beautiful women and the pleasure of the *haute societe Saigonnaise*. At his new post, he started to plot against the Diem regime from which he had now fallen into disgrace.

General Don was known in the army as a master politician who skillfully switched sides to position himself with the winning party. There is a Vietnamese saying *don gio tro co* (to welcome the wind and reverse the flag's direction) and General Don was adept at the game of don gio tro co. His father, Dr. Tran Van Don, was a member of the Southern aristocracy. Dr. Don was one of those Vietnamese for whom some American writers had coined the term "born-again Frenchman," meaning an educated Vietnamese who held French nationality and who occupied leadership roles under the French colonial administration. Dr. Don was a good friend of Tran Van Chuong, the father of Tran Thi Xuan, the future Madame Nhu, whom General Don knew when she was still a student in Saigon. The young Don was attending *l'École des Hautes Études Commerciales* in Paris when World War II broke out. He was drafted into the French Army, sent to a Reserve Officer School and by the time he graduated as an *aspirant de reserve*, the war had ended. Back in Viet Nam, he briefly served as an aide-de-camp to Gen. Nguyen Van Xuan, the polytechnician, when the latter was appointed prime minister of the Provisional Central Government of Cochinchina. Later, Don served in General Hinh's staff and rose to general behind a desk in Saigon.

When it had become apparent that General Hinh had lost his political infighting with Mr. Diem in 1954, Don decided that it was time to switch sides. He pledged allegiance to the new regime and, during a dramatic demonstration of his loyalty, he burned the old French army rank insignia, which had been adopted by the Vietnamese Army. With assistance from Mme Nhu, he was appointed Commander of both I Corps and the First Military Region in Central Viet Nam. In Hue, he gained the favor of Ngo Dinh Can, who intensely disliked the Nhus. General Don retained his job by successfully playing Can against his older brother and sister-in-law. In 1962, however, he was distrusted by Nhu, possibly because he was from the South and also because he had harbored pro-French sentiments. His much talked-about romantic relationship with Mme Nhu herself probably made matters worse. As a result, he was removed from I Corps and put in charge of the newly created Army Command.

By that time, the political situation worsened and the 1963 coup d'etat was in the making. Basically, the coup was triggered by the repression of the Buddhists in Hue on May 8, 1963. At that time, Monsignor Ngo Dinh Thuc was being considered for promotion to cardinal; the Vatican sent a delegation to Viet Nam to inquire about the Buddhist situation in the country. It was certainly not a coincidence that the delegation visited Hue during that year's celebration of Buddha's 2527th birthday. In deference to the Vatican delegation, Can instructed that Hue residents be prohibited from displaying Buddhist emblems during the religious ceremonies. The Buddhists organized a demonstration and requested the right to speak on Hue Radio. During a subsequent melee, regional forces, under orders from Major Si, the deputy province chief in charge of security, shot at the demonstrators, killing eight and wounding several others. The anti-Diem movement quickly spread to the South and reached a climax with the self-immolation of Venerable Quang Duc in front of the Cambodian Embassy on Le Van Duyet Street. Subsequently, many Buddhist monks burned themselves to death in protest and Mme Nhu incensed the Buddhists by describing the monks' suicides as "barbecues." Vu Van Mau, President Diem's foreign minister and a *professeur agrege* of law, resigned after shaving his head like a monk to protest the brutal crackdown on the Buddhists.

I was stunned by the monks' fanaticism because Buddhism was generally viewed as a contemplative, tolerant religion; in Viet Nam all religions, to my knowledge, had always coexisted peacefully. Within my family, for instance, my mother, who was Catholic, never insisted that her sons follow her religion. My paternal grandfather was one of the founders of the Cao Dai Sect, while his three younger brothers were respectively Catholic, Protestant, and a follower of the Hoa Hao Sect. Religious tolerance was an accepted principle in the country and its violation obviously triggered violent behaviors.

In May 1963, my wife gave birth to our fourth child, a son whom we named Dung. The previous year, our second daughter, Bich Nga, had died of meningitis ten days after she was born. Our pain of losing an infant was alleviated by the knowledge that, had she survived the virus attack, her brain would have been permanently damaged and she would have been retarded. Shortly after the birth of our youngest son, my wife consulted an astrologer who predicted that Dung was born under a lucky star and that he would have a good future. Further, since his birth year was in harmony with mine, his coming to life would also benefit my military career.

The astrologer's prediction appeared correct, at least for the immediate future. As the Buddhist crisis escalated and the tensions rose hour after hour, I was informed that I had been selected to attend the U.S. Command & General Staff College (USC&GSC) in the United States. I received the news with mixed feelings. First, I had to temporarily put a halt to my scholastic pursuits. On the other hand, this was an unexpected opportunity to advance in my military career. USC&GSC was a prestigious service school in the U.S. Army where students were hand-picked among the brightest officers in the Armed Forces and were slated for important field commands or high staff positions.

In Viet Nam, candidates for USC&GSC were normally chosen among the officers who had demonstrated their loyalty to the regime; the final list had to be approved by no less an authority than President Diem himself. Thus, I was completely surprised to learn that my name was on the final list of five field grade officers who were to attend the Fall Course at USC&GSC at Fort Leavenworth, Kansas. I guessed that one of the reasons for my selection may have been that President Diem needed loyal officers at home to defend his regime during the time of crisis and that the vacancies could be filled by officers with no definite political affiliations like myself.

To prepare for Fort Leavenworth, the approved students had to attend a crash course in English at the Army Language School. Two months before our departure for the United States, my older brother Tho, who was My Tho Province Chief, received orders to switch job with one of the officers on the approved list. At the time of the battle of Ap Bac, Tho was both province chief and armored regiment commander in My Tho. Along with other officers involved in the operation, Tho had been criticized by the American press for failure to take Ap Bac and subsequently had fallen into disfavor with the regime. Further, by that time, President Diem had become deeply suspicious of the army and had placed loyal officers in sensitive command posts around Saigon. Although Tho had come to the rescue of President Diem during the aborted 1960 coup d'etat, he was from the South, was not a Catholic, or a member of the Can Lao Party. Consequently, as a measure of precaution, Tho had to be replaced by a more reliable officer and Fort Leavenworth was a good alternative for an officer who had served the regime well but who had somehow outlived his usefulness.

In the middle of the political turmoil in Saigon in August 1963, we left for the United States, unsure of what shape the country would be in when we returned the following year.

6

U.S. COMMAND & GENERAL STAFF COLLEGE

THE FINAL LIST OF STUDENTS for the USC&GSC's 1963 Fall Course included two lieutenant colonels and three majors. Since I was the most senior officer, I was the *de facto* group leader.

A few days after we arrived at Fort Leavenworth, we heard the news of the raids on the pagodas in Saigon by armed troops. We learned later that Nhu had ordered his henchman, Col. Le Quang Tung, commander of the Special Forces, to use his troops camouflaged in paratrooper uniform, to raid the pagodas throughout the country. More than 1,400 monks had been arrested and some of them had been beaten. This brutal act of repression, in my opinion, had sealed the fate of the regime and marked the beginning of its downfall. Washington, as a matter of fact, was stunned by the pagoda raids. President Kennedy, at the urging of the McNamara-Taylor mission in Saigon, authorized the suspension of economic subsidies for South Viet Nam's commercial imports and a cut-off of financial aid to the Vietnamese Special Forces, which were under the direct control of Nhu. The financial assistance would resume only under the specific condition that the Special Forces be put under the control of the Joint General Staff. The latter, of course, was controlled by the generals who were plotting against the regime.

In October 1963, Mme Nhu undertook a trip to the United States to explain to the American public the Buddhist crisis and to justify her brother-in-law's repressive measures. We were encouraged by the Vietnamese Embassy in Washington to attend a public appearance of Mme Nhu during her stop at Kansas City, but, citing heavy workload, we decided to stay home. We were, in fact, angry at her verbal abuses toward the Buddhist monks and were also very upset that her husband had ordered the raids on the pagodas.

For the average American, Fort Leavenworth had a bad connotation because it was the name of a federal penitentiary where long-term inmates were incarcerated. It was also the site of one of the most prestigious service schools that had formed great military leaders during World War II and during the Korean War. For Vietnamese officers, Fort Leavenworth was the key that opened high positions in the Army, and was necessary for a successful military career.

The USC&GSC at Fort Leavenworth offered two courses: a regular one-year course and a six-month accelerated course. Since we were attending the latter course, the workload was heavier; we had to spend at least four to five hours every night on homework in order to pass the weekly examination. In addition to staff procedures, tactics, logistics, great units organization, leadership, and management, we also learned the use of tactical weapons on the battlefield. For certain classified courses on nuclear weapons, the "Allied Officers"—as foreign student officers were called—were excused from the class.

There was one general among the Allied Officers in our class. Maj. Gen. Chae mung Shin, a hero of the Korean War, was appointed leader of the Allied Officers group. When the school organized a visit to the Truman Library at Independence, Missouri, General Chae personally thanked the former President for helping the Korean people in their fight against Communist aggression. During a later visit to Washington, D.C., which was organized by the school for Allied Officers in January 1964 (at a period when the American student-officers were studying classified materials at Fort Leavenworth), General Chae again, representing the Allied Officers, laid a wreath at the tomb of President Kennedy.

Because the Fall Course lasted only six months, we had classes on Saturday mornings as well. We usually spent the weekends playing tennis at the school. Occasionally, we would take a bus to Kansas City to eat Chinese food. Once in awhile, the Laotian officers in our class, who seemed to have more money and more free time than we did, were kind enough to give us a ride to downtown Kansas City. Most of the time, however, we stayed at the school to follow the development of the political situation at home. After I learned that Allied Officers could buy liquor duty free, I ordered a case of Scotch and on Saturday nights, I would invite some American classmates living in the BOQ to come over and to have a few drinks. Since many student-officers had previously served in Viet Nam, we would spend the evenings discussing the progress of the war and the current political situation in the country.

At that time, Gen. Le Van Ty, chairman of Joint General Staff, went to the United States to undergo treatment for cancer and Gen. Tran Van Don was appointed acting chairman of JGS. He and his brother-in-law, Maj. Gen. Le Van Kim, a former artillery officer in the French Army, were the main plotters against President Diem. An astute politician, General Kim was the real brains and the *eminence grise* of the coup committee. The titular leader of the coup, however, was Gen. Duong Van Minh (Big Minh), who was the most popular general in the army and who had a strong following among young officers. Since most of the plotting generals were former officers in the French Army, the CIA assigned as a contact with the generals a French-speaking operative, Lt. Col. Lucien Conein, an old Viet Nam hand and also an old acquaintance of several of the generals during the Indochina War.

On November 1, 1963, we were stunned to hear on the radio that the coup d'état against President Diem had taken place; troops and armored units had moved to the capital, shootings were heard around the Presidential Palace, and the situation in Saigon remained confused. In class that day, we had no heart for the material presented since we were busy monitoring the development of the situation in Saigon. Since most of the American officers who attended our class had previously served in Viet Nam or were slated for a tour of duty in Viet Nam, they were also very interested in what was going on in the country.

Toward the end of the day, we learned that the "revolutionary" forces had occupied the Presidential Palace and that President Diem and Nhu had escaped and were in hiding. The next day, we were dismayed to learn that President Diem and his brother had been assassinated in an armored car that transported them from their hiding place in Cho Lon to the coup headquarters at JGS in Tan Son Nhat. Although I was convinced that President Diem and his brother had to be removed from power, I didn't believe they deserved to die, especially under such demeaning circumstances.

A few days later, we received news that Col. Le Quang Tung, the commander of the Special Forces, and the chief of the Navy and a supporter of President Diem, had been summarily executed. Nevertheless, I was so excited by the success of the coup d'état and the great opportunity for the new government to rally the Army and the people to defeat the Communist insurgency that I wanted to go home at once to offer my services to the new government. I was instructed instead to stay at Fort Leavenworth to complete my course, and after that, to attend a short preventive maintenance course at Fort Knox, Kentucky, and then another course at Fort Bragg, North Carolina. I was frustrated to learn that many officers who had participated in the coup had been promoted and were given important commands while I was stuck in the United States.

In November 1963, I witnessed on TV the tragic death of President Kennedy in Dallas. Years later, some Vietnamese people believed that the death of President Kennedy, who approved the coup, and the assassination of his brother Robert Kennedy in 1968, was the result of a curse by the Ngo family, who had also lost two brothers in the November coup d'etat. There was another surprising similarity between the two events: not unlike Major Nhung who reportedly executed the brothers Ngo in the armored car and who was himself mysteriously executed shortly after the coup, Lee Harvey Oswald, who allegedly assassinated President Kennedy, was himself executed shortly after his arrest. These strange parallels appeared to give a certain credence to the curse theory in the minds of superstitious people.

At Fort Leavenworth, we could not escape the controversy and emotion engendered by the Viet Nam War. The faculty included two liaison officers, one from France and the other from Great Britain. The mission of these allied officers was to provide input regarding their country's strategies and experiences relative to their fight against post-World War II's Communist insurgencies in the colonies.The French liaison officer was a lieutenant colonel who had served in the French elite *5ème Régiment Cuirassic* at Thu Dau Mot. I occasionally played tennis with him during the weekends in the fall. We conversed in French and exchanged memories of the Indochina War era and were generally on good terms.

However, French army officers who had suffered the humiliation of the Indochina debacle that culminated in the fall of Dien Bien Phu, tried on every occasion to convince their American counterparts that the same disaster awaited them in Viet Nam. So, one day, the French liaison officer told the three hundred or so students gathered in the school auditorium during a lecture on the Indochina War, that the Americans, like the French before them, would either be killed by tropical diseases, corrupted by the "*con gais*" (girls in Vietnamese) or defeated by the "*du kich*" (guerrilla). I was very angry. After the French officer finished his discourse, I stood and pointed out that he seemed to forget that the situation was completely different; in 1963, the Americans were helping the Vietnamese fight for their freedom and national integrity while during the Indochina War, the French were trying to reestablish their colonialist rule over the Indochinese peninsula. I also warned the American officers about what I dubbed the "loser's complex," or the tendency of the losers to glorify those who had defeated them on the battlefields. I reminded the audience that colonialism was a thing of the past, and that those countries that were still trying to impose their rule on other countries would be doomed to failure and humiliation. The audience erupted into applause.

At the break, many American officers came to me and shook my hand; they congratulated me for speaking out and for providing helpful insights about the differences between the Indochina and the Viet Nam Wars. General Chae, from Korea, also expressed his appreciation for my remarks, which he found pertinent and appropriate. The following week, I wrote to the Vietnamese military attaché in Washington D.C. suggesting that he intervene with proper authorities to have the French liaison officer removed from the school's faculty for having misindoctrinated the elite of the American officers corps, the majority of whom would be seeing combat in

Viet Nam.To my knowledge, the French officer continued to recite, year after year, his defamatory remarks relative to the Indochina War.

In February 1964, we graduated from the Command & General Staff Course and reported to Fort Knox, Kentucky, to attend a two-week Senior Officers Preventive Maintenance Course at the U.S. Armor School. Fort Knox, located thirty miles southwest of Louis-ville, was best known by the average American as the heavily guarded U.S. Bullion Depository where the Treasury kept gold worth bil-lions of dollars. Fort Knox was also the site of the U.S. Armor School that had trained more than fifteen armored divisions during World War II and had formed some of the best armor officers in the world. General George Patton, the World War II hero, was one of them.

The Preventive Maintenance Course was what was dubbed a gentlemen's course. It consisted mostly of lectures and demonstra-tions and did not include any test or examination.Thus, we had ample free time and spent our evenings glued to the TV in the reception room in our BOQ to watch the political developments at home.

One night, we learned of a new coup d'état, this time staged by Gen. Nguyen Khanh, Commander of II Corps in Pleiku and the former Commander of G.M.11 during the last days of the Indochina War. Khanh put most of the generals who had participated in the November 1963 coup under house arrest under the pretext that these generals were pro-French and soft on Communism, having espoused the French-backed policy of "neutralism" vis-a-vis the Communists. General Khanh created a triumvirate to govern the country. It consisted of Gen. Duong Van Minh, Gen. Tran Thien Khiem, a close friend of General Khanh, and Khanh himself. The popular General Minh was kept in place as a figurehead chief of state but Khanh retained all powers.

I learned later, however, that the new coup was in reality orga-nized by the *Dai Viet Quoc Dan Dang* (Great Viet Nationalist Party) that decided to get rid of a group of pro-French generals led by Gen. Le Van Kim, the chairman of the Joint General Staff. After the suc-cess of the coup, the Dai Viet offered the post of prime minister to General Khanh who, in exchange, declared his support for the Dai Viet.

As soon as he was in firm control of the government, General Khanh ordered the execution of Can, the former proconsul in Hue, by a firing squad. It was tragic that the coup d'état (or "revolution" as the generals preferred to call it) and the subsequent counter-coup cost the Ngo family three brothers. The surviving brother, Monsignor Ngo Dinh Thuc, a one-time candidate for cardinal, went into exile in Rome where he had fallen into disgrace with the Vatican. Mme Ngo Dinh Nhu also went into hiding in a convent in Rome. Her daughter Ngo Dinh Le Thuy later was killed in an auto accident in Paris. Decidedly, the curse on the Ngo family did not seem to have relented.

Shortly after General Khanh's counter-coup, U. S. Secretary of Defense Robert McNamara went to Viet Nam and openly hailed General Khanh as a true leader who would successfully lead Viet Nam in its struggle against Communist aggression. Unlike older generals who had conspired against the Diem regime and who at one time or another had served as officers in the French Army, General Khanh was part of a new breed of young generals who did not come from the regular French Army and who had fought in the Indochina War as commanders in the field.

It was not unusual in developing countries that the colorless titular heads of the original successful coups d'état were subsequently ousted by younger, more charismatic leaders. Egypt's Colonel Nasser, for example, emerged as an energetic leader who had, to a certain extent, brought a measure of political and social stability to his country during the turbulent post-World War II era. I served under General Khanh at G.M.11 and knew he was a good field commander. I hoped he would become the Nasser of Viet Nam and would be able to rally the army to defeat the Communist insurgency.

Despite my cautious optimism, I was concerned that the new coup (that General Khanh called simply a "demonstration of force") could engender other coups and that these coups and counter-coups, if not stopped, would plunge our country further into political turmoil and would severely hurt our war efforts. I was also disturbed to hear that many officers who had been promoted during the November "revolution," had been again promoted for siding with the new leaders.

A few days after the counter-coup, one officer in our group, Major Nhien, who served as an intelligence officer at G.M.11 under General Khanh, was ordered home to head the government's Central Intelligence Agency. The remaining officers in our group reluctantly headed for Fort Bragg, North Carolina, for further training.

Fort Bragg, located ten miles northwest of Fayetteville, was named after General Braxton Bragg of the Confederate Army in the Civil War. Known as the "Home of the Airborne" with the Headquarters of the 18th Airborne Corps, Fort Bragg also was the "Home of the Special Forces," a new branch of the Army created by President Kennedy. Its mission was to conduct special operations against potential insurgent forces, mostly in developing countries. Fort Bragg was also the site of the Special Warfare School that developed and taught new concepts and tactics of counter-insurgency operations.

In contrast to Fort Leavenworth and Fort Knox, the Special Warfare School at Fort Bragg was nothing more than a complex of World War II-type, one-story drab army barracks. Although it was early March when we arrived, the camp was caught under a heavy snow storm. Each night a laborer from the facility department had to go to each barrack to shovel coal into the furnaces to keep the building warm.

The commandant of the school was Brigadier General Yarborough, a young and promising officer who had distinguished himself during World War II by his daring operations behind German lines. General Yarborough was reportedly picked by President Kennedy to head the Special Warfare School and to develop and implement the counter-insurgency program in the U.S. Army.

When I reported at Fort Bragg, I was in no mood to study because I was very concerned about the fast-developing political situation at home and because I was physically and mentally exhausted after the tough Command & General Staff Course at Fort Leavenworth. I decided to take it easy and to relax during this less important three-month "Counter-Insurgency Operations" Course.

However, the second night after we arrived at Fort Bragg, the major who headed the Liaison Office of the Special Warfare School, came to see me at my room while I was enjoying a glass of scotch and soda. Visibly concerned, the major finally said that he had seen my records at Fort Leavenworth and that he was certain I would graduate number one among the Allied Officers attending this year's class. I told him I was sorry to disappoint him, but my intention was not to be valedictorian of the allied officers for the coming course. The major explained that historically, officers from English-speaking countries such as the Philippines and India, graduated among the top of the allied officers and that Vietnamese officers had not fared very well in this class. The major also said that he was sure that things would change this time and that I was his choice as the next valedictorian of the Allied Officers. Before he left, he dropped what I would qualify as a bombshell:

"By the way, Colonel Thi, I bet ten dollars on you with one of my colleagues at the Liaison Office and I hope that I will not be disappointed".

I thought the U.S. liaison officer was not fair for having put me in a *fait accompli* situation, but, as the French like to say, "*noblesse oblige.*" I felt that the honor of the Vietnamese Officers Corps was at stake and that I had to do my best to uphold it.

The Vietnamese student group included, besides the four of us who had just come from Fort Leavenworth, one captain and two lieutenants who had previously served as staff officers in the Psychological Warfare section in the provinces. The captain had served under my brother Tho in My Tho; he was a fairly good cook and as we had missed Vietnamese food after eight months away from home, we asked him to buy food at the school commissary and prepare Vietnamese dishes for us during the weekends.

The Counter-Insurgency Operations Course curriculum included a study of Marxist-Leninism, the nature of Communist insurgency, the theory of guerrilla warfare, and counter-insurgency measures. We also studied the teachings of Mao Tse-tung, who proclaimed in part that "the guerrilla lives in the midst of the people like fishes in the water" and that "political power grows from the barrel of the gun." As I dutifully prepared my homework and did the required readings, I received the maximum score on all subjects.

During the second month of our stay at Fort Bragg, I was invited to speak to the students of a middle school in Lafayetteville, a small town near Fort Bragg. I briefly explained to them the history Viet

Nam, how our people fought for one thousand years against the Chinese aggressors, how we were conquered by the French in the nineteenth century, how the French were defeated in Indochina and why the United States became involved in Viet Nam. After my presentation, a young girl asked me which group was the most intelligent, the North Vietnamese or the South Vietnamese.

"As an officer from the South," I replied, "I think that the South Vietnamese are more intelligent."

My answer drew loud applause. I realized at that time that regionalism and North-South tensions were not unique to Viet Nam.

In the middle of the course, while the American student-officers were busy studying classified material, the school organized a one-week trip through the South for allied officers. First, we stopped at the Citadel in South Carolina, where we were introduced to the superintendent of the Citadel, Gen. Mark Clark, a hero of World War II. We subsequently visited various Air Force bases and naval installations in Florida. Back from the trip, we participated in one-week maneuver with elements of the 101st Airborne Division stationed at Fort Bragg. The students were broken into different groups and assumed the role of advisors to various airborne battalions participating in the maneuver.

As an advisor to one maneuver battalion, I was assigned a jeep and a driver. I took advantage of this field exercise to visit the rural areas in the vicinity of Fort Bragg. This was the first time I had been able to see for myself the lifestyle of Black farmers and I was appalled at their poor living conditions. Although it was springtime, it was still very cold in North Carolina. Yet the farmers' houses had no heating and the children had no warm clothes. One sharecropper with ten children to feed told me he worked ten hours per day but was only paid ten dollars for each working day. The U.S. Master-Sergeant who rode with me told me that some of these farmers and their children had not seen a doctor for years and that the Airborne Division often sent their medical teams into neighboring villages to provide medical care to their residents. This was exactly what the American advisors had been asking the Vietnamese government to do all along in order to "win the minds and the hearts"of the Vietnamese people. It was quite a shock to see that the most industrialized nation on earth did not seem to pay much attention to the minds and the hearts of the Black farmers in its own country. "Charity begins at home," goes one American proverb. Because of U.S. global involvement and the higher priority of international politics and security, it was necessary for a superpower to sometimes forgo the welfare of its own people. I thought this was probably one of the causes of the nascent U.S. antiwar movement.

Finally, at the end of the maneuver, each student-advisor was required to make his observations and recommendations to the battalion staff; we were graded on the quality and completeness of the presentation. During my visits to the battalion defensive positions, I noticed that often the battalion had a perimeter of defense exceeding four or five miles encompassing hilly and heavily forested areas. This reminded me of my bad experience at Van Tri in North Viet Nam, where my battery was overrun by elements of the Viet Minh's 42nd Regiment because we had an extended perimeter of defense and because we had no fall back position. Thus, when it was my turn to make the presentation, I told the audience that, based on my unpleasant experiences in North Viet Nam during the Indochina War, the Communist tactics consisted of attacking a weak point of the defense, normally an area located between two units, then once inside the defensive position, one element would destroy the command headquarters while the rest of the attacking forces would spread out and attack the front line units from the rear.

"The Viet Minh called that kind of attack the 'blossoming flower' tactic." I continued. "So, I suggest that you reduce your perimeter of defense and organize a second line of defense around your battalion headquarters. If possible, the battalion executive should have a separate command post to provide for continuous control and command in case the battalion headquarters is overrun. Gentlemen, believe me, I told you all that for my own sake because I know that if the enemy succeeds in breaking through your line of defense, the 'co van' [advisor] would be the first man they would kill."

The audience erupted in laughter. A few days later, the major from the Liaison Office burst into my room. He shook his head and said:

"Colonel Thi, I asked you to try to be number one among the Allied Officers. I did not ask you to be number one for the entire class."

I could not believe it. I graduated at the top of a class of 300 officers of different nationalities, including officers from the United States Army.

Two days later, at the graduation ceremony, General Yarborough, in his commencement speech, stated that it was only appropriate that a Vietnamese officer graduate at the top of a class on counter-insurgency operations due to the fact that Viet Nam was actually threatened by Communist subversion and that Vietnamese officers had gained valuable experiences in their fight against the VC insurgency. Then General Yarborough presented me with the trophy reserved for the valedictorian of the class and after that, he and I climbed on an open jeep to review the graduating students and troops assembled on the parade field of the school.

That night, all officers in my BOQ gathered in my room to empty my case of Johnny Walker.

7

7TH INFANTRY DIVISION

BY THE TIME I FINALLY went home in June 1964, General Khanh seemed firmly in control. He also had the support of the Americans. Khanh kept the popular Gen. Duong Van Minh as a figurehead chief of state, but had him under close surveillance. Gen. Hoang Xuan Lam, who commanded the 23rd Infantry Division at the time, once told me that when Gen. Duong Van Minh spent a weekend in Ban Me Thuot, in the Hauts Plateaux, Khanh called in the middle of the night and instructed Lam to watch and to report all Minh's activities.

The week following my return from the United States, I was assigned to the 7th Infantry Division at My Tho, thirty kilometers south of Saigon. I was excited to be able, at long last, to serve in the Mekong Delta where I was born and raised. The Mekong Delta was rich and fertile, the climate was mild and the people so easy-going and so hospitable that my assignment was a sort of "coming home." It was a blessed opportunity for me to become acquainted again with my own country.

The division commander was Colonel Huynh Van Ton, one of my classmates at Dalat. Ton was a member of the Nationalist Dai Viet Party, which opposed the Diem regime. Under President Diem, army officers affiliated with the Dai Viet were viewed with suspicion. As a consequence, Ton was barred from promotion and remained at the rank of major for many years, despite the fact that he had seen action as a battalion commander during the Indochina War. After the successes of the two coups d'etat in 1963 and 1964 in which he actively participated, Ton had more than made up for his lost time. He rose from major to full colonel within a few months' time and was even on his way to becoming a general. Ton was a protégé of General Khanh. Since the 5th and 7th Divisions were located only twenty and thirty miles north and south of Saigon respectively, these divisions had participated in all coups d'état including the coup against President Diem. For this reason, the command of these divisions was given only to trusted friends and political associates of the power structure.

During the November 1963 coup d'état, Col. Nguyen Huu Co (who later rose to general and became a minister of defense under Gen. Nguyen Cao Ky) neutralized the 7th Infantry Division by taking it over after arresting the division commander, a supporter of Mr. Diem. The plotting generals felt more secure with regard to the 5th Division whose commander, an obscure colonel by the name of Nguyen Van Thieu, had pledged allegiance to the revolution. However, according to the officers who participated in the coup, Colonel Thieu moved cautiously and did not commit himself until he was sure the coup succeeded. This cleverness had served him well as he later outsmarted his contemporaries and became the President of the Second Republic.

Ton appeared happy to see me. He asked me to be his assistant for operations. In that capacity, I would plan and supervise military operations within the division's tactical area. The important post of chief of staff for the division was given to Lt. Col. Pham Van Lieu, who, like Ton, was a member of the Dai Viet. The new province chief of My Tho, Maj. Do Kien Nhieu, was also a member of Dai Viet and a protégé of Ton. A former chief of cabinet of Gen. Duong Van Minh, Nhieu switched sides and became a supporter of Khanh. Two of the regiment commanders in the division were from our class at Dalat and were good friends of Ton. With this impressive cast of characters under him, Ton was ready to play an important role in the political maneuverings in Saigon and his military career appeared to be ready to take off.

With regard to territorial organization, the 7th Division had tactical responsibility over the five provinces of Dinh Tuong, Kien Hoa, Go Cong, Long An, and Moc Hoa. Kien Hoa, also known as Ben Tre, had always been a VC stronghold. One of the richest provinces of the Mekong Delta, Kien Hoa consisted of huge plantations of coconut trees, which could hide entire Viet Cong battalions and were an ideal terrain for ambush. The above five provinces constituted what was called the "Trans-Mekong Tactical Area."

When I joined the 7th Division, the Trans-Mekong Tactical Area was heavily infested with VC local and regular forces and its military situation had become the most serious in the country. A few months before I reported to the division, My Tho's province chief, Lt. Col. Tran Hoang Quan (former commander of the 1st Infantry Battalion on the Mang Yang Pass in the Hauts Plateaux in 1954) was killed in an ambush just a few miles from the city. To assist the 7th Division in its efforts to destroy VC regular units in Dinh Tuong and Kien Hoa Provinces, JGS had attached to the division one Airborne Task Force consisting of two battalions.

On June 23, 1964, President Johnson announced the appointment of Gen. Maxwell Taylor as U. S. ambassador to Viet Nam. General Taylor was a former Chairman of the U.S. Joint Chiefs of Staff and military advisor to President Kennedy. General Taylor's appointment underscored the importance the U.S. government attached to the military situation in South Viet Nam. This also meant that the U.S. would apply a new strategy in the fight against the Viet Cong. General Taylor, in fact, wrote a book, *The Uncertain Trumpet*, in which he developed what was called the strategy of "Graduated Response." This strategy would allow the U.S. to respond in kind to Communist aggression without resorting to nuclear warfare. The flexibility of this strategy would provide the U.S. with the option at any time "to proceed or not, to escalate or not, and to quicken the pace or not."

General Taylor also saw Viet Nam as a welcome opportunity to test his concept of limited war. This concept was adopted by President Kennedy. Based on this concept, President Kennedy created the famous Special Forces for the specific purpose of helping Third World countries fight against what was called brush fire or unconventional warfare against Communist insurgencies.

In the meantime, as assistant for operations to the division commander, three or four times a week, I would direct what were known as "Eagle Flight" operations. I would fly with the Senior Advisor to the division, a full colonel, on a Command & Control (C & C) helicopter over a pre-selected Viet Cong-controlled area to observe suspicious movements. If we detected an unusual activity such as a large movement of sampans, a column of men who dispersed or went into hiding when they heard the noise of our approaching helicopter, etc., we would heli-lift one squad of the Division Reconnaissance Company to the suspected area to search it and to make contact with the enemy. Once contact was made, we would bring in the whole reconnaissance company to mount an assault. It we met an important enemy force such as a regular company or battalion, we would commit a reserve battalion from the division or from the airborne task force. During the morning we would typically drop from five to ten reconnaissance squads in different areas to try to establish contact with the enemy.

In one of these "Eagle Flight" operations in Long An province, the Senior Advisor and I decided to bring in the rest of the reconnaissance company to search a village where one reconnaissance squad reported moderate contact with the enemy. We also decided to land in the vicinity of the village to study the situation. As we walked toward the village, I noticed a dike on the northern edge of the village, which looked suspicious because there were no footprints on it. Intuitively, I enjambed the dike to avoid stepping on a possible bobby trap. Suddenly, I heard an explosion behind me. I stopped, looked back and saw the American colonel lying on the dike, his right leg bleeding heavily. Later, I learned that he had stepped on a string which triggered a hand grenade hidden on the dike. I took the colonel to the American Field Hospital in Saigon in the C&C helicopter. A week later, I went back to see him in the hospital. His condition was not critical but he had to be evacuated to the United States. A few days before his departure, he was awarded the coveted VN National Order, 5th degree, in conjunction with the Gallantry Cross with palm during a 7th Division victory parade in My Tho.

One day, while flying an Eagle Flight mission in Kien Hoa Province, I noticed a monk in saffron robes perched on a small hut at the top of a coconut tree in a small island located in the middle of the Mekong River, just across from the city of My Tho. I was later told that the monk was known as the "coconut monk" because he lived on a coconut tree and sustained himself only with coconut juice. The artillery officers in the division also told me that whenever they fired in support of the outposts on the other side of the Mekong, they had to take special care to avoid firing too close to the coconut monk.

I learned that the coconut monk's real name was Nguyen Thanh Nam. Born into a wealthy Ben Tre family, Nam had studied in France where he received a degree in chemistry. Back in Ben Tre, he created a soap manufacturing plant using coconut as an ingredient. One day, during the Indochina War, he was confiscated by the French during a military operation in Ben Tre to carry food and other supplies for them. It was a common practice of the French Corps Expeditionnaire at the time. The French called these porters "P.I.M.s" (or *Porteurs et Internes Militaires*). The Vietnamese chemist feigned muteness and did not utter a single word during the operation. However, after the French were ambushed in one of these notorious Ben Tre coconut plantations and sustained heavy casualties, the French officers debated among themselves and decided to kill all the surviving P.I.M.s. The chemist stunned the French officers when he spoke in impeccable French, in a Parisian accent, to beg for his life.

After his release, Nam shaved his head and went to That Son Mountains in Chau Doc. There, he meditated for three years under a secular tree near a pagoda on the Nui Tuong Mountain. He subsequently came back to Ben Tre Province and, as a good chemist who had studied the nourishing characteristics of coconut, he decided from then on to feed himself only with coconut ingredients and to remain silent during the rest of his life. His "religion" was a curious mixture of Buddhism, Taoism, Hinduism and Christianity. He also implemented and taught the practice of *"Toa Than Tinh Khau"* (Relax the Body and Close the Mouth) in order to eradicate the three causes of human suffering: body, word, and thought. Occasionally, he would go to Saigon and ask to meet with the President and other foreign dignitaries in order to convey his message of peace. Although the politicians did not take him seriously, he had a following among the young, including, reportedly, draft dodgers. Among his followers was the son of the famous American writer John Steinbeck.

About three months after I arrived at the 7th Division, it suffered a major setback in Kien Hoa province. One battalion of the 10th Regiment was ambushed on its way to the main road after an eventless sector-controlled operation; it suffered over one hundred casualties. Colonel Ton asked me to go to Kien Hoa to handle the medical evacuation and to conduct a pursuit operation the next morning. The 3rd Airborne Battalion, heliborne from My Tho, linked up with the ambushed battalion around midnight and I spent the rest of the night and the next day at Kien Hoa airport evacuating the wounded to Saigon.

The day after the ambush, I dropped two airborne battalions three miles north of the site of the ambush and one Ranger battalion further to the north to cut off the enemy route of withdrawal. In two days, we killed about one hundred VC and captured some forty weapons. In the middle of the pursuit operation, Gen. Tran Thien Khiem, chairman of JGS, accompanied by Col. Nguyen Duc Thang, G-3, flew over to Kien Hoa to assess the situation. General Khiem suggested that I take over the province. Thang also encouraged me to do so.

"Colonel Thi," General Khiem said, "I know that you are ideal for the job because you graduated number one at Fort Bragg."

However, I knew that what was taught at Fort Bragg had nothing to do with the tough terrain of Kien Hoa covered by endless coconut plantations, which constituted ideal sites for deadly ambushes. I knew that if I accepted the post of province chief of Kien Hoa, there would be a great chance I would suffer other tactical setbacks, and my military career would be in serious jeopardy. Further, the current province chief, Lt. Col. Tran Ngoc Chau, was also my classmate at Dalat and I did not want to replace him under such a controversial situation. So, I politely declined. I was happy General Khiem did not insist.

While the military situation deteriorated in the Mekong Delta, new developments in the Gulf of Tonkin pointed toward an escalation of the war beyond the South Viet Nam border. On August 2,

1964, a U.S. Navy destroyer on patrol in the Gulf of Tonkin reported that it was pursued by NVA patrol torpedo boats. Enemy boats were driven off by gunfire and air attacks. On August 4, the U.S.S. *Maddox* and *C. Turner Joy* reported torpedo attacks. The U.S. vessels returned fire. Two NVA PT boats were sunk in this encounter. The next day, the U.S. sent reinforcements to the Gulf of Tonkin and on August 7, the U.S. Congress approved the Joint Resolution to promote the maintenance of international peace and security in South East Asia. This resolution authorized the President to commit the U.S. armed forces for the defense of South Viet Nam or Laos against Communist aggression.

While these incidents indicated a possible enlargement of the Viet Nam War, the political situation in the country was far from stabilized. General Khanh's position had become increasingly precarious due to political infighting. On September 12, 1964, I witnessed the development of a coup d'état and its disastrous consequences.The previous day, we had completed a successful operation in Go Cong Province where we destroyed one local VC company. After the operation, I asked Colonel Ton's permission to spend the weekend in Saigon with my family. I noticed something unusual in Ton's attitude. He seemed to be hesitant. Normally, he encouraged me to take a few days off to relax in Saigon, but that day, he seemed to be preoccupied and elusive. Finally, he let me go and told me to enjoy myself.

The next day, after our family had eaten a good *pho* in downtown Saigon, as we drove by the Saigon Cathedral on our way to my father-in-law's home in Gia Dinh, I was astonished to see that elements of the Airborne Brigade, which was attached to the 7th Division, had taken position around the Cathedral and along Tu Do Street. I stopped, went over to a young lieutenant and asked him what the hell he was doing in Saigon.

"Colonel," he replied, "don't you know that we've participated in a new coup?"

I hurried to the car, turned on the radio and sure enough, Radio Saigon was announcing that a new coup led by Lt. Gen. Duong Van Duc (who was to be relieved of his command of IV Corps) and Maj. Gen. Lam Van Phat (a relative of Ton's wife and recently dismissed as minister of the interior), had taken place and that the "revolutionary" forces occupied most of the Capital, except Tan Son Nhut Airport. Saigon Radio announced the names of generals and colonels who supported the "revolution" and I was surprised to hear that I was one of them. I was ordered on the radio to report immediately to the "revolution" headquarters located at the administration building of Gia Dinh Province.

I drove to my brother Tho's home to discuss the situation with him and to ask him whether his armored units had participated in the new coup. Past experiences had shown that a coup d'etat could not succeed without the participation of tank units. At that time, Tho was the commander of the Armor Branch of the Army and a protégé of General Khanh, the target of this new coup d'etat. Tho told me that on the morning of the coup, Lt. Col. Duong Huu Nghia, an armor officer and close political associate of Colonel Ton, invited him to a poker party. In the meantime, Nghia took over the Armor Command and ordered the armored units to support the new coup. Since General Khanh escaped to Dalat, Tho did not know what to do. He agreed to accompany me to the coup headquarters to inquire about the situation. When we arrived, I saw General Duc, the coup leader, lying on a couch in the reception room with a bottle of Johnny Walker on the nearby coffee table.

Beside General Duc and Colonel Ton, almost all the 7th Division staff was there. Lt. Col. Pham Van Lieu, chief of staff, was busy relaying orders to the troops. Lt. Col. Ly Tong Ba, commander of the armored regiment in My Tho, was particularly exuberant. He told us that revolutionary forces had the situation well under control and that his units occupied all major strategic areas of the capital, except Tan Son Nhut Airport. (Years later, Ba told me he asked instructions from Tho, his titular boss, and Tho had ordered him to go ahead and attack the airport, but I could not confirm Ba's version because by the time Ba disclosed it to me, Tho had already died.)

When I reported to Colonel Ton, he asked me to go back to My Tho at once in order to supervise the territorial defense within the division's tactical area. The situation was critical because the 11th Regiment under Maj. Ngo Le Tue, the Airborne Brigade and elements of one armored regiment, had left the area to participate in the coup. I was relieved that Ton did not get me involved in what he claimed to be a new "demonstration of force."

When I arrived at division headquarters in My Tho, I was surprised to see that Major Nhieu, My Tho province chief and a close political associate of Colonel Ton, had already taken control of the division. I learned that Nhieu had ordered all province chiefs in the division tactical area to report to division Headquarters in My Tho and had held them there pending further developments in Saigon. Among them was Lt. Col. Nguyen Viet Thanh, the Go Cong Province Chief, who was to take over the command of the 7th Division in 1966.

It was only after I arrived at My Tho that I understood the reason for the new coup. The coup was triggered by the firing of Dr. Nguyen Ton Hoang, the leader of the *Dai Viet Quoc Dan Dang* (DVQDD) and a deputy prime minister in charge of pacification. The DVQDD was the parent political organization of the *Cap Tien* (Progressist) Party, whose members were mostly recruited among military officers and middle management civil servants from the South. Mr. Nguyen Ngoc Huy became the new leader of the Cap Tien after Professor Nguyen Van Bong, the founder of the movement, had been assassinated by the VC a few years earlier. Since both Mr. Huy and Mr. Bong were Directors of the National Institute of Administration, many of their former students who were occupying middle and high level management positions in the government were also active members of the Cap Tien. As a result, the movement had grown into a powerful political organization which was viewed with suspicion by General Khanh and his followers.

Since Colonel Ton and most of the participants of the coup were loyal members of the Cap Tien and the Dai Viet, they decided to overthrow General Khanh who had fired their leader and betrayed the Dai Viet. They persuaded Generals Duong Van Duc and Lam Van Phat to lead the coup. Duc, who was in the process of being reassigned from the command of IV Corps and Phat, recently fired from his post of minister of the interior, were glad to accept the offer.

Some speculated that another reason for Colonel Ton's coup was that he was denied promotion to brigadier general. In fact, a few months earlier, he had been invited to meet with General Khanh in Vung Tau where Khanh proclaimed a new Constitution (later called the Vung Tau Constitution), which gave Khanh the title of "Chief of State For Life." Rumor had it that Ton, a staunch supporter of Khanh, would be elevated to brigadier general on this occasion. Lt. Col. Pham Van Lieu, the division chief of staff, ordered that Ton's jeep be decorated with a one-star general's plaque in anticipation of this event when he returned from Vung Tau. However, the staff was surprised that Ton returned without the star and the plaque had to be quickly removed.

As for me, the first night of the coup was a nightmare. Taking advantage of the chaotic political situation in Saigon, the VC attacked or harassed a record number of small outposts within the division's tactical area. At least ten RF outposts were overrun. I spent the night at the division's Tactical Operation Center (TOC) to coordinate artillery and air support for the outposts under attack. It was during that night that I realized the impact of ideological division and political turmoil on the military situation in a country ravaged by Communist insurgency. I realized that we were caught in an insurmountable dilemma; I saw no end to the vicious circle that plagued our country. I was aware that political stability could exist only in truly democratic countries but a developing country at war could never be truly democratic. Even our neighboring countries such as Indonesia, Thailand, the Philippines, Taiwan, and South Korea, which had no war, had never seen democratically elected governments.

The situation in Viet Nam appeared helpless after the overthrow of Diem. President Diem's downfall created a political vacuum that the generals were unable to fill. If, in the late 1950s, President Diem could have declared, like Louis XIV, that *"L'État, c'est moi!"* (I am the State!), in the early 1960s he could have borrowed Louis XV's famous statement, *"Apres moi, c'est le deluge!"* (After me, the deluge!). The generals who succeeded him, in fact, had been trained by the French to be leaders of small units. They lacked the education and political background to assume President Diem's job. (It was during that time that I saw the urgency of improving the education of the cadets at our military academy to better prepare them to assume leadership roles in the army as well in the administration, because in developing countries, the army had always played a primary role in the conduct of national affairs.) "Under Diem," wrote the French journalist Pierre Darcourt,

> there was an idea, a social and economic cadre, a politique and a faith. There was a man: Nhu, who knew how to make himself obeyed and in front of whom, people tremble. The directives he gave were executed. Now, it was the republic of small "*camarades libérateurs.*" Everyone commanded, nobody obeyed. . . .The coup d'état had not been an operation directed "for" something, but "against" an existing régime, the régime of the Ngo family. Overnight, men that nothing had prepared for that, were confronted with the task of elaborating a new doctrine. A task well above their means. . . .[12]

In any event, General Khanh escaped to Dalat during the coup. He was saved by Gen. Nguyen Cao Ky, chief of the Air Force, who threatened to bomb any armored column that dare attack the airport.

Lt. Col. Ly Tong Ba, commanding the armored regiment, later told me that he called General Stillwell at MAC-V to ask for his advice and to inquire about the American attitude with regard to this new coup. Colonel Ba participated in the 1963 coup d'état against President Diem and he knew it would be wise to probe the American side before engaging his troops. Besides, he knew that an attack by armored units on the airport would unavoidably inflict casualties on U.S. Air Force personnel and damage U.S. aircraft. "Colonel Ba, don't shoot," said General Stillwell on the telephone. Ba refused to attack and the coup d'état lost momentum and collapsed.

Colonel Ton took his troops back to My Tho. He was followed by Generals Duc and Phat. That night, I was invited to attend a meeting at Major Nhieu's residence. The atmosphere was subdued and the generals appeared nervous. A few minutes after the dissident generals left for Can Tho, the telephone rang. It was General Khanh who asked to talk to Ton. General Khanh ordered Ton to report to him the next day. I was completely surprised to hear Ton say:

"General, I will report to you tomorrow, but I ask that you give me permission to transfer the command of the 7th Division to Lt. Col. Lam Quang Thi."

General Khanh said he would think about that, but again insisted that Ton go to Saigon and report to him first. I knew I had no chance of getting the command of the 7th Division. Politically, General Khanh did not trust me. Colonel Ton's recommendation made Khanh even more suspicious. The situation was ironic because my older brother Tho was a strong supporter of Khanh (although he had somewhat fallen in disfavor with Khanh after the coup) and my younger brother, Capt. Lam Quang Thoi, was Khanh's own aide-de-camp at the time of the coup.

Brig. Gen. Nguyen Bao Tri, instead, was appointed the new division commander. I had known Tri from when we were instructors at the Command & General Staff College. He was a fine officer who had seen combat in North Viet Nam. Later Thoi told me that General Tri insisted that I be promoted to full colonel before he agreed to take over the division. General Khanh agreed as an accommodation to Tri's request and probably also as compensation for having denied me the command. General Tri appointed me to the vacant position of deputy division commander. General Tri had to replace all the key positions within the division because most of the important former staff officers and some regiment commanders had been implicated in the aborted coup and were awaiting court martial. (With the exception of Lt. Col. Ly Tong Ba, the armored regiment commander, all other officers who participated in the coup would be later discharged from the army.)

About a month after General Tri's arrival, I suggested that we go to Ap Bac to destroy the VC Dinh Tuong Provincial Battalion and to avenge the much publicized ARVN defeat the previous year. The VC claimed victory and a song titled "Ap Bac" was written to commemorate this achievement.

Since I came to the 7th Division, I had considered going to Ap Bac to set the record straight, but the political turmoil at the time prevented this. I had studied the terrain in and around Ap Bac. The village of Ap Bac itself extended about six kilometers from RN4 to the south, to the man-made canal of Ap Bac to the north. The area to the west of the village was an open rice field which could be easily negotiated by the APCs.

My plan called for encircling the VC battalion with one regiment of the 7th Division attacking from the south using RN4 as a line of departure, engaging two Ranger battalions which would be heliborne to the southern bank of Ap Bac canal to the north, while elements of the armored regiment would block in the area west of Ap Bac. The Airborne Brigade was held in reserve. General Tri was receptive because he badly needed a victory to lift the morale of the troops. He also approved my plan of operation for the second Battle of Ap Bac.

As expected, the 11th Regiment met heavy enemy resistance at about two kilometers north of RN4. The two ranger battalions, moving south from their landing zone, sustained heavy contact with the enemy. At that time, we decided to commit the reserve. The 1st and 3rd Airborne Battalions were heliborne to a Landing Zone (LZ) northwest of the village of Ap Bac. They were ordered to attack in a southeasterly direction along the two small canals crossing the Ap Bac area. The Airborne Brigade also met with strong enemy resistance inside Ap Bac.

The battle raged all day; when darkness finally set in on Ap Bac, the famous Dinh Tuong Provincial Battalion left over one hundred dead. This was a significant victory for ARVN, but this time the U.S. media remained curiously silent.

This major victory was soon followed by another military success in Kien Hoa Province. Toward the end of 1964, intelligence reports indicated that the VC had moved their supplies directly from North Viet Nam by boats, which somehow escaped Vietnamese and U.S. naval patrols; the coastal area of Kien Hoa was one of their important staging areas. As a result, we sent the 10th Regiment to search the mangrove area along the South China Sea approximately seventy-five kilometers southeast of Ben Tre. On the second day of operation, the 10th Regiment discovered numerous wooden boxes,which contained a dozen 82-mm mortars with assorted ammunition. It was estimated that the captured mortars could arm one full VC regiment. After that operation, the U.S. Navy as well as the VN Navy inceased their coastal patrols to intercept the flow of supplies from North Viet Nam, but apparently without much success because subsequent search operations discovered other caches along the Mekong Delta's coastal areas.

Unfortunately, while the 7th Division scored significant tactical successes, the country was convulsed by new political turmoil. On December 23, 1964, some young generals arrested five members of the National High Council, a body of respected politicians created in the fall of 1963 to advise and oversee the civilian government. The latter was headed at that time by Chief of State Phan Khac Suu and Prime Minister Tran Van Huong. The arrested members were accused of pro-Communist sentiments by the military.

The following day, Gen. Maxwell Taylor summoned the "Young Turks" who emerged as the new leaders of South Viet Nam and reprimanded them for having created a "real mess" in Saigon. General Taylor complained that in one year he had had to deal with five governments, meaning five different sets of senior generals and five different sets of province chiefs.[13] It was ironic for General Taylor to complain because he was partially to blame for the next political upheaval which was to trigger the departure of General Khanh.

The following passage from *Fire in the Lake*[14] illustrates General Taylor's arrogance and condescension, which were not uncommon in the relationship between American officials and their Vietnamese counterparts:

Taylor exhibited his imperial drive toward the client in the South in an even more obvious way than he suggested toward the enemy to the North. In an extraordinary example of imperial language, Taylor, reprimanding the Young Turks in Saigon—Ky, Thieu, Thi, and Cang—for attempting a coup in December 1964, told them:

"Do all of you understand English? (Vietnamese officials indicating they did, although the understanding of General Thi was known to be weak.) I told you all clearly at General Westmoreland's dinner, we Americans are tired of coups. Apparently, I wasted my words. May be this is because something is wrong with my French because you evidently did not understand. I made it clear that all military plans which

I know you would like to carry out are dependent on government stability. Now you have made a real mess. We cannot carry you forever if you do things like this. Who speaks for the group? Do you have a spokesman?"

Shortly after this incident, the country was again plunged into a new political crisis, this time caused by the armed rebellion of the Montagnards in Ban Me Thuot. In the Hauts Plateaux, the Montagnards, who were trained and paid by the American Special Forces and who constituted what was called the Civil Defense Group (CIDG), overtly revolted against the central government. Under the banner of FULRO, they again demanded autonomy for the Highlands, as they did in 1954 under Diem's government.

Like the French before them, the Americans were sympathetic to the plight of the Vietnamese Montagnards. Belonging to the same Polynesian ethnic group as other Pacific islanders, they were chased from the lowlands by the Vietnamese during the latter's southward expansion. (I was told that in the 1960s, the Filipinos working for U.S. Agency for International Development or USAID in Ban Me Thout could converse with the Rhades, one of the most advanced tribes in the Hauts Plateaux, in their own dialect.) Also like the French Catholic priests who previously lived in their midst and taught them the Bible, the American missionaries tried to convert the Montagnards, who were essentially animist, to Christianity. This was one of the reasons why the Montagnards spoke some French and English but could not converse in Vietnamese.

In any event, when elements of ARVN's 23rd Division in Ban Me Thuot surrounded the dissident garrison, they found many U.S. Special Forces officers and NCOs inside the camp. As Gen. Hoang Xuan Lam, 23rd Division Commander, later recounted, Gen. Nguyen Khanh, then chief of state, called him in the middle of the night and instructed him to attack and disarm the Montagnard garrison. General Khanh also wanted to personally preside over the surrender ceremony inside the garrison the next day. General Lam had to call an urgent meeting with U.S. Special Forces officers to negotiate the terms of the surrender before the American officers agreed to leave the camp. There was a widely circulated rumor at the time that the armed rebellion was staged at the instructions of Gen. Maxwell Taylor, the then-American Ambassador, to exert pressure on General Khanh (whom Taylor bitterly disliked) to leave the country.[15]

Robert McNamara, the secretary of defense under Presidents Kennedy and Johnson, recently wrote a new book, *In Retrospect: Tragedy and Lessons of Viet Nam,*[16] in which he confessed his mistakes for not recommending an early U.S. disengagement. One of the arguments he cited in favor of withdrawal was the political instability in South Viet Nam. Yet there is no doubt in my mind that the United States was, in great part, responsible for this instability because the U.S. government was heavily involved in the overthrow of President Diem's regime. McNamara himself, in 1964, personally hailed General Nguyen Khanh as a hero, who had just staged a successful counter-coup to depose the plotting generals of the November 1963 coup d'état against President Diem. Now, General Maxwell Taylor wanted to get rid of General Khanh by encouraging an armed rebellion by the Montagnards.

With regard to the coup against President Diem for example, one might argue that it doesn't follow that if there had been no U.S. support for coup makers there had been no instability in South Viet Nam. I must admit that, at the time, I was the first to agree that President Diem had to go. In retrospect, I believe, however, that there were other alternatives. First, the U.S. could have used its considerable leverage to pressure Diem into undertaking political reforms.

The following stories by Tran Ngoc Chau, my classmate at Dalat and province chief of Ben Tre under Diem, showed that President Diem was less inflexible than had been portrayed in the U.S. media. During a meeting with President Diem and Mr. Truong Vinh Le, president of the national assembly, just before the August 1963 parliamentary elections, Chau recommended to President Diem to replace a female candidate from Saigon with a local candidate. Mr. Le disclosed that the candidate from Saigon was recommended by Mme Nhu herself. President Diem said that, with regard to local elections, the province chiefs' judgment was more accurate. He then ordered Chau to find a local candidate.

Also in the summer of 1963, after having received an order to remove all Buddhist flags in his province, Chau went to Saigon to see President Diem. He suggested to the President that the order be rescinded. President Diem accepted Chau's recommendation that the national flags fly along the Buddhist flags in front of the pagodas.

Another course of action, in my opinion, consisted of finding a viable alternative leadership among prominent politicians in South Viet Nam. This required building up the potential leader's image and preparing him for the job before approving the coup. The U.S. mistake, in my view, was to rely entirely on the ability of the generals to run the country, or, in the words of an American writer, "to replace bad leadership with no leadership at all."

In any event, in the midst of the new political crisis triggered by the Montagnard rebellion, we were encouraged by the American decision to conduct air raids on North Viet Nam, which had so far remained untouched. After the VC sent its commando units to raid the U.S. compound in Pleiku and an Army helicopter base at Camp Holloway on February 1, 1965, killing nine U.S. soldiers and wounding seventy-six, President Johnson reacted by sending forty-nine U.S. Navy jets, A-4 Skyhawks and F-8 Crusaders from the 7th Fleet carriers—USS *Coral Sea* and USS *Hancock*—to attack NVN barracks and staging areas at Dong Hoi, forty miles north of the seventeenth Parallel. This operation was code-named "Flaming Dart."

General Tri told me that, after learning of the air raid, General Khanh opened a bottle of champagne to celebrate. Flaming Dart was a tremendous boost to the morale of the troops who felt happy that the U.S. was now determined to bring the war to the North and to eventually destroy its will to fight.

Flaming Dart was soon followed by a heavier air raid, named "Flaming Dart II," conducted by 160 U.S. and Vietnamese fighters after the VC attacked the American compound in the coastal city of Qui Nhon on February 11, 1965. In late February, U.S. jet fighters were used inside South Viet Nam for air strikes against VC targets.

The above air raids obviously were part of General Taylor's "graduated response" strategy. Critics of this strategy believed, however, that it was a strategy of reaction rather than action. Rather than seizing the initiative, this strategy consisted of reacting to the enemy. Arthur Schlesinger, Jr., called this strategy a policy of "one more step." It corresponded to his "quagmire model" in which the U.S. was lured into the war not after adequate considerations, but through small decisions. Big decisions are indeed tough to make and politicians feel more comfortable with small decisions, with making "one more step," hoping that the new step would achieve what the previous last step had promised but failed to deliver.[17]

One step led to the other. This "one more step" policy resulted in an increase in the number of U.S. servicemen from 25,000 in 1964 to 429,000 in 1966. The total number of U.S. troops reached 549,000 in 1968 at the peak of the war.

At the time, however, I was very encouraged by these air raids which, I hoped, would destroy the NVA's will to fight. My hope turned out to be premature. As if there were not enough political chaos in our country already, on February 20,1965, Col. Pham Ngoc Thao, a highly controversial figure, staged a "semi-coup" against General Khanh. Thao came from a well-to-do family in Can Tho. He was a nephew of my aunt Di Hai's husband. Although a Catholic and a French citizen, he joined the Viet Minh and served as a Viet Minh battalion commander. (His older brother, Pham Ngoc Thuan, was North Viet Nam's ambassador to East Germany.) In 1954, after the Geneva Accords, Thao rallied to the South Vietnamese government and, under the tutelage and support of Monsignor Ngo Dinh Thuc, President Diem's older brother, Thao was appointed province chief of Kien Hoa. In 1963, he actively participated in the coup d'etat against President Diem. After the coup, he was sent to Washington as military attaché by the generals, who distrusted him. He returned to Viet Nam after General Khanh's successful counter-coup and started to undermine Khanh. Thao was subsequently wounded in Bien Hoa. He was brought to a Saigon hospital where he was killed under mysterious circumstances. Documents disclosed after the war seemed to confirm that Thao was a high-ranking VC intelligence operative who had successfully infiltrated the South Vietnamese government.

The next day, February 21, 1965, Gen. Nguyen Bao Tri took one infantry regiment and one armored squadron to Saigon to support Gen. Nguyen Cao Ky's coup to depose General Khanh. Unlike Colonel Ton, General Tri discussed the move with me beforehand and asked me if I would like to go to Saigon with him. I decided not to become involved and requested his permission to stay home to do the housekeeping while he was away.This time the coup was a success. On February 25, General Khanh left the country as ambassador-at-large after having been elevated to the rank of four-star general. Ultimately, Khanh ended up as a restaurateur in Paris.

In the meantime, my brother Tho came to see me right after the coup and asked for my help because Gen. Nguyen Chanh Thi, the former airborne commander who failed to overthrow President Diem in 1960, wanted to arrest Tho for having supported General Khanh. General Thi, who this time sided with General Ky, was also angry at Tho because Tho had come to the rescue of President Diem in 1960 with his armored regiment. I intervened with General Tri, who was kind enough to take Tho under his protection. I thus returned the favor to Tho without whom I would have been arrested by President Diem's security apparatus after the failed coup d'etat against his regime in 1960. Having a relative on the opposite side of the fence decidedly had its advantages.

In the middle of this new political turmoil, President Johnson started the process of "Americanizing" the Viet Nam War. On March 7, 1965, a Marine force of 3,500 men landed with great fanfare on the beaches of Danang. The Marines were received by a throng of U.S. and foreign reporters with cameras at the ready. As they waded ashore, the Marines were welcomed by Vietnamese schoolgirls in white *ao dai* waving small Vietnamese and American flags. The girls also put garlands around the Marines' necks. The arrival of the Marine Task Force brought the total of U.S. troops to 27,000.

After General Khanh's departure, the Young Turks appointed Dr. Phan Huy Quat, a respected politician, as the new Prime Minister. To prevent other coups, Dr. Quat appointed his friend, Brig. Gen. Vinh Loc, commanding the 9th Infantry Division, as commandant of the Capital Special Military District in Saigon. (Vinh Loc's younger brother had married one of Dr. Quat's daughters.) Col. Tran Van Cuong, IV Corps Chief of Staff and my classmate at Dalat, was recommended to take Gen. Vinh Loc's place, but at the time, Cuong himself was under investigation for having participated in a prior coup. So, General Tri submitted my name as an alternate candidate and I was pleasantly surprised when General Tri announced during a routine morning briefing at the division TOC that I was to be the next 9th Infantry Division commander. I was thirty-two and was very excited at the prospect of commanding an infantry division in combat.

In May 1965, after an emotional send-off at the 7th Division Headquarters, General Tri accompanied me to the division's helipad. He shook my hand and confided that he had personally guaranteed to Maj. Gen. Dang Van Quang, the IV Corps Commander, that I would do a good job and would bring many victories for the 9th Division. I thanked General Tri and assured him that I would do my best not to disappoint him. Then, I took off to assume my new and challenging command. (A few months later, General Tri was appointed III Corps commander and was responsible for the strategic area north of Saigon.)

8

9TH INFANTRY DIVISION

IT WAS RAINING HARD WHEN I crossed into the 9th Infantry Division's territory. It was the first storm of the monsoon season. The visibility was nil and the helicopter pilot lost his direction, so he requested my permission to land near a small watchtower somewhere north of the Bassac River. The chief of the Popular Forces unit that manned this small outpost was startled to see a full colonel dropping unexpectedly from the sky. I inquired about the VC activities in his area and asked him the direction to Can Tho, the IV Corps Headquarters. Then, I climbed back into my helicopter and headed for Can Tho in the middle of the unrelenting monsoon rain.

Maj. Gen. Dang Van Quang, the IV Corps commander, was jovial and courteous. General Quang was a clever officer, who survived the coups and counter-coups by timely siding with the winning parties. He was also reportedly one of the most corrupt officers in the Army. A heavy, corpulent man, Quang was surnamed "Quang Map" (or "Fat Quang"). Quang controlled all the district and province offices in IV Corps, which he sold to the highest bidders. A few months earlier, he had appointed Col. Nguyen Van Minh, his chief of staff and protégé, to the position of division commander of the 21st Division headquartered in Bac Lieu to replace Col. Nguyen Van Phuoc, one of my classmates at Dalat and a veteran of the Indochina War. The wife of the departing commander created quite a scandal when, during the official ceremony of transfer of command, she publicly stated that her husband was relieved of his command because he did not have 2 million piasters to pay Quang.

To Quang's credit, he did not ask me for any money (maybe he knew I had none) for my new job. Instead, he asked me to sign on a piece of paper so he could have his own fortune teller analyze my signature and predict my future as division commander. A few days later, he sent me a personal note telling me my signature was all right but he suggested I raise its tail a little bit so as to have a better ending. I complied because I knew he would watch my signatures on future official correspondence.

The Headquarters of the 9th Division was located in a small island off the city of Sa Dec. Situated on the southern bank of the Mekong River, Sa Dec was originally a province under the French Administration. It was downgraded to a district under Diem's government. Sandwiched between the Mekong and Bassac Rivers, Sa Dec was known for its moderate climate, beautiful flowers, and abundant fruit trees.

The 9th Division's main headquarters was located in the eastern tip of the island. It consisted of two two-story brick buildings built by the French to house the old Sa Dec Provincial Administration. One of the buildings housed the division commander's office and general staff. A second building contained the offices of the special staff including the Department of the Rural Reconstruction, which oversaw the division's pacification program. The division's Headquarters Company as well as the division's clinic were located on a small island northwest of the division's main headquarters. Adjacent to the division's general staff building was located the division Advisory Team complex consisting of prefabricated wood frame buildings.

The division commander's residence, also a two-story brick building, was situated 500 meters west of the division's headquarters. The ground floor was an open area which was divided into a living room and a dining room and the upper floor contained three bedrooms and two bathrooms and a balcony where you could see the tip of the island and the Mekong River, which forked into two branches enveloping the island.

Two days after I reported to the 9th Division, my wife and three children joined me in Sa Dec. My family enjoyed our new home. This was the first time, in fact, that they had lived in such a spacious home and in such a lovely place with water all around and a pleasant climate year round.

At the time I took over the 9th Infantry Division, it ranked as one of the worst divisions in the Vietnamese Army. For the last two years, it had not achieved any significant victory and the troop morale was very low. Gen. Vinh Loc, the division commander, was a cousin of Emperor Bao Dai. Gen. Vinh Loc attended the French Armor School at Saumur. I knew Vinh Loc when we were instructors at the Command & General Staff College. Because he was a cousin of Bao Dai, he was viewed with suspicion by the Diem regime and had remained a major at the Command & General Staff College for many years. After the November coup d'état in which he had actively participated, he was given the command of the 9th Division and rapidly rose to the rank of brigadier general. Finally, in March 1965, after Dr. Phan Huy Quat was appointed prime minister by the generals who had deposed Khanh, Vinh Loc, whose younger brother had married one of Dr. Quat's daughters, was offered the trusted post of commandant of the Capital Special Military District.

Gen. Vinh Loc was also known for his eccentricities. Deputy Division Commander Lt. Col. Dang Dinh Thuy, told me that one day Gen. Vinh Loc instructed a sergeant in his personal guard to wear the rank insignia of a brigadier general to receive and brief new graduates from the Military Academy who were assigned to the division, while General Vinh Loc himself donned the uniform of a sergeant. (When Vinh Loc later commanded the II Corps in the Hauts Plateaux, he paraded in Saigon on Army Days mounted on a Montagnard horse and dressed in traditional Montagnard costume.)

The 9th Division area of responsibility, called the 41st Tactical Area, was located at the heart of the Mekong Delta. It extended from the Gulf of Siam on the west, to the South China Sea on the east. It had a common border with Cambodia to the north. The 41st Tactical Area comprised some of the richest provinces of Viet Nam. The provinces of Vinh Binh, Vinh Long, and Long Xuyen (also known as An Giang), were great producers of rice, fruit, and vegetables. The Chau Doc and Kien Giang Provinces which had common border with Cambodia, exported fish. The province of Kien

Phong, located on the north side of the Mekong River, near the Cambodian border, was famous for its cattle. There was an important cement factory in Kien Giang that produced cement for the whole country. On the other hand, Long Xuyen was the political and religious headquarters for the Hoa Hao religious sect; the village of Cho Moi located on a small island on the Mekong River was known as its Mecca.

The 9th Infantry Division had three regiments (the 13th, the 14th, and the 15th Regiments) and two organic 105-mm artillery battalions. (At the request of the men of the 13th Regiment who believed that the number thirteen was unlucky, the 13th Regiment was later changed to the 16th Regiment and the morale and performance of the regiment noticeably improved.) The total effective force of the division was about 10,000 men. One Ranger battalion (the 43rd Ranger), one armored regiment (with two M-113 APC Cavalry Troops) and one 155-mm artillery battalion were also attached to the division. Each province or military sector within the division Tactical Area had direct control over a number of Regional Forces (RF) companies and each district or military subsector had their organic Popular Forces (PF) platoons. Thus, the total effective force under the division's tactical control, including the RF and PF forces, amounted to about 60,000 men.

After assuming the command of the division, I realized I needed a few quick victories to lift morale. On the other hand, I was aware that the division was not ready to engage enemy regular units. As a consequence, I decided to seek and destroy local VC companies. So, a day after I took over the division, I approved a regimental operation in the Vung Liem-Cang Long area where one enemy company had been identified. The operation area encompassed a border corridor between Vinh Long and Vinh Binh Provinces. The enemy typically escaped to the Vinh Binh side if the operation was launched by the Vinh Long Military Sector, and vice versa. To entrap the enemy, I ordered the Vinh Long Regional Forces to block the enemy route of withdrawal into Vung Liem District, while two battalions from the 14th Regiment would sweep through the area in a westerly direction. My first operation was a success. About thirty VC were killed and fifteen weapons captured. This was a moderate but welcome victory. The next day, I was pleased to receive a message of congratulation from Gen. Nguyen Bao Tri, my former boss at the 7th Division.

The following week, I entrapped and destroyed one VC company along the Kien Phong canal in the heart of the famed Plain of Reeds, which had witnessed many bloody battles between the Viet Minh and the French Corps Expeditionaire during the Indochina War. At the heat of the battle, I decided to land my helicopter near the 43rd Ranger Battalion CP whose troops were engaging the enemy; I stayed with the rangers until the end of the battle, despite the urging of Captain Hiep, the battalion commander, that I leave because it was too dangerous for a division commander.

The morale of the division soared after this second victory and I knew that the 9th Division, from then on, could engage and beat any VC regular units anywhere in the 41st Tactical Area. In the meantime, one incident revealed the corrupt practices within the civil administration. Two weeks after I arrived at the division, the district chief of Hong Ngu, an army captain, requested to see me. Hong Ngu was one of the districts of Chau Doc Province near the Cambodian border where contraband and smuggling were rampant. After the district chief made a brief presentation about the military and economic situation in his district, he presented me with an old box of French biscuits full of 500 piaster bills.

"Colonel! I know you are going to have many victories," said the district chief in a hesitant voice. "This is a small contribution for you to reward your troops when you have victories."

I told the captain to take his French biscuit box and get out of my office or I would have the military police arrest him for attempting to bribe his military superior. Although I felt powerless in eradicating corrupt practices in the parallel civilian hierarchy within my area of responsibility, this incident spread quickly through the grapevine channel and enhanced the morale of the troops.

After my first modest military successes, I decided it was time to take on the VC regular battalions. I also decided that my next target would be the VC Vinh Binh Provincial Battalion and the battle would be set at the famous enemy secret base of the village of Tan Ngai, approximately five kilometers west of the District of

Cau Ke. Tan Ngai, a fortified two-kilometer-long village located on the west bank of Cau Ke River, had been a Communist stronghold during the French colonial days. Tan Ngai so far had remained untouched and it was obvious that any attack on this fortified base would be risky.

I needed the support of armored units if I were to win this important battle. Lieutenant Colonel Tin, the 2nd Armored Cavalry Regiment Commander, assured me that the M-113 APCs would be able to reach the open rice fields directly west of Tan Ngai by overcoming the thick mangroves on the northern bank of the Bassac River, provided that the landing would take place during high tide. I decided to launch the attack by using a combination of naval landing and heliborne operation. My plan called for transporting two battalions of the 15th Regiment and one M-113 Cavalry Troop by the Navy LSTs (Landing Ship, Tank) from the Bassac ferry site south of Vinh Long to a landing site south of the village of Tan Ngai. The 15th Regiment would attack from the south and the APC troop, reinforced with the division's Reconnaissance Company, would take up position west of Tan Ngai and would be held in reserve for the main assault. The 43rd Ranger Battalion would be heliborne to a LZ north of Tan Ngai and would attack in a southerly direction. One battalion from the 15th Regiment would be held in reserve in Cau Ke District, where the division's CP would also be located. To block enemy escape to the east, two RF companies from Vinh Binh Sector would occupy the eastern bank of the Cau Ke River.

Around 6:00 AM. on D-Day, two LSTs disgorged the 15th Regiment and one APC troop near the estuary of the Cau Ke River. At 6:30 AM., I circled the northern area of Tan Ngai and picked up the LZ for the 43rd Ranger Battalion whose first elements landed around 6:45 AM. Immediately after landing, the two battalions of the 15th Regiment, as expected, met strong resistance from the enemy dug in behind dense trees and endless sugar canes fields. The 43rd Ranger also had contact with the enemy and reported a few wounded. In the meantime, the cavalry troop, after some initial difficulties, was finally able to clear a landing path among the mangroves and to reach shore. At around 10:00 am., the APC troop took up position west of Tan Ngai and was ready for the assault.

By that time, it was obvious the enemy was trapped in Tan Ngai and had to fight for its life. Artillery and helicopter gunships were called in to support the attacking forces. At around 3:00 PM., the advance elements of the 43rd Rangers moving from the north and the 15th Regiment attacking from the south, were approximately 500 meters from each other and the enemy battalion dug in between these elements offered furious resistance.

I decided it was time for the final assault. After a heavy tactical airstrike followed by gunship close support, the APC troop went into action, blasting point blank at the VC identified fortifications at the edge of the village with all its organic .50 machine guns while attacking in the direction of the sugar cane fields between the colored grenade smokes that marked the positions of the advance elements of the 43rd Ranger and the 15th Regiment.

It should be noted that the wet terrain and the existence of many rivers and ravines prevented the use of regular army tanks in the Mekong Delta. This was the reason the tank squadron of the 2nd Armored Regiment was put under the control of IV Corps to be used for the defense of Can Tho Airport and also as a reserve for IV Corps. Although the M-113 APC was used for troop transportation and was more vulnerable to recoilless rifle fire than a regular tank, a M-113 Cavalry Troop, in addition to its organic .50 machine guns, was equipped with three 81-mm mortars, one 57-mm recoilless rifle, and one fire thrower. This formidable fire power, combined with timely and skillful tactical maneuvers, was a decisive factor in many victories in the Mekong Delta.

Around 4:00 AM., the battle of Tan Ngai ended. The APC troop and the supporting 9th Division's Reconnaissance Company occupied the assigned target and linked up with the 43rd Ranger and elements of the 15th Regiment. Lt. Gen. John Heintges, Deputy MAC-V, dropped in for a visit and I took him to the village of Tan Ngai to inspect the battlefield first hand. Enemy corpses were all around the dikes and in the rice paddies. I picked up one enemy AK-47 and presented it to General Heintges as a souvenir of his visit.

We suffered about twenty killed and fifty wounded. The enemy left around 150 dead along with numerous weapons, including recoilless rifles and machine guns. The Tan Ngai Battle was the first major victory for the 9th Infantry Division. For all practical purposes, the VC Vinh Binh Provincial Battalion ceased to exist, at least for the time being, for I was aware that the enemy would soon draft young peasants and dig into their local units to replenish the effective force of the badly damaged battalion. But it would take at least six months for the Vinh Binh VC Provincial Battalion to become operational again. In the meantime, the Vinh Binh Province could take advantage of this respite to further its pacification program.

Although I had achieved some significant victories in the first few months of my command and the military situation in the Mekong Delta had remarkably improved, I grew more and more concerned about new political developments in Saigon. On June 19, 1965[18], Pham Huy Quat, unable to govern a country at war, relinquished power to the Army. The Council of Generals appointed Lt. Gen. Nguyen Van Thieu, chairman of the Joint General Staff, as chairman of the National Leadership Committee and Maj. Gen. Nguyen Cao Ky, chief of Air Force, as chairman of the Central Executive Committee. In other words, General Thieu had become chief of state and General Ky had become a prime minister. Generals Thieu and Ky started to enlist the support of the generals and the intense political infighting between these two rivals further divided an already fragmented officer corps.

In July 1965, Chau Doc Province Chief Lt. Col. Ly Ba Pham, called me in the middle of the night to report that, due to logistical problems, the morale of the Cambodian dissident forces called KKs or *Kampuchia Kraom* (Free Kampuchea), which operated in That Son (Seven Mountains) area, had seriously deteriorated. Colonel Pham suggested that they might even rally to the government if the division mounted an operation in the area to surround them and to call for their surrender.

The KKs were loyal to the Cambodian government in Phnom Penh, which gave them money and weapons. Cambodia considered the Mekong Delta part of the Khmer empire and the Cambodian government used the armed KK movement to fight against the Vietnamese "conquerors." The KKs had their secret base in the rugged

That Son area, which was located only a few kilometers from the Cambodian border. That Son Mountains were an ideal secret base for both VC regular units as well as the KK forces because they consisted of multiple huge, deep caverns where the enemy could hide and store supplies. That Son's location near the Cambodian border also allowed the VC to get their supplies in weapons and ammunition from Cambodia and to move to safe sanctuaries in that country in case of important operations by government forces in the area. That Son was the only area in my tactical area of responsibility where I sometimes had to resort to B-52 strikes in support of division operations.

VC units operating in the That Son area left the KKs alone because the latter were also fighting against the government of South Viet Nam. As the U.S. Special Forces started to move into MRIV and to build a chain of outposts along the Cambodian border in 1964 in their efforts to interdict infiltrations of Communist manpower and supplies across the border, the flow of supplies to the KKs was also threatened and their situation became critical. They had lost the support of the local Cambodian population which had grown weary of the war and wanted to be left alone. Colonel Pham had reliable intelligence information that some of the KK leaders considered rallying to the government and were waiting for an opportunity to do so.

The day following Colonel Pham's report, I launched a division operation in That Son, using the 15th Regiment supported by the 2nd Armored Cavalry Regiment. We quickly surrounded the villages located at the foot of the That Son Mountains and used loud speakers to talk the KKs into surrender. Sure enough, around noon, our units received messengers from the KKs who came to negotiate the terms of their surrender. That day, about 200 KK soldiers gave up their weapons and rallied to the government. It was welcome news for the new Thieu-Ky government. It was also a bloodless victory for the 9th Division. This operation was a rewarding experience for me and I have always considered the rallying of the KKs as one of my biggest successes as a division commander.

After this bloodless campaign, which came on the heels of the destruction of the VC provincial battalion of Vinh Binh in June, I had to take care of the other provinces of my tactical area. One such province was Kien Giang. Located on the Gulf of Siam, Kien Giang shared a common border with the provinces of Chuong Thien and An Xuyen to the southeast and south respectively. The last two provinces were part of the 42nd Tactical Area under the control of the 21st Infantry Division. The VC regular units freely moved back and forth between the three adjacent provinces and during the last three months many outposts in the southern area of Kien Giang had come under attack by enemy units coming from Chuong Thien.

Around September 1965, I visited Kien Giang and met with its province chief, Lt. Col. Nguyen Khac Tuan,[19] a classmate of mine at Dalat. Colonel Tuan was an *Adjudant-Chef* (the equivalent of warrant-officer in the U.S. Army) in the French Army when he enrolled at the School of Inter-Arms at Dalat. A very good soccer player (he played for the national soccer team) and a decorated veteran of the Indochina War, he used to tease me at Dalat because I was a rookie with no military experience. Colonel Tuan invited me to the Sector's TOC. After a short welcoming remark, Colonel Tuan let his staff brief me on the military situation and the progress of the pacification in Kien Giang Province.

After the formal briefing, Tuan took me to his private office at the province headquarters and suggested that, since it was difficult to seek enemy regular units, which normally stayed in the Chuong Thien side of the border, I could instead achieve a relatively easy victory by attacking a local company in the village of Kinh Thay Cai, located at the southern border of his province.

Kinh Thay Cai was located near the border with Chuong Thien and could serve as a staging area for the VC regular units which crossed into Kien Giang Province to attack its outposts or recruit new draftees. I was also aware that the enemy's famed secret base of the impenetrable U Minh Forest was only ten kilometers from the target area. It was in this base that my cousin Lam Quang Phong, the former Viet Minh regiment commander, had been sentenced to death by a popular tribunal; he was later rescued by a French military operation.

Back at division Headquarters, I instructed my staff to make the necessary preparations for the Kinh Thay Cai operation to be launched the following week. Kinh Thay Cai (The Canal of Mr. Cai) was a three-kilometer long village. The entire village was traversed by a canal which ran in an east-west direction. As is typical in the Mekong Delta, the houses were built on both sides of the canal and were hidden under thick trees. The main canal was connected to multiple creeks running perpendicular to the canal. These creeks could provide convenient routes of escape to the enemy. They also could be used to provide murderous enfilading fires on the attacking forces.

My plan called for using the Kien Giang Regional Forces to block the enemy withdrawal toward the west and landing two battalions of the 15th Regiment by helicopters in an area to the east of Kinh Thay Cai. The 15th Regiment would attack along the canal in a westerly direction. One APC troop would take up position in the rice fields north of the canal and the second APC troop would block the enemy escape to the south toward Chuong Thien. The 43rd Ranger battalion would be held in reserve at Kien Giang Airport. The operation would be supported by one 105-mm artillery battalion and one 155-mm battery. These artillery units positioned near the Giong Rieng District Headquarters could provide enfilading fire the entire length of the Kinh Thay Cai canal.

At around 7:00 A.M. on D-Day, I circled the operation area in my C&C helicopter with Colonel Conley, the division U.S. Senior Advisor. I picked up an LZ near the tip of a small creek running northward from the eastern end of the main canal. By 8:00 A.M., the landing of the 15th was complete. As elements of the 15th Regiment moved toward the creek, they were pinned down in the open by heavy machine-gun fire. I knew then that what I was facing was not a local company because local units typically were not equipped with machine guns.

"Tuan, is this the local company you were talking about?" I asked Colonel Tuan who was following the progress of the operation at the division CP.

Tuan said he was sorry about the faulty intelligence.

After the artillery had softened the area along the creek, the 15th, supported by attack helicopter gunfire, succeeded in capturing its first objective at the junction of the creek with the main

canal. However, it met increasingly strong resistance as it moved
westward along the canal. I asked Colonel Conley to request U.S.
tactical air support. Meanwhile, the division artillery provided uninterrupted fire along the canal. Despite all the artillery and air
support, by noon, the 15th had only moved about one kilometer
from its first objective. I decided it was time to launch a frontal
attack by the APC troop on the main target. When the squadron
was about one hundred meters from the northern edge of Kinh Thay
Cai, it received heavy recoilless rife fire. Two APCs were destroyed
and a dozen men were killed. Around 3:00 PM., I engaged my last
reserve, the 43rd Ranger.

Due to heavy fire, the Rangers were brought in at an LZ located
one kilometer from the objective. By 4:00 PM., the Rangers started
to attack in the direction of the main canal. Around 4:30 PM., Captain Hiep, the battalion commander, reported that the first assault
was repulsed by the enemy and that the battalion had received
"moderate" casualties. As I circled the battlefield in my C&C helicopter, I grew nervous for I knew that if you could not "solve" the
battlefield by 6:00 PM., the battle would be lost because the enemy,
under cover of darkness, would escape by taking with them all their
dead and wounded. Sensing my concern, Captain Hiep assured me
that he would do his best to capture the objective before nightfall.

"From Panther to Sun I am going to commit my reserve 'child,'"
Captain Hiep said in an unusually calm voice on the radio.[20] "Sun,
don't worry! I am confident I can take the objective before dark."

Captain Hiep was one of the bravest fighting men I had ever
met. A former parachutist, he briefly served in North Viet Nam before the end of the Indochina War. As the 43rd Ranger battalion
commander, he had distinguished himself in numerous battles in
the Mekong Delta and I could rely on him for the most dangerous
and difficult missions. But the Kinh Thay Cai obviously was the
toughest battle he had ever been involved in and I was not sure that
his bravery and coolness under fire were enough for the task ahead.
Somehow, I felt reassured by his calm voice and his confidence.[21]
Captain Hiep made good on his word. His reserve company succeeded in capturing a corner of the village from where Hiep regrouped and attacked the right flank of the enemy. By 7:00 PM.,

Captain Hiep reported there were many VC dead along the canal and that his troops captured two new Chinese 75-mm recoilless rifles mounted on wheels. Soon, the 15th Regiment linked up with the Ranger battalion and both units started the mopping-up operation. During the night, the Viet Cong launched a few counterattacks, which were repulsed by the 43rd Ranger. Later, Captain Hiep told me that he and his U.S. advisor had to hold the two captured 75-mm recoilless rifles the entire night, fearing that the VC would retake them during their counterattacks.

The captured documents indicated that Kinh Thay Cai was occupied by two VC regular battalions: the U Minh Battalion, which was the Kien Giang Provincial Battalion; and the 303rd Regional Main Force Battalion. These two battalions suffered about 200 dead in the Battle of Kinh Thay Cai. We captured around one hundred weapons, including the above-described 75-mm recoilless rifles. We lost twenty-five dead and around fifty wounded. Two APCs were destroyed by recoilless rifle fire.

The next day, Maj. Gen. Tran Thanh Phong, assistant chief of staff for operations, Joint General Staff, flew in to study the battle and to inspect the 75-mm recoilless rifles, which were the first weapons of this kind to be introduced into South Viet Nam by the VC. Major-General Dang Van Quang, IV Corps Commander, also inspected the battlefield and the weapons captured. He took me aside to congratulate me.

"Thi, I congratulate you for this very important victory," General Quang said. "Normally, I would have recommended you for promotion to brigadier general. However you are too young to be general. Instead, I will recommend that you be given the *cravate* of the National Order with the Gallantry Cross with palm."

The *cravate* of the National Order meant the Third Degree of the National Order, which was normally awarded to high-ranking generals. It was presented in the form of a pendant similar to a *cravate* or tie. The second degree and first degree were typically reserved to foreign dignitaries and chiefs of state. The Gallantry Cross with palm that accompanied a "Citation Before the Army" was the highest award for action in face of the enemy. Captain Hiep and his American advisor were also awarded the Gallantry Cross with palm and both of them were also recommended for the U.S. Silver Star medal.

That night, I flew to Kien Giang to have dinner with Colonel Tuan. He opened a bottle of French champagne to celebrate the biggest ARVN victory in his province. We reminisced about our old days at the School of Inter-Arms and did not go to bed until the early hours of the morning.

In February, 1966, at Tet, the Vietnamese New Year, I was promoted to brigadier general. I was thirty-three and one of the youngest generals in the Vietnamese Army. The 1966 Tet was, without any doubt, the best Tet I had ever known.

In retrospect, the victory at Kinh Thay Cai was the result of careful planning and swift execution. It was my experience that a successful field commander should be able to cope with unanticipated situations, and to mass the fire power and the troops available in a timely fashion in order to influence the outcome of the battle. It did not take long for me to learn that speed, flexibility, and mass were the keys to success on the battlefield.

Another battle in Long Xuyen in March 1966 illustrated the tactical concepts of speed, flexibility, and mass.

The night prior to a planned division operation in the enemy base in the Plain of Reeds in Kien Phong Province, I received a call from Lt. Col. Ly Ba Pham, Long Xuyen province chief (and former Chau Doc province chief). Colonel Pham informed me that, according to Catholic priests in the Cai San area, one VC regular battalion had occupied a few canals in this important Catholic resettlement center to draft new recruits for their unit. He also requested that I launch a division operation to dislodge the VC from the Cai San area.

Cai San was one of the most successful relocation projects undertaken by President Diem in 1954 to relocate Catholic refugees from North Viet Nam. Previously an uncultivated area located on the border between the provinces of Long Xuyen and Kien Giang, Cai San had since been improved with multiple irrigation canals and had been transformed into a rich rice-producing region by the hard-working Northerners. Each canal had its own church and the Cai San diocese was under a politically powerful Catholic priest, Father Loc.

I was surprised by the intelligence report from Colonel Pham because the Catholic resettlement center of Cai San, as well as the Hoa Hao-controlled regions in Long Xuyen Province, were the most secure areas of the entire 41st Tactical Area. Since the inhabitants of these regions were staunchly anti-Communist, in the past no Communist units had dared venture into these areas. However, because of the potential political ramifications involved (a VC battalion controlling an important Catholic resettlement center would make headlines in Saigon newspapers), I decided to send the 1st Battalion of the 15th Regiment into Cai San. I also diverted an APC troop from the planned division operation in Kien Phong to Cai San. The above units were placed under the tactical control of the Long Xuyen Province Chief; they were to make a reconnaissance in force in the Catholic resettlement center.

The division operation was launched as planned with the 16th Regiment as the main attacking force. The 43rd Ranger Battalion was held in reserve, this time at Kien Phong Province Airport. Around 4:00 PM., the division met only sporadic resistance from local units in the Plain of Reeds; I decided to fly into Cai San to look at the situation in this resettlement area. Father Loc met me at the local district headquarters and informed me that his Catholic Self-Defense elements reported to him on radio that an enemy unit of battalion size was dug in on the main canal approximately two kilometers from the Long Xuyen-Kien Giang road. Father Loc reminded me of the priest of the village of Cao Xa in Hung Yen, North Viet Nam. The Cao Xa priest led his loyal Catholic paramilitary unit with an iron hand during the Indochina War. He often led night patrols and tended ambushes to destroy Viet Minh units moving around his village. The Catholic priests who immigrated to the South after the 1954 partition of Viet Nam carried on this tradition of self-reliance and determination in their never-ending struggle against the declared enemy of their religion.

The Catholic resettlement of Ca Mau was a case in point. Located north of Mui Ca Mau (or Tip of Ca Mau) in the middle of a VC-controlled area, this strategic resettlement center was put under the command of Father Hoa, a fanatic Chinese- Vietnamese priest who had his own army, supported and equipped by U.S. Special Forces.

These resettlement centers and their fighting priests had constituted the backbone of the Diem regime. In return, they received important financial and military assistance from the government. President Thieu, himself a Catholic, relied heavily on Catholic support to govern the country and defeat the Communist insurgency.

With regard to the VC occupation of Cai San resettlement center, Father Loc was invaluable in providing accurate intelligence reports. He was in constant radio contact with his people who stayed behind to report on enemy activities. He pinpointed the exact location of the VC battalion. Shortly after the 1/15 Battalion had crossed the canal north of the Long Xuyen-Kien Giang inter-provincial road, its forward elements reported heavy contact with the enemy.

I directed Captain Loc, commanding the 3/2 Cavalry Troop, to cross the canal and attack the identified enemy position in front of the 1/15 Battalion. I also asked Colonel Conley, the U.S. Senior Advisor, to divert the helicopters attached to the division operation in Kien Phong for the transport of the 43rd Ranger from Kien Phong to an LZ north of the canal where contact had been established with the enemy. The 43rd Ranger's mission was to block enemy escape to the north. This heliborne operation turned out to be a complicated undertaking since the helicopters had to be refueled en route at Long Xuyen Airport. However, around 6:30 PM., the landing of the 43rd Ranger was complete and the only possible escape route for the VC battalion had been effectively sealed off.

At about the same time, Captain Loc crossed the canal with his APC troops and started the frontal assault on the enemy position in front of the 1/15th Battalion. Since farmhouses on both sides of the small canal that traversed the Catholic resettlement village were only about fifty meters deep, it took less than an hour for Captain Loc to reach the canal after his fifteen APCs blasted enemy machine gun positions with all their fire power. About fifty enemy were killed and twenty weapons captured, including one B-40 anti-tank gun. We suffered only one killed. Documents captured indicated that the VC unit involved in the action was the Kien Giang U Minh 10 Battalion. It had come to Cai San to force young men in the diocese to enlist in the battalion.

Like Captain Hiep, the 43rd Ranger Battalion Commander, Captain Loc was a brave officer. As the commander of one APC cavalry troop, he had distinguished himself throughout the 41st Tactical Area. A highly decorated officer (he was awarded two U.S. silver stars), Captain Loc was expert in the techniques of river crossing by APCs in the Mekong Delta. A few months earlier, at the request of Brig. Gen. William Desobry, the IV Corps senior advisor, himself an armor officer of good standing (General Desobry's armored unit was the first to link up with the U.S. 101st Airborne Division entrapped at Bastogne during the Battle of the Bulge in World War II), Loc organized a river crossing demonstration for U.S. armor officers from the U.S. 9th Infantry Division stationed in My Tho. I knew Captain Loc did not like to be put under the tactical control of the province chiefs and was reticent to execute their orders. This was the reason I had to fly into Cai San to direct the attack, which Captain Loc executed flawlessly.

A lesson I learned from the Battle of Cai San was that in a counter-insurgency situation, an area commander should take necessary steps to provide security to the people; security and popular support are two necessary conditions for winning the "hearts and the minds" of the population. In this instance, while I went after the VC regular units in the Plain of Reeds in Kien Phong with the main division forces, I retained enough troops to protect the Catholic resettlement center of Cai San against enemy incursion.

In this respect I think it is appropriate to discuss U.S. strategies to deal with the counter-insurgency in Viet Nam. I have described General Maxwell Taylor's concept of "graduated response" in Chapter 7. This strategy was developed in his book *The Uncertain Trumpet*. Governed basically by the concept of "flexibility," this strategy allowed the U.S. to respond in kind to communist aggression without necessarily resorting to nuclear warfare.

When the first Marine units landed in Danang in March 1965, their mission was only to defend the airbase under the "enclave" concept which called for the American troops to protect populated areas and important logistical installations in the coastal areas. In order to prevent attacks by commando teams or mortars, the U.S. troops had to patrol a few miles outside the perimeter of defense.

Later, the American forces were allowed to operate fifty miles outside the enclaves to rescue ARVN units under heavy attack from
the enemy.

The American ground troops were allowed to conduct offensive
operations anywhere in South Viet Nam after June 9, 1965. General Westmoreland's concept of "search and destroy," sometimes
called "big unit" warfare, replaced the old concept of enclave. The
objective of this strategy was to inflict defeat on the enemy, rather
than denying him victory. The battle of Pleime in the Hauts Plateaux, where the 1st U.S. Cavalry Division defeated one enemy division in heavy engagements, was a good example of this concept.

Under this concept, General Westmoreland saw the need to fight
on two fronts: conducting offensive operations against NVA and VC
regular units on the one hand, while providing security to the population on the other. Westmoreland compared these two forces as
two fists of a boxer, striking the Communist forces with one hand
while retaining the other to defend and protect the populated areas. I remember General Westmoreland's visit to my division in Sa
Dec in early 1966. In front of my staff and the U.S. advisory team,
he proudly explained his "two-fisted" strategy; he stood behind the
podium of the conference room and alternately punched the air
with both fists like a professional boxer. Watching General
Westmoreland's demonstration, I realized that I had utilized his "two-
fisted" strategy in my division. I remember one character in a Molière
comedy who, after having learned the difference between prose and
poetry, suddenly realized that she had *"fait la prose"* all her life.

However, despite all the exotic names given to these strategies,
the basic flaw of the U.S. policy in Viet Nam was the lack of clarity
of mission. According to former Defense Secretary James
Schlesinger, the use of military power must pass the tests of clarity
of mission and efficiency.

It was disturbing to see that General Westmoreland kept asking
for additional troops without any clear objective. During the Korean War, Douglas MacArthur requested permission to cross the
Yalu River to invade Manchuria. He was fired. General Westmoreland
kept asking for new troops and didn't know what to do with them.
He was later promoted to Army Chief of Staff. This was the sign of

the times. It was unfortunate that we did not have generals in Viet Nam of Douglas MacArthur's caliber who knew what the objectives were and how to achieve them.

It appears to me that after the Korean War, the U.S. Army experienced a general deterioration of military leadership. The U.S. generals who fought in Viet Nam seemed to lack imagination and charisma. They forgot that the most important factor in a war is man, not technology; victory on the battlefield requires traditional leadership, not bureaucratic management. This observation, in my opinion, fittingly describes the performance of U.S. generals in Viet Nam, who seemed to ignore the fact that in unconventional warfare, technology and indiscriminate use of firepower cannot replace the human factors of training and morale.

In retrospect, it is clear that in Viet Nam, the U.S. had no choice but to adopt one of the following alternatives (besides a pure and simple disengagement): 1) To carry the war to North Viet Nam and aim at the destruction of Hanoi government's will to fight; and 2) To support the government of South Viet Nam in fighting a long and protracted war in the South.

The first alternative would have allowed for a quick conclusion to the war. It may have, however, required more than the 549,000 men the U.S. had at the peak of the Viet Nam War. Although there was a risk of intervention by Russia and China, this eventuality was highly unlikely given the animosity between these two countries and given the fact that the destruction of the war-making machine of North Viet Nam would not constitute a direct threat to their security. This alternative was favored by U.S. generals who did not believe in the policy of "status quo" and who, on the contrary, believed that in a war, "there is no substitute for victory." "Had President Johnson changed our strategy," wrote General Westmoreland, "and taken advantage of the enemy's weakness to enable me to carry out the operations we had planned over the previous two years in Laos, Cambodia and north of the DMZ, along with intensified bombing and the mining of Hai Phong Harbor, the North Viet Namese doubtlessly would have broken."[22]

Unfortunately, we did not have the guts to adopt the first alternative. I still believe that the second alternative could have been successfully implemented in conjunction with an intensive and timely Vietnamization program, particularly after the 1968 Tet Offensive where the VC lost one-half of its war-making potential. At that time, in order to appease increased domestic opposition to the war, the U.S. could have effectively reversed to the old "strategy of enclaves." Under this strategy, U.S. troops would concentrate in urban areas along the coastline, while the Vietnamese Army, properly trained and equipped by the U.S., and supported by U.S. air power, would be charged with seeking and destroying enemy regular units.

It was no secret that the Tet Offensive was a major military victory for Allied forces, but at the same time it was a serious psychological setback. After the Tet Offensive, it was obvious that a new strategy was required. Due to increased opposition to escalating the war, alternative # 2 appeared to be the logical solution.

It is interesting that Dr. Alain C. Enthoven of the Pentagon's Office of Systems Analysis had this to say:

> While we have raised the price of NVN's aggression and support of the Viet Cong, it shows no lack of capability or will to match each new U.S. escalation. Our strategy of attrition has not worked. Adding 206,000 more U.S. men to a force of 525,000, gaining only 27 additional maneuver battalions and 270 tactical fighters at an added cost to the U.S. of $10 billion per year raises the question of who is making the war costly to whom.
>
> We know that despite a massive influx of 500,000 troops, 1.3 million tons of bombs a year, 400,000 attack sorties per year, 200,000 enemy KIA, etc., our control of the countryside and the defense of the urban areas is now essentially at pre-August 1965 levels. We have achieved a stalemate for a high commitment. A new strategy must be sought.[23]

The new strategy sought by Dr. Enthoven, in my opinion, could have been the "strategy of enclave" described above. It would permit a reduction in the number of U.S. troops in Viet Nam to approximately 200,000 men and also substantially reduce U.S.

casualties, making the war more acceptable to the American public. Implementation of this new strategy would be conditioned upon an intensive Vietnamization program under which new ARVN divisions would be created. (It was estimated that the cost of forming, training, and equipping five ARVN divisions would be equivalent to the cost of maintaining one U.S. division.) Intensive training of ARVN regulars, as well as RF and PF units, would also be essential for the successful implementation of the "enclave strategy."

Henry Brandon wrote in *An Anatomy of an Error* that he did not believe that the war was lost at home. In his view, the U.S. failure was due to the fact that the American forces did not train and equip the South Viet Namese adequately until 1967-68. He was wrong on his first proposition, but was absolutely right on the second; a growing antiwar movement in the U.S. and the failure to train and equip a strong Vietnamese Army in the 1950s were without doubt two major causes of the Viet Nam disaster. In *The White House Years,* Dr. Kissinger, who, along with North Viet Nam's Le Duc Tho would become the architect of the 1973 Paris Peace Agreement, considered the Vietnamization program as a serious strategy to achieve an honorable peace and not merely a justification for the American withdrawal. [24] Sadly, the latter was to be the case!

The strategy of enclave, while allowing U.S. troops to "stay low-key" and avoid casualties would, on the other hand, eliminate one big mistake made by the U.S. Command in Viet Nam. This mistake consisted of letting U.S. troops assume the major burden of the war and relegating the Vietnamese Army to a secondary role of pacification and static defense. The strategy of enclave, in this instance, could be perceived as a proper alternative if the desired end result was a compromise between a demoralizing withdrawal and an unacceptable escalation.

In short, the Viet Nam War should have been fought by Vietnamese boys, and I am confident that, with adequate logistical and air support, they could have done the job. The defeat of NVN regular divisions in Quang Tri, Kontum, and An Loc in 1972 amply demonstrated that simple fact.

The war of attrition, however, required patience, a quality which unfortunately was in short supply with the Americans. In this kind of war, success or failure is not defined in terms of the number of enemy killed or weapons captured, nor in terms of the numbers of new hamlets pacified. In a war of attrition, we usually fight for time, not space. The problem was that, in Viet Nam, the U.S. did the reverse: it fought for space, not for time.

After the fall of President Diem, his "Strategic Hamlets" concept (based on the success of the counter-insurgency program in Malaysia at the end of World War II), which consisted of relocating people inside fortified hamlets, had been virtually abandoned by succeeding governments. At that time, I failed to understand the simple truth that the government was responsible for providing security to the people in their own villages, and that if it failed to do so, it should leave the people alone.

Under the government pacification program, the villages typically were classified as safe, as located in contested areas, or as in VC-controlled areas. Occasionally, during division operations in sparsely populated contested areas, I directed that the inhabitants be moved into various province-operated refugee camps to shield them from enemy propaganda and taxes. By doing so, I made the same mistakes made by American units which resorted to forced resettlements in their areas of responsibility. The difference was that as a Vietnamese, I should have known the basic feelings, customs, and culture of the Vietnamese peasants who are fundamentally attached to their villages and to the grave sites of their ancestors. Vietnamese peasants feel alienated, even humiliated when they are forced to resettle in new hamlets and, worse, in newly created refugee camps.

Looking back, I think that we failed to understand the true characteristics of a war of attrition, under which time has priority over space. The concept of war by attrition can be summarized in the following manner: if we are determined to hang on, time will work in our favor. Since the VC were constantly on the run and could not patch their wounds, since they had not made good on their promises to protect the population, and because the VC taxes kept increasing, their popular base would be gradually eroded. This tends to accelerate their degradation process. Most important, because time has priority over space, we would not have had to resort to forced resettlements, which alienated the people and were one of the major causes of the failures of the pacification program in Viet Nam.

Meanwhile, however, the political situation in Saigon again gave me cause for concern. Although General Ky appeared to have consolidated his power, the fall of General Khanh triggered a new political crisis. To understand the Buddhist crisis, it is important to remember that six months after he ousted General Duong Van Minh, General Khanh had to cope with student demonstrations demanding that he ease his dictatorial power. The students were joined by the Buddhists who were concerned about their declining influence; they complained that many former Diem Catholic supporters still held important jobs in the government. Not to be outdone, Catholic activists staged their own demonstrations to counter the Buddhists and soon Saigon was engulfed in new turmoil and uncertainty. Khanh had to compromise with the Buddhist leaders, Venerables Tri Quang and Tam Chau, who pledged to support his government in exchange for Khanh's promise to consult with them on all important government decisions.

Consequently, the Buddhists saw the departure of General Khanh as a direct threat to their newly established power. They demanded a return to civilian rule. On March 10, 1966, after General Ky fired Gen. Nguyen Chanh Thi, the I Corps Commander, for having sympathized with the Buddhist dissidents, the United Buddhist Church staged a series of demonstrations in Hue and Danang demanding Thieu and Ky's resignation. Soon the movement spread to Qui Nhon, Nha Trang, Dalat, and Saigon. South Viet Nam was on the verge of collapse, not from a VC victory, but because of new political and religious convulsions.

The military junta replaced General Thi successively with three generals: Nguyen Van Chuan, Huynh Van Cao, and Ton That Dinh. All three generals were from Hue. Chuan and Dinh were Buddhist and overtly sympathized with the dissidents. Cao was a Catholic and had been a strong supporter of President Diem. When Gen. Nguyen Ngoc Loan, chief of police and an emissary of General Ky, went to see General Cao in Danang to discuss the Buddhist situation, the latter believed that Loan intended to kill him. Fearing for his life, Cao sought refuge in the U.S. Marines' compound in Danang, thus giving up his command altogether. Finally, Maj. Gen. Hoang Xuan Lam, commanding the 2nd Division in Quang Ngai, a colorless figure acceptable to both Thieu and Ky and the Buddhist leadership, was appointed new commander of I Corps.

On May 5, 1966, General Ky ordered two Marine battalions airlifted to Danang. In conjunction with elements of the Airborne Division that had been operating in Quang Tri Province, south of the DMZ, the Marines succeeded in recapturing most of the city of Danang and on May 22, the last Danang pagoda surrendered.

Shortly after order had been reestablished in I Corps, Generals Thi, Chuan, Cao, and Dinh were brought back to Saigon to stand trial before the Military Council, which consisted of Generals Thieu, Ky, a few generals from JGS, the four corps commanders and one division commander from each Corps. Gen. Dang Van Quang, the IV Corps commander, appointed me as a member of the Military Council. I remember well the "trial" that took place at the Directorate of Military Training in the compound of JGS. This was the first time I had had the opportunity to witness firsthand the infighting among the generals during the post-Diem period. One by one, the "dissident" generals were introduced in the small room where members of the Military Council were seated in a "U" formation with General Thieu presiding.

General Thi was the first to be introduced. He snapped an impeccable military salute and stood at attention: "Distinguished members of the Military Council," he said, "I have nothing to say for my defense. I feel that I had acted appropriately under the circumstances and I trust your judgment." After a few questions by the Military Council, he again saluted and was escorted out of the room. Although I condemned his overt rebellion against the central government, I was impressed by his dignified attitude and his coolness under adversity. I was annoyed and felt somewhat uneasy when the other generals tried to justify their rebellious acts and asked for the Military Council's clemency. After deliberations, the Military Council approved General Thieu's recommendation to discharge the dissident generals from military service for disciplinary reasons.

After the trial, everyone was happy. We shook hands and hurried back to our units to continue the war, hoping that political stability was at long last established with the installation of the Thieu-Ky government. On the flight back to my division, I couldn't help comparing Vietnamese revolutions and coups d'état with the revolutions in other third world countries where the losers often had to face firing squads. The loser faced no such harsh punishments in Viet Nam, and I think that this may have been the cause of numerous coups, semi-coups, and counter-coups following the overthrow of President Diem.

This also was Frances FitzGerald's opinion. "Preceded by a few titillating moments of suspense," wrote FitzGerald,

> their [the generals] coups were habitually followed by the double ceremonies of weeping and breast-beating on the part of the losers, declaration of unity and harmony on the part of the winners. While the sects with their cosmic concerns murdered each other's members, the generals did little damage within their own ranks. Apart from the case of the unfortunate Colonel Thao, fingered by General Thieu and mysteriously disposed of, there were no killings and not a single suicide among the coups' leaders. The deposed generals were either named ambassadors-at-large or exiled to play endless games of tennis with the American military attaches in Washington and Bangkok.[25]

Toward the end of May 1966, Col. Dang Dinh Thuy, my deputy, was appointed commander of the Army Regional Van Kiep Training Center in Chau Doc Province. I was invited to the ceremony of transfer of command, which was presided over by Gen. Dang Van Quang. As I was heading toward my helicopter after the ceremony, I noticed the Vietnamese Special Forces were undergoing parachute training on the rice fields north of the training center. I had always wanted to be trained as a parachutist but had no opportunity to do so. Since I was not busy that morning, I asked the Special Forces jumpmaster to let me jump. After I received verbal approval from General Quang, I practiced some falling techniques and then boarded the Special Forces' H-21 helicopter to make my first parachute jump. It went very smoothly. I landed softly in the middle of a flooded rice paddy and released my parachute.

I was so elated by this first jump that I asked Master-Sergeant Hoang, the jumpmaster, to let me make another jump. That turned out to be a bad decision, for it almost cost my life. I twisted my ankle as I landed on a small dike with one foot on the dike and the other foot on the rice field. While I was lying on the dike, unable to move, the helicopter pilot, thinking I was injured, set his helicopter down to pick me up. When the helicopter was about one hundred meters from the ground, it blew up my parachute that I forgot to release. In a split second, the parachute lifted me in the air and sent me flying across the flooded rice paddies. I felt my chest hitting the dikes of the rice fields like a motor boat on a rough sea; had it not been for my reserve parachute which served as a cushion, I would have had perished under the shocks.

A few trainees in the camp ran to my rescue and were able to jump into my parachute to stop my crazy cruise across the dropping zone. When I was able to stand up and release my parachute with the help of the trainees, I realized that my field jacket had disappeared. Later, Sergeant Hoang told me I was very fortunate my parachute was not sucked into the helicoper's rotors. It would have meant my certain death.

I've always believed that an army officer not only should be a qualified parachutist, but should be an expert in martial arts. Since I was a child, I had learned Vietnamese martial arts for self-defense. When I was assigned to I Corps in Danang in 1960, I attended a judo class organized for staff officers where I obtained the brown belt. At the time I assumed the command of the 9th Infantry Division, many Korean officers were assigned to ARVN units to teach Korean taekwondo, a martial art which literally means the "art of using feet." There were two Korean instructors at the 9th Division, all fourth degree black belt. One of them, Lieutenant Kim young Ho, was a very skillful taekwondo practitioner. I was very impressed by his demonstrations, which consisted of executing complicated flying kicks and breaking wood and bricks with his bare hands. I encouraged my officers to learn taekwondo and to set an example,

I also practiced three or four times a week with Lieutenant Kim. The Korean instructors also organized a taekwondo class for the sons of the division staff officers, and my oldest son, Tuan, who was nine years old, was one of its early students.

Around June 1966, the district of Sa Dec was elevated to province status. General Ky came to Sa Dec to preside over the ceremony of confirmation of the new province chief. Sa Dec had been a province under the French colonial administration. It was reduced to district status and annexed to the province of Vinh Long under President Diem. General Ky's decision to make Sa Dec a province again was very popular among the Sa Dec residents. I guessed that the decision was politically motivated as Ky tried to muster support for his bid at the presidential election to be held the following year.

The popular celebration took place with much fanfare and pomp, complete with dragon dances and firecrackers. General Ky arrived with most of his cabinet and a throng of Vietnamese and foreign reporters. To help celebrate this joyous event, Col. Nguyen Thanh Chuan, commander of IV Corps Special Forces, suggested I make one more jump to qualify for the Special Forces parachutist wing. Col. Tran Ba Di, my new deputy division commander, volunteered to jump with me. Sean Flynn, the son of the American movie actor and a reporter for the French *Paris Match* magazine, asked my permission to jump with me. Sean Flynn[26] was in Sa Dec to cover the installation ceremony of the new province chief. He had not jumped before but was very eager to try. I agreed to let him jump. I also agreed to let his girlfriend, a French journalist, on board our helicopter to watch him bail out.

Sergeant Hoang dropped us near a division ammunition depot located on the southern outskirts of the city, on the road to the province of Long Xuyen. As soon as I bailed out, I noticed that I was drifting dangerously toward the mine field around the depot. I tried to steer away from it, but because the standard T-10 parachute was hard to direct and because I was a novice, I ended up landing in the middle of the mine field. Fortunately, the mine field was flooded by monsoon rains. As a result, I was able to stand up on landing to avoid a possible explosion triggered by a normal rolling technique. I was also fortunate to land on an unmined spot, otherwise my legs would have been blown up by the mines. Colonel Di and Sean Flynn were more fortunate: they landed a few hundreds meters from the mine field.

Earlier, as I had accompanied General Ky to the helipad after the ceremony, he asked me how long I had been division commander. I told him I had been in Sa Dec for over one year. "Thi," said Ky, "maybe you should take a vacation." I was elated because after a year of constant stress, I needed some relaxation away from the battlefields.

Previously, when I was not busy with military operations, I occasionally took my wife and children to spend half a day on the peaceful island of Phu Quoc in the Gulf of Siam, approximately twenty-five miles off the coast of Kien Giang Province, to which it belonged. Phu Quoc Island was famous its *nuoc mam* (fish sauce), considered the best of the entire country. Although its beaches were muddy like all the beaches in the Mekong Delta (in contrast to beaches in the North and Central Viet Nam which had natural sand) and thus were not favored by vacationers, the tranquil and relaxed atmosphere of the island had been a welcome break for me.[27]

However relaxing these trips might have been, the echoes of war still resonated around me. Because I needed to be in constant contact with the division TOC, the province chiefs and field commanders, a team of radio operators and my aide with the tactical map of my area of responsibility always accompanied me on these trips. Consequently, I considered taking my family to Dalat and Vung Tau to enjoy the mountains and the beaches, but I had not been able to find time to do so. Now that the tactical situation in my area of responsibility had much improved, this could be the opportunity to take some time off.

I could not believe my ears when Ky casually added: "Thi, why don't you take your wife to Hong Kong and Japan for a two-week vacation?"

Toward the end of June 1966, my wife and I left for Hong Kong, the first leg of our vacation trip. We were met at the Hong Kong Airport by an employee of the Vietnamese Consulate who drove us to the Mandarin Hotel, an elegant old British-style hotel located at the center of the business district. To my surprise, we were awakened the next day by the noise of helicopters flying at low altitude. I rushed to my window and saw helicopters landing members of the Hong Kong police force on the roof of a nearby building. Later, I was informed by the hotel personnel that the police had to use this technique to dislodge the Communist Red Guards who occupied the building. It was the time of the Cultural Revolution in China and the Communist activists in Hong Kong, brandishing Mao Tse tung's red bibles, paraded en mass to support the new revolution. I didn't expect to witness in Hong Kong the combat environment and the heliborne operations I wanted to get away from.

We were met at the Tokyo airport by an employee of the embassy who took us to a hotel on Ginza Street. I truly enjoyed my new VIP status. It was obvious that the Consulate in Hong Kong and the Embassy in Tokyo were not clear with regard to my mission, but I guessed that, to be on the safe side, they were willing to go the extra mile to accommodate me at a time when the government back home was run by the military. Further, since the overthrow of the Diem regime, our embassies must have been hard put to keep track of all the coups and counter-coups and it would be wise to treat army generals with consideration. Who knows? An obscure general today could be somebody important tomorrow.

Fortunately, the situation remained calm until I rejoined the 9th Division. In October 1966, I turned my attention to Vinh Binh Province where the central government had intensified its pacification program. To pacify the Viet Cong-controlled area in the southern part of the province, it had become necessary to destroy the Viet Cong regular units in the area. Since its defeat in the Tan Ngai Village in Cau Ke District the previous year, the VC Vinh Binh Provincial Battalion had withdrawn to the coastal area of Long Toan to be resupplied in men and matériel. The latest intelligence reports indicated that this battalion had received new weapons and was operational again. Its main mission was to disrupt the pacification program in Vinh Binh.

Two months earlier, the 9th Division's 14th Regiment, in a joint operation with elements of the 21st Division, discovered an important weapons and ammunition cache in the Vinh Binh coastal area. That day, our air reconnaissance detected enemy ships unloading ammunition in a mangrove area northeast of Long Toan. I requested helicopters from IV Corps to transport one battalion of the 14th Regiment to search the area, but since the 21st Division was operating in the Ba Xuyen Province, just across from the Bassac River that day, General Quang decided instead to heliborne one battalion of the 21st Division.

It was no secret that Gen. Nguyen Van Minh, the 21st Division commander, was a protégé of Quang and the Long Toan search operation was an occasion for Quang to help Minh achieve an easy victory. Thus, I called General Quang to protest his decision to introduce outside forces into my area of responsibility without my consent. At the time there was a fierce competition between division commanders; our respective tactical areas were considered inviolable and the incursion of outside units into our jealously guarded fiefdoms was unthinkable. (This static mentality fortunately would change during the North Vietnamese 1972 and 1975 offensives when it was necessary to deploy units from different corps and divisions into areas under attack.)

Realizing he had made a mistake by not consulting with me beforehand, General Quang agreed to lift one battalion of the 14th Regiment to search the area in conjunction with elements of the 21st Division. After the discovery of the important cache described earlier, it was decided to send a joint team from the 21st and the 9th Divisions to Saigon to make a presentation to the press.

To destroy the newly reconstituted VC provincial battalion, I decided to lure it into the open. In order to do that, I instructed the Vinh Binh province chief to construct an outpost on the VC main supply line between the Cau Ngang District and the Long Toan VC secret base. This outpost was to be occupied by one Vinh Binh RF company. I ordered one battalion of the 14th Regiment to provide protection during the construction. I was certain that the VC Vinh Binh Provincial Battalion would have to remove the outpost from its crucial supply route at all costs if it were to survive. I instructed my staff to prepare plans to trap and destroy the enemy in the open in case it launched the attack on the outpost. Since the Cau Ngang-Long Toan area consisted of open rice fields with occasional sand dunes running parallel to the coastline, an ideal terrain for the use of armor, I decided to use the entire Armored Cavalry Regiment as the striking force.

As expected, two days after the construction of the outpost had been completed and the 1st Battalion of the 14th Regiment (1/14) which had been providing protection, had left, the enemy struck. Around midnight, my TOC reported that the Vinh Binh RF company manning the outpost was under strong attack. I called the province chief and told him to hold at all cost; then I instructed my staff to strike the next day.

Around 8:00 AM, the 43rd Ranger was heliborne from Vinh Long Airport to Long Toan to block the enemy withdrawal to its secret base to the southeast. One battalion from the 16th Regiment was brought in an area northeast of the outpost while the 1/14 was to link up with the outpost under attack. The 2nd Cavalry Regiment rushed to an area southwest of Cau Ngang to attack along the sand dunes in a northeastern direction. The VC battalion was effectively trapped in the open and was decimated. They left more than one hundred dead and we captured many weapons. A few prisoners were also captured. Friendly casualties were light. The next day, I received a message from General Westmoreland congratulating me for the "tactical ingeniosity" displayed in the Long Toan operation.

Vietnamese field commanders not only had to wage the war against Communist insurgency and implement the pacification program in their areas of responsibility, but they were also affected by political infighting within the Army. To make matters worse, they were sometimes subject to the arrogance of their American advisors. In his voluminous *A Soldier Reports* General Westmoreland told how he "rebuked" the Minister of Defense for not complying with his instructions regarding the promotion of Vietnamese officers. Westmoreland wrote: "Cajolery and encouragement were sometimes insufficient. When I discovered, for example, that the ARVN had abandoned a program I had espoused of drawing officer candidates from men of demonstrated ability in the ranks rather than soliciting only the educated elite from the cities, I rebuked the Minister of Defense, General Nguyen Van Vy."[28]

Cultural differences caused misunderstanding and friction, but I believe Americans' reluctance to learn other countries' culture and language is the reflection of their arrogance. I would say that the situation resulted from a basic American ethnocentric attitude regarding other countries, which consisted of judging other people by using American customs and standards. Americans in Viet Nam seemed to ignore the simple truth that effective inter-cultural communication requires that communicators make a sincere and honest effort to understand and recognize cultural differences and eliminate nationalistic ethnocentric attitudes. Incidents relative to cultural variances abounded in Viet Nam and these, more often than not, resulted in frustration and anger and may have played into the hands of Communist propaganda.

During an early stage of U.S. involvement in Viet Nam, for example, a U.S. senior advisor in a light infantry division near the DMZ, held a routine inspection of the weapons of a division's unit and noticed a dirty rifle. He wiped its grease on the division commander's hand to demonstrate his point. This might not be considered unusual or impolite as far as the U.S. advisor was concerned, but this gesture constituted a supreme insult for the Vietnamese. The Vietnamese division commander slapped his American advisor and was later relieved of his command.

I experienced the same frustration at the 9th Division. In 1967, the problem of "ghost effectives" (unit commanders reporting imaginary soldiers to pocket their salaries) was so serious that, under American instigation, the ARVN Inspector General was instructed to inspect the effective forces of different units selected at random. One day, it was decided that the 15th Regiment of my division was to be inspected at Long Xuyen Province. Lt. Gen. Nguyen Van La, the Inspector General, was accompanied by a U.S. brigadier general acting as a liaison officer with the Vietnamese Joint General Staff.

The purpose of the inspection was to determine whether the number of troops inspected corresponded to the regiment's reported effective. The U.S. general, however, displaying supreme arrogance, made comments about the physical presentation of the regiment, which, by the way, had returned from an operation the day before. He pulled soldiers' hair which, he commented, was too long or the soldiers' uniforms, which, he said, missed a couple of buttons. He acted like a commander inspecting his troops in a parade, and as though General La and I were his subordinates or we did not exist at all. I took General La aside and suggested that the American general be advised that he had overstepped the boundary of his authority and decency, and that he should stop his uncalled-for behavior at once. A few months after that incident, Nguyen Cao Ky told me during a meeting at IV Corps Headquarters at Can Tho, that General Westmoreland had informed him that I had become "anti-American."

It was ironic that while I had won many battles with my division and had tried, if not to eradicate, at least to minimize the corruption within the 41st Tactical Area, I was under political pressure from all sides. I had been considered anti-Thieu and anti-Ky by these two generals. Now, I was labeled anti-American by no less a personality than the Commander of MAC-V. I decided to keep my calm and do my job without paying attention to rumors and political infighting. In retrospect, I am glad I survived all these political attacks without losing my honor as an army officer and my hope for a better future for the army and for the country.

Some American authors have described American arrogance in the relations of the United States with its client state, South Viet Nam. They called this attitute "imperialism." Imperialism, in this context, doesn't mean expansionism or conquest of new territories as the term implies. It is perceived instead as synonymous with pre-World War II concept of "colonialism," which reflects mainly an attitude of arrogance and condescension inherent in any "master-subject" relationship. Henry Kissinger reported, for example, in the *White House Years* that when President Nixon learned that President Thieu refused to sign the first version of the 1973 Paris Agreements, he told Kissinger he would take some harsh actions against Thieu: "Brutality is nothing," said President Nixon. "You have never seen it if this son-of-a-bitch does not go along, believe me."[29]

This said, I must acknowledge, however, that while there may be friction and misunderstanding at the higher echelons, the genuine camaraderie and esprit de corps between ARVN unit commanders and their "counterparts" in the field were the rule rather than

the exception. The majority of U.S. advisors were dedicated officers who tried to bridge the gap of cultural differences and to help.
The presence of the advisory team in a combat unit considerably
contributed to the morale of the troops because they knew that, in
case of heavy engagements, they coud rely on U.S. air support and
medevac. And many victories couldn't have been achieved without
the dedicated officers and men of the advisory teams. Unfortunately,
by the time the advisor began to learn how to carry out his mission,
his year was up and it was time to go home.

I believe that special credit should be given to province and
districts advisors who worked tirelessly to improve people's lives in
an effort to "win the hearts and minds" of the peasantry. Col. Edward Metzner, who spent seven years as a principal advisor to districts and province chiefs, expressed the feelings of these advisors
in these moving terms:

> In spite of the sad outcome and the emotional scars left by
> our futile, costly effort, I still firmly believe that our Viet-
> nam cause was an honorable one and that most of those
> who gave of themselves in Southeast Asia and were touched
> by the people there feel the same way. If the stilled voices in
> the hamlets could speak, I believe they would testify loudly
> that they keenly appreciated the effort. Although we cannot
> take pride in the part our precipitous abandonment played
> in the final outcome, there is much to respect in the way
> America's young sons responded earlier when sent to pre-
> vent that very outcome.[30]

During the summer of 1965, political developments at home and in
the United States were far from encouraging. As mentioned earlier,
after Generals Thieu and Ky came to power in June that year, the
political situation in the country became precarious. The dissident
Buddhist movement put the government on the verge of collapse.
Soon after the central authority in I Corps had been reestablished,
General Thieu and Ky enlisted supporters in the Army in an effort
to enlarge their political base. The Thieu-Ky rivalry would deeply
divide the Army and adversely affect its morale.

To add to our problems, the antiwar movement in the United States intensified and exerted mounting pressure for a U.S. disengagement from Viet Nam. The antiwar and pro-Viet Cong movement had also sprung up in Europe, where Bertrand Russell, the famous British mathematician, and Jean-Paul Sartre, the founder of the French existentialist movement, both Nobel Prize laureates, had set up a "tribunal" to try the "war crimes" in Viet Nam. I was particularly dismayed and angry at Jane Fonda's trip to Hanoi where she was photographed with NVA anti-aircraft gunmen who had shot down U.S. planes in North Viet Nam. American servicemen in Viet Nam also were very angry; they believed she was a traitor to her own country.

On the other hand, I had the privilege of meeting many Hollywood celebrities who came to Viet Nam to show their support for U.S. war efforts. During their Viet Nam tour, these "hawk" actors visited not only American troops but various U.S. Advisory teams attached to Vietnamese units. Henry Fonda visited Sa Dec one day in 1966 and Col. Bob Bringham, the division senior advisor, invited me to have dinner with him. When I accompanied Henry Fonda to his hut where he was to spend the night, we discussed the progress of the war and the antiwar movement in the United States. At that point, I asked Mr. Fonda his opinion with regard to his daughter's trip to Hanoi. He said he was very angry at her. He also expressed hostility toward French actor Roger Vadim, her daughter's husband at the time. I was under the impression that Henry Fonda thought that Vadim had a bad influence on his daughter.

A month after Henry Fonda's visit, I unexpectedly ran into John Wayne at Can Tho Airport. John Wayne went to Viet Nam to direct his film *The Green Berets*. After Colonel Bringham introduced us, we shook hands and I told Mr. Wayne I was a great admirer of his. I also told him how much I appreciated his support for the war efforts in Viet Nam.

A few months after Henry Fonda's visit, I met Robert Mitchum in Sa Dec. Mitchum was surprised when I told him I was honored to meet a great colleague and counterpart. He had a good laugh after I explained that I admired him in his role as the 9th Infantry Division commander in Normandy in *The Longest Day*. Robert Mitchum was interested when I informed him that there were three "9th Divisions" in Viet Nam: the ARVN's 9th Division that I commanded, the U.S. 9th Division, which was operating in the My Tho area, and the VC 9th Division operating in III Corps area, near the Cambodian border.

James Gardner also visited, but my most memorable experience with Hollywood stars was, without any doubt, my meeting with Jennifer Jones. After a dinner at the U.S. Advisory team compound, I invited Ms. Jones and Colonel Bringham to my residence to have a *digestif*. She was very relaxed and gracious. Holding my youngest son Dung on her lap, she inquired about our family and about Vietnamese customs and traditions. I recall that, right after our marriage, my wife, who was a fan of Rock Hudson, and I went to a theater in Saigon to see the film *The Sun Also Rises*. Ms. Jones was so exquisite in her role as a nurse in the film. It had never entered in our mind that one day, we would have the honor of receiving her in our home.

Toward the end of 1966, General Quang was relieved of his command by General Ky for corruption. At that time, General Ky and General Thieu were actively seeking the support of field commanders for the upcoming presidential election; since Quang was a supporter of Thieu, he was targeted by Ky. Thieu made Quang his special assistant for security. Quang was replaced by Gen. Nguyen Van Manh, a protégé of Gen. Nguyen Huu Co, the minister of defense. Manh, Co, and President Thieu had been classmates at the Officers Course at Hue. Before he enrolled at the Officers Course, Manh had participated in a revolutionary movement and had been jailed by the French.

Manh was very intelligent. He had a good sense of humor and liked to tell jokes. He had served most of his career as a staff officer at the Joint General Staff and had yet to demonstrate his skill as a field commander. In fact, he had not achieved any significant victories as the commander of the 23rd Division at Ban Me Thuot in the Hauts Plateaux, but as everywhere else, good connections helped. Soon, I received damaging information about his immediate entourage. Just two months after he assumed the command of IV Corps, my Military Security Office reported that one of General Manh's brother-in-laws had gone to the province of Chau Doc, near the Cambodian border, where he was suspected of setting up a contraband operation. However, the Chau Doc province chief, who happened to be a classmate of the new Corps Commander at the Officers Course in Hue, fearing for his own job, decided to ignore this suspicious activity. I instructed the division's Military Police to watch General Manh's brother-in-law and to arrest him immediately if he was caught in his contraband activities.

I might have over-reacted because I hadn't caught the man in the act; my instructions somehow got to General Manh and he decided that I had to go. One day, General Thang dropped in to see me in Sa Dec. He informed me that Manh had accused me of corruption during a meeting of the Military Council in Saigon. He had also submitted to the Council a written report from the Vinh Binh province chief, also a classmate of Manh in Hue, to the effect that I had instructed him to give to the division 50,000 piasters (approximately one hundred U.S. dollars) from the fund of the province's "Committee of Support for Battlefield" to celebrate the victory of the Long Toan operation. (At that time, each province was authorized to raise a fund for the support of military units on the occasion of Tet or successful military operations and that this fund usually amounted to many millions of piasters.) Although 50,000 piasters was a nominal amount, General Thieu, Chairman of the Military Council, jumped on this to get rid of me, whom he suspected of being a Ky supporter. Fortunately, I had instructed Col. Tran Ba Di, my deputy, to keep all receipts from the units that were recipients of the fund. I gave General Thang copies of the receipts to submit to the Military Council. Later, Thang informed me that Thieu was livid when he read the documents Thang presented to the Military Council. Although Thieu could not fire me, he decided that Manh had done nothing wrong either.[31]

In January 1967, I had the pleasure of welcoming to my division Lt.Gen. Chae mung Shin, the commander in chief of Korean Forces in Viet Nam and my former classmate at Fort Leavenworth. South Korea contributed the second most troops to the Viet Nam War after the United States. Korean troops under General Chae consisted of two infantry divisions (the Black Horse Division and the Tiger Division) and one Marine Brigade. The two infantry divisions operated in the coastal area north of Nha Trang, in Military Region II. The Marine Brigade was stationed in Hoi An, south of Danang, in Military Region I. The Korean troops were known for their motivation and their expertise in close combat. Although their main mission was to support the pacification program in the coastal areas of Central Viet Nam, they were involved in tough combat situations toward the end of the war.

General Chae came to pay me a courtesy visit and also to preside over my testing for the first degree blackbelt in taekwondo. After I executed a few patterns, sparred with other candidates and broke a few bricks and wood panels, General Shin awarded me the 1st degree blackbelt. I was surprised when he asked me to stand still after he had presented me the blackbelt that bore my name in both Vietnamese and Korean. An aide handed a paper to General Chae, who proceeded to read in a solemn voice a Korean Presidential Citation awarding me the Order of Chung Mu, the highest Korean decoration. The citation praised my performance in the fight against Communist aggression and my cooperation with the Korean Forces in Viet Nam in our struggle for the common cause. Then he put around my neck the yellow cravate of the much coveted Order of Chung Mu and we embraced heartily. Afterward, General Chae confided to me that he knew I would do well after he heard my remarks at Fort Leavenworth directed at the French liaison officer. General Chae, long after Viet Nam, remained one of my best and respected friends.

In January 1967, I was instructed to secure the canal of Mang Thit, which links the Bassac and Mekong Rivers, in order to facilitate the rice traffic to Saigon. The opening of the important Mang Thit canal was to be a showcase of the ambitious 1967 pacification program in the Mekong Delta. An important battle took place around Mang Thit in March, but since this battle—which was the subject of a controversial book by an American author—will be used to illustrate the role of the U.S. media in the Viet Nam War, it will be the subject of the next chapter.

The military situation remained relatively quiet in my tactical area as we entered the new year of 1967; however, the increasing rivalry between Thieu and Ky was having a disastrous effect on Army morale. After they were appointed chairmen of the "National Leadership Committee" and the "Central Executive Committee" respectively by the Military Council following the resignation of Dr. Pham Huy Quat's government, Thieu and Ky lost no time trying to enlarge their political bases, primarily among the military hierarchy. Division and corps commanders were especially courted by both.

Furthermore, the Vietnamese media seemed also to enjoy spreading false rumors about power plays among general officers. For example, when General Thieu returned to Saigon after a visit to my division in late 1966, a reporter asked him if there was any truth to the rumor that I had planned to kidnap him during his visit. This question was ridiculous, but intentional or not, it intensified discord and suspicion within the military leadership, which in turn adversely affected the morale and effectiveness of the Army.

A few months after this incident, Gen. Nguyen Duc Thang, minister of Rural Reconstruction and a strong supporter of Ky, came to see me during one of his routine inspections of the pacification program in the Mekong Delta. To my surprise, he informed me that, had it not been for his personal intervention in my behalf, Ky would have already fired me because he suspected me of staging a coup d'etat to overthrow him. This was beyond my comprehension because at that time I was an unknown brigadier general without political ambition and without any political base or following. I inferred from this information that petty infighting within the higher echelons of the Army must have been viciously ruthless.

At the beginning of 1967, General Ky, in his position as prime minister, had control of the government. Further, he had the support of the Americans and seemed to have the upper hand in the bid for the presidency. He started to get rid of Thieu's supporters in preparation for the coming elections. Gen. Nguyen Huu Co, minister of defense and a supporter of Thieu, was ordered by General Ky to remain exiled in Hong Kong after an official visit to Taiwan where President Chiang Kai-shek awarded him one of the highest decorations of the Republic of China. Gen. Tran Thien Khiem, chairman of JGS and Gen. Do Cao Tri, one of ARVN's best field commanders, were appointed ambassadors to Washington and Seoul respectively.

Setting aside the political infighting, I decided to concentrate on my job as commander of a division in combat. In early October 1967, I scored another victory, this time at the heart of the old Viet Minh secret base of the famed Plain of Reeds in Kien Phong Province. Every year, in the rainy season, the Mekong River overflowed its banks, flooded the rice fields and interrupted ground traffic in the riverine provinces. In 1967, Kien Phong was hit the hardest; unusually heavy rains flooded the entire province. Hundreds of thousands of inhabitants whose houses were submerged by water had to be evacuated to the city of Kien Phong. As the VC had nowhere to go, they sought refuge on the top of the trees in the Plain of Reeds. I saw this as a unique opportunity to wipe out the VC infrastructure in the province.

To this end, I requested the support of the U.S. Special Forces, which provided a few inflatable air boats equipped with one machine gun in front and mounted with a propeller in the back. These watercraft could negotiate shallow waters. These boats were directed at the VC hiding places by helicopters and observation planes to capture the enemy or to shoot if they encountered resistance. Occasionally, the helicopters were shot at by the Viet Cong perched on the trees. The helicopter gunships then would swing into action and the air boats would come to pick up the enemy dead or wounded or to capture prisoners. In one month, we killed over 200 VC and captured many prisoners. We suffered no casualties. I considered this operation one of the most successful campaigns during my command of the 9th Division. Misfortune for some may mean opportunity for others. The French have a saying: "*A quelque chose, malheur est bon.*" (For certain things, misfortune is good). Although, floods had always caused hardship to the civilian population, they, however, could be exploited to inflict devastating damage to the Communist military and political infrastructure.

In the meantime, the infighting between Generals Thieu and Ky and their jockeying for power continued in earnest. Political maneuverings reached a climax at a meeting of the Military Council held in May 1967 to appoint a military candidate for the upcoming September presidential election. As a general and division commander, I was invited to attend the meeting. I knew that Ky was the favorite: during his two years as prime minister of South Viet Nam he had dispensed favors to friends and appointed his protégés to strategic positions within the Army and the government. Ky cultivated a special relationship with Gen. Cao Van Vien, chairman of JGS, and had the support of Gen. William Westmoreland, commander of U.S. Forces in Viet Nam. Other members of the Council and I thought that Ky would be a logical choice and that our meeting was convened merely to confirm his candidacy. But we were wrong for not considering Thieu's shrewdness and Machiavellian political maneuverings. He knew that the majority of the Council favored Ky; he also knew that the Council members wanted to maintain a semblance of unity in the Army. So Thieu threatened to run as an independent candidate if the Council chose Ky to represent the Armed Forces in the next election.

After heated discussions, the generals called for unity and ultimately decided that both Generals Thieu and Ky would run on the same ballot for President and Vice-President respectively. As a concession to Ky, Thieu would concede the important policy-making role to Ky. Thieu wept openly, thanked each member of the Council. Everyone was happy that a split in the Armed Forces had been avoided. We all shook hands and rushed back to our units to continue the war, hoping again that we would finally have a strong government capable of rallying the Army and the people, and with the help of the Americans, of defeating the Communist insurgency.

Unfortunately, this was not to be. We prevented a division within the Armed Forces by imposing a *mariage de raison* that didn't work. The generals still were divided into opposite factions. The few, like myself, who did not support either were regarded with suspicion by both sides. Although Ky lost most of his political power under Thieu, he retained the loyalty of the Air Force. On the other hand, the rift between Thieu and Ky revived the old spirit of regionalism and kindled the traditional antagonism between North and South. Since Ky was from North Viet Nam, he had the support of the majority of Northerners in the Army and in the government; while Thieu, who was born in Phan Rang, a city located at the border between Central and South Viet Nam, and who married a Southerner (Mme Thieu was from My Tho), had the support of Southerners and Centrists.

As expected, Thieu and Ky easily won the presidential election in September 1967. As a concession to Ky, Thieu appointed one of Ky's supporters, Mr. Nguyen Van Loc, a Southern lawyer, as the first Prime Minister of the Second Republic. But Loc was soon replaced by Gen. Tran Thien Khiem, a good friend and supporter of Thieu. General Khiem was a survivor, an opportunist, and clever politician. During the 1960 coup d'etat, as commander of MRIV in the Mekong Delta, he rushed his troops to Saigon to rescue President Diem. In 1963, he actively participated in the coup which overthrew the Diem regime. When Khanh came to power in 1964, Khiem was promoted to full general and became the chairman of JGS. Ky, who intensely disliked Khiem, sent the latter off to Washington, D.C., as ambassador after Khanh relinquished power to the young generals in 1965. Now that Ky had lost power, Khiem returned and was to play an important role in the Second Republic until its demise in 1975. Gen. Do Cao Tri also was recalled from Seoul to take over the all-important III Corps whose units were responsible for the security of the Capital.

To borrow from General Taylor, "the house was cleaned and turned over" one more time. Supporters of General Ky were replaced by Thieu's friends and associates. New province chiefs and division and corps commanders were appointed. Previously uncommitted officers had to switch sides and pledge allegiance to the new leadership if they wanted to retain their posts. For those, like myself, who remained neutral, we knew we were on borrowed time.

9

THE BATTLE OF MANG THIT

IT IS NO SECRET THAT the U.S. media was hostile to the Viet Nam War. The war was presented from unfavorable angles, with the media sensationalizing the news and distorting the truth if necessary, to achieve its antiwar objectives. I believe that the media played a major role in the final downfall of South Viet Nam. A Vietnamese journalist who was sympathetic to the Communist cause during the war and who escaped to Paris after the fall of Saigon said: "A physician who makes an error kills his patient; a general who makes an error kills one division; a journalist who makes an error kills an entire country." And this was exactly what happened in Viet Nam. Gen. Vo Nguyen Giap stated in a French television broadcast that his most important guerrilla during the Viet Nam War was the American press. This was a tragic compliment.

As a division commander, I had an interesting experience with a self-proclaimed Viet Nam expert. Harvey Meyerson, a professor at the University of Hawaii, decided one day to go to Viet Nam and write a book about the war as it was a fashionable thing to do in those days. However, in lieu of traveling all across the country as other correspondents did, he chose to stay in one province to observe the progress of the pacification program and the war in that province. He tried, from these observations, to reach conclusions about the Viet Nam War as a whole. The province he chose happened to be Vinh Long, located between the Mekong and Bassac Rivers. Vinh Long was one of the seven provinces in my tactical area. Meyerson came to Vinh Long a few times and in 1970 published a book entitled *Vinh Long*[32] which described the pacification progress in the province.

In 1967, President Johnson, under pressure to win the war after having committed American troops, decided to intensify the pacification program. He sent Robert Komer, his White House assistant for pacification, to Saigon with the rank of ambassador. Komer was to work under General Westmoreland but would have full authority to coordinate the pacification efforts in the country. A key point in the reorganization was the creation of a new agency called CORDS (Civil Operations and Revolutionary Development Support). Under the new concept, some of South Viet Nam's provinces would have military senior advisors, with civilian deputies, while some other provinces would have civilian senior advisors, with military deputies.

One of the goals, and the showcase, of the 1967 pacification program would be the reopening of the thirty-mile-long Mang Thit-Nicolai canal for rice traffic. This canal had been designed at the turn of the century by a French engineer named Nicolai. The Mang Thit canal runs parallel with, and about ten kilometers east of, RN4 in Vinh Long Province. It directly connects the Bassac and Mekong Rivers. This canal traversed many VC- controlled areas and was closed for traffic during the 1963 and 1964 political upheavals. Since then, the rice traffic had to make a long detour to Long Xuyen Province, near the Cambodia border, where it accessed the Mekong River and reversed its course to finally unload at a ferry site across the Mekong River from the city of Vinh Long. From there, rice was transported by trucks to Saigon and Cho Lon. It was estimated that the reopening of the Mang Thit canal would save two and a half days travel time for Saigon-bound rice traffic; this would constitute a tremendous boost to the local economy.

Among the sixteen provinces of the Mekong Delta, Vinh Long, with a total area of 1,600 square kilometers, ranked twelfth in size. However, with a total population of about 500,000 and located at the very heart of the Delta, at midway between the Lower Delta and Saigon and between the South China Sea and Cambodia, Vinh Long took on a strategic importance, both militarily and economically.

I must admit that since I assumed the command of the 9th Division, I had not paid adequate attention to the pacification program

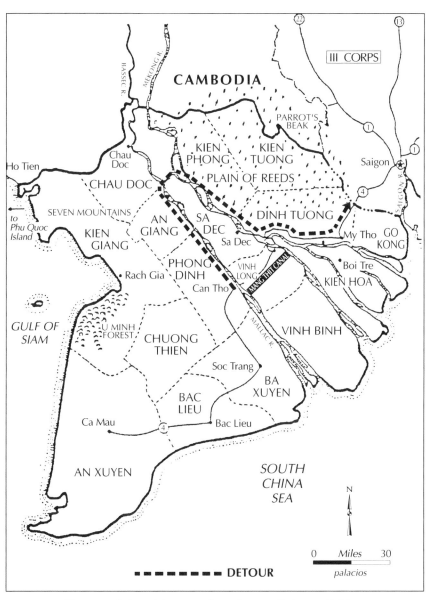

Detour of rice shipment from Lower Delta to Saigon

in my tactical area. I considered that the main mission of a division commander was to destroy the VC local and regular units and the implementation of the pacification program was mainly the responsibility of the province chiefs. In my opinion, this division of responsibility made sense because different intelligence collection agencies, Rural Reconstruction cadres and the Provincial Reconnaissance Units (PRU) were coordinated at province and district levels. The latter units were paid by the Americans and were created under the controversial Phoenix Program to identify and eliminate the VC political and administrative infrastructure in the province. The use of these units was at the discretion of the province chiefs and their senior advisors, who reported directly to Corps and Military Regions.

In November 1966, Gen. Nguyen Duc Thang, minister of rural reconstruction, informed me that the reopening of the Mang Thit waterway would be one of the top government projects for 1967 and that it would be of the utmost importance that I take every measure to bring that project to fruition. On December 16, 1966, a meeting was convened in Vinh Long to discuss the implementation of the Mang Thit project. Present at the meeting were General Thang and his advisor, Brig. Gen. William Knowlton, Gen. Nguyen Van Manh, IV Corps commander and his advisor, Brig. Gen. William Desobry, myself, and the division senior advisor, Col. Bob Bringham, and Lt. Col. Huynh Ngoc Diep, the province chief, accompanied by his pacification staff and the U.S. provincial advisory team.

It was agreed during the meeting that the Mang Thit project would be carried out in three stages: First, the 9th Division would mount a regiment-sized operation to destroy VC regular units in the area; then, the division would leave one battalion to protect the construction of eleven outposts to be occupied by provincial RF and PF units; in the third stage, Rural Development teams would implement the pacification program, including the construction of self-help projects in the villages and the election of local officials. It was also decided that the canal would be opened for commercial traffic by the middle of 1967.

To destroy the VC units and administrative infrastructure along the canal, I ordered the 16th Regiment to conduct a search and destroy operation along the waterway and then to leave one battalion to secure the construction of the outposts. I instructed the regiment commander to constantly change the defense position to avoid a coordinated attack by the VC.

On March 23, 1967, the first battalion of the 16th Regiment (1/16), which had been operating on the canal for six weeks, moved to a location one kilometer south of Cau Moi Bridge, the headquarters of the 16th Regiment. Capt. Ly Duc, the battalion commander, a veteran of the Indochina War, decided to occupy a defensive position of about 700 meters square. The exterior perimeter of defense espoused on both sides the contours of small ravines which crisscrossed the thick jungles on both sides of the Mang Thit canal. The back of the battalion was protected by the Mang Thit canal itself. Due to the large size of the defense position, Captain Duc deployed all his companies on the perimeter of defense and used the headquarters company as the battalion reserve. During the next two days, Captain Duc improved his defense positions by clearing the fields of fire up to fifty meters. He also installed two double barbed wire fences and planted trip flares and claymore mines in front of the perimeter of defense. Squad size ambush teams were also sent forward to detect any enemy movement toward the battalion. As it was a full moon, Captain Duc felt confident that he would have a few peaceful days because the VC rarely attacked in bright moonlight.

By midnight, however, a VC commando probed the 1st Company on the southern perimeter of defense. 1/16 suffered one dead and one wounded. The enemy left one dead.

At 11:00 PM. on March 24, the 2nd Company on the left flank was probed with small automatic rifle fire. Although there were no casualties, Captain Duc knew the enemy was attempting to identify his defense lines for a coordinated attack.

On Easter eve, Saturday, March 25, at 9:00 PM., a grenade trap exploded in front of the defense line. Although a reconnaissance team was sent out and found nothing unusual, Captain Duc sensed the attack was imminent. He called his ambushes and saturated the thick jungles in front of the 1st Company with artillery fire from Tam Binh District, five kilometers southwest of the 1/16 position. Duc also put his battalion in full alert.

At 1:00 AM. on Sunday, the enemy attacked in force. The attack was preceded by heavy mortar fire on the artillery positions in Tam Binh and Minh Duc (seven kilometers north of 1/16 position). Captain Duc asked his advisor, Capt. Bob Graham, who commanded a four-man advisory team, to request "Spooky" air support. ("Spooky" was the name given to an AC-47 flare and gunship equipped with Gatling guns which could fire 600 rounds per second.) Every night, it was customary to have one Spooky in air alert so it could be quickly directed to an outpost under attack anywhere within the IV Corps area. After some initial confusion regarding communication frequency, Captain Graham was finally able to contact Spooky on the 9th Division's channel and to guide its gunfire immediately in front of the 1/16. At the same time, artillery platoons (two 105-mm guns each) at Tan Binh and Minh Duc provided uninterrupted close support fire around the perimeter of defense despite the fact that Tan Binh District itself was under intense enemy mortar counter-artillery fire.

At 1:30 AM., 3rd Company on the right flank reported being under heavy attack. A few minutes later, Captain Duc lost contact with 3rd Company. He immediately dispatched a relief team which succeeded in restoring 3rd Company's front line. Around 2:00 AM., 2nd Company on the left flank fell back under repeated enemy assaults. Duc sent the battalion's executive officer with a new relief team to aid the 2nd Company defense. The relief team had to cross in the dark and under intense fire the treacherous "monkey bridges" (*cau khi*) built over small internal ravines. It reached 2nd Company's position just in time to beat off a new assault. At 4:00 AM., U.S. Skyraiders, guided by Captain Graham as well an Air Force observation aircraft, started to strafe enemy positions along both flanks of 1/16 Battalion. From then on, it was obvious the attack had failed because the VC had to withdraw before daybreak to avoid annihilation by artillery and air strikes.

I closely followed the development of the situation of 1/16 Battalion in the division's TOC. Studying the map of the Mang Thit area, I predicted that the enemy would have to withdraw to their base area in Hoa Binh village, approximately five kilometers to the south of 1/16 Battalion's position, in order to regroup and patch up their wounded. As a result, I decided to conduct a pursuit operation that was launched at once. The main attacking force would consist of the 16th Regiment with two battalions: the 2/16 and the 3/16, reinforced by the 2/2 and 3/2 Cavalry Troops. The 1/14 and 43rd Ranger Battalion were held in reserve at Vinh Binh and Vinh Long airfields respectively.

Around 7:00 A.M., I circled the target area in a C&C helicopter to pick up the LZ for the 3/16 battalion. Hoa Binh village was about six kilometers long and had a Y configuration. The left side of the Y and its tail flowed west into the Mang Thit canal opposite the district town of Tam Binh. I guessed that the enemy, after withdrawing from Mang Thit, must have concentrated on the north branch of the village because it was the most direct escape route from Mang Thit. Consequently, I chose LZ Alpha in an open area near a small feeder ravine running in a north-south direction, approximately 200 meters from the main northern "tree line" of Hoa Binh village. The vegetation on both sides of the ravine would provide cover and protection for the attacking troops

After the LZ was softened by preemptive airstrikes, the first lift of the 3/16 was brought in. One helicopter from this first lift was hit and damaged by enemy machine gun fire and could not take off. Lt. Col. Jack Dempsey, commanding officer of the 13th Army Aviation Battalion in Can Tho, went down to pick up the crew of the downed helicopter. His helicopter was hit and set afire by recoilless rifle fire from the northern edge of Hoa Binh Village. He died in the firefight. Colonel Dempsey's death triggered a frantic rescue operation. Jet fighters from other Corps areas were diverted to Hoa Binh to destroy the enemy positions and to protect the rescue operation. Maj. James Eberwine, 657th Medevac Company commander, landed near the downed helicopters and succeeded in rescuing four men who were nearest to his landing site. As he attempted to take off, his helicopter was hit by recoilless rifles fire and burst into flames. Capt. Tom Mitchell, senior advisor to the 3/16, who had landed with the first lift, crawled back to the downed helicopters to try to rescue the survivors. He was shot dead by enemy machine gun fire.

With regard to my pursuit operation, the situation was far from bright. In fact, it appeared bleak.We had three helicopters destroyed.

There were now fourteen Americans on the LZ. Two U.S. officers were killed. Most of the other U.S. personnel were wounded and could not be evacuated. The first elements of the 3/16 were pinned down in the open by intense enemy fire. Col. Bob Bringham, my senior advisor, grew nervous. "General Thi," he told me on the intercom of our helicopter as we circled the LZ, "I think that you and I will be in big trouble if we don't take Hoa Binh today."

According to my plan, the 2/2 Cavalry Troop would cross the Mang Thit canal north of Tam Binh District, then regroup around LZ Alpha and be ready to support the final assault on Hoa Binh. So, I directed it to speed up to the site of the downed helicopters to rescue the survivors, but the mud and thick mangroves in the area north of Tam Binh turned out to be insurmountable obstacles to

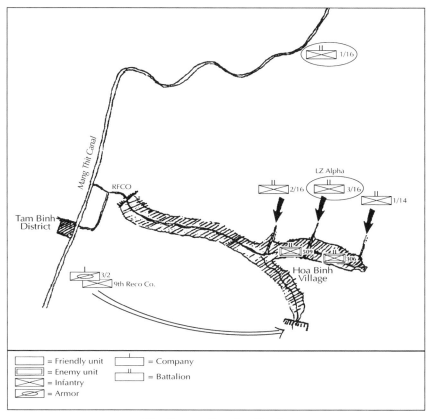

The Easter Sunday Battle

the 2/2 Cavalry Troop. But the 3/2 Cavalry Troop succeeded in crossing the canal south of Tam Binh and occupying its assigned blocking positions south of Hoa Binh Village. Its main mission was to block any attempt by the Viet Cong to escape to the south.

Finally, around 10:00 A.M., using a smoke helicopter supported by gunships to provide cover for the rescue operation, four helicopters of the 657th Medevac Company succeeded in landing and picking up all the dead and wounded.

In the meantime, the rest of the 3/16 Battalion was helilifted to an area about one kilometer north of LZ Alpha. Then the 2/16 Battalion was brought in to an area west of the 3/16. Since the rice fields north of Hoa Binh were flooded by heavy monsoon rains, the men of the 16th Regiment had to progress very slowly with water reaching their waist. The regiment was to attack along two ravines along to the western edge of the Hoa Binh Village.

To physically coordinate the assault of these two battalions, Major Thanh, the 16th Regiment Commander and his senior advisor, Major Palenchar, and their staffs were helilifted into the operation area with the 2/16 Battalion. Normally, regiment commanders would direct their battalions from an advanced CP, but in case of heavy contacts, I wanted them to be with their troops so that they could accurately assess the situation and make quick decisions.

After regrouping at their respective landing sites, the 2/16 and 3/16 launched their assault to occupy the northern tips of their assigned ravines. However, Major Thanh reported that the 16th Regiment met with heavy enemy resistance and was pinned down. I decided it was time to commit the 1/14 Battalion from Vinh Binh. This battalion was to attack along a small creek running north-south into the eastern edge of Hoa Binh.

Although the enemy ferociously fought back the 16th Regiment's multiple assaults, by 7:00 PM., the 1/14 Battalion succeeded in capturing the eastern edge of Hoa Binh; from there it provided effective enfilade machine gun fire support to the 16th Regiment. By 8:00 PM., the battle was over.

Captured documents indicated that enemy forces in Hoa Binh consisted of the Vinh Long 509th Mobile Provincial Battalion and the crack 306th Regional Regular Battalion. The latter was ordered to move from its usual operational area in Chuong Thien Province, south of the Bassac River, to Vinh Long Province, to disrupt the important Mang Thit project.

Below is the result of the so-called Easter Sunday battle:

Casualties:

U.S	ARVN	VIET CONG
4 KIA	24 KIA	184 KIA (plus an estimated 100 dead carried away)
12 WIA	69 WIA	2 CAPTURED

Weapons lost

U.S.	ARVN
1 M-1 Rifle	1.45 Caliber Pistol

Viet Cong Equipment Captured:

2 BARs	1 Czech Lt Machine Gun
2 Chinese Lt Machine Guns	4 SKS Rifles
6 Russian Rifles	3 Flare Pistols
5 U.S. M1 Rifles	5 Pistols
8 U.S. M1 Carbines	2 U.S Thompson Sub-machine Guns
1 U.S. M2 Carbine	2 Russian B-40 Rocket Launchers
3 Russian AK-47 Rifles	1 82 mm Mortar Sight

(Plus miscellaneous communication equipment and ammunition.)

By any standard this was a successful operation for two reasons: First, the pursuit operation, given the fluid enemy situation and the lack of up-to-date intelligence, is generally considered by tacticians as one of the most difficult military operations; second, the Mekong Delta village, unlike its North Vietnamese counterpart, is built along the intricate contours of multiple canals and ravines. It usually extends over many kilometers without well-defined boundaries. Consequently, it was practically impossible to surround and destroy the enemy within the confines of any given Delta village. I have never heard or witnessed, during my twenty-five-year military career, any instance where the enemy was encircled and totally destroyed in a Mekong village or hamlet.

This was also the opinion of Gen. Creighton Abrams, the deputy commander of MAC-V. General Abrams came to the CP of the 1/16

Battalion two days after the 9th Division's attack on Hoa Binh to study the Battle of Mang Thit. Abrams, a tough and laconic man who, in the words of Admiral Zumwalt, "ate people alive," shook my hand after the visit and simply said: "General Thi, you have a great outfit." Yet, in his book *Vinh Long*, Harvey Meyerson, university professor turned journalist then tactician, had this to say about what he called "The Easter Battle": "Tactically,. . .the battle was a failure. The enemy was trapped in broad daylight. Escape routes were obvious and limited. There was plenty of time, the entrenched Viet Cong should have been surrounded. . . ." [33]

Worse, intentionally or by mistake, Meyerson omitted to show in his map entitled "One-Way Traffic" (as it describes the Easter Battle) the blocking position of the 3/2 Cavalry south of the Hoa Binh village. Although the division's Reconnaissance Company, which accompanied the 3/2 Cavalry, had set up ambushes along the main possible escape route on the south branch of the Hoa Binh canal, it did not make contact during the night following the Easter Battle, since the enemy had dispersed in small groups and escaped under cover of darkness. It has been my experience that, for an operation in the Delta to be successful, you must trap the enemy early in the morning so you can bring in reinforcements to destroy it before it can escape when darkness sets in; it is futile to mount a pursuit the next day because by then the enemy has dispersed in small elements to regroup a few days later at designated locations.

Another discrepancy was that, contrary to what was indicated in *Vinh Long*, the 43rd Ranger Battalion was not committed in the Easter Battle. The reason was the 1/14 Battalion was able to seize the eastern edge of the village and provide enfilade supporting fire to the 16th Regiment. Consequently, it was not necessary to commit the Rangers. Yet in his book, Meyerson conveniently included the 43rd Ranger Battalion as part of the attacking force to prove his point that an overwhelming attacking force failed to trap and destroy two VC battalions. [34]

Meyerson's one-sided reporting was not an exception. It seemed to be the rule for American journalists reporting on the Viet Nam War.

In analyzing U.S. broadcasts and printed material during the Viet Nam War, I've discerned some unwritten rules:

1 – When comparing the Viet Cong and North Vietnamese with the Allied Forces, praise the first and criticize the latter.

2 – When comparing the U.S. forces with ARVN, praise the first and criticize the latter.

3 – When reporting on ARVN or GVN, use the following epithets and, if possible, in the same order: a) corrupt; b) repressive and c) inefficient.

Along these guidelines, the My Lai massacre, for instance, received ample coverage while the Viet Cong atrocities (such as the murder of 4,000 civilians in Hue during the 1968 Tet Offensive) were hardly mentioned. The Viet Cong was often depicted as a highly motivated fighting man while the U.S. soldier was plagued with drug and other discipline problems. In the contrast between a VC and an ARVN soldier, the former was depicted (in a *Newsweek* article) as a "lion," while the latter was called a "rabbit."[35]

General Westmoreland complained in his book *A Soldier Reports* about government officials in Washington trying to act as field marshals. But the situation became worse when journalists and academicians started to act similarly. With regard to my performance as a division commander and the conduct of the pursuit operation leading up to the Easter Sunday Battle, it was fitting that if there was no evidence of corruption or repression, then there must have been incompetence. The details of the operation were distorted and some omitted to prove that the Easter Battle had failed to encircle and annihilate two entire VC battalions in a Delta village. Then, the operation was conveniently labeled a "gross tactical failure."

After the fall of South Viet Nam, the U.S. media, which had vociferously accused the Nguyen Van Thieu government of dictatorship and corruption, was conspiciously silent about the fact that the Hanoi regime had sent hundreds of thousands of army officers and officials of the former government to numerous "re-education camps" established throughout Viet Nam. The media also remained silent when the Communists used chemical warfare to kill Hmong tribes in Laos who had previously collaborated with the Americans during the Viet Nam War. There was little media reaction to the slaughter of one-third of the Cambodian people by the genocidal regime of Pol Pot.

In her book *Dictatorship and Double Standard*[36] Jeanne Kirkpatrick, former U.S. ambassador to the United Nations, explained this political phenomenon by stating that in the 1960s and 1970s there appeared on the American political scene, a new class of intellectuals, politicians, professors, journalists, and clergymen who tried to bring rationalism into politics. The new rationalist politicians in the United States conceived an abstract political regime in which basic citizen rights must be respected. The tragic mistake of this neo-rationalism is that it wanted to impose on emerging nations an idealistic political system, which required constant adjustments even in Western democracies, and which was completely detached from the experiences and political realities peculiar to each of these countries.

This neo-rationalism was not a new invention. Karl Marx had conceived an idealistic and classless society in which every man would work according to his capacity and consume according to his needs. However, instead of letting the historical process produce such a utopian society according to his dialectic concept, his disciples such as Lenin, Stalin, Mao Tse-tung and Ho Chi Minh resorted to pure violence to force social change while these countries were still at a pre-industrial stage of development. The collapse of the Communist empire in the former Soviet Union and East European countries proves that an idealistic society imposed by force can be a costly undertaking.

The new class of intellectuals in America became frustrated and reacted strongly when they saw that social and political realities in the emerging nations did not fit into preconceived political structures. Because rationalist political theories are too abstract and have no relation to political realities, they cannot be applied to new developing nations. This in turn caused frustration among the new class of American liberal politicians and pushed them to work toward the overthrow of anti-Communist regimes in these countries.

The U.S. media during the Viet Nam War was caught in the above political game and it worked hard to discredit the GVN and its Army. Meyerson's *Vinh Long* was only a small contribution to the greater political scheme of the rationalist movement of the 1960s.

2ⁿᵈ Brigade, École Inter-Armes, 1950. I am 3ʳᵈ from right, front row. My brother Tho is 5ᵗʰ from left. Second-Lieutenant Nguyen Van Bich, Brigade Commander, is at center.

Tet 1967. Vacation in Dalat with my son, Tuan, Colonel Bringham (2ⁿᵈ from left), and Major Palenchar.

Touring Australian Service Academies, July 1971.

La Vang Cathedral in
Quang Tri after recapture
of the city by ARVN
troops in September
1972.

Hue, July 1973. Visiting servicemen's dependent quarters with my wife.

September 1973. With Brigadier-General Luong,
Airborne Division Commander, after parachute
demonstraion in Hue.

June 1974. With General Lan, Marine division commander. In background are ammunition and Chinese rations retrieved from a sunken NVA ship, north of Hue.

June 1986. VN Armed Forces Day in New Orleans, Louisiana, with General Westmoreland and General Nguyen Cao Ky. I am at General Westmoreland's left.

10

1968 TET OFFENSIVE

ON JANUARY 30, 1968, THE second day of the new Year of the Monkey, at 2:00 AM., my aide awakened me and reported that the VC had simultaneously attacked the capital cities of Vinh Long, Vinh Binh, and Kien Giang. The situation was particularly critical in Vinh Long where the enemy occupied most of the city and part of the airport, which was defended by a U.S. Army aviation unit. The 1968 Tet Offensive in the Mekong Delta had begun. In the evening of January 29, General Manh, IV Corps Commander, had called to inform me that the VC had attacked a few cities in Military Region II, and that I should take necessary measures against a possible enemy attack in the Delta. Consequently, I ordered that all leaves for the traditional Tet festivities be suspended immediately and all units put in the highest alert status.

For the Vietnamese, Tet is Christmas, New Year, and Thanksgiving combined. Tet is the occasion for people to relax after one year of hard work, for the peasants to thank "Heaven and Earth" for a good harvest and to celebrate, for the members of the family to get together and to pay respect to the ancestors, and mostly for the children to put on new clothes and to receive "lucky money" in small red envelopes from their parents and friends of the family. Thus, it was customary for the government and the VC to declare unilaterally a three-day truce on this occasion so that soldiers could celebrate this important holiday with their families after one year of fighting. Normally, one-third of the soldiers in each ARVN unit would rotate to spend time with their loved ones on this important holiday.

For me, it was also a chance to relax and get away from the battlefields. The previous Tet, I took my oldest son, Tuan, to Dalat. We flew to this beautiful resort station in a military Cessna. I also invited Colonel Bringham, the division Senior Advisor and his Operations Officer, Major Palanchar, to come along. The mayor of Dalat, an army officer, was kind enough to provide us with a villa and a sedan. We spent two wonderful days visiting the Vietnamese Military Academy and other tourist attractions; we ate French food at exotic restaurants built on small hills with breathtaking views. I was tempted to repeat the experience this year, but something told me to stay home. This turned out to be one of the best decisions I made in my life.

The day before, the first day of the New Year, contrary to habit, I donned my army fatigues and flew out to visit my regiments. My wife had suggested that I stay home because it was a popular belief that anything you do on the first day of the Tet would impact your activities for the rest of the year. Thus, if I went out to inspect my units that day in combat uniform, I would have to fight the VC all year long. I disregarded my wife's advice because I did not believe in superstitions. Now that the enemy had attacked all over my tactical area, I painfully realized the relevance of certain popular beliefs.

When I arrived at the division TOC, the atmosphere was gloomy. The city of Vinh Long was completely isolated. Except for the military installations and the province chief's residence, the city was practically under VC control. Lt. Col. Huynh Ngoc Diep, the province chief, who was lightly wounded in an ambush on January 6, 1968, just fifteen kilometers east of Vinh Long, appeared to have lost control of the situation. At the airport, the enemy occupied part of the runway. All access routes to the city were blocked by VC units.

I was especially concerned about the fate of the Vinh Long archbishop and thousands of residents who had taken refuge at the historic Vinh Long Cathedral located at the crossroads of RN 4 and the Vinh Long-Sa Dec axis. The Cathedral had been built by Monsignor Ngo Dinh Thuc, archbishop of Vinh Long and President Diem's older brother. It was a showcase for the growing influence of Catholicism in the Mekong Delta under President Ngo Dinh Diem. At that time, high government officers and high ranking officers in the Armed Forces had been selected to go to Vinh Long Cathedral, under the over-all supervision of Monsignor Thuc, for an indoctrination course on the theory of *"Personalism"* or *"Nhan Vi,"* which had constituted the philosophical foundation for President Diem's Can Lao Party.

Monsignor Ngo Dinh Thuc lived in exile in Rome after the 1963 coup d'état which overthrew his brother's regime, but the Vinh Long Cathedral remained a historical landmark in the Mekong Delta. The Cathedral was now occupied by a VC unit, which practically controlled all access to the city. Any effort to bring in reinforcements and supplies to the city would require that the Cathedral be retaken. I was faced with a dilemma because any attack would inevitably cause substantial loss of life among the refugees and heavy damage to the Cathedral.

In Vinh Binh, the situation was also bleak. The enemy occupied most of the city, including the official residence of the province chief, who had escaped to the Sector TOC from which he was trying to rally his troops. Fighting was going on inside the city and, again, I was concerned about the inevitable damage to the beautiful Cambodian pagodas located within the city proper.

Chau Doc Province reported only small unit infiltrations at the northern section of the city. The city of Kien Giang on the Gulf of Siam was also under attack; however, the province chief appeared to have the situation under control. Sporadic fighting took place around the city of Kien Phong near the Cambodian border, but overall the situation was considered not serious. The only encouraging news was that the province of Long Xuyen, where the Hoa Hao population was strongly anti-Communist, had remained calm.

While I was following the tactical situation at the provinces under attack, I heard the sounds of gunfire in the direction of my residence. Then, one of the TOC telephones rang and an agitated Col. Tran Ba Di, my deputy, handed the phone to me. "Help! help! Come back!" I heard the voice of my wife yelling in the phone, "the Viet Cong are attacking our house!"

I dashed outside and grabbed a light machine gun positioned in the bunker at the division Headquarters's main gate. Leaving my security detail behind, I rushed to my residence while bullets were flying around me. "Halt!" yelled the guard at the front gate of my residence. "It is the General!" my aide yelled back. I hastily put the machine gun in position at the side yard directly in front of the rear gate, ready to beat back any new assaults. At the same time, the two armored vehicles I had earlier sent out to patrol in the city of Sa Dec had returned and took up position behind my residence. I ordered my aide and the security detail to man the machine gun, then I dashed inside my house. Fortunately no one was hurt. By that time, the gunfire had died down. The enemy must have known that reinforcements had arrived and that it would be suicidal to attempt a second assault; thus, the VC commando unit had already retreated.

I instructed the security detail to search the area behind my residence. My men discovered a dozen bodies; they captured a few armed VCs hiding under a bush just a few meters from where I stood. I sometimes wondered why these VC didn't shoot the division commander they were sent out to kill and to make good on Hanoi Radio's announcement the next day that I was killed along with a few other division commanders. According to astrologers my wife had consulted, 1968 was supposed to be a bad year for me, because I was also born the Year of the Monkey. Somehow, my family and I survived unscathed from a raid on our home. But it was a close call.

The VC prisoners were very young, possibly fifteen or sixteen years old. By their own account, they were drafted into a commando company from the province of Kien Phong a few months before Tet. After some intensive training, they were told they would cross the Mekong River during Tet to attack an "American facility" in Sa Dec. At around 2:30 A.M. on the second day of Tet, they reached their objective and launched the attack shortly after arrival. Unfortunately, the company commander was wounded during the first assault and they had to withdraw and regroup. By the time they were ready to launch a new assault, the objective had been reinforced with machine guns and armored vehicles, so the acting company commander gave orders to retreat.

Later my wife told me that, after I left the house to go to division Headquarters, the security squad that guarded our residence was put on alert on my aide's instructions. Although most of the members of the security squad had been wounded in combat and were detached to my residence before being discharged for disability, they still could shoot and perform under fire. However, it was mere luck that the soldiers who mounted guard at the rear gate during the first attack inflicted casualties to the attacking force, including the company commander.

When fire broke out, my wife took the children to the bunkers I had built downstairs as a protection against enemy mortar fire. She grabbed a grenade from a guard and was ready to hurl it at the VC if they broke into the house. She also handed a pistol to Uncle Four, who had come from Bac Lieu with his wife a few days earlier to spend the Tet with us. "Can you shoot?" asked my wife. "Yes, I can still shoot," answered Uncle Four, who had seen action at Verdun as a soldier in the French Army in World War I, "but I doubt I can hit anyone anymore."

Noticing an army radio set on the ground near the bunker, my wife grabbed the radio handle, pressed the speaking button and directed the armored vehicles to return at once because the house was under attack. (After I received the earlier call from General Manh regarding a possible VC violation of the Tet truce agreement, I sent these vehicles to patrol the city of Sa Dec to detect any enemy infiltration.) The patrol commander recognized the northern accent of my wife, but could not acknowledge because my wife, in her panic, kept pressing the speaking button. He returned to our residence, although he was instructed by the province chief to report to Sa Dec Sector Headquarters. For us, it was a fortunate decision because it saved our family from massacre at the hands of young VC militiamen.

After I gave instructions to the division Reconnaissance Company to mount a pursuit operation, I went back to the division TOC. Fighting was still taking place in Vinh Binh and Kien Giang, but the situation appeared to be under control. In Vinh Binh, units of the 14th Regiment had retaken the major part of the city and most of the Cambodian pagodas, which incurred only light damage. In Kien

Giang, the 15th Regiment in conjunction with RF units cleared the commercial district and were battling the enemy at its southern outskirts.

In Vinh Long, the situation remained precarious. Although the VC had been evicted from the airport, they still controlled most of the city and were still occupying the Cathedral. Heavy fighting took place in the commercial district and armed helicopters had been called in to support counterattacking units from the 16th Regiment, causing heavy damage to the city. Important enemy concentrations in the southern section of the city had been reported. There was also an unconfirmed report that VC Gen. Tran Van Tra, commander of the troops of the Front for the Liberation of South Viet Nam (FLSVN) was personally directing the attack on Vinh Long and had established his command post in a villa south of the city perimeter. It was obvious by now that Vinh Long was one of the enemy main targets for the Tet Offensive. The capture of this strategic city would cut off traffic from the Delta to Saigon and all supplies to different units of IV Corps.

Around 10 AM. I flew to the naval assault squadron located three kilometers west of the city since heavy fighting prevented my helicopter from landing at Sector Headquarters. I borrowed a small patrol boat from the squadron to reach the province chief's residence, which also housed the Sector Headquarters. Like most provinces in the Delta, the residence of the Vinh Long province chief was located on the bank of the Mekong River, thus it was easily accessible by boat. This residence was certainly one of the most beautiful in the entire Delta. Surrounded by an eight-foot concrete wall, the whole complex originally consisted of a main two-story administrative building and a one-story detached office building which had been converted into the Sector Headquarters. Under President Diem, Mme Ngo Dinh Nhu built a modern two-story villa where she occasionally spent her weekends away from the political infighting among members of her husband's family.

As I was ready to disembark, the squadron commander, a young Navy lieutenant, came to see me. "Sir, I would like to present you with a small gift," he said, pulling from his pocket a white object, which looked like the tooth of a tiger attached to a silver chain.

"This is a talisman that has protected my life," continued the lieutenant, "but now, your life is more precious than mine since the future of the seven provinces under your command rests on your shoulders." I thanked the lieutenant for his thoughtfulness and put the lucky charm in my fatigue pocket. Since then, it has accompanied me in all of my operations and, true to the lieutenant's wishes, it has brought me luck. I still have this talisman that I keep in a safe place at our home in California as a precious souvenir of those turbulent years.

The situation was not encouraging. At Vinh Long Sector's TOC, I was met by Maj. Bui Van Hai, the Deputy Sector Commander and my classmate at Dalat. Hai had served as a sergeant in the French Army before attending *l'École Inter-Arms*. He reported that friendly units had difficulty in dislodging the enemy from the commercial buildings in the central sector of the city. Also, according to Major Hai, a VC unit of platoon size was still occupying the Cathedral where an estimated two thousand residents had taken refuge. Major Hai was convinced that an all-out VC attack on the Sector Headquarters could happen at any time. Captain Loc, commanding the 3/2 Calvary Troop, reported that some of his APCs were damaged by direct enemy rocket fire while providing close support to one battalion of the 16th Regiment and the 1st Battalion of the 15th Regiment. (The 1/15 had been operating in Vinh Long province under the command of the 16th.) The mission of these units was to evict the enemy from the commercial center. After the briefing, I wanted to go to the commercial district to make a personal assessment of the situation but heavy engagements on the street adjacent to the Sector Headquarters prevented me from doing so.

Back at Sa Dec, I instructed Col. Tran Ba Di, my deputy, to go to Vinh Long to take charge of the operations to evict the VC from the city. Colonel Di had risen through the ranks and had a tremendous amount of combat experience. He had been province chief and regiment commander and was a competent and promising officer. Di had just returned from the United States where he attended the Command & General Staff College at Fort Leavenworth, Kansas. It was difficult to find a better officer to take charge of Vinh Long at this critical time and I had the utmost confidence in Colonel Di's ability to carry out his difficult mission. To reinforce Colonel Di's attacking force, I directed that one battalion from the 15th Regiment be transported by helicopters from Long Xuyen to Vinh Long at once. Lt. Col. Nguyen Van Thi, the 15th Regiment Commander, would be in charge of the offensive operation under the overall supervision of Colonel Di, who would also have full authority over the province's RF and PF units.

The next day, I flew again to Vinh Long to review the situation in that city. This time, I was able to land directly in front of Sector Headquarters. During the night, Colonel Di had dislodged the VC from the surrounding area and was in the process of directing a counterattack to destroy the enemy entrenched in the commercial district. I borrowed a jeep from the Sector and drove to the center of the city. I was shocked at the devastation caused by street combat. Rocket fire from armed helicopters and machine gun fire from attacking units erupted as I reached the downtown area. Buildings were burning. Civilian casualties were piled on wheelbarrows and evacuated to the city hospital.

Except for occasional terrorist attacks in which enemy agents in civilian clothes riding motorcycles hurled a hand grenade into a U.S. compound or detonated a homemade mine in front of a crowded restaurant, the urban population in Viet Nam so far had been largely untouched by the war. No more! The VC Tet Offensive had brought the war to the cities and caused incalculable devastation and suffering.

Can Tho, the seat of IV Corps Headquarters, was also under heavy attack by regular VC units. According to the latest reports, the 21st Division had to mount massive heliborne operations to evict the enemy from its fortified positions in Can Tho's southern suburbs. Even Saigon was not spared by the Tet Offensive. A VC sapper unit penetrated the compound of the U.S. Embassy on Tu Do Street, only a few blocks from the Independence Palace; the latest reports from international news services provided conflicting accounts of the above attack.

In any event, when I returned to Vinh Long Sector, I met with a U.S. colonel who commanded a brigade of the U.S. 9th Infantry Division headquartered just outside of the city of My Tho in the 7th

ARVN Infantry Division's tactical area. The American officer requested permission to engage elements of his brigade along the river east of the airport, running in a north-south direction. The objective of the operation was to destroy Viet Cong units south of the airport and to relieve the pressure from U.S. aviation units occupying the airport. The U.S. 9th Infantry Division was specially trained in combat operations in the Mekong Delta and was equipped with an impressive armada of assorted river boats and vessels. I was very happy to get help from a friendly unit and as this was the first time the U.S. 9th Infantry Division was to be engaged in my tactical area, I was curious to watch its technique of riverine operations. Unfortunately, the U.S. brigade involved in the operation incurred heavy casualties and had to withdraw after two days of engagement.

On the afternoon of February 2, 1968, Maj. Gen. Tran Thanh Phong, chief of staff at the Joint General Staff, called me to inquire about the situation in Vinh Long. I told him the situation was critical but assured him that I would use every means available to evict the enemy from the city. I asked General Phong about the conflicting reports on the VC attacks in Saigon. Phong informed me that a VC unit had attacked the Joint General Staff Headquarters in Tan Son Nhut; reserve Ranger units were engaged to dislodge them from the Army Language School located on the northeastern section of the Joint General Staff compound. General Phong told me that fighting was taking place in various parts of the Capital and that I should not rely on Saigon to provide logistical support at this time. According to General Phong, the situation in the Imperial City of Hue was critical. The enemy occupied most of the city and the 1st Infantry Division Headquarters, trapped inside the Citadel, was under heavy attack.

The next day, I relieved the Vinh Long province chief of his command. Lt. Col. Huynh Ngoc Diep, a reserve officer who had attended *Le Cours d'État-Major* (Staff Course) in France, was a fine administrator and a good staff officer, but he had limited combat experience. He panicked and lost control of the situation during the first hours of the VC offensive.[37] I recommended to General Manh, IV Corps Commander, to replace Diep with Lt. Col. Duong Hieu Nghia from my staff.

Nghia was a controversial figure in the Vietnamese Army. A member of the Dai Viet Party, he had actively participated in the overthrow of the Diem regime. He was responsible for escorting President Diem and his brother, Mr. Nhu, from their hiding place in Cho Lon to JGS Headquarters in Tan Son Nhut in an armored personnel carrier. President Diem and Mr.Nhu were murdered during the trip, but there was no evidence that Nghia was involved in the killing. Nghia also played an important role in the failed coup against General Khanh in 1964 for which he was court martialed. Released after General Khanh's departure, he was assigned to my division where he worked in the Inspector's Office. Although concerned about his political affiliations, I decided that he was the right man for Vinh Long because he had combat experience and was on good terms with the Hoa Hao sect, having previously served as a district chief in the province. Besides, he was the only staff officer available for the job and the choice was rather limited during this time of emergency.

That night, as I sat in my office reviewing the tactical situation in my division area, I felt the heavy burden of my responsibility. The city of Sa Dec itself had been spared but my own residence had been attacked by a sapper company. The situation in Vinh Binh and Kien Giang was still unclear. A large section of Vinh Long and its strategic Cathedral were still under VC control. Further, I was practically cut off from Saigon and Can Tho, which were also under attack. Units battling VC in the cities badly needed food and ammunition. There were wounded to be evacuated and killed to be buried. Sipping a glass of tea and studying the tactical map on the wall of my office, full of red flags depicting enemy positions, I suddenly felt very alone. I had responsibility for about 60,000 men, including RF and PF forces. Staff officers reported hourly to me on the situation in the seven provinces under my jurisdiction. They made recommendations, but I—and I alone—was responsible for the outcome of this historic battle to retake the cities under attack while minimizing losses to my men and to the civilian population. In a brief moment, I acutely felt the famous "loneliness of command" experienced by so many commanders in times of crisis or when they had to make important decisions.

It turned out that Colonel Diep was not the only victim of the Tet Offensive. General Manh, the IV Corps Commander, asked to be relieved of his command after his Headquarters in Can Tho was shelled by the VC and the flagpole destroyed by one mortar shell. Manh was very superstitious. He believed the destruction of the flagpole was a warning that his life was in danger.

My friend, Maj. Gen. Nguyen Duc Thang, replaced General Manh. Although Thang was a good friend of General Ky and had served as minister of rural reconstruction in his government, President Thieu appointed him to the job, probably under pressure from the Americans who considered Thang an honest, capable, and hard-working officer.

In the meantime, the situation in Vinh Long improved slightly. The enemy had been evicted from the city proper, but was still holding the villages immediately south of the city perimeter. Worse, the Cathedral was still in the hands of the enemy. As a result, troops fighting around Vinh Long could not be resupplied by that route and food supplies for infantry units and artillery ammunition were dangerously low. Small arms ammunition could be supplied by helicopters but the scarce number of Chinook helicopters available was inadequate to transport artillery ammunition.

Rice was available to the infantry units fighting in Vinh Long, but soldiers engaged in uninterrupted street combat didn't have time to cook. My wife had a brilliant idea: she suggested that I instruct the province chief to reopen the bakery in Sa Dec to make bread for the units. My wife operated an orphanage to take care of the children of soldiers killed in combat and she had obtained donations of flour from American humanitarian organizations. So she supplied the bakery with flour from the orphanage and every morning, I loaded my C&C helicopter with hundreds of loaves of bread which I dropped on the battalions of the 15th Regiment fighting around Vinh Long.

One day, as I landed in the southern outskirts of the city, the 1st Battalion of the 15th Regiment was launching an assault on an enemy unit inside a small cemetery on the south side of the canal which surrounded the city. After the sound of a trumpet announcing the assault, soldiers of the 1/15, covered by the battalion's machine guns, charged the enemy positions while firing M-1 carbines at point blank. I admired these men who attacked without hesitation, although they were outgunned by the enemy who was armed with the deadly Chinese AK-47.[38] The VC were finally evicted from the cemetery, leaving a dozen dead, but the 1/15 battalion commander, Major Huynh, an officer of the Engineer Corps who volunteered to serve in an infantry unit, was wounded from a bullet in the head and had to be evacuated by helicopter to Cong Hoa Military General Hospital in Saigon.

Medical evacuation was, in fact, a critical problem during the Tet Offensive. Usually, soldiers wounded in action were evacuated to MRIV's General Hospital in Can Tho. However, since the start of the Tet Offensive, the Regional General Hospital was overcrowded with soldiers from the 21st Division and from other Regional Forces belonging to the province of Can Tho. Further, most Chinook helicopters were diverted to resupply operations and were not available for medevac.

My wife transformed her orphanage into a small field hospital to accommodate approximately 200 soldiers wounded during the first wave of the Tet Offensive. She enlisted the help of officers' wives who gladly contributed their time and labor to her makeshift hospital. My wife asked Mr. Nguon, the local pharmacist, to donate antibiotics, serum, and bandages.

My wife also handled the funerals for officers and soldiers killed in action (KIA). One day, she told me how frustrated she was when two women came to the funeral of an officer killed in Vinh Long: both claimed to be the legal wife of the deceased. In a lighter note, she also related the story of a wounded sergeant who received a visit of two women who both claimed to be his wife. Frustrated, the sergeant climbed on the roof of the clinic and threatened to jump to his death if the women did not leave him alone.

Had it not been for my wife's devotion, the number of KIAs would have been higher. My wife's training as a social worker served her and the division well.

It was obvious that to solve the logistical problems in my tactical area, it was necessary to retake the Vinh Long Cathedral immediately. To avoid casualties to the civilian population which had taken refuge inside the Cathedral and also to avoid damage to the Cathedral itself, I ordered the 15th Regiment to surround the Cathedral but to leave an escape route for the VC along a small creek. The 15th Regiment was also directed to mount small ambushes along the creek to destroy the escaping enemy. The 15th Regiment would use loudspeakers to tell the enemy to surrender or face destruction. Sure enough, the second night the enemy left under cover of darkness. Although the 15th Regiment ambush teams failed to destroy the escaping enemy, the Cathedral was retaken without bloodshed and ground resupply operations began.

Intelligence reports indicated that VC regular units had retreated to their secret base, a marshy area about fifteen kilometers south of Vinh Long. Because this enemy staging area was unpopulated, I requested a B-52 bombing run on the enemy concentration. (This was my first B-52 request in my tactical area outside the rugged and cavernous Seven Mountains near the Cambodian border in Chau Doc, which served as a permanent VC base.) Elements of the 15th Regiment sent in to reconnoiter the target area after the B-52 mission reported many enemy bodies and weapons. General Thang and I flew into the area to personally assess the result of the B-52 strike. VC bodies and weapons were scattered all around as we walked on a small dike which traversed the target area. Limbs and body parts hung on the trees. The B-52 strike apparently had caught the enemy off-guard while they were recuperating.

A few days later, General Thang came to see me in Sa Dec when I was directing a search and destroy operation between Vinh Long and Sa Dec. He told me that he was going to Saigon to see General Khiem, the prime minister. He also informed me that, due to the critical situation around Can Tho, he would ask General Khiem to let me assume command of the 21st Infantry Division whose headquarters was located in my hometown of Bac Lieu and which had the tactical responsibility for the city of Can Tho, the seat of IV Corps Headquarters.

I told Thang I did not want to go to the 21st Division because I hadn't finished destroying enemy units around Vinh Long and Sa Dec. It should be noted that Gen. Nguyen Van Minh, the 21st Division Commander and Thieu's protégé, had been appointed Commander of the Capital Special District in charge of the defense of Saigon and the surrounding areas a few days earlier. Since the enemy was still occupying Can Tho's suburbs, Thang needed someone he could trust.

While walking with me to his waiting helicopter, General Thang said: "Thi, I've made my decision. I am sure you know the saying '*Chon mat goi vang,*'[39] don't you?"

After Thang left, I called my brother Tho, a protégé of Khiem. I asked him to tell Khiem that I did not want to go to the 21st Division before the situation in my tactical area was corrected. Beside, after three years as division commander, I wanted something more challenging. Although I didn't say it, Tho knew I was aiming for the command of an Army Corps.

Meanwhile, the situation around Sa Dec suddenly worsened. The 1st Battalion of the 16th Regiment made heavy contact with the enemy. Captured documents revealed that the local VC units had been reinforced by a regular battalion from Kien Phong Province. I ordered the Sa Dec province chief to launch a sector operation to search and destroy enemy forces north of the city. In addition to its RF organic Battalion, Sa Dec Sector would have operational control of the 1/16th Battalion, one artillery battery, and the 3/2 Cavalry Troop, which I diverted from Vinh Long. Strong enemy resistance was encountered and artillery support was needed to destroy enemy machine gun positions. Since the artillery battery was positioned just behind our residence, my family was frightened by the detonations and could not sleep at night. Fortunately, the Sa Dec Sector operation caused heavy casualties to the enemy and forced it to withdraw.

Things were looking up. The situation in Vinh Binh, on the South China Sea, was very encouraging. The 14th Regiment, reinforced with the 2/2 Cavalry Troop, chased the enemy ten kilometers south of the city and captured many prisoners and weapons. The dry, sandy terrain near the sea was very favorable to armored units operations, and enemy units dug in on the sand dunes were easy targets for the 2/2 Cavalry Troop and were destroyed one by one.

Although General Thang was very pleased with the progress of the pursuit operation in Vinh Binh, he decided to relieve the province chief, Lieutenant Colonel Quy, for having failed to defend the province headquarters during the first wave of assault. Thang knew that this was a sensitive matter for me, because Quy previously had obeyed General Manh's instructions to file a complaint against me regarding the so-called illegal use of the provincial "Fund For Support Of Battlefield." Quy was replaced by Lt. Col. Ton That Dong, a veteran of the Indochina War and my classmate at Dalat.

Near the end of January 1968, the situation was well under control. The VC had retreated in every city under my jurisdiction. Everywhere, division units were mounting pursuit operations to destroy the enemy in their staging areas. To boost the morale of the people and the troops, General Ky, vice president, and Gen. Cao Van Vien, chairman of the Joint Chiefs of Staff, decided to fly into Vinh Long and from there to drive to Can Tho on RN 4. Again, they were followed by a throng of Vietnamese and foreign reporters. I was glad the trip was a smooth ride and the convoy reached Can Tho without incident.

On February 18, 1968, the VC launched what was known as the Second Tet Offensive. However, the small units they were able to assemble for this second offensive were quickly destroyed and by the end of February, the much celebrated VC Tet Offensive had practically ended.

In May 1968, General Thang was removed from the command of IV Corps. A good friend of General Ky, Thang had been sent to Can Tho to replace General Manh at the heat of the Tet Offensive, but since the situation had now stabilized, his presence at IV Corps was no longer needed. Also in May, I was made a major general. Since I was the senior division commander in IV Corps, I would have been the logical choice to replace Thang. Because Thieu still suspected I was a backer of Ky, he reassigned me instead to the post of superintendent of the Military Academy in Dalat. Thieu made it a point to trust only the cadets of his Brigade when he was instructor at *l'École Inter-Arms*. Consequently, most of the corps commanders were chosen from his former students. It was no secret that, in the Vietnamese Army and throughout the Republic of Viet Nam, the most powerful men were the four corps commanders. They were called "the four pillars of the dynasty" by the Vietnamese press and "warlords" by American reporters. The corps commanders formed the most exclusive group in the country and had direct access to the President. As they also accumulated the function of "Representatives of the Government" in their Military Regions, they had authority not only over the military but also controlled the political and economic matters within their Region. Consequently, with regard to non-military matters, the province chiefs usually bypassed the division commanders by reporting directly to the corps commanders.

Maj. Gen. Nguyen Viet Thanh, who replaced General Thang as IV Corps Commander, however, was an exception. He was not Thieu's former cadet at *l'École Inter-Arms*. Although Thanh was rather a colorless officer, he was considered one of the most honest generals in the Army.

As for me, I had a special relationship with General Thanh. He had come to my rescue with his infantry company when my artillery battery was overrun by the Viet Minh's 42nd Regiment in Hung Yen Province in North Viet Nam during the Indochina War. Also, one day my battery was requested to provide support to Thanh's company which was under attack by a Viet Minh unit across from the city of Hung Yen. That day, Thanh's company had established defensive positions on the river dike when a Viet Minh company launched the assault on his unit. Thanh was lucky because the enemy didn't know that the rice paddy near the dike had been harvested just the day before. As a result, the Viet Minh had to charge across a vacant field and were almost decimated to the last man. The remnants of the Viet Minh company, which consisted mostly of the fire support elements, were partially destroyed by my battery fire.[40]

I received the news of my assignment to the Vietnamese National Academy while conducting an operation to repacify the Mang Thit River, which had been temporarily abandoned during the VC Tet Offensive. The 16th Regiment, provincial RF units and Rural Reconstruction teams went back into the Mang Thit area without any enemy resistance. Most of the pacification areas in the country had been reoccupied shortly after the Tet Offensive and the pacification program was made easier because the VC had lost more than one-half of their strength during their attack on the cities. However, the foreign media later hailed the temporary disruption of the government pacification program as one of the VC's biggest victories during the Tet Offensive.

In the previous chapter, I mentioned what I perceived to be the bias of the U.S. media with regard to the Viet Nam War. The Tet Offensive, in particular, provided an opportunity for American reporters to substantiate, at the cost of accuracy, their belief that the war was unwinnable. In retrospect, I think that the U.S. media's coverage of the Tet Offensive was, in fact, a classic case of irresponsible reporting and should merit further discussion.

The first example was the much publicized execution of a VC officer. When Police Chief Nguyen Van Loan executed a VC officer who had killed some of his officers during an engagement in Cho Lon, the sprawling Chinese suburb south of Saigon, the U.S. media transformed it into a sort of *cause célèbre* for antiwar activists. Not satisfied with broadcasting reruns day after day of the devastating sequence of the execution by an Associated Press correspondent titled "Pictures of an Execution," NBC went into great detail to make these pictures more dramatic to the American public. On the NBC *Special on Viet Nam*, broadcast March 10, 1968, with Frank McGee as anchorman, viewers could see the entire footage showing the VC officer lying dead on the street with an enormous pool of blood forming under his head.

In the heavily damaged Ben Tre province, an unnamed U.S. advisor, in response to reporters' remarks about the destruction of the city during the Tet Offensive, stated that "it became necessary to destroy Ben Tre in order to save it." This unfortunate remark has since been used time and again by antiwar activists and politicians. In his book *Reporting Vietnam*, William Hammond wrote, "The *New York Times* seized upon the remark as soon as it appeared. So did *Time*. From there it passed into the lore of the war to become one of the most serviceable icons of the antiwar movement." [41]

In *Big Story*, Peter Braestrup, who was bureau chief of the *Washington Post* in Saigon during the Tet Offensive, described how Associated Press correspondent Peter Arnett reported the attack on the U.S. Embassy on Tuesday night, January 30, 1968. [42] The fact was that all nineteen men who constituted the VC sapper team were killed and that they were never able to enter the embassy. Yet, based on conversations between U.S. Military Police personnel outside the wall surrounding the embassy, AP's Peter Arnett reported that the VC had been inside the embassy.

On January 31, 1968, at 2:09 A.M. New York time, AP broadcast the following news: "A Viet Cong suicide squad blasted its way into the U.S. Embassy compound. . . and fought for seven hours before being wiped out by American forces. . . . Some sources, including a U.S. captain, reported some of the communist invaders got into the first floor of the embassy building. But General William G. Westmoreland. . . said the building was not penetrated."

At 6 A.M. EST, Arnett cabled that the Viet Cong had failed to penetrate the building, but the next day, February 1, at 6:48 A.M., AP still refused to make the correction. "Reports conflicted," said AP, "as to whether the commandos got inside the embassy building. Bunker (the U.S. Ambassador) said the Viet Cong were never able to enter the building offices. A U.S. captain at the same time said some had penetrated the first floor. A major overruled him, saying they did not. Vietnamese police said they did."

"As a result," wrote Peter Braestrup, "in U.S. eastern morning newspapers, and in most of the country's other morning editions, the impression given by AP was that:1) the Viet Cong had seized the embassy itself; and: 2) Westmoreland was lying when he said they had not."

Breastrup explained the irresponsible reporting of the Tet Offensive as a "case of journalistic reaction to surprise" and that "newsmen were willing, even eager to believe the worst." It would be closer to the truth, in my opinion, to understand this type of reporting as an effort to substantiate the media's basic premise that the Viet Nam War—in fact any war aimed at stopping Communist aggression in Third World countries—could not be won. Every news story that could support that premise, whether verified or not, could be put to good use. The VC attack on the U.S. Embassy and its reported success in penetrating the building, which showed that the enemy could strike virtually everywhere in the country at will and that the United States was losing the war, were a welcome opportunity that had to be used at all cost, including sacrificing the accuracy or even distorting the truth for the benefit of sensationalism.

In fact, nothing was further from the truth than the affirmation that the Vietnamese population supported the VC. The failure of the VC during the Tet Offensive and the subsequent destruction of more than one-half of their war-making potential were due largely to the loyalty of the population toward the government. Popular uprisings in the cities and urban centers that the VC expected would support and bring to fruition their Tet Offensive simply did not materialize. In fact, at Hue, the VC summarily executed about 4,000 people whom they accused of opposing the "revolution." The loyalty of the urban residents toward the government and their non-cooperation with the VC were the most important factors causing the disaster for the latter. Yet, according to the *Washington Post*, if the VC were able to enter Saigon, this was because they had the support of the population and even the support of some sympathetic elements in the ARVN. To my knowledge, there was not a single ARVN unit defecting to the enemy during the Tet Offensive. Also according to *Newsweek*, the VC could not have attacked Saigon and other cities without at least the passive support of the population. According to this line of reasoning, a good portion of the population in the South during the American Civil War must have been sympathetic to General Sherman's army.

The basic truth that the urban population did not support the VC was disregarded because it contradicted the basic premise mentioned earlier. This is another case of "advocacy journalism" where a fact that contradicts the reporter's belief is disregarded.

The battle for the recapture of the Citadel of Hue was another interesting case of "advocacy journalism." American television reported only the fighting of the U.S. Marines to retake the Citadel. Yet, ARVN had eleven infantry battalions participating in the battle (versus three U.S. battalions) and suffered 384 killed among the 500 KIA suffered by all Allied Forces in Hue. According to Peter Braestrup, the following statement was made by Mr. Dean Rusk, the Secretary of State, to a New Jersey delegation on February 10, 1968: "With very few exceptions, South Viet Nam troops fought with courage and persistence. Their records in the last twelve days should lay to rest once and for all the myth that the South Viet Nam troops won't fight." This statement was not mentioned by the U.S. correspondents when they reported on Mr. Rusk's speech. Braestrup also reported that when Ambassador Komer, in a press conference about the effects of the Tet Offensive on the pacification program, stated that only thirty-five out of fifty-one ARVN battalions had returned to the pacification areas, this statement was quickly reported by all correspondents, including the *New York Times* and the *Washington Post*.

In the case of the battle for the Hue Citadel, the fact that ARVN units did fight with "courage and persistence" contradicted one of the U.S. media's unwritten rules: When comparing U.S. forces with ARVN, praise the first and criticize the latter; it therefore had to be disregarded.

Theoretically, "revolutionary warfare" had to go through three distinct stages: a) guerrilla warfare in which the insurgency forces adopt their usual "hit-and-run" tactics; b) conventional warfare in which the enemy stays and fights; and c) popular uprising which results in the toppling of the government. The goal in the first phase is to inflict casualties on the enemy while avoiding contact. The objective in the second phase is to control the ground while fighting under conventional conditions. The ultimate objective of the revolutionary warfare is to topple the government by a combination of military pressure and popular uprising.

Before the Tet Offensive, the VC never reached the stage of conventional warfare. In 1968, they decided to skip the above phase (*"dot giai doan"* or literally "burn the stages"). The Tet Offensive turned out to be a military disaster for the VC. Unfortunately, the U.S. media's biased coverage of the Tet Offensive transformed it into a major VC psychological victory and made it a turning point in the Viet Nam War.

In all fairness to the U.S. media, I recognize that it was not alone in biased reporting on the Viet Nam War. French journalists were also biased, but for a different reason. The French, who had lost the Indochina War, would never admit that the Americans would succeed where they had failed. Jean Lacouture was openly sympathetic to the Viet Cong and North Viet Nam. The late Francois Sully and

Bernard Fall, who both became American citizens, were also very critical of American policy in Viet Nam. Bernard Fall in particular, strangely enough, considered the Viet Nam War as moral depravity. "Saint Augustine lived a debauched life before his conversion," he wrote with Marcus Raskin in the *Viet Nam Reader*. "If debauchery is a necessary prerequisite to redemption, then the situation in Viet Nam is ripe for the next step."[43]

It is significant to note that after the war, some "antiwar" journalists realized that they were wrong and had fallen prey to Communist propaganda. One of these men is Michael Novak, a nationally syndicated journalist. Under the headline "Tyranny in Viet Nam Brings a Protester to Recant," Novak wrote in the *San Jose Mercury News* on July 27, 1984:

> The North Vietnamese boast that from the first day they held their infiltrators into South Viet Nam under tight Marxist discipline. After the war, they had no scruples to murder or keep imprisoned the gullible South Vietnamese who joined the Front without being Marxist. . . .What hurts my conscience though is not the dire strategic threat to innocent people, but rather the painful sufferings of the Vietnamese, North and South. Marxism is a harsh matter. The Gulag has been extended beyond USSR to oppress an additional 58 million human beings. . . . It is late, very late, to say we were wrong. Never to say so would be unconscionable complicity.

Novak was right. For the people of South Viet Nam, these conscience-soothing recantations, although admirable, indeed came too late. By intention or ignorance, the U.S. media, by practicing one-sided journalism, acted as North Viet Nam's "most important guerrilla" during the Viet Nam War in the words of General Vo Nguyen Giap.

After the war, I have talked and written to many former U.S. advisors and Viet Nam War veterans. Most of them resented the U.S. media's biased reporting on the war. A U.S. colonel who served many years in an advisory capacity in various Mekong Delta provinces wrote in a letter to me: "I agree entirely that the U.S. media was distorted, negative and bears an undisputable responsibility for the loss of Viet Nam. Between the media performance and the immoral actions of the U.S. Congress in 1973, '74 and '75, I still feel great anger and shame."[44]

In 1998, I was invited to address the U.S. Viet Veterans in Houston, Texas, on Memorial Day. I told them that they fought well for a good cause and that one of the reasons we lost the war was the U.S. media's hostility and biased reporting. After my speech, many veterans came to tell me they agreed.

11

VIETNAMESE NATIONAL MILITARY ACADEMY

TOWARD THE END OF MAY 1968, after a brief ceremony when I transferred the command of the 9th Infantry Division to Col. Tran Ba Di, I bid farewell to my staff and province chiefs. Then, I boarded a helicopter for my trip back to Saigon. I asked the pilot to circle the city of Sa Dec, then follow at low altitude the Mekong River up to Vinh Long before heading north to Saigon: I wanted to see for the last time the land where I had spent three challenging and rewarding years and where many of my men had fought and died for a lofty goal not all of them fully understood. As our helicopter climbed to a cruising altitude, I saw Vinh Long gradually disappear behind the Mekong River, which looked like a tiny white ribbon down below. Overwhelmed with emotion and memories, I felt tears in my eyes.

Saigon still wore the scars of the Tet Offensive. Although some of the buildings that were damaged during the Viet Cong attack had been repaired, around Tan Son Nhut Airport piles of rubble and remains of buildings which had burned to the ground were still evident. Certain buildings wore the impact of machine-gun fire on the walls or had the roofs destroyed by mortar shells. Tanks positioned in strategic areas of the city gave the impression of a city under siege. Had I not known there was an enemy attack a few months earlier, the presence of these tanks in strategic areas of Saigon would have led me to believe that another coup d'etat was taking place in the Capital.

The day after I returned to Saigon, I telephoned Colonel Cam, President Thieu's chief of cabinet, to request an interview with the president before I reported to my new post; this was customary in the Vietnamese Army for general officers to report to the president (who was also commander in chief of the Armed Forces) when assuming a new position. Colonel Cam returned my call the next day and informed me that the president was "too busy" to receive me.

The next day, I paid a courtesy visit to Gen. Cao Van Vien, chairman of JGS. General Vien received me in his huge office on the second floor of the Headquarters building. I knew General Vien from when we were both students at the Faculty of Letters in Saigon. At the time he commanded the Presidential Guard Brigade. A self-made man, he was eager to achieve scholastic recognition and his goal was to obtain a *license en litterature*.

General Vien was a Diem loyalist but his career, strangely enough, took off after the fall of President Diem. Shortly before that, Vien was appointed commander of the Airborne Brigade, which was considered the main striking force of any coup against the regime. President Diem believed that, as the airborne commander, Vien would be in a position to ward off any coup attempt. However, the Airborne Brigade remained neutral to the end. Vien was briefly arrested but was allowed to retain his command by the plotting generals who were impressed with his military rectitude and his apolitical stance. He was subsequently made commander of III Corps, north of Saigon, then elevated to chairman of JGS by President Thieu who wanted an unobtrusive man at this post so he could bypass him and deal directly with the corps commanders.

In fact, General Vien, once a sergeant in the French Army, was a colorless officer with no political ambition. A yoga expert, Vien preferred the practice of this discipline over inspection trips in the field. To use a Vietnamese Army slang-phrase, this man liked to *che du* or to "cover himself with an umbrella," meaning that he was unwilling to take any responsibility. Whenever a corps commander asked him for advice, he typically referred him to the President. He was installed as chairman of JGS for nine years because of these very qualities.

General Vien was very jovial that day. He invited me to sit at the large coffee table beside his desk and asked about my age. "You are very young, Thi, and you have all the future before you," said

General Vien. He then complained about corps commanders who bypassed him to report to the Presidential Palace. "When birds have all the feathers," General Vien said bitterly, "they will take off. I guess you would do the same." During our conversation, General Vien disclosed that he had, on numerous occasions, offered his resignation to the president because he wanted to give his job to younger generals. I did not know if I should believe him, since many felt that Mrs.Vien had taken full advantage of her husband's position to make a fortune in illicit real estate dealings and that she was not likely to give up these profitable activities.

After a few days in Saigon where my wife and I took the kids to Chinese restaurants in Cho Lon and to downtown cinemas to enjoy the current cowboy films, I flew to Dalat to assume the new job of Superintendent of the Vietnamese National Military Academy. For many officers, military schools (except for a few lucrative training centers where one could make money by cheating on draftees' food allowances and by getting kickbacks from contractors) were the last places in the Vietnamese Army they wanted as an assigment. The service schools usually served as sinecures for unwanted officers; for province chiefs or district chiefs who had been relieved of their function because of corruption; for inept unit commanders who had suffered severe setbacks on the battlefields; for officers who had fallen into disgrace or were considered politically dangerous to the regime; and for officers who needed a place to vegetate before they retired.

For me, however, the Military Academy was the best alternative to the command of an Army Corps. Dalat was a beautiful place to live and I looked forward to enjoying this wonderful resort city with my family after three years of fighting in the Mekong Delta. Second, I would be able to put my personal imprimatur on the future leaders of the Armed Forces and of the country as well. Lastly, the Military Academy, at that time, was about to convert from a two-year to a four-year program; this included a heavy academic curriculum and I was excited to be in charge of the implementation of this crucial program.

Dalat had grown beyond recognition since my days as a cadet at the School of Inter-Arms. Modern villas had sprung up around Ho

Xuan Huong Lake located in the middle of the city. (Later, I was told that the most beautiful ones were owned by General Khiem, the Prime Minister, and by other high-ranking generals). The old Lang-Bian Palace Hotel overlooking Ho Xuan Huong had been converted into a modern two-story masonry hotel which often served as a convention center for important national and international meetings. A new golf course was built on the rolling hills west of Ho Xuan Huong Lake. Behind the golf course was the Catholic University of Dalat, built in 1957 under President Diem. It had approximately 1,500 students and offered courses in business administration, political sciences, education, and sciences.

Dalat, with its mild climate and academic environment, had also attracted military schools. The Psychological Warfare School was created in Dalat in 1964 to train "psywar" officers for the Armed Forces. The school offered a two-year curriculum which included the study of Marxism, political science, communications, and humanities. It emulated the Psywar School of the Republic of China in Taiwan, which provided advisory assistance to the Dalat Psywar School's staff and faculty. After their defeat at the hands of the Communists, the Republic of China decided to form the Psywar branch within its Armed Forces to handle the crucial task of political indoctrination of the troops. Not unlike the powerful political commissars in the People's Liberation Army who, as representatives of the Communist Party, were responsible for the political correctness of their units, the psywar officers in Taiwan's Armed Forces were members of the Kuomingtang and were responsible for moral actions within their units.[45]

The Command & General Staff School had also moved to Dalat under the Joint General Staff's plan to concentrate institutions of higher military learning to that resort city. I suspected, however, that the main reason was that the generals wanted to move the school away from Saigon because they had grown wary of its students who, in the past, had participated in numerous coups in the Capital.

Interestingly enough, the commandant of the Command & General Staff School was a naval officer, Adm. Chung Tan Cang. A protégé of Nguyen Khanh, Cang was exiled to the remote city of Dalat after

Khanh was deposed by General Ky. Although Cang had no background in army staff procedures and tactics, he was appointed commandant of a school which trained army officers destined for important staff functions and battalion and regiment command. When I paid a courtesy visit to Admiral Cang, I jokingly told him that there were too many naval officers in Dalat (the Psywar School was also commanded by another naval officer, Capt. Lam Nguon Tanh) and that their logical place should be in the sea and not on a mountain. We had a good laugh.

The Military Academy had undergone a complete transformation. The old barracks of the former School of Inter-Arms, to my chagrin, were in disrepair and were now occupied by the school service company. The new school complex was built in the late 1950s under President Diem. It occupied Hill 1515 located immediately northwest of the old complex. Under the original plan, four three-story student barracks, a student mess hall, and classrooms were built around an interior court where students marched in parade to their lunches during week days. A two-story office building for staff and faculty was built on an adjacent promontory. In the middle of the building was a rotunda structure used as a reception and display area. Later, I moved my office to the rotunda, which had a commanding view of the valley and pine forests. The reception and display area subsequently moved to the new academic building next to the library. In front of the office building was the Le Loi parade field where graduation ceremonies took place.

When I joined the Military Academy, it was in the middle of a new expansion plan with assistance from the United States to accommodate the new four-year curriculum. An American construction company, under a U.S. military assistance program, was putting the finishing touches on a "heavy" engineering laboratory, which included an underground firing range, a two-story classroom building, a two-story library and a cafeteria. The new buildings were concrete. Soon, the laboratory received modern civil, electrical, and mechanical engineering equipment, most of it coming directly from the U.S. Military Academy at West Point. Included among the new equipment was a wind tunnel, which was the first of its kind in an engineering school in Viet Nam. The library also received thousands of books in all disciplines from the United States. Fortunately, the US military assistance program also provided for an American librarian to train my staff on library procedures and management.

It should be noted that President Diem, in the late 1950s, had already seen the benefits of a four-year program and had decreed that the cadets at the Military Academy spend four years at the school. However, increased Viet Cong activities compelled the government to reduce the program to three, then to two years. Now, under pressure from the Pentagon to upgrade the quality of the Vietnamese Officer Corps, which was viewed as necessary for the successful prosecution of the war against the VC, the Vietnamese government agreed to the new four-year program, despite the fact that there was an urgent need for new career officers.

To help with the implementation of the new program, a six-man U.S. advisory team had been assigned to the academy. The team was headed by Colonel Wyrough, a West Point graduate and a former aide to Gen. Creighton Abrams, deputy commander of U.S. Forces in Viet Nam. The team also included one army officer with a doctorate in civil engineering and an air force officer with a doctorate in social sciences. This advisory team gave invaluable help to my staff and faculty with regard to the preparation of the four-year curriculum and the installation of heavy equipment in the new science laboratory.

According to the new curriculum, the cadets' schedule was divided into two parts: the academic season and the military season. The academic season started in January and lasted through September and was succeeded by the military season, which took place during the winter. During the military season, the cadets learned the techniques of warfare: weapons, survey, communication, tactics, arms, and services. The cadets spent most of their military season in the field. The senior class trained at the Ranger School at Duc My and visited various army training centers during their military season.

At graduation, cadets selected their units according to their ranking. Traditionally, cadets graduating in the top of their classes chose to serve in the Airborne and Marine Divisions. About ten to twenty percent of the graduating class was allocated to the Air Force and Navy.

Many valedictorians who selected to serve in combat units died shortly after their graduation. In 1971, for example, 2d. Lt. Nguyen Duc Phong, Class 22B (Class 22 was split into Class 22A which graduated after two years; and Class 22B, which was the first class to follow the four-year program), was killed by a recoilless rifle shell just a few months after graduation, when he charged on enemy positions at the head of his armored unit during the Cambodia invasion. Phong was selected to attend graduate schools in the United States in order to become a teacher at the academy. He declined the offer and chose instead to serve in a combat unit. It was a tragic loss for his family and also for the army as Phong was an exceptionally gifted student and was destined for a brilliant career. He had a very modest background. His father worked as a laborer in the French Lycée Yersin and put all his hopes on him. I was shocked to receive the news of his death. Sometimes, I had to believe that exceptional men often die young.

Although I was an ardent supporter of the four-year program, there were enormous problems which needed to be resolved. The most important was the lack of qualified academic instructors. To reinforce the academic faculty, JGS assigned 100 reserve officers who were college and high school professors before being drafted into the Army. However, most of these teachers were formerly trained under the French system and were not familiar with American methods of education, including the system of credit, that the Vietnamese Military Academy had adopted. Therefore, to upgrade the school faculty, I recommended to JGS to send career officers, including graduates of the four-year program, to graduate schools in the United States.

Another pressing problem was the granting of degrees to the graduating cadets. Although Gen. Tran Thien Khiem, the prime minister, was in favor of granting a degree to graduates of the four-year program, he met strong opposition from presidents of civilian universities. To help win them over, he suggested that the presidents of the Universities of Saigon, Hue, Can Tho, and Dalat and the Director of the Phu Tho Engineering School be invited to the Military Academy to make a personal assessment of the four-year program.

I knew I would have a hard time selling the Military Academy since, apart from Dr. Le thanh Minh Chau, president of the University of Hue and holder of a doctorate in English from an American university, the other presidents were trained under the French system. It was common knowledge that there was a strong rivalry, even open hostility, between professors educated under the French system and the relatively few American-trained educators. I was further aware that civilian professors were hostile to the idea of a competing degree-granting military institution.

Moreover, I was informed that normally any accreditation committee would look at the following factors: student selection, curriculum, faculty quality, and facilities. I had a good corps of cadets who, in addition to the *tu-tai 2* in math or science, had to pass a competitive examination before being admitted to the school. I also had the best engineering lab and the most modern library in the country. The curriculum was also considered adequate for a degree in general engineering. The credit system that we adopted was somewhat revolutionary in Viet Nam since civilian universities still maintained the old system of a one-time final examination at the end of the school year. I was convinced, however, that this new system was more realistic and flexible than the French system and that it could be sold to the accreditation committee. The lack of an adequate number of instructors with a doctoral degree could be a problem. However, we had addressed this by sending qualified instructors to graduate schools in the United States and Australia and also by hiring qualified part-time visiting lecturers from the University of Dalat.

It felt odd preparing for the accreditation committee's visit. Only a few months earlier, I had fought against the Communist insurgency in the Mekong Delta; and now, I was actively involved in another war that my military training and background had not prepared me for: the war for academic recognition for a new crop of cadets destined for leadership role in the army and in the government.

True to expectations, the delegation was impressed with the military academy. After a short briefing in my office where we presented our curriculum and the general description of our facilities, we took the delegation to the heavy laboratory. The visitors could not believe their eyes when they saw our cadets busily experimenting with modern engineering training equipment. The director of the engineering school at Phu Tho, Saigon, the top engineering school of the country, swallowing his pride, requested permission to annually send his students to the military academy to practice at our lab. I jokingly replied that I would welcome his students in exchange for the granting of an engineering degree to my cadets.

After the visit to the lab, the delegation visited the academic building. They were surprised to see that our classes consisted of no more than twenty cadets, contrary to the large size (one hundred or more) in the classes at their own institutions. Specifically, in the math classes, the visitors were favorably impressed to see that all the students were busy solving calculus problems on the long blackboard running the length of the classroom.

I reserved the last visit for the library where the librarian and his American advisor made a presentation on the operation of the library, including the new book indexing method. The only problem with our new library was that it did not have any books in Vietnamese. I assured the delegation that I would take immediate steps to acquire Vietnamese books which were deemed relevant to the academy's curriculum.

Over lunch, the delegation expressed their general good impression of the way we ran the academy. The selected luncheon menu added to the good feelings of everyone. Dr. Le Thanh Minh Chau was particularly complimentary of the academy. He stated that the academy education system was the way of the future and that he was very happy that the military academy had pioneered this new system. However, it took two more years before the government decided to award the degree of *Cu Nhan Khoa Hoc Ung Dung* (Bachelor Degree in Applied Sciences) to our graduates.

To improve the quality of the academic staff, I made two crucial appointments. Lt. Col. Dao Mong Xuan, chief of staff of Tuyen Duc Sector (Dalat and surrounding districts) was transferred to the academy as the new chief of staff. I met Xuan in Hung Yen Sector, North Viet Nam, in 1953. A graduate of the School of Inter-Arms, Xuan had distinguished himself as an infantry company commander. I also appointed Col. Nguyen Van Su, an instructor at the Command

& Staff College, as the new Commandant of cadets. Colonel Su, who had served in the 1st Artillery Battalion during the Hauts Plateaux campaign in 1954, was an able, hard-working officer and very strict with discipline. In my judgment, he was the best choice for this important position.

While I was busy dealing with issues at the academy, my wife and children enjoyed our more relaxed lifestyle in Dalat. Our residence was a spacious two-story French villa located on a small hill overlooking the green plain of Da Thien to the north, covered with endless cabbage and artichoke fields. The villa had a large courtyard planted with tall pine trees and a cherry tree which blossomed in the spring. Tuan, our oldest son, enrolled at the all-boy *Tran Hung Dao* High School, while our daughter Ngoc attended a private school for girls near our residence. Dung, our youngest son, attended the French *Petit Lycée Yersin*, the parent elementary school of the *Grand Lycée Yersin*. He became a member of the Boy Scout Club of Dalat and often went camping in the rolling hills around Ho Xuan Huong Lake on weekends.

One of my first visitors at the academy was Mr. Zimmerman, the *Proviseur* of the French Lycee Yersin. Mr. Zimmerman had fought in the French Resistance during World War II and had lost his left arm. He invited me and my wife to have lunch with him.

Another guest at the luncheon was the Vietnamese Archbishop of Dalat. As always, a French *repas* lasted forever. After a good *aperitif*, we recounted war stories. Even the archbishop, with the help of a glass of French *Pernod*, recounted his actions during World War II along with the European campaigns he had participated in as a Catholic chaplain in the French Army. Our conversation became more animated with the good *vin rouge de Bordeaux* which accompanied a voluminous Dalat steak and an excellent *Camembert*.

In the fall of 1968, the Academy prepared to admit the freshman class, Class 25. We organized written entrance examinations at major cities: Saigon, Danang, Nha Trang and Can Tho. The turnout was impressive. For the 400 slots for the freshmen class, there were about 4,000 applicants. This high turnout was due to the fact that many young men—quite a few of them university students—had witnessed the VC terror tactics in urban centers during the Tet

Offensive and decided to serve in the Army to fight against the Communists. Further, for these young men who chose to serve in the armed forces, the degree-granting military academy was the best option for a successful military career.

An incident we experienced during our second weekend in Dalat made me aware of a crucial problem at the military academy. As my family rode on the east shore of Ho Xuan Huong Lake in our unmarked sedan, an army jeep cut in front of us and pulled over to the curbside. The driver, a young army lieutenant, signaled for us to stop behind his car. Angrily, I jumped out of my sedan, went to the young officer and, grabbing his collar, I pulled him out of his jeep and dragged him to the military police car which followed my sedan. I instructed my aide-de-camp to escort the infringing officer to Dalat Sector Headquarters and to put him in military confinement for fifteen days for disorderly conduct in public.

Later, I was informed that the young officer involved in the incident was an officer of a Ranger battalion in MRII. He was on leave in Dalat to attend his father's funeral. Frustrated to see civilians driving around in beautiful cars with complete indifference to the lot of soldiers like himself who daily risked their lives to protect them, he decided, on the spur of the moment, to stop a car at random and to lecture its occupants on their responsibilities toward the army. It was unfortunate for the officer that the car he stopped happened to be the sedan of the new superintendent of the Military Academy.

It was more disturbing to me that that young officer was a graduate of the academy; the incident revealed an urgent need to refocus on leadership training at the school. At the Command & General Staff College at Fort Leavenworth, Kansas, I had learned the American concept of military leadership. But since graduates of the Vietnamese Military Academy had been called upon to assume high positions in the government (the president, the prime minister and many province and district chiefs were former cadets), I decided to do research on the subject of leadership and to come up with a concept suitable not only for the army, but also for the leaders of a developing country, which had little or no tradition of democracy and which, at the same time, had to fight a war against Communist insurgency.

I learned that there were two theories of leadership: the old theory of the leader as a symbol and the more modern theory of the leader as a result of interactions between different interest groups within a particular social setting.

According to the symbol viewpoint, the leader is an extraordinary person endowed with certain abstract qualities. A person is a leader because he or she is intelligent, courageous, and knowledgeable. Under this theory, the leader identifies with the Freudian concept of "super-ego" or father-image, symbolizing moral authority. In retrospect, the symbolic leader also identifies, in certain aspects, with the Asian concept of the moral leader, particularly with the Confucian leader, although the latter has to go through stringent phases of self-development in order to ultimately achieve "peace under heaven."

Modern psychological theories of leadership, on the contrary, maintain that the leader must be placed in his own functional context and that one cannot consider a leader without the social environment within which he must act. In essence, these theories hold that the leader and those he leads must be bound together and united by common aspirations and ideals. The leader is not someone who is intelligent, courageous, and knowledgeable, but rather because his intelligence, his courage, and his knowledge can be used to satisfy the needs and aspirations of a specific social environment.

The view of the leader as a symbol usually results in damaging consequences. This occurs because, separated from the environment, the leader no longer knows the needs and hopes of the people he leads. Indeed, he often opposes those very needs and hopes. This leads to dictatorship. On the other hand, if one holds that the leader is a person chosen to satisfy the needs of a group of people and that the leader is merely a result of passive interactions among the motive forces of a given social environment, then the other calamity might result: demagoguery. In order to achieve enlightened leadership, in my opinion, both the foregoing extremes must be avoided.

The enlightened leader springs from a particular environment and continues to have frequent contact with that environment in order to satisfy its legitimate ideals and hopes. At the same time, he must be resolved to lead the group to achieve loftier, more distant goals than the frequently limited ones held by the group. The enlightened leader, especially a leader of a developing country, must be a person who can maintain an intimate and understanding link with his or her environment and also one who can lead and maintain discipline in that environment while progressing toward greater goals.

In short, I believed that culture and democracy are the destiny of developing nations in Asia. "The enlightened leader is not a dictator, nor yet a demagogue," I wrote in an article at that time, "but, rather, a person who can both embody the profound ideals and hopes of a social group and have the ability to rise above the environment to lead the way into history."[46] Of course, one cannot expect a young lieutenant to "lead the way into history," but he can be expected to "maintain an intimate and understanding link" with his environment. To do otherwise would be to play into the hands of the Communists, who stressed that the guerrillas live within the people like "a fish within the water."

After I developed and published my concept of leadership, I made it a point to teach it to my cadets. Although my concept was not officially approved by the Training Directorate of the Joint General Staff, it was generally accepted by most military schools. I was a frequent lecturer on the subject of leadership at the VN Command & General Staff School and the Air Force Academy. Occasionally, I was invited to speak at the University of Dalat on the topic of Leadership and Management for its School of Business.

In addition to academic excellence, I endeavored to develop physical skills and self-confidence for the future leaders of the army. To accomplish this, I encouraged the cadets to obtain a black belt in either taekwondo or in judo, before graduation. One benefit that many people do not expect from martial arts, is that it not only equips practitioners with physical skills, but also instills important moral principles such as self-confidence and self-discipline. Taekwondo practitioners are further required to uphold certain moral rules. Among these is the pledge to defend the country, and to defend the weak against aggressors.

To implement my black belt program, I requested and received approval from Gen. Chae mung Shin, the commander of South Korean Forces in Viet Nam, to transfer Captain Kim young Ho, my former taekwondo instructor at the 9th Infantry Division, to the Vietnamese Military Academy. To keep myself in good shape and also to set an example, I practiced with Captain Kim every day.

In the spring of 1969, I passed my exam for the second degree black belt. General Chae came to Dalat to preside over my demonstration. We had lunch at the Hotel Palace with representatives of the Korean community in Dalat.

Around December 1968, Gen. Do Cao Tri, commanding general of III Corps headquartered in Bien Hoa, north of Saigon, invited me for dinner at the Hotel Palace when he came to spend a weekend in Dalat. The last time I had had dinner with General Tri was when my wife and I were vacationing in Kyoto, Japan. This time, however, there was a change in our relationship as Tri's current wife, the daughter of the late governor of North Viet Nam, Mr. Nguyen Huu Tri, was a cousin of my wife.

During dinner, General Tri offered me the command of the 5th Infantry Division, also headquartered in Bien Hoa. The previous month, President Nixon had won the presidency and promised to accelerate his "Vietnamization" program and to gradually withdraw U.S. troops from Viet Nam. As ARVN was expected to assume more responsibilities in the conduct of the war, General Tri said he needed experienced division commanders. I politely declined the offer because I was committed to bring to fruition the expansion program of the military academy. Besides, Tho, my older brother, was commanding the III Corps' 18th Infantry Division and my assuming the command of the 5th Division could be interpreted by a hostile press as a manifestation of a oligarchic system in the army.

In May 1969, I was invited to visit Thailand's service academies. This was to be the first of a series of visits to service academies of allied South East Asian countries. Colonel Wyrough was to accompany me during the trip. I invited my wife and my daughter to join me in Bangkok. Our daughter Ngoc was very excited about the trip because this was her first voyage abroad. My wife and daughter traveled by Air Viet Nam, while Colonel Wyrough and I boarded a U.S. Air Force plane for a direct flight to Bangkok. Mrs.Wyrough, who lived at the U.S. Clark Field Air Force Base in the Philippines with her children, also joined us at Bangkok.

An old classmate at Dalat, Nhan Minh Trang, now a Congressman, cabled a friend of his in Bangkok, Mr. Danu, asking him to take care of us during our sojourn in Thailand. In 1964, Mr. Danu, a half-brother of Prince Sihanouk and his Finance Minister, defected to Viet Nam following a discord with his half-brother. At that time, Trang was the Chief of Cabinet of General Nguyen Khanh, the new strongman of South Viet Nam. Trang flew to Kien Giang to meet Mr. Danu and made arrangements for him to escape to Thailand, where he amassed a huge fortune through real estate ventures.

We were met at Bangkok International Airport by a Thai army colonel, a friend of Mr. Danu. Later, we discovered that the colonel was the son of the then-Thai Prime Minister. The colonel informed me that Mr. Danu would like to invite me and my family to stay at the Rama Hotel, one of the most luxurious hotels in Bangkok, but we politely declined. Instead, we registered at a modest hotel in the commercial district. As my wife, my daughter, and I were unpacking our baggage, the Thai colonel came back and insisted that we move to the Rama Hotel. Reluctantly, we re-packed and followed the colonel to the Rama Hotel. We were stunned when the colonel led us to a huge presidential suite. The suite consisted of two bedrooms, a dining room and a living area, all nicely decorated. Our daughter, Ngoc, was intimidated by the suite's impressive setting and was afraid to sleep alone in a huge bedroom. I asked the colonel to give us a smaller unit, but he answered that it was Mr. Danu's wishes and he did not have authority to make any change.

That night, we had dinner at the luxurious hotel restaurant near the indoor swimming pool. The chef at the restaurant was a Frenchman. We ordered soup and steak and a French bottle of red wine and enjoyed the good food and relaxed atmosphere of a country which had endured no war in its entire history. As we were ready to leave, I asked the restaurant attendant to give me the bill. When he discovered that we occupied the presidential suite, the attendant told us that we did not have to pay anything and that any expenses we incurred during our stay at the hotel would be taken care of by Mr. Danu. Later, I learned that Mr. Danu was the owner of the Rama Hotel.

The next day, I visited the Thai Chulachomklao Royal Military Academy in Bangkok. The Thai Military Academy also offered a four-year curriculum and, like its counterpart in the Philippines and South Korea, but to a lesser degree, was organized on the U.S. model of West Point. After a tour of the facilities and visits to classrooms, the general, the superintendent of the Academy, invited Colonel Wyrough and me to lunch.

The morning of the third day, I visited the Thai Air Force and Naval Academies also located in Bangkok. All the visits took place in the morning because the superintendents of these academies usually spent their afternoons on the golf courses. All Thai service academies offered a four-year program and a bachelor's degree to graduating cadets. Because of the small size of the Thai Armed Forces, in my opinion, the merging of the three service academies into a single inter-arms institution would be a more economic alternative. This would not take into consideration, however, of the traditional rivalry between the arms and services within Thai Armed Forces.

That night, the Danus invited us to dinner in a European restaurant. Mr. Danu suggested that we stay over the next day, a Sunday, so he could take us to the beach south of Bangkok. I told him we had already booked for the return trip to Saigon for the next day. I could not believe my ears when Mr. Danu replied that he would charter an Air Viet Nam plane to Saigon on Monday, if we decided to go to the beach on Sunday. Again, we declined. It was ironic that the most lasting impression of my trip to visit Thai service academies were not from the academies themselves but from the royal treatment we received from a Cambodian refugee who had become highly successful in a new land.

I had always believed that an army officer should be a qualified parachutist. Thus, after I returned from Thailand, I recommended to JGS to include two-week parachute training in the four-year curriculum for the senior class at the Airborne Division Training Center in Saigon. Gen. Cao Van Vien, chairman of JGS, the former airborne commander and an expert skydiver, readily approved. A medical team from the Airborne Division, headed by Lt. Col. Hoang Co Lan, came to Dalat to give physical examinations to the cadets of Class 23 to qualify them for parachute training. I requested that

Dr.Lan bring along a jumpmaster and one parachute, for I decided to make a demonstration jump to boost the morale of the cadets and to initiate the parachute training program.

However, because the wind speed had unexpectedly risen to approximately twenty knots (one knot equals 6,080 feet per hour) and that it would be too dangerous to jump under these conditions, Dr. Lan, who was an experienced parachutist, suggested that I cancel my jump. Col. Ngo Le Tue, my deputy, suggested that I reschedule. But, a cancellation would be damaging to the new parachute training program and an irreparable loss of face for the new superintendent.

As we circled the campus, Aspirant Thuan, the jumpmaster, released small paper flags to test the wind. The winds were so strong that the flags were lost. Thuan suggested that we return to Cam Ly airfield. I asked him whether I had any chance to land anywhere within the academy. Thuan replied that, if I kept pulling the main parachute rope toward me with enough strength, I had a fifty percent chance of landing within the academy. He warned that the landing would be very rough and that I might be injured. "Sir, I await your decision," concluded Thuan. "Let's go!" I replied as calmly as possible. Thuan signaled me to take position at the door and hooked up my parachute cord to the static line of the aircraft.

We made a final circle, past the Farraut Farm; as we approached Doi Bac Hill, just north of the academy, I felt a light pad on my shoulder followed by the shout "Go!" I threw myself outside and immediately felt the shock of the T-10 parachute opening above me. I saw the academy come toward me at high speed. Remembering Aspirant Thuan's instructions, I pulled one of the two parachute cords toward me with all my strength to amortize the wind, and before I knew it, I felt a shock in my back. I had landed against the back wall of the parade stand with my parachute dangling from its roof. A cadet rushed forward to help release my parachute. I walked away unscathed.

In October, Colonel Wyrough and I were invited to visit the Philippines Military Academy. We flew by helicopter from Dalat to Cam Ranh Bay where we boarded a U.S. Air Force plane which took us directly to Clark Field. The U.S. ambassador in the Philippines, who was en route to Baguio for a golf tour, graciously offered us two seats on his personal plane. Baguio, a beautiful mountain resort station where the Philippines Military Academy was located, had served as General MacArthur's general headquarters during World War II. Baguio was located approximately one hundred miles north of Manila. We were joined at Baguio by Col. Nguyen Huu Boi, the Vietnamese military attaché in Manila. He drove from Manila to pick us up for our return trip.

Brigadier General Garcia, the superintendent of the Academy, received us in his office and then took us to view the classrooms and student barracks. At noon, we watched the cadets marching to lunch in parade uniform, which was a replica of the uniform of West Point cadets. The Philippines Military Academy seemed like West Point in miniature; its four-year curriculum was almost a carbon copy of West Point's. Before we departed, General Garcia suggested that we go to his office to change into civilian clothes for our trip back to Manila because, according to General Garcia, there were recent activities along the road by the Huk Communist guerrillas. Colonel Boi and I brought Colonel Wyrough to Clark Field and continued to Manila where I spent the night.

The next day, Colonel Boi drove me to Clark Field for my trip back to Viet Nam. This time, we landed at Saigon's Tan Son Nhut International Airport. I was surprised when Vietnamese custom officers would not let me leave because I had exited illegally when I left Viet Nam through Cam Ranh Bay, a U.S. military base that did not have a Vietnamese custom office. Finally, after some clarification, I was released to join my family who were waiting for me.

In November 1969, I made another trip to the military academies in Taiwan, South Korea and Japan. Again, Colonel Wyrough accompanied me. Before my departure, Gen. Chae mung Shin, the commander of ROK's forces in Viet Nam, invited my wife and I to have lunch with him at his residence in Saigon.

It was always a pleasure to meet with General Chae. During the luncheon, we reminisced about our student days at Fort Leavenworth, Kansas. General Chae, whose country was at one time a Japanese colony, had shared my feelings and sympathized when I stood and spoke against the French liaison officer who painted a gloomy, distorted picture of the Indochina War at the U.S. Command & General Staff College in 1963. Since that day, General Chae and I had become good friends. But, I was startled when, after lunch, General Chae presented me with two new pieces of Samsonite luggage. General Chae also told me that he would send Capt. Kim young Ho, my taekwondo instructor, to Seoul to meet me when I arrived. Captain Kim would serve as my aide and tour guide during my stay in South Korea.

The first leg of my trip was to Taiwan. We were met at the airport by Colonel Nu, the Vietnamese military attaché in Taipei. In the afternoon, Colonel Nu met me at my hotel and we drove around Taipei. This was my first visit to the Republic of China and I was impressed with its economic achievements. Taipei was a prosperous city with high-rise buildings in the central business district and large apartment buildings with green open spaces in outer areas. The second day of our stay, we visited the Military Academy at Taipei and attended a luncheon with the chairman of Taiwan's Joint Chiefs of Staff. The Chinese have a tradition of offering many toasts to their guests and each time, we had to empty our glass in one breath.

The following day, we flew to Kaohsiung, located at the southern tip of the island, and one of Asia's major container ports, to visit the Naval Academy.We flew back to Taipei the next day with the chairman of Joint Chief of Staff who came to Kaohsiung to participate in a military exercise. A lasting impression I retained from my visits to Taiwan military academies was the stress placed on academic excellence and the political and moral indoctrination of their cadets. Their faculty, in fact, had an impressive number of teachers with doctoral degrees, many of whom were graduates of U. S. universities.

The warmest welcome I received was in South Korea. I was a recipient of the Korean Chung Mu decoration and was the sole Vietnamese general with a black belt in taekwondo. Captain Kim and the Vietnamese military attaché in Seoul met Colonel Wyrough and me at Kimpo Airport and we drove to the Seijong Hotel in downtown Seoul. Seoul had grown beyond recognition. It was very different from the city I had visited in 1958, which had still borne the signs of the last war's ravages. High-rise office buildings, luxury hotels and restaurants had sprung up in the commercial district. Everywhere, one could feel an atmosphere of confidence and optimism in a country which had finally risen from the ashes of a bloody civil war.

The Koreans, in my opinion, are among the most hospitable people in the world. However, they sometimes, unknowingly, embarrass their guests in their efforts to please them; they had placed a Vietnamese flag and a two-star flag in front of my hotel room. I also noticed a security guard in civilian clothes discreetly posted at the stairway. The next morning, as I went down the stairway for breakfast, I was startled to see a throng of reporters in the lobby, cameras at the ready. They asked me the purpose of my visit, my first impression of Korea, and about the performance of Korean troops in Viet Nam. I remarked that I had many Korean friends, that I was very impressed with the progress of post-war reconstruction of Seoul, and that the Korean troops had been most effective in their support of our pacification program. In conclusion, I thanked the Korean people for helping our country in the war against Communist aggression.

The official schedule, to Colonel Wyrough's frustration, called for us to visit the headquarters of the Korean Taekwondo Association before the Korean Military Academy. Different countries have their own priorities. For South Korea, taekwondo, obviously, had priority over other activities. Gen. Choi hong He, President of the association, received us at the new taekwondo building. I was taken aback when, after brief welcoming remarks, General Choi signaled his aide to bring one wood board, possibly two inches thick; he then announced to the audience that I was going to break that board. Although I would have preferred otherwise, I had to oblige.

I took my jacket off, stood parallel to the board and in view of the cameras, swung my right hand and hit the board at its middle, the most vulnerable spot. I felt the impact and my hand hurt as if it had hit a rock. I tried another swing. The board was still intact. I decided to take a last chance. If I still failed, so be it! After all, I hadn't come to Korea to break a board. This time, I decided to give a greater twist to my swing. Taekwondo, in fact, is a very scientific form of martial art. It is based on the physical principle that, given the same mass, the force generated varies in direct proportion to acceleration. Of course, a greater twist to your arm has the effect of increasing the acceleration. So, I pulled back my right hand toward my left shoulder, twisted it and, with a large swing, I hit the middle of the board with all my strength. I remember the eerie feeling of my hand sailing smoothly through the broken fibers of the board and almost hitting the two Korean blackbelters holding it. Applause rose from the audience amid the flashes of cameras. I felt relieved as did Colonel Wyrough and the Vietnamese military attaché. General Choi congratulated me and presented me with a certificate for an honorary third degree black belt. Later, the Korean driver, a former soldier who had served in Viet Nam, took my hands with his two hands and effusively offered his congratulations.

Like the Philippines Military Academy, the South Korean Military Academy was a replica of West Point with similar cadet uniforms and a four-year curriculum. However, because the country was under the ever-present threat of invasion from North Korea, cadets were well motivated and disciplined. Martial arts, especially taekwondo, for obvious reasons, occupied an important place in the physical education curriculum.

The next day, Colonel Wyrough and I flew to the Demilitarized Zone (DMZ), stopping first at the headquarters of the U.S. Army Corps that controlled the two U.S. infantry divisions manning the DMZ. The Corps Commander was Lieutenant General Yarborough, the former commandant of the Special Warfare School at Fort Bragg, North Carolina, where I had been a student in 1964. He was glad to see me again. After a brief presentation at his headquarters, General Yarborough offered to take Colonel Wyrough and me in his helicopter to the "international village."

Panmunjung, headquarters of the International Armistice Commission, was located in the DMZ; it consisted of a group of tents occupied alternately by the representatives of the Allied Forces and by the members of the North Korean and Chinese delegations. Since there were cases of foreign visitors being kidnapped by North Koreans and dragged into their tents at this international village, I was constantly surrounded by the U.S. Military Police.

The last leg of our trip was to Tokyo. The military academy we visited the next day, officially named the "Self Defense Forces" Academy, was located just outside of Tokyo. Unlike other Asian military academies I had visited, the Japanese Self Defense Academy offered a five-year curriculum with an emphasis on academic achievement. The U.S.-imposed Constitution after the war had restricted the Japanese military to merely a self-defense role. This, visibly, had an impact on the Academy which appeared to place more emphasis on academic achievement than military skills.

I returned to Dalat in time to prepare for the graduation of Class 22-B, the first class to graduate under the new four-year program. The commencement exercise at the Military Academy was the event of the year for the city of Dalat. For one day in December, *Le Tout Saigon* was present. The president of the Republic, the vice president, the prime minister and his cabinet, the diplomatic corps, military attaches, U.S.and Vietnamese generals, local dignitaries, and, of course, the press, descended on Dalat. For the academy, however, it was a nightmare. We had to marshal all the transportation available in Dalat to shuttle dignitaries from the small Cam Ly airport to the academy. The protocol involved along with security issues was a headache for the academy staff.

In his address, President Thieu expressed his pleasure at presiding over the graduation of the first four-year class; he urged the cadres to use their military skills and technical knowledge to serve the country and the people. Then he officially declared that the graduating class would be named after Brig. Gen. Truong Quang An, the late commander of the 23rd Infantry Division in Ban Me Thuot killed early that year along with his wife in a helicopter crash during a visit to the division units on the Vietnamese New Year.

After President Thieu's address, the valedictorian of the graduating class ordered his fellow cadets to fall on their knees with the command: "Kneel down, Gentlemen!" I invited President Thieu to give the new epaulettes of second lieutenant to the valedictorian while academy instructors did the same for other cadets. After the officers returned to their seats, Phong, the valedictorian, stood up and shouted: "Stand up, Officers!"

Then, following a long-established tradition, the valedictorian took a bow and shot an arrow in each of the four cardinal directions to signify that the new officers were ready to go out and to serve their country. The graduation ceremony terminated with a taekwondo demonstration and the enactment of the historic battle of Dong Da, near Hanoi, where Nguyen Hue, one of Viet Nam's most celebrated heroes, soundly defeated the Chinese on the fifth day of the lunar calendar Year of Binh Ty in 1879.

At the conclusion of the graduation exercise, I invited President Thieu and other dignitaries for refreshments at the cafeteria in the new academic building. President Thieu took this opportunity to discuss the progress of the pacification program with Ambassador Bunker and the commanders of the four Military Regions. Around noon, the guests departed and I was relieved and happy that everything had worked according to plan. I was also very proud to have had a part in this innovative program.

In January 1970, Colonel Wyrough left the Academy to assume command of a U.S. independent infantry brigade on the coastal area of Phan Thiet, 150 miles south of Dalat. It was a much sought-after command by colonels itching for promotion to brigadier general.

About two months later, Colonel Wyrough invited me to visit his brigade. Only the previous month, a Viet Cong sapper unit had infiltrated the base, killed some soldiers and caused damage to helicopters. It was a serious setback for the new commander and he needed a victory to put his career back on track. This was the reason he wanted me to come to Phan Thiet: to assess the tactical situation and advise him on how to achieve that needed victory.

Colonel Wyrough's brigade consisted of three infantry battalions, one artillery battalion, and one armored unit. A detachment of helicopters was also attached to the brigade. Two infantry battalions occupied various Fire Support Bases (FSB) west of RN1, which linked Saigon to the coastal areas of Central Viet Nam. One battalion was held in reserve at the rear base. After a tactical briefing at his headquarters, Colonel Wyrough took me to his FSBs to inspect their defensive systems. Before returning to the headquarters, we flew over the brigade's area of responsibility to survey the terrain.

A few miles south of the brigade's rear base was the old Communist secret base of Le Hong Phong, named after a Viet Minh hero of the Indochina War. Like many other secret bases, including the famous "Iron Triangle" west of Saigon, near the Cambodian border, Le Hong Phong base had been completely leveled by American engineer units using huge bulldozers to fell trees and bushes and clear the area. The area immediately west of RN1 consisted of bare rolling hills which were excellent terrain for the deployment of armored units. Further west there were moderate to high mountains covered with dense vegetation which constituted ideal hiding places for enemy regular units.

In my opinion, the best terrain to engage the enemy was the flat area near the population centers along RN1 and the open area immediately west of it. I suggested to Colonel Wyrough to organize a striking force consisting of an infantry unit reinforced by armored elements. The infantry element of the striking force should be able to be helilifted at a moment's notice to any point within the brigade's area of responsibility. The armored unit should be able to link up with the heliborne elements within a short period of time. Whenever a RF or PF outpost of the Phan Thiet province located along RN1 was attacked, Colonel Wyrough should consider the possibility of helilifting the striking force west of RN1 to block an enemy retreat and to attack it from behind. I advised Colonel Wyrough to use the "Eagle Flight" tactic of helilifting small reconnaissance units on known enemy supply routes; once contact had been established he should engage the striking force to destroy the enemy. In other words, tactical successes could only be achieved by massing the force and the firepower at the proper point and at the proper time.

I didn't know if Colonel Wyrough followed my advice or not. To my knowledge, he did not achieve any noticeable successes during his command. At the end of his tour of duty in Viet Nam, he was transferred to a staff job at the Pentagon.

Although I was immersed in the new expansion program of the Vietnamese Military Academy, I reserved a portion of my time to increase the defense of the academy, which, in my view, was vulnerable to a Viet Cong attack. Under the cover of a dense pine forest bordering the northwestern side of the campus, the Viet Cong could launch a company size attack without being detected. The academy's two organic RF companies were inadequate to defend the entire complex whose perimeter amounted to about three miles. Elements of these two companies occupied the Doi Bac Hill immediately north of the academy and manned two bunkers, one near the Le Loi parade field, and one at the old academy campus.

I instructed Col. Nguyen Van Su, the head of the Military Department and commandant of Cadets, to use the cadets for the defense of the new academy complex. I also directed Colonel Su to stage a defense exercise once a month so each cadet would know exactly what he was expected to do in case of an attack. Staff and faculty personnel were divided into three shifts; each shift took turn sleeping at the academy and being prepared to participate in the defense under the overall control of the Head of the Military Department. A TOC was also set up at the Military Department to coordinate the defense. I made it a point to sleep at my office at least two nights a week to heighten the awareness of the threat of a Viet Cong attack. Often, Tuan, my oldest son, would accompany me.

One Sunday night in February 1970, the Viet Cong struck. They sent a commando team with the mission to kill me. Around 2:00 AM., the commando team consisting of a dozen men, taking advantage of the heavy fog in the valley, sneaked past the Doi Bac Hill north of the academy, and succeeded in infiltrating the defense perimeter without being detected. They rushed toward my office on the second floor of the administrative building and sprayed it with bullets. The timing was bad—both for the enemy and for me— because earlier that day, I took my wife, my daughter Ngoc and, my youngest son Dung, for a one-day vacation to Nha Trang, thirty miles east of Dalat. Tuan did not want to go along so I asked Colonel Thanh, my chief of cabinet, to make arrangements for him to sleep at the academy while I was away because I felt that it would be safer for him to spend the night there.

Around noon on Monday, as our helicopter bringing us back from Nha Trang landed on the Le Loi parade field, I saw broken glass and other debris around the administrative building. I knew that something terribly wrong had happened during my absence.

Dung jumped out of the helicopter and rushed toward my old office, yelling: "Brother Tuan! Brother Tuan! Where are you?" There was a large hole in the west wall of the office and all the windows were broken. Dung thought that his brother must have been killed by the blast. My driver, who was waiting for us at the helicopter pad, rushed toward me and yelled that Tuan was safe.

Colonel Thanh later reported that Tuan had decided to stay home after he lost a few Chinese chess games, since it was past midnight and too late to go to the academy. We all thanked God for saving our child. Tuan, no doubt, would have been killed had he slept at the academy that fateful night.

Maj. Cao Thien Yet,[47] a civil engineering instructor and duty officer that night, was killed during the commando attack.

On the night of the attack, Lt. Col. Nguyen Dinh Toan, deputy commandant of cadets, was on duty at the academic building. Hearing the fire fight at the administrative building, he got in his jeep and raced toward the building, in time to meet the retreating commandos in the driveway. He exchanged fire with the attackers, forcing them to escape to the west. By that time, the cadets had taken position on the perimeter; Cadet Bui Le, from the sophomore class, was manning a bunker near the west wing of the administrative building with one of his classmates, when a grenade landed at his feet. Fortunately, it didn't explode. Looking up, he saw a Viet Cong standing at the bunker opening. He instantly pulled the trigger and killed the Viet Cong commando with one bullet from his Garant M-1 rifle. I recommended him for the Vietnamese Gallantry Cross. He was perhaps the only cadet in the annals of military academies cited for heroism in combat while still at the school.

I was certain the Viet Cong would come back. I also guessed that the next time, they would change their avenue of approach and would come from the south along the Da Thien plains near the atomic plant. I instructed Col. Dao Mong Xuan, my chief of staff, to install barbed wire across the valley floor to the south and to post a squad size ambush inside the barbed wire. Since nothing occured within the next two months, Colonel Xuan recommended that I cancel the ambush. However, I decided to continue it for another month.

Sure enough, the VC struck again. A few days after my decision to retain the ambush, Colonel Xuan awoke me around 3:00 AM. "General!" Colonel Xuan yelled on the phone, "The Viet Cong attacked again. Our ambush reported contact with possibly one Viet Cong company." I dropped the phone, put on my fatigues, jumped in my "armored" jeep and rushed to the academy. (A few months after I joined the academy, I instructed my headquarters company to equip one jeep with a .50 machine gun and two-inch thick steel plates to protect against small arm fire because I had a presentiment that I would need that armored vehicle some day.) Although Colonel Xuan advised me that fighting was taking place in the valley and that it would be safer for me to make a detour, I decided to take the shortest route, hoping I could influence the outcome and the armored jeep could provide some protection in case we had to fight inside the academy.

I went directly to the academy's TOC. Colonel Su reported that earlier the ambush team detected enemy infiltration through the barbed wire. They immediately detonated two Claymore mines inside the barbed wire fence. Two VCs were reported killed while the rest of the enemy unit, regrouping on the western slope of the valley, was exchanging fire with the ambush team about two hundred meters away. I knew that my defense scheme had worked and that the VC were cornered. I instructed Colonel Su to follow the development of the situation. I also ordered Colonel Xuan to mount an assault with the RF company which had been held in reserve.

I left the TOC and drove to the bunker overlooking the valley with my aide. It was almost dawn. As I tried to locate the VC position on the opposite slope with my binoculars, one B-40 recoilless rifle shell landed a few meters in front of me. Fortunately, no one was hurt. I directed the soldiers who were manning the machine gun at the bunker to return fire. I instructed my aide to bring in a loud speaker to call the VC to surrender. The VC replied with a new burst of automatic rifle fire in our direction. It was almost daytime. I ordered the assault. By that time, the cadets had taken position on the edge of the valley. They were thrilled to observe a live assault with RF soldiers firing their guns at point blank while advancing in formation toward the enemy defensive position. There was no doubt this assault in formation was the most realistic and most instructional demonstration any academy could offer to its cadets. Results of the assault: Enemy: twelve KIAs. Friendly: no casualties. A pursuit operation launched immediately after the assault captured two more VCs who belonged to a sapper company of Tuyen Duc (Dalat) Province.

To prevent other VC raids on the academy, I instructed the school engineer platoon to build a dam across the valley in front of the concrete bunker southwest of the parade field. Soon, the northern portion of the valley was transformed into a beautiful lake where cadets could swim and fish during weekends.

In March 1970, Gen. Creighton Abrams visited the academy and presented me with the U.S. Legion of Merit for my performance at the academy. The citation read in part that "Assigned to the Vietnamese National Military Academy in the midst of a second joint Viet Nam-United States attempt to expand and convert the Vietnamese National Military Academy from a two-year candidate school to a four-year degree-granting academic institution, General Thi immediately grasped the new ideas and tasks required in such development. Under his guidance the academy graduated its first four-year students with a degree equivalent to a Bachelor of Science in General Science."

In November 1970, the Pentagon invited me on a tour of U.S. service academies. Colonel Fye, my new advisor, Navy Captain Nguyen Van, head of the faculty department, and Col. Nguyen Van Su, commandant of cadets, accompanied me on this trip. Gen. Nguyen Van Vy, minister of defense, allocated me a special fund to purchase gifts for officials at the U.S. service academies. I directed my chief of cabinet to buy highly acclaimed lacquered artworks manufactured by the Thu Dau Mot-based Thanh Le lacquer firm. To add an exotic touch to my gifts, I also ordered my aide to acquire Montagnard-made fabrics and bronze bracelets, which were treasured by American tourists in Dalat.

The first leg of our trip was to Honolulu, where we stayed for two days as guests of the Pacific Theater Command. The day following our arrival, we received a briefing at the headquarters of the

Pacific Theater Command and subsequently went on a sightseeing tour of Pearl Harbor Bay.

We were met at San Francisco International Airport by a U.S. major general from the U.S.VI Army at the Presidio. We drove to Fort Mason, near the Presidio, where we stayed during our sojourn in San Francisco. The next day, a Saturday, the Chief of Staff of VI Army invited us for a cruise on San Francisco Bay. Some staff officers and their wives were also invited. We boarded a small army boat at the foot of the Golden Gate Bridge and cruised toward Bay Bridge. As we approached Alcatraz Island, our host informed us that the former prison had been occupied by armed members of an Indian tribe who had claimed ownership of the island. On the return trip, we were served lunch on the boat and I took that opportunity to present my gifts to the U.S. general and his wife, who appreciated Thu Dau Mot lacquer and Montagnard fabrics. That afternoon, Colonel Fye, who grew up in the Presidio, offered to take us on a tour of this historic army base, possibly the most beautiful army base in the United States.

There was no official schedule the next day, a Sunday, but the VI Army was kind enough to put at our disposal a sedan with a driver. At Capt. Nguyen Van's suggestion, we paid a visit to Vietnamese teachers at the Monterey Army Language Institute. (Captain Van had attended the Naval Post-Graduate School at Monterey.) At that time, a large number of American officers were learning Vietnamese to prepare for their tour of duty in Viet Nam. Consequently, the U.S. Army had recruited many Vietnamese to teach the language at the Monterey Language Institute. The Vietnamese teachers had been out of Viet Nam for many years and had many questions about the war and the political situation in the country.

The next day we flew to Denver to visit the Air Force Academy at Colorado Springs. We had been advised by the Pentagon not to wear uniforms during our trips in the United States (to avoid possible embarrassment from growing antiwar movements following the Cambodian invasion in May and the Kent State University shootings), so we traveled in civilian clothes as simple businessmen. I was met at the Denver International Airport by my wife's younger brother, Air Force Maj. To Tien Phat and my wife's brother-in-law, Capt. Tran Dat Minh. Phat was liaison officer at Lowry Air force Base in Denver and Minh was attending an X-Ray technician course at a nearby Army hospital.

On the afternoon of our arrival, Captain Van and I were invited to play tennis with two cadets. The Air Force Academy must have inquired in advance about my hobbies. Even though Captain Van was an excellent tennis player and I was a fairly good one, we lost the match. The Air Force cadets, I jokingly told Captain Van, had failed to display their sense of diplomacy on this occasion. After the match, the tennis coach at the academy commented that I had an "unpredictable forehand." I took it as a compliment, but I didn't know how it was intended.

The next day, we were received by the superintendent of the Academy, an Air Force lieutenant general; afterward were invited to tour the academy facilities. I was impressed by the academic curriculum, considered one of the best of the country and by the original architecture of the academy cathedral whose structure was flexible enough to accommodate all faiths. After watching the cadets' daily parade, we were hosted at a lunch in the cadets mess hall by the Superintendent. During the luncheon, I learned that the Air Force Academy was very proud of its football team, which at that time ranked among the top ten college football teams in the country.

In the afternoon, our schedule called for us to board a glider and to take off from a dirt runway outside the academy. I was somewhat apprehensive about riding on an airplane with no engine and with a cadet at the wheel. I was instructed to sit in the cockpit; the Air Force cadet was already comfortably installed in the back. I looked at the young man to whom I trusted my life and was reassured by his calm appearance. A Cessna pulled us into the air and as soon as we reached the required altitude, we were cut loose. The cadet maneuvered the glider toward the freeway below and explained, through the intercom, the techniques of gliding. He also described the scenery below. Suddenly, everything around me seemed unreal and I had the eerie feeling of floating weighlessly in the air like a big kite. It was a wonderful experience.

In the evening, the commandant of cadets, Brigadier General Olds, hosted the dinner. General Olds was a Viet Nam War hero.

During a mission in North Viet Nam, the then-Colonel Olds, simulated a low speed flying aircraft to attract North Viet Nam's fighter ace, Capt. Khong Van Tuyen. He skillfully maneuvered his F-4 at full speed to position himself behind the North Vietnamese and with one air-to-air missile, he sent the latter swirling toward the earth to his death. Later, Hanoi organized a national funeral in honor of its fallen hero.

During dinner, General Olds said that U.S. pilots on missions in North Viet Nam were not allowed to bomb "targets of opportunity" such as supply ships in Hai Phong Harbor or the intense dike network which protected the Red River Delta. I had fought in North Viet Nam during the Indochina War and knew firsthand that the dike system in the Red River delta was very vulnerable and subject to frequent flooding. I agreed with General Olds that the destruction of these dikes would cause irreparable damage to this rich, rice-producing area and consequently, affect the outcome of the war in the South. The destruction of the dikes would cause death and misery to the civilian population; on the other hand, it would likely shorten the war and save the lives of thousands of allied soldiers. Unfortunately, the politicians in Washington apparently chose to sacrifice victories in order to maintain the "status quo." This remains incomprehensible.

It was ironic that President Nixon, in a memo released by the National Archives, complained that his commanders had played "how not to lose" for so long that they had forgotten "how to win." To render justice to the generals, I agree with General Westmoreland that the U.S. needed to rethink its Viet Nam policies. It had to do away with the "status quo" and to resolutely carry the war to the North. Although President Nixon later ordered B-52 runs on North Viet Nam, this move was not so much to win the war, but to induce the enemy to sit at the negotiation table.

To make matters worse, the war in Viet Nam was directed not by generals in the field, but by the Pentagon and the White House. When it was decided to conduct limited raids north of the 17th parallel for example, Washington reserved the right to approve all targets in North Viet Nam. The target list was revised twice a month for the Secretary of Defense by the Joint Chiefs of Staff. It had to be evaluated by the Defense Department's I.S.A (International Security Agency) Office and approved by the Secretary of Defense, the State Department and the White House before the targets could be bombed. Once, a mission was canceled at the last minute because officials in Washington discovered a small cabin in the target area on an aerial photograph. Targets were carefully scrutinized if they were located in an area within ten miles of Hanoi and four miles around Hai Phong. Like General Olds, American pilots reported that, in many instances when they could not locate assigned targets, they had to release their bombs in the South China Sea rather than strike at targets of opportunity that were not on Washington's approved target list.

After a one-day visit at Fort Collins, a major army base approximately sixty miles north of Denver, we flew directly to New York. We were met at the airport by Major General Knowlton, superintendent of the U.S. Military Academy at West Point. My wife's younger sister, Nga, and her husband, who worked as assistant to the Vietnamese permanent observer at the United Nations, were also there to meet me. I had known General Knowlton when he was advisor to my friend, Minister of Rural Development Nguyen Duc Thang, under the Ky government. I was present at the ceremony in Can Tho where General Knowlton was awarded the Viet Nam National Order for his contribution to the pacification program. His son, who served as a sergeant in the Special Forces, also received a gallantry cross on that occasion.

I was moved by General Knowlton's thoughtfulness for having taken time to meet me in New York. He insisted I stay with him at the official residence of the superintendent of the Academy instead of at the VIP guest house located just outside the campus. It was a great honor for me as General Knowlton's residence was once occupied by General MacArthur when he had been superintendent of the U.S. Military Academy, right after World War II. I was glad I had reserved the most beautiful lacquer and the most elaborate Montagnard fabrics for the Knowltons.

After dinner, General Knowlton and I walked his dog and we strolled *incognito* around the campus along the Hudson River. General Knowlton explained details of this historic site; it was an exciting experience and I realized, long afterward, that that night's walk was one of the most memorable times of all my visits to the U.S. service academies.

The next day we had an official tour of the academy; we watched the cadets' daily parade and then had a luncheon with the cadets in their huge mess hall. Back in 1963, when I was a student at the U.S. Command & Staff College at Fort Leavenworth, Kansas, I visited West Point during a trip organized by the school for allied student officers. Physically, there was not much change at the academy, but the military curriculum had received a profound impact from the Viet Nam War. Most of the instructors appointed to West Point had served in Viet Nam and had brought back their experiences.

Another difference was that there was, for the first time, a Vietnamese cadet at the U.S. Military Academy. His name was Nguyen Minh Tam. He had been a first-year cadet at the Vietnamese Military Academy when he was selected to attend West Point under an exchange program approved by the U.S. Congress. During lunch, I sat with General Knowlton on the mezzanine in the mess hall with a dominating view of the cadets below. Since my visit took place two days before the Army-Navy game, the mess hall walls were covered with "Sink Navy" signs.

There was a tradition at West Point that allowed a foreign cadet to ask a visiting dignitary from his own country to pardon all cadets who were punished on the day of the visit. Thus, Tam stood up in the middle of the lunch and asked for my official pardon. I turned to General Knowlton who gave me a discreet sign of acquiescence. I then solemnly declared my pardon to the thunderous applause of the 4,000 cadets down below.

General Knowlton gave an official reception that night in my honor at the Officers open mess. I stood in line with General Knowlton and Mrs. Knowlton and we shook hand with our guests. I was surprised at the number of officers I had known in Viet Nam who came to the party. I was also surprised to see that many American officers had married Vietnamese women and their wives were happy to speak in Vietnamese with me and to inquire about the political and military situation at home.

The next day, a Saturday, we flew to Washington, D.C., where we were met at the airport by Col. Nguyen Linh Chieu, the Vietnamese military attaché. We spent Sunday sightseeing and visiting friends. Early Monday, Colonel Chieu picked us up at our hotel and we went to the Pentagon to see General Westmoreland, the new Army Chief of Staff. We discussed the progress of the conversion of the Vietnamese Military Academy to a four-year degree granting institution, of which General Westmoreland was one of the strongest supporters. We also discussed the progress of the pacification program and the war in general.

That evening, we were hosted to a dinner at the Officers Club at an army base near Arlington. The dinner was organized by Colonel Wyrough[48] and other officers who had served in Viet Nam. At the Officers Club, I met with old Viet Nam friends, most of whom complained bitterly about the conduct of the war and expressed concern about the growing anti-war sentiment in the United States.

The next day, we drove to the Naval Academy at Annapolis. The atmosphere was somber at the academy because its football team had been defeated by Army over the weekend. After a courtesy visit to the vice-admiral, uperintendent of the Academy, we were given a tour of the classrooms and other facilities by a naval officer and Midshipman Tran Van Truc, the son of Adm. Tran Van Chon, chief of the Vietnamese Navy. Like Tam at West Point, Truc was the first Vietnamese to attend Annapolis. Admiral Zumwalt, commander of the U.S. Navy in Viet Nam and a good friend of Admiral Chon, was instrumental in Truc's admission at Annapolis.

After the tour of the academy, our delegation was hosted to a luncheon with the midshipmen. Contrary to the cheery ambiance at West Point, the atmosphere at the midshipmen mess hall that day was understandably subdued. I wished the Pentagon had reversed the schedule of our visits so we could have visited Annapolis prior to the Army-Navy game.

We were scheduled to fly back to San Francisco the next day, but I received a message from the Pentagon stating that the under secretary of the defense in charge of training wished to see me to hear my preliminary report on my visits. I told the under secretary that I noticed a general relaxation of rules in the U.S. service academies, possibly due to the permissiveness permeating American society. I suggested that the service academies might consider including a liberal arts degree in its curriculum, and that, additionally, martial arts training would be beneficial to the cadets.

Back at the remote mountain city of Dalat, I was not immune from the ramifications of political infighting in Saigon. When Vice President Ky visited the Military Academy and challenged me to a tennis match, it was reported to Saigon that I had remained on friendly terms with Ky. When the Air Force Cadet School in Nha Trang invited me to attend the graduation ceremony of its new officers and Ky was the presiding dignitary, it was reported to Saigon that I had attended a "secret" meeting with Ky in Nha Trang. This was brought to my attention when General Tho, who at the time commanded the 18th Division in III Corps, informed me that he was told by Gen. Do Cao Tri, the III Corps Commander and a staunch supporter of Thieu and Khiem, that I had secretly met with Ky on many occasions. General Tri made it clear that it would be in my best interest to put a stop to these meetings.

In the summer of 1971, I was invited to visit Australian service academies under the sponsorship of SEATO (Southeast Asia Treaty Organization). I flew on Air Viet Nam from Saigon to Singapore where I stayed overnight. In the evening, the Vietnamese Charge d'Affaires gave me a tour of the city and we had a delicious dinner at one of the best Chinese restaurants in the city.

The next day, I boarded a Qantas plane for the trip to Sydney where I was joined by Colonel Alexander, my new advisor. After a two-day sojourn in Sydney, Colonel Alexander and I flew to Canberra, the capital of Australia. That evening, the Vietnamese Embassy had a party in my honor. All military attachés of non-Communist countries stationed at Canberra were invited. During the reception, the military attaché from South Africa took me aside to express his country's support for our fight against Communist insurgency. He was disappointed that his country had not been requested to send troops to fight against the common enemy.

The reception at the Vietnamese Embassy provided the opportunity for me to meet Vietnamese students at Canberra who volunteered to prepare traditional Vietnamese dishes, including the very popular *cha gio* (spring roll). One of these students was Kieu My Duyen, a well-known reporter who was studying journalism in Australia. On this occasion, Miss Duyen gave me information concerning the Military Establishment in Australia. She also interviewed me about Australian Forces in Viet Nam.

The next day, I visited the Australian Royal Military Academy and the Air Force Academy in Canberra. The Director of the Military Academy had previously served in Viet Nam and knew many of our generals. He took me by surprise by asking me to address the cadets during my visit. I began my speech by thanking the Australian government for sending the equivalent of an infantry brigade to Viet Nam to fight against our common enemy. I praised the performance of Australian troops, known for their expertise in jungle warfare. I also spoke on the domino theory which held that the fall of Viet Nam would trigger the collapse of neighboring non-Communist countries, and that, consequently, it was in Australia's best interest to help our country in its fight to contain the spread of Communism in South East Asia. I concluded by telling the cadets that they could be proud of their country and their Armed Forces and that the Vietnamese people were grateful to Australia for its help. In the afternoon, I spoke to the cadets of the Air Force Academy outside of Canberra.

What struck me during these visits was that Australian service academies had almost done away with any semblance of harshness; the cadets were treated as gentlemen. Following the path of the British Military Academy of Sandhurst, Australian cadets spent only two years at the academy, and thus were not granted the baccalaureate degree upon graduation.

The following day, Colonel Alexander and I drove to Melbourne, approximately 250 miles south of Canberra. Although it was July, it was winter in Australia and we could see snow on the tops of the mountains to the west. I was surprised that we didn't see any kangaroos.

The Australian Army detached a major to serve as our escort officer during our stay in Melbourne. In the evening, we attended a dinner at the exclusive, all-male Melbourne sport club, where we watched a "trotting" race and what was called an "Australian-style football" game. In this game, the players could kick or throw the ball forward (and not backward). To me, it looked like the European rugby game. As it was raining, the players had to slug it out in the mud.

Back in Dalat, I drafted a report to the Directorate of Training/Joint General Staff. I also wrote an article entitled: "Military Academies and the Challenge of the Seventies" that was published by the U.S. Command & General Staff College.[49] It reads in part:

> Across the board, the older, developed states are less demanding of their cadets than are the newer or emerging nations. A Canadian officer, a graduate of Canada's Royal Military College, was astounded to observe the strict regimen of cadets in Viet Nam. He remarked that: "Our cadets in Canada are far too soft."
>
> . . . . In the realm of academic attainment, one sees the same general phenomenon. The emerging nations attach much status to education and place great stress on producing a highly educated corps of professional officers. This is especially true in Asian countries where Confucius long ago stressed the importance of learning, and where societies are strongly degree-oriented. They require cadets to stay at their academies at least four years and, in some cases, five. In the developing countries, academy graduates are destined to play a key role not only in the defense of their countries, but they also might well become the leaders of these countries. So, it is self-evident that these young men should be given a good moral and academic education.
>
> Wealthy nations—with the notable exception of the United States—seem to consider that educating a soldier is a waste of money. . . .
>
> Now, compare the results. All governments expect the graduates of their academies one day to lead their respective armed forces. These are the men, then, who will inspire or fail to inspire the defense of their nation. In the dark hour of peril, which comes sooner or later to every country, they must shoulder the lonely burden of high command. Will they be ready?

A society, like a person, can expect to receive no more than it is willing to give. The cadet is malleable; the new graduate will largely reflect the attitudes and principles he developed while at the academy. Those countries whose cadets receive an inadequate education in an easy environment of luxury and privilege should not be dismayed to find themselves saddled with professional soldiers both ignorant and lethargic.

The tour of foreign military academies had been an eye-opening experience. I learned how military academies reflected the attitudes, traditions, and needs of their parent societies. I was convinced that for developing countries, where leaders were often selected from the ranks of the armed forces, investment in the education and leadership development of a cadet was of prime importance.

While working to improve these two aspects of cadet formation, I also watched the progress of the war and kept abreast of the new tactics and techniques employed in the battlefields. In the spring of 1970, I asked Colonel Fye, my advisor, to make arrangements for us to visit some U.S. units in the First and Second Military Regions.

The first leg of our trip was the town of An Khe in the Hauts Plateaux where I had been involved in some of the bloodiest battles toward the end of the Indochina War in 1954. It was at the Hill of Deo Mang, about seven miles east of An Khe, where General Khanh's G.M.11 lost one infantry battalion and one artillery battery after an attack by one Viet Minh regular regiment. It was west of An Khe, between the city of Pleiku and the Hill of Mang Yang, where my battery was stationed, that the French G.M.100, fresh from the war in Korea, was almost entirely decimated in one of the bloodiest ambushes in the history of the Indochina War.

Artillery guns of all calibers were blasting away the hills north of An Khe without interruption when we landed at the headquarters of a U.S. Brigade located in that town. The colonel who commanded the brigade explained that he had received instructions not to take chances, and that firepower should be used to the utmost at reported enemy concentrations before sending in U.S. infantrymen to reconnoiter the area. "Gentlemen," said the brigade commander, "from now on, firepower is the name of the game!"

The U.S. colonel, in my opinion, described the main difference between the two wars by this simple statement. I remembered that during the Indochina War artillery ammunition had to be dropped by parachutes to my battery trapped in Cho Noi, North Viet Nam, and later on Mang Yang Hill, and that, as a consequence, artillery ammunition was used only in cases of actual contact with the enemy; harassing fire on suspected enemy positions was limited due to difficulties of resupply. (The French did not have transport helicopters for resupply missions during the Indochina War.)

The same tactics of saturating contested areas with artillery bombardment was used by the 101st Airborne Division that we visited at Phu Bai, approximately twenty kilometers south of Hue. Colonel Fye was glad to see his brother, an artillery colonel at the 101st Airborne. After a brief meeting with the division commander, we toured the division's FSBs which had been built on the hilltops west of Phu Bai. These FSBs were part of a string of fortifications designed to protect the populated areas of the coastal towns of MRI. The unpopulated areas west of the FSBs extending to the Laotian border were designated "Free Fire Zones." In these free zones, firepower could be used without restraint. Little did I know then that I was to be in charge of the defense of this strategic area and would witness some of the bloodiest fighting during the last days of the Viet Nam War.

Frances FitzGerald, the noted American journalist in Viet Nam, offered an interesting explanation of the American colonialist attitude in Viet Nam which, in my opinion, was reflected in the concept of the Fire Support Base. "Covered with righteous platitudes," she wrote,

> theirs [the American view] was an essentially colonialist vision, born out of the same insecurity and desire for domination that had motivated many of the French. When their counterparts did not take their instructions, these advisors treated the Vietnamese like bad pupils, accusing them of corruption and laziness, and attempted to impose authority

over them. And when the attempt at coercion failed, they retreated from the Vietnamese entirely, barricading themselves behind American weapons and American PX goods, behind the assumption of American superiority and the assumption that the Vietnamese were not quite human like themselves.[50]

The concept of the Fire Support Base adopted by U.S. troops in Viet Nam undoubtedly mirrored this colonialist attitude, the "Fort Apache mentality," which considered any people outside the Fire Support Base as expendable because they were "not quite human" like the Americans, who barricaded themselves behind barbed wire and Claymore mines.

In Hue I met Maj. Gen. Ngo Quang Truong, who commanded ARVN's 1st Infantry Division, an elite Vietnamese unit considered by the U.S.media to be the equal of any American division in Viet Nam. A reserve officer from Thu Duc, Truong had a remarkable military career. I knew him from back in 1964 when Truong was a captain commanding the 5th Airborne Battalion, which was part of an airborne brigade attached to the 7th Infantry Division. And now, seven years later, he was a major general and division commander.[51]

Truong invited me to fly to Quang Tri in his C&C helicopter. During the trip, he briefed me on the success of the pacification program in his tactical area. He was very proud of the fact that all the populated areas on both sides of RN1 had been under government control. Little did we know then that North Viet Nam was feverishly preparing for its Great Offensive, that the populated areas south of the Demilitarized Zone (DMZ) were to become the sites of some of the deadliest battles of the Viet Nam War and that Truong, as I Corps Commander, was to assume a major role in the battle to recapture the city of Quang Tri. Neither did I know then that I would return to this region to serve under him.

In May 1970, President Nixon ordered U.S. troops to cross the Cambodian border to capture Viet Cong stocks of weapons and to destroy their ammunition depots and supplies along the Ho Chi Minh Trail. ARVN's III and IV Corps also participated in the Cambodian invasion. ARVN units were to remain in Cambodia after the

U.S.withdrawal to shore up the new government of Gen. Lon Nol, who had deposed Prince Norodom Sihanouh in a bloodless coup. Maj. Gen. Nguyen Viet Thanh, IV Corps Commander, was killed while directing his troops in Cambodia. His C&C helicopter ran into a gunship and burst into flames. His advisor, a U.S. colonel, was also killed in the accident. General Truong replaced General Thanh as the new IV Corps Commander. In a period of just seven years, Truong rose from battalion commander to corps commander.

The problem with this meteoric promotion was that Truong, like many other general officers, didn't have time to attend advanced military training. In fact, of the four corps commanders prior to the fall of South Viet Nam in 1975, only one had attended the Command & General Staff College. These general officers doubtlessly were gifted tacticians and battle-hardened combat veterans, but they would have been better generals had they received advanced staff and leadership training. Military leaders cannot improvise. They have to learn their trade and master the fundamentals of warfare. As in other professions, military leaders must be technicians before becoming artists or geniuses.

In early 1971, the U.S. withdrew 235,000 troops from Viet Nam. In reaction to the Cambodian invasion, the Cooper-Church Amendment prohibited the deployment of U.S. troops outside of Viet Nam. In February 1971, at the instigation of President Nixon, President Thieu sent two ARVN divisions into Low Laos in the direction of the strategic town of Tchepone located near the Ho Chi Minh trail in order to destroy NVA supplies and ammunition. ARVN troops battled 30,000 NVA regular divisions and suffered heavy casualties: 3,000 KIAs and 7,000 WIAs. The Cambodian and Laotian invasions were aimed at temporarily disrupting NVA's logistical system to buy time for an orderly U.S. withdrawal from Viet Nam.

On February 23, 1971, Gen. Do Cao Tri, the dashing III Corps Commander, was killed in a helicopter accident while directing operations in Cambodia. Francois Sully, a reporter for *Newsweek* who rode with General Tri, was also killed. General Tri was possibly the best field commander in the Vietnamese Army. His strong leadership and tactical skills were instrumental in the successful initial breakthrough of III Corps armored task forces through NVA's front east of the Cambodian city of Kratie. According to reliable sources, General Tri was slated to replace Cao Van Vien as chairman of the Joint General Staff.

The deaths of two corps commanders in a short period of time caused vacancies to open, but I was eliminated from consideration because I did not belong to President Thieu's inner circle. However, on National Day, November 1, 1971 (anniversary of the overthrow of Diem's government), I unexpectedly received a kind of windfall profit from the Thieu-Ky rivalry. As Thieu's term was nearing completion, he skillfully maneuvered to obtain the support of the Armed Forces which formed the backbone of his regime. Fearing a new split among the generals and possible renewed support for Ky, Thieu generously dispensed promotions a few months before the elections. As a result, I was pleasantly surprised to receive a call from Colonel Cam, President Thieu's chief of cabinet, congratulating me on my promotion to the rank of lieutenant general. I was thirty-nine. It was unheard of that a young officer without political affiliations, without a mentor in the Army or the government, could rise to the second highest rank in the Army. On this occasion, my brother Tho also was promoted to the rank of major general.

In a regime where corruption and factionalism were rampant, as was often the case in emerging nations, one could still succeed by sheer hard work, determination, and a little good luck. Thieu, Ky, Khiem, and Vien and many other generals did not come from rich, powerful families. Their parents belonged to that ill-defined middle class consisting mostly of small farmers, teachers, and low ranking civil servants. By sheer ambition and luck they attained the highest positions in the Armed Forces and in the government. I felt strongly that this social mobility and the opportunity offered to young people from every social and ethnic background, were good incentives for continuing this difficult and seemingly endless war.

Back in the fall of 1971, General Abrams had asked me whether I would be willing to provide facilities for a crash course in Staff Procedures for selected field grade officers from the Cambodian Army at the Military Academy. Although the United States was heavily involved in Cambodia after the overthrow of Norodom Sihanouk and was providing military assistance to the Cambodian

Army, it obviously did not want to attract attention to a staff course designed for high-ranking Cambodian officers. The remote city of Dalat was an ideal site for such a course. I agreed to General Abrams's request, despite the fact that I had to provide additional security to our Cambodian guests. The course was presented in French and the instructors were French-speaking U.S. officers from MAC-V, Saigon.

At the opening ceremony, I made welcoming remarks in French. The class consisted of a dozen colonels and one brigadier general. Most of them had served as NCOs in the French Army during the Indochina War. Most of them also spoke Vietnamese. The Cambodian general, who would be appointed ambassador to Saigon a few months after the course, had previously served in a French armored unit in Vung Tau.

The following weekend, I invited the Cambodian officers to a formal reception. I also invited the French *Proviseur* of Lycée Yersin and other French professors and their wives so my guests could converse in French with them. I was astounded when the Cambodian general stood and, after having proposed a toast to the friendship between our two countries, concluded his remark by shouting: *"Vive la France!"*

In mid-November, to keep myself abreast of the new military developments in Military Regions III and IV and also to assess the performance of the graduates under the four-year curriculum, I visited ARVN units which were participating in the Cambodian operations. The first unit I visited was my brother's 18th Infantry Division under III Corps. Tho had his CP at Tay Ninh, one hundred miles northwest of Saigon. The 18th Division was operating in the area north of the famous "Parrot's Beak" on the Cambodian border, a Viet Minh stronghold since the Indochina War.

Tho was complimentary of the conduct under fire of the new military academy graduates. After a briefing on the tactical situation of his area of responsibility inside Cambodian territory, Tho opened a bottle of French cognac and proposed a toast to our reunion and to our new promotions. Afterward, I suggested we visit the 18th Division's units operating inside Cambodia, but Tho rejected the idea. Since there were no major contacts with the enemy that day, he suggested instead that we pay a visit to our grandfather's grave located in a rubber plantation outside of the city of Tay Ninh. Although I outranked him, he was my older brother and *en famille*, he had the last word.

The trip to the rubber plantation triggered many memories. I remembered the journey Tho and I had made thirty years earlier to attend our grandfather's funeral. We were two frightened boys from Bac Lieu traveling at night on a horse-drawn carriage on a tiger-infested backroad to attend a secret funeral of a grandfather who died in exile in Thailand. And now, these two boys, both generals, returned to pay respects to a grandfather they did not know well. The grave, located between two neat rows of rubber trees, was well maintained and beautifully decorated. A few members of the family that I had never met were there to greet us. I guessed that Tho advised the family of our visit. After Tho introduced me to the family, we burned three incense sticks, bowed three times and planted the incense sticks in a small jar at the foot of the grave. We then bid farewell to the family and departed followed by an escort of MPs.

The next day, I flew to Kien Giang Province in MR IV to visit my former division which was operating in the famous U Minh Forest area. Brig. Gen. Tran Ba Di, commanding general of the 9th Infantry Division, received me at his CP. He introduced me to his staff, most of whom had served under me. After the usual briefing, General Di and I flew to the Cambodian town of Naek Luong located on the left bank of the Mekong River, midway between Chau Doc and Phnom Penh. We were met by Col. Huynh Van Chinh, commanding the 16th Regiment, whose mission was to provide security to the naval convoys transporting supplies to the Cambodian capital.

From Naek Loung, we flew directly to Phnom Penh International Airport. We were met by a Cambodian captain and forward elements of the 9th Division. General Di had to go back to Kien Giang to direct the division's operation in the famed U Minh Forest. This was my first visit to Phnom Penh. Although I had crossed Cambodia with my artillery battery to participate in operations in Laos in early 1954, we had traveled on RN13 which ran through the eastern part of Cambodia along the east side of the Mekong River. Anti-

Vietnamese sentiments ran high at that time and a parade of a Vietnamese artillery battery through a Cambodian city almost triggered a war. Things had changed so much. Now ARVN troops were everywhere in Phnom Penh. Elements of the Vietnamese Air Force were controlling the air traffic at the airport and our Navy was escorting fluvial convoys into the Cambodian capital; in fact, the personal pilot of Lon Nol, the new Cambodian leader, was a Vietnamese Air Force officer.

I asked to visit the museum. I was disappointed to see only a few remaining relics of the once flourishing Khmer civilization. Maintaining a museum in a war-torn country was an almost impossible task. Compared to the museum in Saigon, however, the Phnom Penh museum was in much better shape because Cambodia had remained relatively unaffected by the Indochina War. Unfortunately, the French Colonial Administration, over time, had shipped to France some of the most valuable relics and historical documents relating to the ancient Khmer civilization as well the civilization of other Indochinese States. Some of these relics disappeared during the Japanese occupation in 1945; the result was that the former colonies were plundered of many of their priceless historical treasures.

From Phnom Penh I flew to a fortified outpost built by the 21st Infantry Division in the heart of the U Minh Forest. Maj. Gen. Nguyen Vinh Nghi, the 21st Division commander, met me and gave me a tour of the imposing military fort. The base was occupied by a RF company and one 105-mm artillery platoon. It was a triangular structure built with large trees from the surrounding U Minh Forest which provided effective protection against Viet Cong 82-mm mortar fire. The fortifications were surrounded by large water-filled ditches which provided a natural barrier against enemy assaults. On the other side of the ditches was a mine field protected by a dense network of barbed wire.

General Nghi invited me to ride in his helicopter for our trip to Bac Lieu, my natal province. Bac Lieu had changed a lot since my last visit in 1957. The main avenue next to the old province administrative quarters had been blocked off to accommodate new construction for the 21st Division Headquarters and other organic units.

Under President Diem, Bac Lieu was downgraded to district status. Although it had been recently elevated again to province level, it had not recovered from long neglect. The streets, unkempt, were further damaged by armored vehicles and other heavy trucks from the 21st Division.

The next morning, Colonel Ninh, Bac Lieu province chief, drove me to the home of the Lam Quang family in the small village of Vinh Trach approximately five kilometers southeast of the city of Bac Lieu. We were met in front of the former mansion of my great grandfather by a dozen elders of the village. The village chief introduced each one as I shook hands with them. Most of these gentlemen were my relatives and had known my grandfather and my father.

The old two-story mansion where I had spent my weekends when I was a child was now occupied by a PF platoon and was so dilapidated that it was merely a shadow of itself. The brick wall surrounding the old mansion still bore the impact of machine gun bullets. The huge garden full of fruit trees was now a muddy yard with two concrete bunkers covered with barbed wire. The families of the PF soldiers who occupied the mansion cooked their meals in the living room where my great grandfather used to receive his tenant farmers. I remembered a scene in the movie *Gone With the Wind* where Scarlet returned to what remained of the old family mansion after the war. The difference was that in my case, the war had not ended and the family mansion was still occupied by the soldiers.

Colonel Ninh told me that the previous year, President Thieu came to the village of Vinh Trach to preside over a ceremony of distribution of lands to the farmers under his *Nguoi Cay Co Ruong* ("Farmers Own Land") land reform program. When he was informed that most of the lands he distributed belonged to my family, he told the province chief: "I am sure Tho and Thi will not be very happy about this program."

In February 1972, President Nixon and Dr. Kissinger made a historic visit to China. It was a diplomatic breakthrough with incalculable consequences for the Viet Nam War. I had hoped that President Nixon would be able to persuade the Chinese, an arch-rival of the Soviet Union, to stop their support for the North Vietnamese, who at the time were siding with the Soviet Union.

In March 30, 1972, the North Vietnamese Army (NVA) launched their overall offensive in three areas: Quang Tri in MRI, Kontum in MRII, and An Loc in MRIII. The most important offensive, however, was in the northern province of Quang Tri. In mid-April, I was ordered to report to I Corps Headquarters in Danang as Deputy Corps Commander. I was replaced at the Military Academy by Maj. Gen. Lam Quang Tho, my older brother.

The night preceding the transfer of command of the Military Academy, Col. Nguyen Van Su, the commandant of cadets, was killed under mysterious circumstances. Somebody hurled a hand grenade at the room where he slept at the academic building. Subsequent investigations by the Army Security Agency failed to resolve this murder case. As I stated earlier, Colonel Su was an artillery officer who had served with me at the 1st Artillery Battalion during the Indochina War. I brought him to the Military Academy as the Commandant of Cadets because he was a disciplinarian and a very hard-working officer. I felt very saddened by his death.[52]

12

MILITARY REGION ONE

AFTER A BRIEF CEREMONY IN which I transferred the command of the Military Academy to my brother Tho, I boarded a C-123 transport aircraft for my trip to Danang, where the headquarters of MRI was located. Normally, the pilot would stop at Nha Trang to refuel, but as the weather forecast for MRI was good, he decided to go directly to Danang without refueling. This turned out to be a monumental mistake that almost cost our lives.

As we approached the city, it was unexpectedly struck by a heavy storm. The visibility was zero and the aircraft was caught in heavy turbulence. The passengers, about one hundred of them, were mostly soldiers rejoining their units after a few days leave in Saigon, servicemen's dependents visiting their husbands fighting in Quang Tri and Thua Thien Provinces, and also a few reporters getting a ride to the front. The children started to panic and cry while their mothers tried to calm them. Other women prayed in silence, their hands nervously manipulating their rosaries. Sitting in the front seat just behind the cockpit, I saw the crew chief, an Air Force major, open the cockpit window in an attempt to orient himself amidst the storm. I knew that we were in trouble. I was particularly concerned that, by circling over Danang, the aircraft could bump into the Hai Van Chains just north of the airport.

Quietly, I went into the cockpit and asked the major if we had any chance of landing in Danang with the aid of navigational instruments. "General," the major replied, "I have no radar contact with the ground control tower." I asked him if he could change direction and try to land in Chu Lai, approximately thirty miles to the south. "General," he said apologetically, "we have no fuel left." I then asked him as calmly as I could under the circumstances what he proposed to do. He said he would attempt a descent and if he missed the runway, he would direct the aircraft toward the ocean and try a forced landing on the beach.

As the aircraft started its painful descent shaking violently in the middle of the turbulence, I looked out my window, holding my breath and trying to catch a glimpse of Danang hidden somewhere under the thick layers of cloud and rain. The few minutes seemed like an eternity. Suddenly, I saw the red tile roofs of houses somewhere around Danang. In a split second, the aircraft landed. It then stopped in the middle of the flooded runway, incapable of taxiing to the airport terminal because we had run out of fuel. It was a close call.

When I reported to Lt. Gen. Hoang Xuan Lam, I Corps Commander, the battle was raging around Quang Tri, which was defended by the untested 3rd Infantry Division. General Lam had graduated from the *École de L'Arme Blindée* at Saumur, France. He was the commander of the 2nd Infantry Division at Quang Ngai, south of Danang, when the Buddhist movement erupted in MRI in May 1966. He was appointed I Corps Commander after other generals failed to restore order.

General Lam had been criticized by the U.S. press for the fateful invasion of Low Laos in February 1971 where ARVN troops suffered heavy casualties. The objective of the incursion, according to the White House and the Pentagon, was to destroy NVA's supply line to the South. President Nixon and Dr. Kissinger reasoned that if successful, the attack into Cambodia and Laos would secure the safe withdrawal of the remaining American troops in South Viet Nam.

However, the troops' movements, logistical preparations, and, most of all, the speculations of the American press, had alerted the enemy of the incoming attack. (The attack didn't start until February 7, but by February 1, the *Washington Post*, the *Baltimore Sun*, and the *New York Times* reported the possibility that a strike into Laos was imminent). [53] As a result, NVA had concentrated a powerful antiaircraft defense system in the area. Over one hundred U.S. helicopters were shot down during the first week and consequently the Americans substantially cut down on the number of helicopters available for troop transport and medical evacuation. Finally, on March 6, ARVN launched a successful air assault into Tchepone, the objective of the attack, and discovered a large number of enemy bodies. However, by then NVA was able to move their supplies to the South through a new road which bypassed Tchepone.

In *Reporting Viet Nam*, William M. Hammond reported that when transmitting President Nixon's compliment to Ambassador Bunker for the successful air assault on Tchepone, Dr. Kissinger noted: "The president made the additional comment that our worst enemy seems to be the press."[54]

In any event, when I entered his office, General Lam was talking on the phone to Gen. Cao Van Vien, the chairman of the Joint General Staff. General Lam seemed to be upbeat. He motioned for me to sit down while he continued his conversation with General Vien. I overheard his optimistic report that our armored brigade had just inflicted heavy damage to NVA armored units northwest of Quang Tri, on the north side of the Thach Han River. After the first serious setbacks, this was good news for ARVN.

After the irreparable losses incurred by the Viet Cong in the failed 1968 Tet Offensive, North Viet Nam decided to launch the 1972 Great Offensive to capture South Viet Nam by force. In lieu of continuing the traditional communist strategy of guerrilla warfare culminating in a popular uprising, NVN was determined to hurl its regular divisions across the DMZ and to fight a conventional warfare similar to the Korean War.

On March 30, 1972, after heavy artillery preparations on ARVN's 3rd Division positions, NVA's crack divisions, 304, 308 and 324B, supported by one artillery division and two armored regiments, crossed the Ben Hai River, which separated the two Viet Nams under the 1954 Geneva Peace Agreement. This major offensive coincided with the arrival of the first seasonal monsoon storms which prevented tactical air support to the defending units.

ARVN's regular forces in the Quang Tri province at the time of the attack consisted of the 3rd Infantry Division reinforced with the 147th Marine Brigade, the 5th Ranger Group, and the 1st Armored Brigade. The 3rd Division was the youngest division in the Vietnamese Army. The majority of its soldiers were deserters, draft dodgers, and other undesirable elements, who were sent to the northernmost province of South Viet Nam as a punishment. Yet, it was the fate of this division to receive the brunt of NVN's bloodiest offensive of both the Indochina and the Viet Nam Wars.

Since the departure of the 3rd U.S. Marine Division from the area under Nixon's Vietnamization Program the previous year, ARVN's 3rd Division had to spread out thinly to cover the chain of former U.S. bases south of the DMZ. The 57th Regiment and the 2nd Regiments had been respectively assigned the tactical areas east and west of RN1 from the DMZ to the Cam Lo River. The 56th Regiment's mission was to defend the area west of Cam Lo and to secure the strategic RN9. The 147th Marine Brigade assumed tactical responsibility for the area west of Ai Tu between the 56th Regiment positions and the Thach Han River.

After two days of fierce resistance, the 57th and 2nd Regiments, outgunned and outnumbered, were ordered to fall back to the new defense line of Dong Ha and RN9 south of the Cam Lo River. The 147th Marine Brigade and the 56th Regiment also had suffered heavy casualties and had to abandon two strategic positions on the western flank of the 3rd Division. To make matters worse, Lt. Col. Pham Van Dinh, the 56th Regiment Commander, surrendered to the enemy at the former U.S. Camp Carroll with the remnants of his regiment. Colonel Dinh was a hero during the 1968 Tet Offensive at Hue. His elite reconnaissance company, surnamed *Hac Bao* (Black Panther) company, was the first unit to raise the Vietnamese flag on the Phu Van Lau Citadel. His surrender was a serious blow to the morale of the 3rd Division.

As mentioned earlier, bad weather in the two northern provinces of Quang Tri and Thua Thien denied ARVN forces crucial close air support. To compound the problem of fire support, our counter-artillery fire had been ineffective because the enemy's 130-mm artillery guns could reach a distance exceeding 27,000 meters, while ARVN's two 175-mm batteries stationed at Dong Ha and Camp Carroll had been neutralized during the first days of fighting. Further, the enemy had in their arsenal the highly mobile 122-mm missiles. Consequently, on the battlefield, with regard to artillery fire power, ARVN units were outgunned both in quantity and quality.

Another major problem was that ARVN divisions were overextended to cover the old U.S. FSBs after U.S. troops had departed under the Vietnamization Program. As a result, there were not enough troops to constitute adequate reserve forces which could be used to counterattack enemy penetrations. The left flank of I Corps area was thus very vulnerable to enemy envelopments.

On April 2, the 3rd Division Headquarters at Ai Tu, which had received uninterrupted enemy artillery bombardment since the beginning of the offensive, moved to the Dinh Cong Trang Citadel at Quang Tri. To shore up the defense of the area north of Quang Tri, I Corps ordered the 258th Marine Brigade, which was held in reserve in the Hue area, to move to Dong Ha and be put under the tactical control of 3rd Division. The Airborne Division, minus one brigade, was held in reserve at My Chanh, at the border between Quang Tri and Thua Thien Provinces.

On April 15, a day after my arrival in Danang, I flew to Hue to assess the tactical situation at the two northern provinces of MRI. At I Corps Forward CP, I was informed that the NVA attacking force consisted of three regular infantry divisions reinforced with two armored regiments plus an undetermined number of independent infantry and sapper regiments. The 3rd Division, reinforced with two Marine Brigades, the 1st Armored Brigade and one Ranger Group, retreated under the first waves of attack and was defending the city of Quang Tri, located south of the Thach Han River. Brig. Gen. Vu Van Giai, the division commander, holed up inside the Quang Tri Citadel with his staff, was busy rallying his troops to beat back NVA's multi-division assaults with the help of U.S. Naval gunfire, B-52 sorties, and limited tactical air support.

The situation around Quang Tri appeared very fluid. It changed every hour and it was hard to make an accurate assessment of the situation on the ground.

A few days after I arrived in I Corps Forward CP, President Thieu, Prime Minister Khiem, and General Vien flew to Hue to evaluate

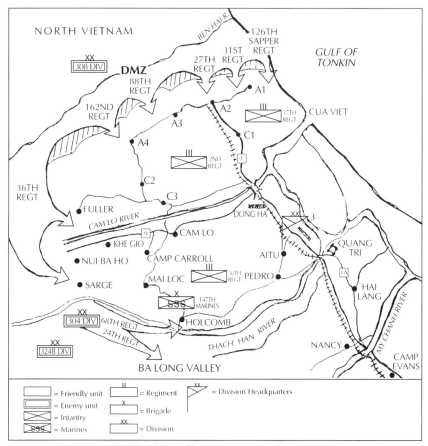

NVN's 1972 offensive across the DMZ

the situation in MRI. We met at I Corps Forward CP inside Hue Citadel. The atmosphere of the meeting was somber as the situation in Quang Tri had become hopeless.

During the meeting, Lt. Gen. Du Quoc Dong, the Airborne Division commander, and Lt. Gen. Le Nguyen Khang, the Marine Division commander, were openly critical of the way I Corps conducted the defense of Quang Tri. At one point, General Lam offered his resignation to President Thieu. Finally, it was decided that the 1st Airborne Brigade, which had participated in the successful defense of the city of An Loc in MRIII, would be airlifted to Hue to reinforce the Airborne Division once the situation in An Loc improved and that I Corps should resume its offensive operation to link up with the 3rd Division as soon as possible.

The encouraging news for I Corps was that Saigon finally realized that the enemy's main direction of attack was the two northern provinces. As a result, Saigon will concentrate all available B-52 sorties to the Northern Theater. In March 1972, NVA launched a simultaneous three-pronged offensive on Quang Tri in MRI, Kontum in MRII, and An Loc in MRIII and the Vietnamese Joint General Staff was unable to figure out the enemy's main direction of attack. Also due to the close proximity of An Loc to the capital, JGS was understandably concerned that the fall of An Loc would place the three attacking NVA divisions at a striking distance from Saigon. The intensity of the attack, the massive use of artillery and missiles, the heavy casualties of the 3rd Division, and the fact that the attack on Quang Tri was directed by NVA High Command itself, convinced President Thieu that the two northern provinces were the main objective of the enemy's so-called Great Offensive.

After a few days in Hue, I returned to Danang as General Lam did not need me at his forward CP. Toward the end of April 1972, I successively received the visits of General Weyand and Gen. Alexander Haig.

General Weyand was deputy to General Abrams, commander of U.S. Forces in Viet Nam. General Weyand once commanded an army corps in MRII and had participated in the Viet Nam peace negotiations in Paris as military advisor to Mr. Kissinger. We flew to Hoi An, the capital city of Quang Nam Province, just south of Danang, to be briefed on the situation in this crucial province. The province chief was Col. Le Tri Tin, an artillery officer.

Colonel Tin reported increased enemy activities in the strategic Que Son Valley, thirty miles southwest of Danang, since the departure of U.S. troops from the region. The 2nd ARVN Division had to spread to its limits in order to occupy the old U.S. FSB's. To compound the problem, the 4th Regiment of the 2nd Division had been sent to the Northern Theater to help stop the NVA offensive in Quang Tri; as a result, the 2nd Division had to operate with only two regiments.

During our flight back to Corps Headquarters, General Weyand asked me about the progress of the Vietnamization Program. I told him that although our troops were overextended to cover all the former U.S. positions, we would still be in a position to defend ourselves if we had continued U.S air support. We discussed the progress of the Paris Peace Conference and agreed that the outcome of the current NVA offensive would have a decisive impact on the bargaining table.

General Haig, a major general at the time, came to MRI to make a personal assessment of the tactical situation. He was assistant deputy to President Nixon and was participating in the Viet Nam Peace Conference in Paris. I briefed him on the general situation in MRI; General Haig asked a few questions, then left for Hue. I was aware that General Haig had had an exceptional career. Although his highest command was only an infantry battalion in MRIII, he rapidly rose to the rank of general under the tutelage of Dr. Henry Kissinger who brought him to the National Security Council as his assistant. Little did I know then that this man would be elevated directly to a four star general and become the Army vice-chief of staff. He would be appointed commander in chief of NATO forces, then secretary of state and he would be embroiled in a controversial role in the aftermath of President Nixon's resignation following the Watergate scandal.

One week after I reported to I Corps, Navy Captain Ho van Ky Thoai, the commandant of Navy in MRI, invited me to visit the naval installations in Tien Sa on the east side of Danang Bay. I was struck by the strategic value of this area. I knew that ultimately, we had to fight a last ditch battle to defend the important enclave of Danang and Tien Sa would be an ideal place from which I Corps could conduct the defense of the enclave. During my visit to the United States in 1970, I observed firsthand the fast growing antiwar movement in the country that, in my opinion, would eventually cause the United States to disengage from Viet Nam. I knew that President Nixon's "Vietnamization Program" would not work because it was too little and too late. I was certain that we had to fight alone to defend that last enclave of MRI. Tien Sa would be the fateful place where we would fight our last battle.

The Tien Sa-Son Tra area reminded me of Bataan in the Philippines where American and Philippine troops fought their last battle before surrendering to the Japanese in World War II. A small peninsula surrounded on the north side by the Danang Bay and along the west side by the Da River, which constituted a natural barrier to infantry attack, Tien Sa was also protected from direct fire by a small hill located behind the Navy headquarters building. On the other hand, due to its location on the ocean front, the Tien Sa-Son Tra peninsula could be resupplied by sea.

Thus, I directed I Corps Engineer units to excavate under the hill behind Captain Thoai's headquarters and to construct an underground CP from which we could direct our last battle that I was sure was coming.

In the meantime, the situation at Quang Tri had worsened. Despite a heroic defense, casualties began to mount and on May 1, NVA divisions, spearheaded by armored units, crossed the Thach Han River and encircled the 3rd Division inside the Citadel. Judging the situation hopeless, General Giai ordered the evacuation of the Citadel and withdrew his troops to the next line of defense south of the My Chanh River, which was defended by the Airborne Division and one Marine Brigade. The Airborne Division with two brigades was responsible for the area south of My Chanh and west of RN1. The Marine Division with one brigade and reinforced with a Ranger Group was responsible for the area south of My Chanh and east of RN1.

On May 2, the remnants of the 3rd Division, the 1st Armored Brigade, the 5th Ranger Group, and the two Marine brigades had to fight their way back against pursuing NVA units along that fateful portion of RN1 located between Quang Tri and My Chanh. The withdrawal was rendered more difficult by thousands of refugees from Quang Tri who fled south to escape the war. Many perished under artillery and missile concentrations along this section of RN1, which was subsequently littered with charred corpses and burned vehicles. That section of RN1 was later known as "The Freeway of Horror."

That night, stragglers and deserters from withdrawing units caused quite a commotion in Hue. Gangs of looters and gunmen ran rampant in the commercial district, burning the market place and creating anarchy in the Imperial City. Often discipline breakdown follows a retreat. I recalled that French Marshal Pétain sent deserters to firing squads to reestablish discipline after the first setbacks at Verdun during World War I. General Lam refused to take the same radical measures and I Corps's MPs had a hard time rounding up the rioting stragglers in Hue in order to reestablish order.

General Giai, 3rd Division commander, was escorted to Saigon to stand trial at a military tribunal for withdrawing without permission. He was later sentenced to a jail term. Brig. Gen. Nguyen Duy Hinh, an armor officer, was named new commander of the 3rd Division whose remnants had been moved to Danang for refurbishing and retraining. Replacements arrived from MRI recruit training centers. Weapons and materials were flown in from Saigon to replace the ones lost at Quang Tri and Dong Ha.

Looking back on the fall of Quang Tri, I believe that one of I Corps' mistakes was to put too many units under the tactical control of the 3rd Division. General Giai and his small staff, holed up in the Quang Tri Citadel, which was under constant enemy artillery bombardments, were unable to adequately control all the subordinate units; this resulted in confusion, even chaos. New boundary lines should have been redrawn to relieve tactical pressure from the embattled 3rd Division. The Marine Division, with two brigades participating in the defense of the area north of Quang Tri, should have been assigned a tactical area, so it could be in a position to better coordinate and support its organic units. In retrospect, I found it difficult to understand why General Khang, commanding the Marine Division, readily surrendered his authority by agreeing to put his two brigades under the command of the embattled 3rd Division.

At any rate, it was obvious that General Lam's days as I Corps Commander were numbered. Three days after the fall of Quang Tri, Lam was relieved of his command and reassigned as assistant to the prime minister for anti-narcotics operations. This was a position newly created for generals who were in disgrace. In the meantime, I took over as Acting I Corps Commander pending the appointment of a new corps commander. I immediately ordered two RF battalion groups from Thua Thien Province to reinforce the Marine Division on the My Chanh new defense line, east of RN1, the defense sector west of RN1 being held by the Airborne Division with two brigades. I also requested additional B-52 sorties on enemy lines of communication and Naval gunfire from the U.S. 7th Fleet on enemy concentrations north of Quang Tri.

Staff officers speculated that I would be the logical choice to succeed Lam. General Khang, the Marine Division commander, told me he believed I would make a good corps commander but that he would have a problem with my nomination because I was his junior in rank. That night, Col. Duong Thai Dong, who represented the artillery command at I Corps Forward CP, came to see me in my office. Colonel Dong was my deputy when I commanded an artillery battery in North Viet Nam. Subsequently, he succeeded me as commander of the 4th Artillery Battalion in Pleiku in 1954. Dong was known in the Army as one of the best *tu vi* (astrology) experts. He disclosed that he had been requested the night before by Saigon to look into my *tu vi* to see if I could defeat the current NVA offensive and that he had filed a favorable report for me. "General," said Dong with a mysterious smile, "I think your time has finally arrived!" I thanked Dong for his favorable report, but I knew that as long as President Thieu remained in power, I would not have the opportunity to command an army corps.

Sure enough, on May 3, Lt. Gen. Ngo Quang Truong, the recently appointed IV Corps commander, was again appointed the new commander of I Corps. Because he was junior to both General Khang, the Marine Division commander, and General Dong, the Airborne Division commander, the latter two generals had to be reassigned. General Dong, a protégé of President Thieu, was appointed III Corps commander and General Khang became inspector general of the Armed Forces.

Col. Le Quang Luong who, as commander of the 1st Airborne Brigade, had distinguished himself during the defense of the city of An Loc, was elevated to the rank of brigadier general and succeeded General Dong as commander of the Airborne Division.

General Khang, the Marine Division commander, was replaced by Col. Bui The Lan, who was promoted to brigadier general. Lan served as chief of staff of the Marine Division. He had no combat experience and his new promotion was somewhat controversial. In the view of many officers in the Marine Division, a more logical choice would have been Colonel Tri, the deputy division commander, a highly decorated officer and recipient of two U.S. Silver Stars. There was an unwritten rule, however, that the commandant of the

Marine Division was traditionally an officer from the North, possibly because the majority of the soldiers in the division were from North Viet Nam. The only problem with Colonel Tri was that he was from the South.

The reshuffle of the command structure in MRI also affected the elite 1st Infantry Division. Maj. Gen. Pham Van Phu, commanding general, 1st Division, was appointed commandant of the Quang Trung Training Center near Saigon and was replaced by the newly promoted Brig. Gen. Le Van Than, an artillery officer.

The day after General Truong took over I Corps, he asked me to assume the command of the Southern MRI Theater which covered Quang Nam, Quang Tin, and Quang Ngai Provinces. At that time, beside the 3rd Division, I had the 2nd Infantry Division with two regiments (the 4th Regiment had been sent to Hue to reinforce the Northern Theater), and one Ranger Group. The 2nd Division was responsible for the two southern provinces of Quang Ngai and Quang Tin. Its headquarters was located at Chu Lai, thirty miles south of Danang. The 3rd Division's tactical responsibility included the province of Quang Nam and the city of Danang itself. Its headquarters was located on a small hill west of Danang Airport.

A week after I assumed responsibility for the Southern MRI Theater, I survived a helicopter accident. In the morning of that fateful day, I went to the VC-infested Que Son Valley, south of Danang, to visit the 5th Regiment of the 2nd Division operating in the area. After a short stop at the old U.S. FSB Ross about 2 miles west of the district of Que Son where Col. Tran Van Cam, the 2nd Division deputy commander, briefed me on the progress of the operation, I decided to visit one battalion which had a slight contact with the enemy. Colonel Cam suggested that I skip that visit because it was too dangerous, but I wanted to see the terrain of that area known to be the stronghold of NVA's famed 711th Division.

We landed in a small clearing marked with a smoke grenade. The ground was almost completely covered with tall trees and dense vegetation. It was an ideal place for a secret base. It was no surprise that it was traditionally used by the VC as a rest area and as a corridor to access the coastal areas in Southern MRI. I was met by the battalion commander who took me to his front units. Small arms fire resonated in the distance. The captain reported that his men were firing on small groups of fleeing enemies. I was proud of the men of the 2nd Division who were searching for the enemy in the treacherous Valley of Que Son.

When we left, the pilots tried a vertical take-off to avoid enemy fire. At about 1,500 feet, the helicopter sputtered. The chief pilot reported a mechanical failure. He told me he would try to bring the helicopter to the rice fields near RN1, where it would be safer to perform a crash landing. By the time we reached the flat area east of the highway, the helicopter engine had stopped entirely. I clung to my seat and watched the helicopter free falling on the rice paddies below.

The helicopter crashed near a small dike; its rotors collapsed and broke. I saw the pilots rushing outside then crawling on the wet rice paddies away from the helicopter. I unbuckled and left the site of the accident, happy to be alive.

In June, I received the visit of Gen. Paul Vanuxem, a retired French general who was a good friend and advisor to President Thieu. When the then-Colonel Vanuxem opened the *Cours d'État Major* in Hanoi in the early 1950s, President Thieu, then a captain, was one of his students. During the Indochina War, Vanuxem was one of those promising colonels Gen. de Lattre de Tassigny, commander in chief of French Forces in Indochina, selected to command a Groupement Mobile in North Viet Nam. I remember that the French press at that time dubbed these Groupement Mobile commanders "de Lattre's marshals," in allusion to Napoleon's field marshals during France's First Empire. Not only a good tactician, General Vanuxem was unique in the French Army in that he held an *agrégation en philosophie*, France's highest academic title. (An agrégation was higher than a doctorate and was usually a requirement for university professors.)

General Vanuxem was also a very good friend of Viet Nam. He came to the country every year to see President Thieu and to watch the progress of the war. All his children were born in Viet Nam, which they considered their second country. Once, General Vanuxem sent his son to Viet Nam during a summer break to practice parachute jumping and to train with the Vietnamese Airborne

Division. His daughter also volunteered at Cong Hoa General Hospital in Saigon. It was reported that President Thieu, at one point, had even approached the French government to appoint General Vanuxem French ambassador to Viet Nam.

Col. Nguyen Ngoc Khoi, mayor of Danang, organized a dinner in honor of General Vanuxem. This was the first time I met the French general. Vanuxem asked me about my military career and whether I had served in North Viet Nam during the Indochina War. I told him I was an obscure battery commander in the Red River Delta and did not have the privilege of attending his *Cours d'État Major* in Hanoi. As I knew he was an *agrege de philosophie*, I asked him his thoughts on the formation of career officers, especially the advisability of providing future military leaders with a solid academic background including an equivalent to a university degree. I was disappointed that General Vanuxem still belonged to the French *Ancienne École* which refused to see the necessity of an adequate academic education for future military leaders.

During dinner, General Vanuxem told me he had just returned from a trip to the newly liberated city of An Loc with President Thieu. He was very impressed by the heroic stance of the Vietnamese garrison. In fact, at one time during the attack, Viet Cong T-54 and T-76 tanks were dangerously closing in on the underground command post of Brig. Gen. Le Van Hung, the 5th Division Commander. Col. Le Nguyen Vy, the deputy division commander, personally destroyed one PT-76 tank with a M-72 anti-tank rocket in front of General Hung's bunker.[55] General Vanuxem was deeply touched when he was presented with a Vietnamese flag which had withstood the enemy attack and artillery bombardments.[56] After his visit to An Loc, General Vanuxem wrote an article in the French newspaper *Carrefour*, in which he compared the successful defense of An Loc to the Russian stand at Stalingrad during World War II. General Vanuxem's comment reflected the indisputable truth that An Loc was the greatest feat of ARVN's arms, where courage and determination have not been equaled in the history of the Indochina Wars.

To understand the battle of An Loc, it is necessary to compare it with another siege which took place eighteen years earlier when

French troops battling the Viet Minh fought for fifty-five days to finally lose the battle of Dien Bien Phu and eventually the war itself. A comparison of forces and terrain would reveal the following differences and similarities between the earlier battle and the battle of An Loc.

The French had 15,000 men defending Dien Bien Phu whereas, at the peak of the battle, ARVN had only 6,350 men in An Loc.

The attacking forces were two divisions, plus a number of independent regiments, totaling about 30,000 troops in the case of Dien Bien Phu. In the case of An Loc, the attacking forces were also two divisions totaling about 18,000 troops, not counting the civilian labor force and other blocking forces which in both sieges probably numbered 5,000 to 10,000 men.

At Dien Bien Phu, the French had a perimeter of defense measuring sixteen by nine kilometers, but An Loc had a defense perimeter only one-tenth as large. In other words, in the early stages of the siege there were points within Dien Bien Phu well beyond enemy artillery range; such was never the case at An Loc.

Dien Bien Phu had the disadvantage of being on a valley floor, subject to deadly artillery fire from enemy batteries well bunkered inside the surrounding hills. Although the topography of An Loc was somewhat different, the city of An Loc itself was no less vulnerable as it was the only open terrain in the middle of a forest of impenetrable bamboo and rubber plantations.

At Dien Bien Phu, the French had twenty-eight artillery guns (twenty-four 105-mm and four 155-mm) and twenty-four 120-mm mortars. In An Loc, during the most critical days of the battle, only one 105-mm gun was available to provide close support. The other guns had been destroyed by enemy artillery during the first attack. The French had tanks at Dien Bien Phu whereas the Viet Minh had none. In the case of An Loc, the reverse was true.

What were then the causes of the success of the defense of An Loc? First, it was the determination of ARVN troops. The French had at Dien Bien Phu some of their best units (paratroopers and legionnaires), but they also had many hill tribe paramilitary units called the *partisans* who deserted en masse after the first waves of attack in which they were exposed to the Viet Minh's deadly artillery fire. (It is significant to note that the garrison of An Loc received some 70,000 rounds of artillery, or three times the number that was fired into Dien Bien Phu.)

Second, it was the fire support available, mainly B-52 sorties, that made the biggest difference between Dien Bien Phu and An Loc. Day after day, B-52 sorties hit NVA assembly areas, logistical installations, even the first echelon assault units. B-52 strikes were so accurate that they could hit enemy troops 1.5 kilometers from the An Loc defense perimeter and disrupt enemy offensive schemes.

At that time, one captured communist document stated that "Saigon's Infantry + American Firepower = National Liberation Army (NLA)." An Loc, and as we shall see later, ARVN's successful defense of Kontum and recapture of Quang Tri, unequivocally demonstrated that "Saigon's Infantry + American Firepower > NLA + NVA."

The following day, I invited General Vanuxem to visit the 2nd Division at Chu Lai. As we approached the Valley of Que Son, I told General Vanuxem through the helicopter inter-com: "It is exactly 7:58. Look carefully at the ridge of that mountain just north of Que Son district town. In exactly two minutes, you will witness some spectacular events."

At precisely 8:00 A.M., the mountain suddenly exploded before our eyes. A quick string of successive explosions followed by fire and then by white smoke engulfed the ridge of the mountain while below we could see the units of the 2nd Division moving from their positions to begin the uphill assault. General Vanuxem had witnessed for the first time a B-52 strike. "*Mon général*, I have never seen anything like this before," said Vanuxem. "It certainly was spectacular."

The C&C helicopter transporting us was a marvelous machine. It was equipped with sophisticated communication systems that allowed the commander to talk directly to ground troops, to the TOC at Headquarters and also to the forward air controller who directed the tactical close air support. The chopper also was equipped with two M-60 machine guns which could occasionally be used to advantage against the enemy troops on the ground.

As our helicopter was about to land at Chu Lai, headquarters of the 2nd Division, I heard on my radio that there was an engagement on the route to Bong Son, northwest of Quang Ngai Province. An armored column consisting of one APC troop and one RF company was stopped by heavy machine-gun fire. I directed the chopper pilot to head toward Bong Son Valley. Circling the target area, I spotted a camouflaged machine gun in a cemetery on the east side of a small abandoned pagoda. I told General Vanuxem that I wanted to land in front of the armored column to talk to its commander, but I did not want to unnecessarily expose him, a retired general, to possible machine gun fire. "*Mon general*, I will follow you wherever you go," replied Vanuxem.

We landed in front of the APCs and I instructed its commander to launch his assault while aiming his gunfire at the target that I would pinpoint for him. We climbed back into our C&C and circled the small pagoda at low altitude, north of the route to Bong Son. I directed my door gunners to take turns firing phosphorous tracking bullets to identify the enemy machine gun.

Down below, the APCs moved in formation, blasting away at the machine gun which was identified by phosphorous bullets fired from my C&C's M-60 machine guns. The attack was successful. Two Viet Cong were killed and a few were captured. General Vanuxem, a noted tactician, commented after we landed at Chu Lai that the operation was a remarkable example of coordination between firepower and troop maneuver.

In the meantime, the situation on the Northern Theater was very encouraging. During the month of May, the situation was stabilized along the My Chanh River. The enemy had to stop to await resupplies. The weather had cleared up and tactical air support and B-52 sorties had taken a heavy toll on the enemy. In June, the Airborne and the Marine Divisions conducted successful heliborne raids on selected enemy targets north of My Chanh. And in early July, these two crack divisions, refurbished and reequipped, finally crossed the My Chanh River abreast, to launch the counter-attack to recapture the city of Quang Tri. Although heavily outnumbered—by that time NVA's order of battle consisted of the 304th, 308th, 312th, 320d, and 325th crack divisions—the Airborne Division on the west of RN1 and the Marine Division on the east, supported by U.S. air power, had caught the enemy off-balance and they quickly regained some strategic terrain north of My Chanh. The morale was high and ARVN's counter-offensive appeared unstoppable.

The initial successes of our counter-offensive in the Northern Theater also had a contagious effect on the morale of the troops south of Hai Van Pass. The situation in the two southern provinces of MRI was relatively calm, and we followed with excitement the tactical developments in other parts of the country. The favorable news of the counterattack north of the My Chanh River, the liberation of the city of An Loc and the successful defense of Kontum in MRII by ARVN's 23rd Division (whose commander, Brig. Gen. Ly Tong Ba, had skillfully used his armored reserve unit to counterattack and destroy NVA's 2nd and 10th Divisions) had brought excitement and elation to the residents of Danang. People were proud of the military feats of their armed forces and especially the successes of the two elite ARVN Airborne and Marine Divisions north of Hue.

During the summer break of 1972, my wife and children joined me in Danang. However, there was one problem. According to experts on Chinese geomancy, the official residence of the deputy Corps commander on Gia Long Street had in the past brought bad luck to its residents. The property used to be the official residence of the corps commander, but after a string of corps commanders had been disciplined and discharged from the army during the 1966 Buddhist insurrection, and especially since the death of Gen. Phan Dinh Soan in a helicopter accident in 1967, it had been left vacant.

General Soan, the deputy MRI commander, a U.S. colonel from the Corps Advisory Team, and other staff officers died when the helicopter that took them for a visit to a U.S. battleship hit a cable near the landing pad and fell to the sea. It took local fishermen over a month to retrieve their bodies. General Soan's remains had been brought to the residence on Gia Long street for funeral proceedings. Rumor had it that it had been haunted ever since.

A naval officer I knew from the 7th Division in My Tho, Commander Thiep, insisted that I vacate the property on Gia Long Street. Thiep commanded a Naval Assault Squadron in My Tho and had participated in many operations with the 7th Division. He was now director of the Port of Danang and lived in a beautiful villa with a good view of Danang Bay. His wife had died the previous year of a heart attack. He had no children and as the villa was too large for him, he invited me to stay with him temporarily. I gladly accepted his offer because I liked the view of Danang Bay and Thiep's company.

Shortly after I moved to Commander Thiep's villa, I again changed residence. An old classmate at the *École Inter-Arms*, Le Van Phuoc, invited me to move to his residence also located on the bay front. Phuoc was province chief of Vinh Long at the time of the coup d'etat against President Diem. He was subsequently discharged from the army by the leaders of the coup because he was a supporter of Diem. A very astute officer, Phuoc cultivated a good relationship with Shell Oil Company when he was province chief of Vinh Long. After he left the army, he got a job with Shell and had since moved up the corporate ladder.

Now, he was regional director of Shell in MRI and lived in a luxurious three-story villa with a gorgeous view of the bay. Mrs. Phuoc was an educated woman and an accomplished hostess. Phuoc also had an excellent cook who could prepare a variety of French dishes. This was too much temptation for me to resist. It turned out that my stay with Phuoc was my most enjoyable time during the turmoil and confusion which followed the fall of Quang Tri. In the evening, after a long day visiting units on the front, I sat with Phuoc on the third-floor balcony, reminiscing and admiring the beauty of the sunset on Danang Bay.

Mrs. Phuoc offered to accommodate my wife and children during the summer break, but I did not want to take advantage of the Phuocs' hospitality so I moved back to the residence on Gia Long Street. Commander Thiep insisted, however, that we should chase out the devils before my family arrived. To do that, he hired an expert in magic art to perform required rituals to rid the house of evil spirits. Sure enough, my wife and children did not experience any ghostly appearance and they enjoyed every minute of their stay in the Gia Long residence.

I soon discovered that Commander Thiep was not the only high-ranking officer who believed in chiromancy and magic arts. One day, my wife and I were invited for lunch by Gen. Nguyen Duc Khanh, the 1st Air Division commander, and his wife. General Khanh had

attended the French Lycée Pascal in Nha Trang from which he graduated with the French baccalaureate degree in mathematics. Drafted
into the army, Khanh was sent to France to be trained as a fighter
pilot.

Khanh was a great believer in chiromancy. His master was a Mr.
Diem, possibly the most famous chiromancy expert in Viet Nam at
that time. Cu Diem—as his disciples respectfully called him—in
fact, had an impressive list of clients, which included such powerful
men as President Thieu himself and Prime Minister Khiem. Cu Diem,
thus, had gained increasing personal power as he had the ears of
the president; this was another reason that many generals wanting
a promotion actively courted his favors.

The day General Khanh invited us for lunch, I was busy visiting
the 2nd Division in Quang Ngai, so I told my wife to go to the Khanh's
residence first and to wait for me there. Mrs. Khanh introduced my
wife to *Cu Diem* as the wife of a businessman from Saigon and asked
him to make a prediction for her future. *Cu Diem* looked at my wife
for a moment but did not utter a single word. Finally, when I arrived, Mrs. Khanh introduced me to *Cu Diem* as my wife's true husband.

"This is very good! This makes sense," said *Cu Diem* at long
last, "the husband of this lady [pointing at my wife] must be a general or a cabinet minister or above; a lesser husband would have
perished because she has very powerful stars. And if I did not want
earlier to give you my prediction that was because I did not want to
tell you that a simple businessman would not survive the *sat phu*
[husband-killer] power of this lady."

Since that day, to my chagrin, my wife occasionally reminds me
of her newly discovered cosmic might.

In any event, my family enjoyed their vacation in the cosmopolitan city of Danang, the second largest city of South Viet Nam
after Saigon. Both the United States and France maintained a Consulate in the city. Dung, my youngest son, enrolled in summer classes
at the French Petit Lycée to improve his French. He was also a
frequent patron of the *French Centre Culturel* which frequently
showed French movies. Danang also had many French restaurants
where we could enjoy good French cuisine. One of these restau-

rants, La Moraie, overlooking Danang Bay, to my delight, served an excellent couscous.

Finally, by July, the 3rd Division became operational again. Brig. Gen. Nguyen Duy Hinh, the new division commander, worked hard to raise the morale of the division, which had suffered a heavy blow after the retreat of Quang Tri. To ward off enemy missile attacks on Danang Airport, the 3rd Division launched sweeping missions in the area around Danang.

In July, the enemy mounted a heavy attack on the district of Ba To located on the valley floor bordering the Plateaux GI near the Laotian border. The population of this remote district, accessible only by helicopter, consisted of 10,000 hill tribe people. The district was defended by a Ranger Battalion and two local RF companies. Most of the soldiers were Montagnards from a local tribe. The Ba To garrison, supported by tactical air, repulsed the attack, causing heavy casualties to the enemy.

I flew into Ba To with Colonel Loi, the Quang Ngai province chief, the day after the attack, to study the situation and to present awards to the heroic defenders of Ba To. Ms. Kieu My Duyen, the journalist I had met at the Vietnamese Embassy in Camberra, Australia, requested my permission to accompany us to Ba To. What I witnessed and heard in this remote district was one of my most unforgettable memories of the war. The district chief reported that the attack was so intense that the soldiers' wives and children had to pitch in and fight. He introduced me to a little Montagnard girl, possibly eleven or twelve, who had braved enemy fire to supply ammunition to her father manning a machine gun on the defense perimeter. Touched by the story of the heroic Montagnard girl fighting alongside her father, I turned toward Ms. Kieu My Duyen and said: "Please tell the people in Saigon, the politicians who oppose the war and those who want to negotiate with the enemy to form a coalition government, that a little hill tribe girl, poor and illiterate, did not ask why she fought. She knew that the only way to save her district and her family was to fight against the oppressor."

In August 1972, to relieve ARVN's pressure on the Northern Theater and to delay their advance on Quang Tri, NVA launched their offensive in the Que Son Valley south of Danang. NVA's 711th

Infantry Division, supported by elements of an armored regiment, overran the 5th Infantry Regiment of the 2nd Division which held the old FSB Ross, two kilometers west of the district town of Que Son in Quang Nam Province. The district headquarters was also overrun. Elements of NVA's 711th Division were now pushing eastward in an effort to cut off RN1 between Quang Nam and Quang Tin.

The following day, I flew to the 2nd Division Forward CP at FSB Baldy, located on a small hill near RN1, to evaluate the situation. As I walked toward the Division CP, two Communist 82-mm mortar shells exploded about one hundred meters from me. Luckily, no one was hurt.

The division staff briefed me on the latest tactical developments. They were far from optimistic: The 6th Regiment and two Ranger battalions were having heavy contact with the enemy and could barely hold the high ground located on the east side of a small creek which ran in the northerly direction, almost parallel to the railway and RN1.

After the briefing, Mr. Thomas, Senior Advisor to Quang Tin Province, expressed his concern that the provincial town of Quang Tin would be the next target if the 711th NVA Division was not expelled from Que Son. Mr. Thomas was an old Viet Nam hand. He had worked in the U.S. Consulate in Hanoi during the Indochina War. I told him I was confident that, with the reinforcement of the 4th Regiment from the Northern Theater and with adequate air support, I could retake both FSB Ross and the district town of Que Son.

"General Thi," Mr. Thomas said unconvinced, "I think you are being too polite."

Brig. Gen. Phan Hoa Hiep, the 2nd Division commander, requested authorization to appoint Lt. Col. Vo Vang, my assistant, as the new 5th Regiment commander. I readily acquiesced to General Hiep's request because the 5th Regiment, badly mauled at FSB Ross, needed to be regrouped, refurbished, and retrained in the shortest possible time in order to become operational again. I knew Col. Vo Vang could do the job. Vang, a highly decorated officer, was an instructor at the Military Academy. He had distinguished himself as the commander of a Ranger Battalion during the 1968 Tet Offensive in Hue. (His battalion participated in the bloody combat for the recapture of the Hue Citadel.) When I was assigned to MRI, I took Colonel Vang with me because he was familiar with the terrain and the tactical situation in the area.[57]

Back at Corps Headquarters, I called General Truong in Hue and requested that the 4th Regiment be returned to the 2nd Division that day so that a counterattack could be launched the next day to recapture the district town of Que Son. I also requested, through a U.S. Advisory Team's channel, two B-52 "boxes" along the west side of the creek where heavy enemy concentrations had been reported. (In U.S. military jargon, one B-52 "box" is usually one rectangle of one by two kilometers drawn on the intended target to be saturated with B-52 bombs.) This B-52 strike was to take place in the early hours the next day in preparation for a counterattack, which would be carried out by a newly constituted mechanized task force consisting of the 4th Regiment and one tank squadron.

Around 1:00 AM., I received a call from General Phan Hoa Hiep reporting that the situation was very critical and that he expected an imminent enemy attack on FSB Baldy. Unexpectedly, and like a bombshell, Hiep offered his resignation. Hiep was an armor officer and a protégé of General Lam, the former I Corps Commander. He seemed to be competent and aggressive but his resignation was a big disappointment; it also came at the worst possible time.

After I spoke with General Hiep, I called General Truong in Hue and requested that a new division commander be appointed immediately to replace Hiep. Truong asked me if I had any candidate for the job. I told him that Col. Tran Van Nhat, the province chief of An Loc, seemed to be the right man. I had never met Colonel Nhat but I was impressed by press reports that indicated that Nhat's sense of duty and determination were instrumental in the successful defense of An Loc. Nhat, in fact, was on leave in Saigon when NVA's divisions were closing in on An Loc. Without hesitation, Nhat rushed back just in time before NVA laid siege to the city. In my opinion, the 2nd Division needed that type of leadership to be able to face more crises that I knew were coming.

The B-52 strikes took place at 4:00 AM. After the usual artillery preparation, the Ranger Group in the north and the 6th Regiment in the south crossed the creek to conduct a frontal attack, while the 4th Regimental Task Force, reinforced with an armored squadron, enveloped the enemy forward elements by using a provincial road north of the provincial city of Quang Tin; they then rushed toward FSB Ross. Taken by surprise, the enemy gave up their positions west of the creek. The 6th Regiment reported eighty-two NVA bodies with assorted weapons and equipment on a small hill overlooking the creek. Later, we found that they belonged to the enemy crack 30th Regiment of the 711th Division. Next day, when Colonel Nhat reported to me at I Corps Headquarters, the Ranger Group had already recaptured the district town of Que Son. Later in the day, the 4th Regimental Task Force retook FSB Ross without serious enemy resistance.

After its defeat in the Que Son Valley, NVA's 711th Division shifted its activities south and captured the district of Tien Phuoc toward the end of August. As the tactical situation had worsened in Quang Ngai, the 2nd Division did not have enough troops to mount a counterattack on Tien Phuoc. Consequently, the mission of recapturing Tien Phuoc was transferred to the newly reconstituted 3rd Division. After some hard fought battles, elements of the 3rd Division entered Tien Phuoc in early in October. It was a major victory for the 3rd Division and its new commander. The Tien Phuoc victory also confirmed the operational status of the 3rd Division, which had come a long way in a short time.

Finally, some good news that lifted the morale of the whole country! On September 15, ARVN troops, after bloody combat, had retaken the Citadel of Quang Tri, the last bastion of NVA south of the Thach Han River. The Quang Tri Citadel consisted of a fortress of approximately 500 meters square surrounded by a five-meter-thick wall. Surrounding the wall was a fifteen-meter-wide moat. Between the wall and the moat, the 3rd Division had installed a thick barbed wire fence. The 3rd Division's engineer company reinforced the division's TOC located in the middle of the Citadel with steel plates and its roof with fifteen layers of sand bags. After their occupation of Quang Tri following the retreat of the 3rd Division, NVA forces,

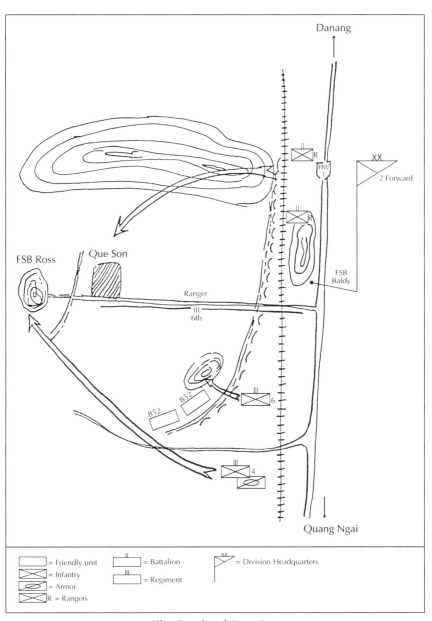

The Battle of Que Son

estimated to be of regiment size, inherited all these improvements, which they used to repel repeated attacks of ARVN troops.

The attack on the Citadel was carried by the Marine Division, which assigned the western sector of the objective to the 258th Marine Brigade and the eastern sector to the 147th Marine Brigade.

On the night of September 14, under cover of artillery fire, the 3rd Marine Battalion from the 147th Brigade blew a hole in the Citadel's wall where attacking forces had rapidly gained a foothold on the southeastern corner of the fortress. During the night, the Marines fought block by block and used hand grenades to annihilate the last enemy pockets of resistance. Finally, on September 15, after forty-eight days of uninterrupted fighting, the Vietnamese Marines, like their U.S. counterparts in World War II in Iwo Jima, raised the national flag on the main headquarters of the Citadel and on its surrounding walls.

It should be noted that the Airborne Division had been first given the mission to take the Citadel, but it had the disadvantage of having to secure its left flank against a possible NVA attack from the western mountains. As the attacking forces were approaching Quang Tri, the Airborne Division's left flank became longer and more units had to be used to secure it. As a result, the Airborne Division did not have enough troops to launch an effective assault on the Citadel. On July 27, after twenty days of unsuccessful assaults, the Airborne Division relinquished the mission of retaking the Citadel to the Marine Division.

Unlike the Airborne Division, the Marine Division east of RN1 did not have to be concerned with its flanks. This was the reason General Truong reassigned the main mission to the Marines after the paratroopers failed to take the Citadel. It was common knowledge that there was a rivalry between these two elite ARVN general reserve divisions; the credit given to the Marines for the Quang Tri victory was considered unfair by many officers in the Airborne Division. To add insult to injury, Brig. Gen. Bui The Lan, commanding the Marine Division, was later promoted to major general, while Brig. Gen. Le Quang Luong, the commander of the Airborne Division and the hero of An Loc, was ignored.

Without question, the recapture of Quang Tri was a personal victory for General Truong, the rising star in the Vietnamese Army. With that victory General Truong reached the zenith of his military career. Sir Robert Thompson, who directed the successful counter-insurgency campaign against the Communist guerrillas in Malaysia after World War II and was now an advisor for President Nixon, openly called General Truong one of the world's finest generals. He stated that he would not hesitate to put British troops under General Truong's command. An article in *Time* magazine even speculated that Truong was a likely candidate to replace President Thieu. Of course, President Thieu was not amused. A suspicious man, Thieu began to keep Truong under his watchful eyes.

The triple victory of An Loc, Kontum, and Quang Tri clearly demonstrated that ARVN, with U.S. air support, could beat NVA's finest divisions, supported and supplied by Russia and China. It was the coronation of a young army that had come of age. In 1952, when I was assigned to an artillery battery in North Viet Nam, the Vietnamese National Army still operated at battalion level under the tactical control of French officers while the Viet Minh was hurling entire divisions at the French units defending the Red River Delta. Twenty years later, ARVN units successfully repulsed NVA's multi-divisional offensive on three separate fronts.

The entire country was proud of its Army; people realized for the first time that a well-trained, motivated, and properly equipped National Army with adequate logistical and fire support could gain the upper hand against a highly indoctrinated Communist army in conventional as well as unconventional warfare.

In this regard, I think it is appropriate to elaborate on the enemy's motivation. The VC's and the NVA soldier's behavior, in fact, was strictly conditioned by a sophisticated system of political indoctrination. The following story, however, shows that this system was not without shortcomings: When I commanded the 9th Division in the Mekong Delta, one day, I overheard an interesting radio debate on the operation frequency during a Vinh Long Sector-directed operation:

"You, mercenary," shouted the VC, "you should be ashamed to be the lackey of U.S. imperialists."

"You, bastard, listen to me," retorted the RF soldier. "I can say, 'Down with Nguyen Van Thieu.' Can you say the same thing about Ho Chi Minh?"

The VC radioman must have been confused because he abruptly stopped the debate. Maybe the political cadre of his unit hadn't discussed such thing as freedom of expression under a socialist regime.

The communist system of political indoctrination is based on the psychology of hate and the politics of control. The VC and his NVA counterpart were taught to hate the "American imperialists" and their "Vietnamese lackeys," the "Thieu-Ky-Khiem clique" and its "fantoche" government, the "reactionary" forces in the cities and the "cruel and oppressive" officials in the villages. To insure compliance with the party line, a party apparatus parallels the normal chain of command, from party cells in small units to the highest levels of command within the army structure.

However, all this can hardly be sufficient: in the battle of An Loc and during the heavy engagements around Quang Tri in 1972, ARVN soldiers discovered bodies of NVA tank drivers chained to their tanks. One can't deny, however, that the VC and NVA soldiers, tightly controlled, mentally and physically, were able to incur hardship and generally perform well in battle. Overall, I believe that ARVN units were better trained than NVA and VC forces; before 1973, when we still had adequate U.S. air support, the casualty ratio was typically three to one in our favor. And to this day, I am certain that, had we continued to receive American fire support, we could have stopped and crushed the NVA's offensive during the critical months of February, March, and April 1975. Unfortunately, that was not the case. We demonstrated earlier that "Saigon's Infantry + American Fire Power > NLA + NVA." Because one critical variable was missing in this strategic equation, we inexorably ended up losing the war.

13

I CORPS FORWARD

SHORTLY AFTER THE VICTORY OF Quang Tri, General Truong asked me to assume the command of the Northern Theater. Since the recapture of the Quang Tri Citadel in September, the situation had stabilized along the Thach Han River, north of Quang Tri. There were only small unit-sized contacts in the mountains west of RN1, as the Airborne Division and the 1st Division were expanding westward in an effort to capture as much ground as possible before a peace agreement was reached in Paris.

Because the Airborne and the Marine Divisions were overextended and had suffered heavy casualties and because we had no more strategic reserves, we were unable to cross the Thach Han River to recapture the city of Dong Ha and the territory extending from the Thach Han to the Ben Hai River. This river constituted the southern limit of the old DMZ as specified by the 1954 Paris Peace Agreement.

My new title was Commanding General, I Corps Forward. I had a staff and a reduced headquarters unit, including a communication detachment. Col. Le Khac Ly, valedictorian of the first class at the National Defense College, and a native of Hue, was assigned as my chief of staff. The Corps Forward Command organization was later confirmed by an order from the Joint General Staff. It would be used in MRs whose size, geographical features, and tactical situation would prevent the main Corps Headquarters from effectively controlling the operations in the entire MR. On the surface, this new command structure seemed to make sense, as MRI, with a total number of five divisions and two distinct theaters, was no doubt the most important MR in the country, and an additional command structure to handle the two northern provinces appeared justified. However, I had a feeling that this new alternate organization was specially created to fit my rank and to avoid having to appoint me as commander of another army corps. I took solace in the fact that history has shown that there is a political side to most important military decisions. And in Viet Nam, as in most other developing nations, the political aspect seemed to carry more weight. Although, for political reasons, I was denied the command of a corps, I was nonetheless very proud to have under my command the three finest divisions of the Vietnamese Army.

In the meantime, the negotiators in Paris appeared to be heading toward some kind of peace agreement. In January 1973, the Paris Agreement was finally signed after the Americans exerted heavy pressure on President Thieu and after President Nixon wrote a personal letter to Thieu assuring him of continued American support and assistance in the post-settlement period. In his letter, President Nixon also promised that the United States would intervene militarily in case of severe violations of the Agreement by North Viet Nam.

Toward the end of January, President Thieu ordered I Corps to capture the strategic port of Cua Viet on the mouth of Quang Tri River before January 28, 1973, the date of implementation of the Paris Agreement. During the 1972 Offensive, the port of Cua Viet, where NVA's 5th Naval Regiment was stationed, had been heavily used by NVA to bring their supplies by naval and commercial ships from Hanoi. The capture of this strategic port would prevent NVA from building up their supply reserves for a new offensive in the event they decided to violate the Paris Agreement.

At the time of the peace accord, the tactical situation was somewhat stabilized along the Thach Han River, west of Quang Tri City, and to the east along a line roughly perpendicular to the coast line. Cua Viet was twenty kilometers north of the line of contact. The attack was to be carried out by the Marine Division because Cua Viet was located in the latter's zone of responsibility.

The attack was scheduled to begin on January 26, two days before the 1973 Tet. To carry out the mission of capturing Cua Viet,

General Lan, the Marine Division Commander, organized a special task force consisting of the 4th Marine Battalion and elements of the 1st Armored Brigade. As the task force was put under the command of Colonel Tri, the deputy division commander, it was called "Task Force Tango," named after its commander.

In order to seize the objective before January 28, first, we had to break through the enemy line and then to rush the armored task force along the coast all the way to Cua Viet. To "soften" the area around the objective, I requested twelve B-52 "boxes" in two days. At the same time, naval gunfire from the U.S. 7th Fleet were requested north of Quang Tri River to prevent the enemy from reinforcing Cua Viet.

At dawn on January 26, after an intensive artillery preparation, Task Force Tango broke through the enemy line. Taken by surprise, the enemy offered only scattered resistance. Serious fighting took place south of Cua Viet, but Task Force Tango quickly eliminated these pockets of resistance and by 8:00 AM. on January 28, forward elements of Task Force Tango entered Cua Viet, just before the Paris Agreement went into effect. At first, a few enemy soldiers came over to chat with the Marines and asked for cigarettes and rations. They looked sick, dirty, and now they seemed genuinely happy that the war was over and they could at long last go back to their families. Things, however, changed dramatically the next day. The NVA High Command sent over a former ARVN officer, Lieutenant Colonel Dinh (who had surrendered with his regiment to the enemy in April 1972 at the former U.S. Camp Carroll) to talk to our officers and pledge them to lay down their arms and join the enemy ranks. Then women and children were brought in from nearby villages. They surrounded the Marines and asked them to lay down their weapons. At noon, the women and children disappeared and NVA began to shell Task Force Tango, first with mortar, then with deadly artillery and rockets. Without American support—because the war was theoretically over— surrounded and outnumbered, Task Force Tango had to withdraw with heavy losses.

The period following the Paris Agreement was known as the "land-grabbing" period as both sides tried to occupy as much land as possible before an international control organization was put in place. Every day, elements of the Airborne and the 1st Divisions had to fight against infiltrating NVA elements which encroached on our territory. Soon, it was apparent that the Paris Agreement was completely ignored by NVN, which began to violate it right after it had been signed. Cities, district towns, and even schools were shelled, bridges were destroyed and government officials in rural areas were murdered.

The Paris Agreement allowed the Americans to withdraw from Viet Nam, but failed to require the withdrawal of an estimated 125,000 to 145,000 NVA troops from the South. (The Agreement had only this to say on the matter: "The question of Vietnamese armed forces in South Vietnam shall be settled by the two South Vietnamese parties in a spirit of national reconciliation and concord, equality and mutual respect, without interference, in accordance with the post-war situation. Among the questions to be discussed by the two South Vietnamese parties are steps to reduce their military effectives and to demobilize the troops being reduced. The two South Vietnamese parties will accomplish this as soon as possible.")

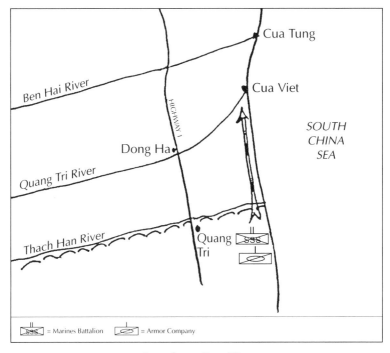

Attack on Cua Viet

The Paris Agreement was an American creation that allowed the United States to disengage "with honor," but did not solve the basic issue over which the war had been fought for a quarter of a century. This issue, according to Arnold R. Isaacs, a noted author on Viet Nam, was who would rule in South Viet Nam. "And this was not decided," wrote Isaacs, "just deferred to negotiations between two sides whose perceptions contained no visible basis for compromise. To negotiate a settlement would require bridging a gulf of hate and suspicion that was as wide as a million graves."[58]

To make matters worse, the International Commission for Control and Supervision (ICCS) created to help enforce the agreement, was organizationally deficient. From the beginning, it was obvious that such an organization could never fulfill its mission. The ICCS was composed of four members: two from Communist countries (Poland and Hungary) and two from non-Communist countries (Canada and Indonesia). Frustrated, Canada later withdrew from the Commission and was replaced by Iran. Every decision, to be enforced, had to be unanimous. But it was a known fact that there could never be unanimity between Communists and non-Communists in dealing with such issues as war and peace. Soon it became apparent that the Communist members in the Commission made every effort to help NVN "legally" violate the very agreement they were supposed to enforce. All requests for investigation of violations were turned down by the Hungarians and the Poles. Often, the Indonesian and Iranian officers had to conduct their field inspection trips alone and their observations, of course, were declared invalid and set aside.

Not only did the Communist members in the Commission fail to carry out their mission, they constituted a hazard as far as South Viet Nam's security was concerned. For example, every day, one could see Hungarians and Poles going around freely snapping pictures of airports, bridges, and military installations. They had direct radio communication with Hanoi. In Quang Tri, they went back and forth across the river to exchange intelligence information with NVA officers, while the non-Communist members could not visit NVA sectors without prior permission. It had become a pattern that whenever the Polish and Hungarian delegations withdrew from certain areas, these places would soon come under attack. Although we were aware of the Hungarian espionage activities, we could not confiscate their materials because of the diplomatic status accorded ICCS delegations.

Col. William E. Le Gro, G-2, Defense Attaché Office (DAO), mentioned that a report submitted by the National Police of MRI to the National Police headquarters in Saigon cited the following specific espionage activities of the Hungarian delegation:

February - Colonel Markus, Chief of Hungarian ICCS group at Quang Tri, together with Lt.Gyori and Sergeant Szabo toured Phu Vang and Phu Thu Districts of Thua Thien Province, using maps and camera to record the RVNAF defensive positions in the area.

March - LTC Markus, with camera and maps, was stopped at an RVNAF checkpoint on a road leading to the forward positions of the 3rd Infantry Regiment, 1st ARVN Division. A few days later, LTC Markus and another member of his team drove from Hue to Quang Tri, recording on maps the GVN positions and installations along Highway 1. On the last day of the month, LTC Markus and CPT Gyula Toser were seen photographing all bridges on Highway 1 between Hue and Danang.

April - Three Hungarian field grade officers arrived in Quang Tri from Saigon and, guided by LTC Markus, drove around the ruined city taking pictures of the Marines positions.

May - Hungarian Signal Sergeant Toth and two other members of the Danang team drove from Danang to Hai Van Pass, taking pictures of the Nam O bridge, the Esso gasoline storage area, and RVNAF military installations en route. Later in the month, Major Kovacs, chief of the Hungarian unit at Phu Bai was observed photographing, with a photo lens, aircraft landing and departing Phu Bai Airbase. He was also seen using binoculars and recording the locations of the RVNAF defenses around Phu Bai. Also in May, LTC Varkegyi and Lt. Borkely from Saigon toured the Hai

Van Pass with Major Kovacs-taking pictures of all RVNAF installations.

June - Another delegation visited from Saigon. Brigadier-General Csapo, Colonel Vida and three others were given the tour to the Hai Van Pass by LTC Horwath (Chief of the Hue unit) and Major Kovacs. Using a map to note the locations, the party took pictures of installations all along the way.

There was no connection, but during the last week of June enemy sappers got to the fuel storage area at Camp Evans northwest of Hue and the ammunition storage at Phu Bai. About 8,000 gallons of gasoline burned at Camp Evans; 4,000 tons of ammunition blew up at Phu Bai.[59]

To add confusion to an already complicated situation, the Paris Agreement prescribed the creation of a four-party Joint Military Commission (JMC), consisting of the United States, GVN, NVN, and the Provisional Revolutionary Government (PRG). The JMC was charged with the search for dead and missing-in-action (MIA) soldiers. Additionally, there was a two-party military commission (GVN and PRG) whose mission was to accompany the members of the ICCS on their inspection trips. However, except during the exchange of POWs in Quang Tri after the Paris Agreement was signed, I never saw these commissions in the two northern provinces of MRI.

The Communists, in addition to killing government officials and children in remote areas, shot at American search teams who went into the countryside looking for remains of Americans MIAs. A four-party JMC team was attacked by the Viet Cong in Binh Chanh, Gia Dinh Province, in December 1973, while on a mission searching for MIA's graves; a U.S. officer and a Vietnamese officer were killed, four Americans and three Vietnamese were wounded. In complete disregard for the Paris Agreement, NVN forces on April 7, 1973, shot down an ICCS helicopter that bore all prescribed identification signs while transporting its members for deployment at Lao Bao (Quang Tri), killing or wounding nine members of this organization.

Even Dr. Henry Kissinger—who co-authored the Paris Agreement with Hanoi's Politburo member Le Duc Tho—readily admitted these violations by NVN. As preparation for his post-Agreement meeting with Le Duc Tho, for example, Kissinger had this to say:

> To make our point, I had brought along a compilation of North Vietnamese violations in the two weeks since the signature of the Paris Agreement. The list left no doubt that Hanoi accepted no constraints of any of the provisions it has signed so recently. We had incontrovertible evidence of 200 major military violations. The most flagrant were the transit of the Demilitarized Zone by 175 trucks on February 6 and the movement of 223 tanks heading into South Viet Nam through Laos and Cambodia. Transit of the DMZ by military vehicles violated Article 15(a), on the wording of which we had spent nearly two months and which banned all military traffic, as well as requiring the concurrence of Saigon for civilian traffic. It also violates the explicit stipulation that new military equipment could be introduced into South Viet Nam only on the basis of one-for-one replacement through previously designated international checkpoints (Article 7). The movement of tanks through Laos and Cambodia violates Article 20, according to which all foreign troops were to be withdrawn from Laos and Cambodia and the territory of these countries was not to be used as a base for encroaching on other countries. When the tanks reached South Viet Nam, they would be also violating Article 7's prohibition of new matériel.[60]

Kissinger also related the following discussion with Le Duc Tho on June 13, 1973, in Paris, relative to the implementation of the provisions of the Paris Agreement:

"It is a contribution to the history among states," Kissinger said, "to find 350 tanks, 300 pieces of long-range artillery and several battalions of anti-aircraft guns and missiles classified as civilian goods not subject to the restrictions of Article 7."

Le Duc Tho began his response by saying: "Your intelligence service has been mistaken. I would like to point out your intelligence service sometimes mistakes an elephant for a tank." Kissinger asked him if he was pumping water through his newly built oil pipe-line so that the elephants in South Viet Nam had enough to drink. Le Duc Tho was quite blunt: "You have seen it wrong. But I think you understand also that, militarily speaking, the PRG must have some reserves. So now if the Saigon administration continues its military operations, the reserve will be sufficient to cope."

"Would he," Kissinger asked, "do his utmost to keep all elephants in North Laos?" "When the elephants are hungry and thirsty," said Le Duc Tho laughing, "they must look for food and drink."

When Kissinger protested these violations in Hanoi in February 1974, Vice Foreign Minister Nguyen Co Thach stated that the tanks probably were carrying civilian goods to the civilian population, which prompted Kissinger to write: "Hanoi's solicitude for the com-fort of the fewer than two million South Vietnamese under its con-trol was remarkable; it has shown little evidence of it while the war was still going on."[61]

To compound the problem, the antiwar movement that origi-nated in university campuses had now spread to Congress. Some usually staunch anti-Communist senators such as Richard Russell and John Stennis joined the ranks of their antiwar colleagues, who included, among others, Senators J. William Fulbright, Albert Gore, Sr., Frank Church, George McGovern, and Wayne Morse. Even gov-ernment officials who had previously supported the war efforts such as Robert McNamara, McGeorge Bundy, James Schlesinger, and Clark Clifford, had changed sides. Frances FitzGerald called these new converts "rationalists" to distinguish them from what she called "ideologists" who stood firm to the end in their support of the war efforts. "While the ideologists continued to hold fast," wrote FitzGerald, "the rationalists had had second thoughts."[62]

All of this led to a new antiwar policy and a major cut in foreign aid. The Second Supplementary Act, for example, prohibited the use of funds appropriated by the act to "support directly or indi-rectly combat activities in or over Cambodia, Laos, North Viet Nam and South Viet Nam." On June 29, 1973, Congress prohibited any military activity in the Indochinese Peninsula after August 15. These decisions sent a clear signal to Hanoi that they could freely violate the Paris Agreement without fearing reprisal.

Because the U.S. Congress prohibited any U.S. military activity in the entire Indochinese Peninsula, the violations of the Paris Agreement soon spread to Laos and Cambodia as well. For example, in violation of Article 20 which required withdrawal of foreign troops from Cambodia and Laos, NVN moved one infantry division into South Laos right after the signature of the Paris Agreement. NVN's refusal to withdraw its troops from Cambodia, on the other hand, posed a serious threat to the security of South Viet Nam, because the presence of NVN's troops would tip the balance in favor of the Khmer Rouge and would help open a new front on the southwestern flank of South Viet Nam. It would also help channel supplies and matériel for the National Liberation Front and NVN's troops through the strategic port of Shihanoukville in the Gulf of Siam.

That a small country such as North Viet Nam could afford to be so arrogant and to humiliate the most powerful country on earth showed how low America's prestige had fallen. Hanoi could afford to be insolent because it knew America had no more stomach for the war. It also knew that for the American people the war was over and they were now concerned with more urgent economic and political problems at home. In the 1970s, the American people, indeed, had to cope with urgent domestic problems and an emerging global energy crisis.

In retrospect, the post-Paris Agreement period was also a time of confusion and misunderstanding for everyone concerned. The relationship between the military commissions (JMC and two-party military commission) and the ICCS had never been clearly defined; there were also serious conflicts among the members of ICCS itself: conflicts, of course, between Communist and non-Communist members; misunderstandings between U.S. and ARVN officers, the latter unable to understand why these same American officers who, only days earlier, were still their advisors and through whom they requested logistical assistance and fire support, suddenly let them down and now appeared too friendly toward their former enemy. One story that circulated at that time around the Saigon cocktail circuit held that after VC Gen. Tran Van Tra, head of the PRG delegation (Tra was in charge of the 1968 Tet Offensive in Saigon and became Saigon's military governor after the fall of South Viet Nam in 1975) expressed his love of classical music, the Americans presented him with a stereo set and assorted classical music recordings.

There were also misunderstandings between the Iranian and Indonesian officers. The Indonesians considered the Iranians too soft toward the Communists. There were even conflicts between NVA and PRG soldiers. For example, during the exchange of POWs on the banks of Thach Han River under the supervision of ICCS, the NVA POWs caused much embarrassment to the Communists when they refused to cross the river because they saw PRG flags on the north side. Since Hanoi had always denied the presence of their troops in South Viet Nam, the PRG delegation had to send for a North Vietnamese officer to explain to the POWs that the PRG flags were a mere facade and that the whole situation was actually under NVA's control. Finally, the NVA POWs relented and crossed the river "to return to the PRG's ranks."

Shortly after the Paris Agreement was signed, the central government decided to reestablish the provincial government of Quang Tri which had *de facto* disbanded during the 1972 Great Offensive. Since the city was completely destroyed during the war, a new administrative complex consisting of prefabricated buildings was erected north of My Chanh River. Col. Do Ky, chief of staff of the Marine Division, was appointed new Quang Tri Province Chief. Since both Prime Minister Khiem and General Truong—who was also a government representative in MRI—were busy, I presided over the official ceremony confirming Colonel Ky in his new function. When it was time for me to speak, I simply wished good luck to Colonel Ky and handed him the official seal of Quang Tri Province. During the reception following the official ceremony, Mr. Thomas, the new U.S. Consul in Hue and former advisor to Quang Tin Province, commented that it was probably the shortest speech he had ever listened to during his diplomatic career in Viet Nam.

On Armed Forces Day, June 19, 1973, President Thieu, Prime Minister Tran Van Khiem accompanied by his cabinet, and General Vien, the chairman of the Joint General Staff, came to Hue to preside over an award ceremony for the troops in MRI. There was a parade of MRI units in front of the Citadel and General Truong asked me to command the troops participating in it. He also informed me that I would receive the Gallantry Cross with palm along with the division commanders. I told him, to no avail, that I did not want any new award.

After the ceremony, I drove to the airport with Prime Minister Khiem who was also Minister of Defense. I took this opportunity to request a transfer to a job in Saigon. After all, I told him, the war had ended and General Truong did not need a three-star general in Hue. Like General Vien, General Khiem was an unobstructive man. He was appointed prime minister for this very quality because President Thieu, who liked to run the show by himself, did not want independent, assertive people under him. As expected, General Khiem was non-committal, although I had a gut feeling that he was sympathetic to my situation. Further, Saigon was awash with rumors there was a rift between President Thieu and his prime minister whom Thieu considered a potential rival. As a result, General Khiem remained very cautious and did not want to get involved in the appointment of general officers, particularly those who, like myself, were considered politically unreliable by the Thieu regime.

That night, however, Mr. Hoang Duc Nha, the youthful Minister of Information, had a party for the general officers of MRI at the Hue Cercle Sportif. After dinner, we went to the terrace and listened to songs by singers from Saigon while watching the sampans crisscrossing lazily on the Perfume River. Nha was President Thieu's nephew. A U.S.-educated and ambitious man (he was considered, along with General Truong, a possible replacement for Thieu by U.S. media) he took great pains to court the general officers.

By the summer of 1973, I became increasingly weary of the precarious situation in the country and of the lack of U.S. action in face of increasingly blatant violations of the Paris Agreement by NVA. I was well aware that, for the Communists, peace is considered only as a temporary phase of relative military quiescence, an expedient breathing space to be used for revising tactics and refurbishing arms for renewed fighting under more favorable conditions. Although I was reassured by Vietnamese politicians who visited me in Hue that President Nixon had written President Thieu a letter in which he promised to intervene in case of serious violations, I had a sad feeling that the Americans had left for good and that we had to fight the next battle alone, which, I was sure, was in the making.

The Paris Agreement, however, provided me with a welcome respite to enjoy the charm and beauty of the Imperial City along with the hospitality of its residents. My wife and children, who joined me during the summer break, loved the city, the romantic yet elegant Perfume River with its exotic sampans, which Mr. Pham Quynh, the noted French language writer and a former prime minister in the Imperial Court, compared to the gondolas of Venice; they also loved the old Citadel and its historic monuments and the numerous imperial tombs around Hue. We lived in a charming two-story French villa located on Nguyen Hue Street in the old residential quarter. From the veranda on the second floor, we could see the left bank of the Perfume River, the red-roofed houses hidden behind blossoming flame trees and the historic Ngu Binh Hill which guarded the southern entrance to the Imperial City. In front of the villa, there was a big longan tree whose sweet, seedless fruits were the delight of my children during the summer.

On Sundays, I used to take my family to the Canh Duong beach north of the Hai Van Pass. Located between two rocky promontories, Canh Duong beach, with its weeping willow trees, natural white sand, and crystal clear water, was possibly the most beautiful beach in Viet Nam. The Airborne and the Marine Divisions had built a complex of thatch-roofed huts on the beach which they used as a recreation center for officers and troops. On Sundays when we were at the beach, the frogmen from the Naval Assault Squadron at nearby Dam Cau Hai Bay, loved to demonstrate their skills by diving under the rocks of the promontories to hunt for red lobsters which we steamed and ate on the beach.

During that first summer following the Paris Agreement, I was host to artists, government officials, businessmen, politicians and friends. Since the Huong Giang (Perfume River) Hotel, the only viable hotel in Hue, had been neglected during the war and was in an advanced state of disrepair, I invited the visitors to stay with us in our villa. Many foreign journalists also came back to monitor the implementation of the Paris Accords. They took this opportunity to tour some of the historic sites they were unable to visit during the war. My guests even included a delegation of movie actresses from Taiwan headed by Tham Thuy Hang, Viet Nam's leading actress. Col. Ton That Khiem, the Thua Thien province chief, organized a luncheon in their honor at the beautiful Tu Duc Tomb's reception hall built on an artificial lake covered with blossoming lotus trees. My wife and children, who knew most of the Chinese actresses through the popular Kung Fu movies, were delighted to be able to meet them in person.

My cousins from France, whom I had not seen for many years, also visited us in Hue. They had left Viet Nam in the 1950s and now that the war had ended, they returned to the country to visit family members. One day, I invited one of my cousins to visit the ruins of the city of Quang Tri, which was destroyed during the war. As our helicopter landed near the Citadel, my cousin starred in disbelief at the ruins. I told her this was all that remained of the old city. Suddenly, as if all this destruction and horror were too much for her, she started to weep uncontrollably.

Foreign tourists also flocked to Hue in the summer of 1973 to visit the Citadel and other historic sites. Fortunately, right after the Paris Agreement, Hue received monetary assistance from the U.S. Government earmarked for the restoration of major Vietnamese war-damaged cities. The restoration of Hue called for repainting the Citadel, the facade of public buildings and schools and the kings' tombs outside of Hue. The engineer in charge of this program, Truong Van Thong, was a native of the southern province of Bac Lieu. Thong had studied in France and since he spoke fluent French and English and since there was no government tourist agency in Hue, Thong also served as a *de facto* tour guide for foreign tourists. One young French journalist who came to Hue to study Vietnamese royal architecture was so impressed with the performance of ARVN troops and the number their casualties during the war that she volunteered to donate her blood for the Vietnamese combatants.

During that brief post-Paris Agreement period, Col. Ton That Khiem, the province chief, introduced me to a few members of the Hue intelligentsia. My wife and I enjoyed the company of Dr. Nguyen Van Vinh and Dr. Nguyen khoa Nam Anh and their wives. Dr. Vinh had his own practice and Dr. Anh was director of the Hue Hospital.

Both of them taught at the Faculty of Medicine of Hue University. Often when my family rejoined me at Hue, my wife brought along specialties of the Mekong Delta such as the *oc len* (small snails growing on the delta groves) and *con duong* (palm-grubs growing inside the delta water palm trees). The *oc len* steamed with coconut and the *con duong* sautéed with butter were the delight of my friends. In return, they took turns cooking Hue specialties in our honor; these gatherings remained some of our most cherished memories of our sojourn in the Imperial City.

The graduation at Hue University was a yearly event. After the graduation exercise, Dr. Chau, President of Hue University, offered his guests a French luncheon at his residence. That evening, we boarded a large barge near the Cau Truong Tien Bridge. From the barge anchored in the middle of the Perfume River, we ordered a variety of foods from the multiple sampans cruising in a leisurely manner on the river. We spent most of the evening discussing the history, culture, and traditions of the Imperial City. I remember one day I asked Dr. Chau, who had a doctorate in English, to translate into English a line in the famous poem describing the sounds of a Hueen night:

> *"Tieng chuong Thien Mu, canh ga Tho Suong."*

The trick in this sentence is the two words *"canh ga." Canh,* literally, means soup; *ga* means chicken. But *canh* has also another meaning. A night is divided into many *canh* (or watches) and *canh ga* means the early morning marked by cock's crow. A few years earlier, however, one Vietnamese congressman during a visit to a U.S. university, when asked to translate the above sentence, volunteered the following translation: "The bell of Thien Mu, the chicken soup of Tho Suong." The incident had been widely reported in the Vietnamese media and created a sort of national embarrassment; but Dr. Chau readily admitted that it was impossible to correctly reflect the exquisite poetry of this sentence in any foreign language. As a consequence, he politely declined to offer his own version.

In early August, General Truong directed me to take the Bach Ma (White Horse) Mountain north of Hai Van Pass. The occupation of Bach Ma, a strategic observation post, would allow us to control RN1 from Hai Van to Phu Bai during the dry season. (Permanent clouds made Bach Ma useless during the rainy season.) Bach Ma was a resort station built under the French Colonial Administration to accommodate vacationing French civil servants during the hot summer months. Famous for its year-round cool climate and its gorgeous view of the South China Sea, Bach Ma was also a short distance (thirty miles) from the beautiful Canh Duong beach. It was no surprise that it was the preferred vacation spot for the French colony.

I directed Colonel Khiem, Thua Thien Province Chief, to provide one RF company which would be helilifted to Bach Ma after VNAF's fighter bombers had "softened" the area. The first lift landed without incident. I directed my pilot to land with the second lift near what looked like an old French residential quarter. From the Bach Ma peak, I had a breathtaking view of the South China Sea and the Dam Cau Hai Bay down below. The old French villas were almost completely destroyed. The foundations, overgrown with shrubs and vegetation, were all that remained of this once beautiful colonial resort station.

Toward the end of August, bad weather and seasonal clouds prevented resupplies to the RF company on Bach Ma and on October 12, the RF company abandoned their position in face of a relatively weak Viet Cong attack. The bad weather that closed in on the mountains in the fall prevented us from recapturing Bach Ma. Further, by that time, we faced renewed NVAs attacks in the Truoi area and had neither time nor resources to go back to Bach Ma.

In September, the Airborne Division celebrated its anniversary. Following the French tradition, every arm or branch of ARVN had a patron saint: Vietnamese paratroopers adopted the Archangel Michael as their patron. Like the Archangel Michael, who was brave and who chased the evils from the heavens, the paratroopers were the bravest soldiers of the armed forces and were committed to chase the VC from the Republic. Because the paratroopers descended from the sky to fight the enemy, they were dubbed "the angels with red berets" by an admiring civilian population. Consequently, every year, the Airborne Division celebrated September

29, the Archangel Michael day, which was also the Airborne Division's official anniversary. The 1973 festivities, however, were organized with more fanfare than in previous years because this was the first peaceful anniversary that the paratroopers had enjoyed in many years.

As for the paratroopers, there was no celebration without a parachute demonstration. Thus, General Luong decided to have a big demonstration on the Perfume River in front of the population of the Imperial City. To accommodate the VIPs, our engineer units erected a stand on the south bank of the river in front of the provincial administrative building. Among the guests were the members of the ICCS in Hue, including the Poles and Hungarians. The Airborne Engineer company also had pneumatic boats at the ready to pick up the parachutists after landing. General Luong invited me to jump with him in the first lift; I happily obliged.

On Yom Kippur, October 6, 1973, Israel's most important holiday, Egypt and Syria, without warning, launched a coordinated attack on Israel. In the first four days, Israel had to withdraw with heavy losses. After one week of fighting, Israel regrouped and counterattacked on the Golan Heights. In the Sinai, Israeli armored units broke into Egyptian defense positions, crossed the Suez Canal and surrounded one Egyptian army corps. This three-week war, known as the Yom Kippur War, occurred at the worst possible moment for Viet Nam, as U.S. military aid all over the world was diverted to Israel and Mr. Kissinger, busy with his "shuttle diplomacy" in an effort to negotiate a settlement, had no time for NVN's increasing violations of the Paris Agreement.

Around this time, I received a call from an old friend, Dr. Lan Phuong. Dr. Lan Phuong was now working for the French Pharmaceutical company Roussell in Saigon. She and her boss'wife would be in Hue the following week to visit and distribute pharmaceutical products to flood victims in Quang Tri and Thua Thien Provinces. Since the villages affected by the flood were inaccessible by road, the only way to reach the victims was by helicopter; the Army was the only organization who could provide this.

I flew Dr. Lan Phuong and Mrs. Ormancy, the wife of the director of Roussell, to the most affected villages located in the coastal

area east of RN1 between Hue and Quang Tri. This region had to
endure annual flooding during the monsoon season, but the 1973
flood was one of the worst. Over fifty percent of the villages in this
area were under water. After the war came the flooding, and then
famine and disease! It appeared that there was no end to the suffering of the residents of this poor region, one of the most destitute in
Viet Nam. A couplet of a folk verse fittingly describes the conditions of the people in this area:

> *"My native village is very poor, my dear!*
> *In the winter, we lack clothing; in the summer, we lack*
>   *food."*

Although I knew Mrs. Ormancy's visit was calculated public relations, I was impressed by her dedication and compassion for the
poor peasants and fishermen of these two northern provinces who
had suffered more calamities than other regions of Viet Nam. Dr.
Lan Phuong worked tirelessly to distribute medicines to the flood
victims and to explain how to use these products. She volunteered
to examine the sick victims, mostly children and old men. For these
people, most of whom had not seen a doctor in their life, Dr. Lan
Phuong and Mrs.Ormancy's visit was a godsend.

Toward the end of 1973, I received an invitation from the Royal
Council to attend the birthday of the mother of former Emperor
Bao Dai. I considered it a honor to be invited and looked forward to
seeing the former Queen Mother.

Duc Tu, as the former Queen Mother was formally addressed,
lived in a modest home in An Cuu, in the southern suburb of Hue.
Colonel Khiem, Thua Thien Province Chief, himself a member of
the royal family, once told me that he had received instructions
from President Thieu to disburse to Duc Tu a monthly allowance so
she could maintain a decent lifestyle.

Duc Tu came from a modest peasant family from Vinh Loc District, south of Hue. Although she was in her early 70s, she still radi-
ated a natural charm and simplicity which made you instantly feel
at ease. I was to discover that she was both witty and politically
savvy.

The former Queen Mother received me in a large reception room decorated with relics and pictures of the royal family. She waved me to a seat next to her and asked me how old I was. I told her that I was the same age as Prince Bao Long, Emperor Bao Dai's oldest son (who was forty-one). She looked at me with an air of amusement and sympathy:

"General, you are so young," the Queen Mother finally said, "Why don't you have a *nang hau* [concubine]?"

I must admit that I was not prepared for this line of questioning. I knew that it was customary for mandarins in the old Imperial Court to have many *nang hau.* I was also aware that old traditions had changed, that Duc Tu was rather a "progressive" woman, and that Emperor Bao Dai himself had no (legal) concubines. I decided, however, to put her to task:

"Duc Tu," I replied, "I thank you for your thoughtfulness. And I certainly would appreciate if you would introduce me to some attractive young person from this much celebrated Imperial City."

"General, aren't you afraid I will relate this to *Madame the General*?" asked the Queen Mother.

"Duc Tu," I said, "I would like to respectfully remind you that it was your idea in the first place."

We had a big laugh. Sipping a glass of lotus tea, Duc Tu then inquired about my family and my background. By that time, I felt completely at ease with her.

"Duc Tu," I said, "the Lam Quang family in South Viet Nam is somewhat equivalent to the *Ton That* [royal family] in Hue."

"Is that so?" inquired Duc Tu with an air of incredulity.

"Duc Tu," I said, "I was just kidding. You know very well that there is no monarchy in a former French colony.[63] Now most of the big families in the South, who used to be big landowners, had lost their properties under government agrarian reform programs. Both my paternal and maternal families have been affected by these reforms."

Soon, luncheon was served. The members of the royal family were gathered around a huge table on which were displayed dozens of different dishes meticulously arranged on tiny bowls and plates. Duc Tu took time to explain to me some of the most exotic

Hue specialties, which were prepared only for certain official occasions.

When I later bade goodbye to the Queen Mother, she expressed her wish to see my family the next time they came to Hue.

Toward the end of December 1973, General Truong went on a two-week mission in South Korea. I was appointed Acting I Corps Commander and returned to I Corps Headquarters in Danang. One of our patrol boats, a PCE (Patrol Craft, Escort) on a routine patrol mission in the Paracel Islands, approximately 400 kilometers east of Danang, reported Chinese vessels in the area. President Thieu, who was vacationing in Phan Rang, his native province, asked Admiral Tran Van Chon, the Navy commander, to come to Phan Rang and report on the situation in the Paracels. After hearing Admiral Chon's report, President Thieu ordered the Navy to intercept the Chinese vessels and to escort them out of our territorial waters.

On January 1, 1974, a Chinese patrol boat opened fire. Our PCE fired back and destroyed one Chinese vessel, but was hit by a Chinese missile and sank. The captain of the PCE was killed instantly at his command post. I sent a patrol of F-5 jet fighters to destroy the Chinese Task Force involved in the attack. However, by the time they reached the islands, the F-5s ran low on fuel and had to return to their bases without engaging the enemy.

Unknown to me, the Chinese had every intention of controling the Bien Dong (Eastern Sea) with its huge oil reserve estimated at tens of billions of barrels. The Chinese missile that sent our naval vessel to the bottom of the sea turned out to be the opening salvo of the war for the conquest of the Paracels and—much later—of the Spratly archipelagoes. I was to learn years later that Hanoi had already conceded the Paracel Islands to Communist China as compensation for Chinese military assistance during the Indochina War. In a letter to the Chinese government dated September 14, 1958, Phan Van Dong, then prime minister of NVN, officially confirmed China's territorial rights on the above islands, despite the fact that both the Paracel and Spratly archipelagoes had been historically considered an integral part of Viet Nam.

On February 1974, NVA's 324B Division launched a series of small attacks in the 1st Division's sector west of Phu Bai airport.

The 324B Division had been reorganized and had now assumed control of five regiments: its organic 803rd and 812th Regiments and three independent infantry regiments, the 5th, 6th, and 271st. The 324B Division's objective was to capture the strategic western chains of foothills south of Phu Bai. Many hills were lost then recaptured. The inconclusive engagements lasted the entire spring. Toward the end of June, the 54th Regiment of the 1st Division, after some hard fought hand to hand combat, regained possession of the important high ground that controlled the Phu Bai area and its airport.

While skirmishes took place west of Phu Bai airport, I had to divert time to attend social functions in Hue. In the spring of 1974, Mr. Ormancy, and his wife, accompanied by Dr.Lan Phuong, came to see me. Mr. Ormancy was very eager to visit Hue after he heard favorable impressions from his wife about the Imperial City. Like the Parisians who escaped to the countryside during summertime, the French who lived in Saigon flocked to Dalat or Hue whenever possible to avoid the traffic and air pollution of the capital. The French were particularly attracted to the charm and beauty of Hue, which had become a "must" for French tourists in Viet Nam after the Paris Agreement.

To promote tourism and to introduce the Ormancys and other French tourists in Hue at the time, I borrowed a boat from the local River Assault Squadron and took the French delegation on a cruise of the Perfume River which was reminiscent of the cruises on *bateaux mouches* on the Seine in Paris. We departed from the Cercle Sportif late in the afternoon and steamed slowly upstream to the famous Thien Mu Pagoda, west of the Citadel, where the sailors using the ship's flood light created an impressive *effet de lumiere*. This short trip was a success and during the summer of 1974 even more French tourists flocked to the Imperial City to discover its charm and elegance.

During a brief stay in Saigon the following week, I accepted an invitation for lunch from the Ormancys. After the aperitif, the Ormancys took me to a restaurant run by a French Corsican in the old port of Khanh Hoi, across the Saigon River, to eat Maroccan *couscous*, my favorite dish. In the middle of the luncheon, Mr.

Ormancy proposed a toast and released what I considered a time bomb:

"*Mon general*," said Mr. Ormancy, "I would like to take this opportunity to offer you the position of Director of Personnel at Roussell. This position requires an honest person with proven managerial skills. And I know you are that person. You don't have to give me an answer right now, but please think about it. I will keep this position for you for six months."

I thanked Mr. Ormancy for his thoughtfulness. I told him that his offer was very tempting and that I would discuss it with my wife and would let him know my decision soon. By any standard, the position of Director of Personnel at Roussell was one the best one could hope for in Viet Nam at that time. Roussell was the largest foreign pharmaceutical company in Viet Nam. The Director of Personnel controlled, not only Roussell's permanent employees, but also an important team of highly paid *visiteuses medicales*, female agents who introduced new pharmaceutical products to the physicians. This position also was very political, because wives of high government officials, including reportedly the wife of General Vy, the Minister of Defense and even President Thieu's wife, were on Roussell's payroll. This was considered a public relations necessity and the cost of doing business in Viet Nam. The job of Director of Pesonnel at Roussell was a high paying job as its salary was almost three times the salary of an ARVN lieutenant general.

If I resigned from the Army as a lieutenant general, I was entitled to almost one hundred percent of my army salary. Additionally, I would have at my disposal a chief of cabinet, one aide-de-camp and one driver. Further, at that time, I had bought a one-quarter-acre lot on the northern bank of the Binh Loi River, just north of Saigon, on which we had grown banana and papaya trees. On the lot, I had a trailer given to me by my U.S. advisor at I Corps Forward Command. Each time I had a few days vacation in Saigon, I never missed going to my trailer in Binh Loi to rest and to enjoy the relaxing atmosphere of the countryside. My new job at Roussell would allow me more time to enjoy Binh Loi with my family and I looked forward to this.

I was also fully aware that as long as President Thieu was in office, I had no future in the army. My wife and I, thus, came to the conclusion that it was the proper time to leave the army and to accept Mr.Ormancy's offer. This had not been an easy decision, for the army had always been my life and my *raison d'être*.

Toward the end of the spring, I informed General Vien of my decision to leave the army and to ask him to give a favorable recommendation to my written request. General Vien simply told me that he would submit my request to the President. Shortly afterward, I formally sent my written request for resignation and informed Mr. Ormancy of my decision. President Thieu, however, refused to act on my request. Although President Thieu did not want to use me in the army, he probably felt more comfortable with me in it than outside of it.

A possible alternative—which had been often used in the past—would be to get rid of politically unreliable generals by sending them overseas as ambassadors-at-large. President Thieu probably considered this alternative: shortly after his visit to Hue, his special assistant, Nguyen Van Ngan, also came to Hue and met with me. Mr. Ngan originally was Assistant to Mr. Nguyen Cao Thang, a confidant of President Thieu. Mr. Thang put Ngan in charge of relations with Congress. Thang was one of the richest men in Viet Nam and a very controversial figure.

Thang owned the big *Office Pharmaceutique du Viet Nam* (OPV) which reportedly received a large portion of its revenues from illegal drug sales to the Viet Cong. He was also notorious for tax invasion. (Thang was also rumored to have bought a house for Thieu in Switzerland.) Thang made all the behind-the-scene manipulations whenever there was a vote on crucial issues. For example, Alfred McCoy in his book *Politics of Heroin: CIA Complicity in the Global Drug Trade,* stated that

> during the debate over 1971 election law it was an Independence Bloc member, Representative Pham Huu Giao, who floor-managed the passage of Article 10. This controversial clause required a minimum of 40 congressional signatures on every nominating petition for the upcoming presidential

election and made it possible for Thieu to eliminate Ky from running. Early in the debate, Representative Pham Huu Giao reportedly tied down a few tribe votes for a little as $350 apiece and most of the Cambodian minority's ballots for a mere $700 each. However, in the three days of intensive bargaining preceding the final balloting, the price jumped from $1,000 to $1,800 for the final handful that completed the proposal's winning tally of seventy-five votes. . . . Loyalty to Thieu seems to have its benefits. . . .[64]

Ngan was appointed to the post of special assistant to the president after Mr. Thang died of cancer. However, Ngan did not enjoy the same relationship that his predecessor had enjoyed with the president. Further, intense infighting between him and General Dang Van Quang, special assistant for National Security, one of the most corrupt men in Viet Nam under the Thieu regime, had somewhat weakened his position. In any event, Mr. Ngan took me aside and confided that he had recommended to President Thieu that I be appointed to the vacant post of Ambassador to South Korea. I thanked him for his thoughtfulness, but, as always, I remained skeptical about President Thieu's intentions.

A few months later, I was invited to attend a lecture by Dr. Phan Quang Dang, the deputy prime minister in charge of Pacification and Rural Development, at Hue University. Dr. Dang, a U.S.-trained physician, was a prominent leader of the opposition under the Diem regime. Dr. Dang liked to talk to university students to keep them abreast of political issues and the progress of the pacification program. He seemed to have a genuine concern about the needs and aspirations of the younger generation. He told me he had proposed to President Thieu that the Directorate of Youth be elevated to a ministry and that I be appointed Minister of Youth because, in his opinion, I had the required leadership qualities and could be a role model for young Vietnamese. I thanked Dr. Dang for his thoughtfulness. I also told Dr. Dang that I agreed that a Youth Ministry should be created. As for me, I would love to serve as the new Minister of Youth if I was offered the job. However, my ministerial appointment, like my proposed ambassadorship, had fallen through the crack of political discrimination and personal animosity.

In early June, I received orders to release the 1st Airborne Brigade to the strategic reserve controlled by the Joint General Staff. As a result, the Marine Division, reinforced with the 15th Ranger Group and the 1st Armored Brigade, was extended to cover the sector left by the 1st Airborne Brigade. The Marine Division also had operational control of Quang Tri's seven RF battalions.

To cover his new area of responsibility, General Lan, the Marine division commander, positioned the 258th Brigade with one M-48 tank company attached, defending the area east of Quang Tri. The 369th Brigade was assigned the center sector, including the city of Quang Tri and RN1. To the west of 369th Brigade, was the 15th Ranger Group positioned along the Thach Han River. The area left and south of the 15th Ranger Group, formerly occupied by the Airborne Division, was assigned to a task force under the control of the 147th Brigade and consisting of two Marine battalions, one RF battalion and elements of the 1st Armored Brigade. As reserve, General Lan had one Marine battalion and two tank companies positioned at the central location east of An Lo to cover the approaches to Hue.

The Airborne Division, minus one brigade, was responsible for the Song Bo corridor northwest of Hue. It was repositioned around Hue because, according to General Truong, the paratroopers could move out of the Northern Theater at any time.

In the summer of 1974, as usual, my family joined me in Hue during the school break. My children were eager to come back as they had fallen in love with the relaxed atmosphere and the hospitality of the Imperial City. For Tuan, my oldest son who was sixteen, this would be his last vacation in Viet Nam. My wife's sister, who lived in California, agreed to take him in charge, and he was due to leave for the United States in the fall to further his studies.

As I had promised *Duc Tu*, the Queen Mother, my family visited her at her residence shortly after they arrived in Hue. Duc Tu was visibly moved. She embraced the children and caressed the hair of my daughter Ngoc. "She is so tall for a fifteen-year-old girl," marveled Duc Tu. I knew she must have missed her great-grandchildren, who lived in France. (Ngoc's classmates at Gia Long High School didn't believe her when she told them later that she had had an audience with the Queen Mother.)

In July, I received a visit of five French cadets of the French École Militaire of Saint-Cyr. The cadets were all Eurasian. They were born from French fathers who had served in the French Corps Expeditionnaire and Vietnamese mothers. General Vanuxem made the arrangements for them to visit the land of their mother and to learn a few lessons from the war. I took them to Quang Tri to see what was left of the city. I also showed them the Citadel and described the counterattack to recapture it from NVA. The French Saint-Cyriens were visibly touched by the scenes of destruction of this war-ravaged land where their mothers had once lived.

After Quang Tri, we paid a courtesy visit to the Airborne and Marine Divisions. The cadets were impressed with the professionalism displayed by combat-hardened veterans in these two ARVN elite units. As most of our officers spoke French, they were able to answer their questions and share combat experiences with the future elite of the French officer corps.

While I was enjoying a period of calm following the signing of the Paris Agreement, I kept an eye on NVA's activities and I became increasingly alarmed at evidence that they were preparing for a new attack. It was the calm before the storm, but I felt frustrated and powerless to deal with these increased activities since the United States' inaction in face of NVN's repeated violations indicated that it had decided to look the other way and to leave South Viet Nam to its fate.

Shortly after the signing of the Agreement, with the connivance and support of their comrades in the ICCS, the NVA feverishly prepared for a new invasion. Directives No.2 and No.3 of 1973 from the Communist Central Office in South Viet Nam (COSVN) showed how the communists viewed the Paris Agreement: "Only consider the Paris Agreement as a new human factor, as a new weapon, which will benefit the building and development of the armed forces, the building and enlargement of the liberated zone. . . . Use the armed struggle as support, in all military actions; before, during and after the attack, use arguments, based yourself on the provisions of the Agreement to justify even the annihilation of the enemy unit. . . ."[65]

At the convention of the North Viet Nam Labor Party held February 11, 1974, Le Duan, first secretary of the NVN Communist Party, exposed the objective of the Communists when he called for strengthening the "aid to the revolution in South Viet Nam to proceed toward the reunification of the Fatherland." It was also Duan who openly called for the "fulfillment of international duty toward the revolution in Laos and Kampuchea."

The 1974 Directive No 4-74 of COSVN was more explicit. It urged its cadres and troops to vigorously push on with acts violating the cease fire, launch attacks at battalion and regiment levels against the Armed Forces of ARVN and simultaneously plan strong military activities in 1975, "of sufficient size to settle the question definitely."

The Communists began building a sophisticated network of routes across mountains and creeks to bring supplies to MRIII around Saigon. Their engineer units worked feverishly day and night to cut roads through forests and hills. Echoes of detonations could be heard every day beyond the range of mountains west of RN1. Three engineer and transportation divisions were activated to hasten the building of more roads and to expedite the flow of supplies moving south. These divisions were under the NVA High Command and comprised four engineer and four transportation regiments each. Not content with the old Ho Chi Minh trail on the Laotian border, the Communists built a new road east of the Annamite Mountains, running parallel to our RN1. This new road, dubbed "Ho Chi Minh East" by the Americans, permitted supplies to be delivered directly to Communist troops fighting in South Viet Nam.

Nguyen Khac Ngu, a noted historian, in his book *The Last Day of the Republic of Viet Nam*[66] (based in part on NVA General Van Tien Dung's post-war memoirs *The Great Spring Victory*[67]) described NVN's efforts to build this new strategic road.

Gen. Van Tien Dung wrote in his memoir that the number of workers building this new road amounted to tens of thousands. According to CIA documents, in 1973 alone, the Communists infiltrated more than 70,000 people.

In addition to these two roads running southward, the Communists also built or repaired a sophisticated system of lateral roads which permitted them to bypass and envelop every large city in South Viet Nam. To name a few, these included in MRI, the important Provincial Road 14 which linked Ashaw Valley to the strategic area of Truoi, south of Hue, and the area south of Hai Van Pass via another road named Col de Bay. The communists also repaired the old road linking Ho Chi Minh trail to the district towns of Ben Giang and Thuong Duc, south of Danang, and to the strategic Que Son Valley. NVA units feverishly repaired the Dong Ha and Khe Sanh airfields heavily damaged by U.S. bombings. They established an interlocking system of anti-aircraft weapons around these airports in order to protect these important bases. It is significant to note that in Quang Tri alone, NVA had eight anti-aircraft regiments with armaments ranging from 12.7-mm machine guns to SAM missiles.

In the middle of NVA's frantic build-up in preparation for a new invasion, the news from the United States was discouraging. On April 4, 1974, Congress again cut military aid to South Viet Nam for fiscal year 1974-75 from one billion to $750 million. Out of this $750 million, 300 million was appropriated as salary for the personnel employed by the Defense Attaché's Office (DAO) in Saigon. Significantly, Israel received $2.1 billion in military aid during the three-week Yom Kippur War in 1973. In other words, South Viet Nam, over one year, received 21% of what Israel obtained for three weeks. In reality, due to the Arab oil embargo followed by escalating prices, the military aid for South Viet Nam was worth only one-quarter of its pre-embargo value. "The economic aid was cut," said President Thieu on a TV broadcast, "the military aid was cut, and we have no means to fight."

The results of these cutbacks coupled with inflation were immediately felt on the battlefield. Each infantryman, for example, could only spend one hand grenade and eighty-five rifle bullets per month. Each 105-mm howitzer, the main artillery weapon in our arsenal, could now fire only ten rounds per day. The artillery units were short of trucks and prime movers to tow the guns. In 1974 in MRI, no artillery battery was capable of carrying its basic load of ammunition. The logistical situation was bad enough in the regular army, but it was worse in the RF. When we decided in 1974 to create RF battalion groups to increase the efficiency and mobility of the RF forces, we had to activate RF artillery batteries by combining two static artillery platoons to support these RF groups. But the shortage of trucks was so acute that none of these artillery batteries ever received a single truck to tow their guns, let alone carry their ammunition.

Transportation units experienced the same shortage of trucks and "petroleum, oil, lubricant" (POL), whereas in 1972 we could move any unit from one area to another; after 1974, the shortage of trucks and POL greatly jeopardized the movement of troops and our tactical mobility. In Saigon, the ambulance units were so short of gasoline that in order to evacuate the wounded they had to tow four ambulances in a row with a 2 1/2-ton truck. Not only were we short of trucks, the lack of spare parts also became acute in 1974. It was estimated that the lack of spare parts alone caused at least fifty percent of trucks and other vehicles to be inoperative. The most critical items were engines, batteries and tires. Very often one would observe 2 1/2-ton trucks running with six tires instead of ten. The 1st Logistical Command in Danang set up a plant to retread old tires, but it was destroyed by Communist sappers. Sapper attacks on ARVN logistical installations were high on the list of Communist priorities. During the first months of 1975, Communist sappers destroyed an important bomb depot in Danang Airbase and five million liters of POL in Pleiku. Consequently, a significant number of RF units were assigned to guard logistical installations and airbases instead of being used for mobile operations.

The "one for one" replacement authorized by the Paris Agreement never materialized. A tank, APC, truck, or bulldozer destroyed by a mine or lost in an accident was never replaced. By the end of 1974, the 10th Combat Engineer Group in Danang, for example, had fewer than ten operational bulldozers.

While army combat units badly needed ammunition and trucks, the Air Force also was acutely short of POL and spare parts; it had to ground a total of 224 aircraft: AD-6 fighters, C-47s, C-11-Gs, and C-123 transports. The grounding of transport aircraft dangerously affected our strategic mobility. While in 1972 we were able to lift one entire regiment (the Airborne Division with two brigades was flown in from Saigon to Hue in a few days), after 1974, it was estimated that our air transport could only move a battalion from one area to another. The helicopters available for troop transportation and supplies were also critically reduced. In MRI, we could barely move one infantry company at a time. Even the C & C helicopters assigned to each division commander could not fly more than thirty hours per month or one hour per day.

In terms of naval fire support, the situation dramatically changed: whereas in 1972 the U.S.7th Fleet could provide massive area fire up to twenty kilometers inland, after 1974 the naval gunfire support was practically nonexistent. The entire Vietnamese Navy had five old destroyers with guns which could reach targets only five to seven kilometers inland. It is significant that the VN Navy received only eleven million dollars as military aid for fiscal year 1974-75 (out of a total of $450 million for ARVN) and subsequently had to eliminate most of its river squadrons.

The Navy units most affected were the "River Assault Groups" whose mission was to intercept Viet Cong weapons traffic and transport of personnel on the multiple rivers and canals which crisscrossed the Mekong Delta. Due to the lack of spare parts, for example, only thirty percent of the famous turbo-propelled PBRs (Patrol Boat, River) left by the Americans were available for operations in 1974.

More importantly, radar stations located in the coastal cities of South Viet Nam, transferred by the Americans to the Vietnamese Navy, often could not be used to detect NVN transport of weapons and supplies due to a lack of electronic components. The Vietnamese Navy also did not have an adequate number of patrol boats to intercept suspicious foreign ships moving along the Vietnamese coastline. Consequently, by 1974, NVN was able to supply by sea weapons, food, and ammunition to their troops in the South.

On the political front, it appeared there was no end to South Viet Nam's misfortune. The Watergate scandal that broke out in the summer of 1974 came at the worst possible time. President Nixon, who was trusted by the Vietnamese people for his unswerving support, was now so politically weakened that his promise to intervene in case of grave NVAs violations had become almost irrelevant.

Gerald Ford who succeeded President Nixon (who resigned in August) was an unelected President and thus had no mandate to support South Viet Nam's war efforts. On the other hand, he also had to face a new Congress dominated by antiwar liberal Democrats.

To make matters worse, the internal political situation in Saigon suddenly deteriorated in September. Political dissidents and opposition parties, encouraged by the weakening of President Thieu's position, organized numerous antigovernment movements: Popular Front Against Corruption; Front For Coalition and Reconciliation; Front Against Hunger.

The Popular Front Against Corruption, headed by a Catholic priest from Quang Tri, Father Tran Huu Thanh, was the most powerful opposition movement. Father Thanh's anticorruption drive struck a sympathetic chord with the common people. Because corruption was one of the causes of the final collapse of South Viet Nam, I think it is appropriate to discuss the causes and practices of corruption under President Thieu.

Corruption was a way of life in developing countries and Viet Nam was no exception. If "absolute power corrupts absolutely," corruption also appears to vary in inverse proportion to the level of a country's economic prosperity. As a rule, corruption tends to increase with the worsening of the country's economy. In Viet Nam the economic situation deteriorated rapidly after 1973. Like other countries, Viet Nam was also affected by the 1973 Arab oil embargo and the subsequent global energy crisis. The rice shortage of 1972 caused by a poor harvest throughout Asia compounded the problem. Most importantly, however, the withdrawal of 500,000 U.S. troops caused mass unemployment (estimated at one-fifth of the work force) and accelerated the deterioration of the general economy. The resulting inflation was so bad that in 1974 civil servants and soldiers found themselves unable to support their families. They often had to moonlight to make ends meet. Corruption was necessary for survival in South Viet Nam's war-ravaged economy.

There was also an interesting social factor contributing to the practices of corruption in Viet Nam. Unlike wives in other Asian countries, the Vietnamese wife, under a deceiving appearance of docility and submission, held tremendous power. With the increasing economic difficulties experienced by the country in the early 1970s, the wives had to work, operate businesses, or indulge in other financial transactions in order to contribute to the family's income. Consequently, they gained increasing power and had a voice in their husband's important decisions. The wives of top government officials became so powerful that they practically ran their husband's businesses. They made all the behind-the-scene manipulations, sold offices and, of course, collected the money. In other words, they acted as their husband's power brokers. This allowed their husbands to avoid getting personally involved in political corruption.

Interestingly enough, the term "housewife" in Vietnamese is "*noi tro.*" "Noi" means "interior" and "tro" means "support" or "assistance." The problem began, however, when the *noi tro* evolves into a "*noi tuong*" ("tuong" means "general"). It became a disaster when the "noi tuong" or "general in charge of the interior" began to get involved in "foreign affairs" by selling highly coveted positions in the government and the Army.

Mme Vien, wife of the chairman of the Joint General Staff, for example, was known to have engaged in illegal real estate transactions. Mme Khiem, the wife of the prime minister, on the other hand, was known to exploit the administrative authority of her husband and was the behind-the-scene power broker for appointments to the posts of province chiefs, district chiefs, and the chiefs of provincial police departments.

The wife of the president was no exception. While Mme Vien's activities were confined within the Army, and Mme Khiem was involved in the appointments of province and district chiefs, Mme Thieu dealt with wealthy Chinese businessmen from Cho Lon and shared the profits from imports, exports, and international trade. One such businessman was the famous Ly Long Than. In his book *Nhung Ngay Cuoi Cung cua VNCH* (The Last Days of the RVN), Nguyen Khac Ngu reported that Than owned the largest textile company in South Viet Nam, called VINATEXCO, located on the outskirts of Saigon. During the 1968 Tet Offensive, VINATEXCO plants were heavily damaged by rockets from U.S. gunships because they were occupied by the Viet Cong. President Thieu subsequently instructed the Ministry of Economy to intervene with the U.S. Embassy for war reparations. With the help of the ministry, Ly Long Than inflated the damages and used only half of the money to repair the textile plants.

Another profitable transaction involving Mme Thieu and Ly Long Than was the trade in various metals salvaged from war matériel and ammunition, such as copper (bullet cases and artillery shell cases), steel (military vehicles, tanks, navy ships), aluminum (aircraft). Ly Long Than, using Thieu's authority, bought these materials at low prices and exported them to Japan on special ships flying South Korean or Panamanian flags.

Nguyen Khac Ngu also reported that Mme Thieu and Ly Long Than were actively involved in the trading of Viet Nam piasters on the Hong Kong market. As a matter of fact, during the war, Viet Nam piasters were highly priced in Hong Kong because the Communists needed the currency to spend in South Viet Nam. Mme Thieu and Ly Long Than not only sold Viet Nam piasters at a high profit, but were able to obtain U.S. dollars in exchange that they could transfer to their foreign bank accounts.

Corruption under Thieu's regime had taken such immense proportions by 1974 that even his staunchest supporters, the Catholics, began to dissent and overtly criticize him. They believed some sort of coalition government was inevitable and they wanted to position themselves for eventual participation. They also reasoned that Thieu's autocratic and corrupt regime did not have a chance to successfully wage the upcoming political struggle against the Communists. It should be understood that before 1974, while people still enjoyed an acceptable standard of living and relative security, corruption was somewhat tolerated. But with the departure of U.S. troops and the subsequent increase in unemployment and deterioration of the country's security, people resented corruption and social injustice and they demanded reform. Father Thanh's movement was a reflection of genuine popular discontent.

First, the movement aimed its criticism against Prime Minister Tran Thien Khiem and demanded his resignation. But Khiem, an astute politician, was able to ward off the attack by promising to cooperate with the Catholics by providing them with documents relative to Thieu's corruption. This turned out to be a good move because it left him untouched. It also helped implicate Thieu, whom Khiem hoped eventually to replace. As a result, Father Thanh publicly accused President Thieu and his immediate family of corruption and asked for his resignation. Father Thanh's Text of *Accusation No. 1* was largely circulated within the Army and among the general population.The treatise denounced the fact that President Thieu owned many houses in Viet Nam and abroad; that he was personally involved in narcotics traffic; that the *Vi Dan* (For the People) hospital (the largest and most modern hospital ever built in Viet Nam and whose administration and operations were directly supervised by Mme Thieu) was a center of corruption and favoritism; and that Mme Thieu's brother-in-law monopolized the import of fertilizer, which he sold at exorbitant prices.

With regard to the Army, Father Thanh demanded the removal of Gen. Nguyen Van Toan, II Corps commander, and Gen. Nguyen Vinh Nghi, IV Corps commander. Both of these generals—strong supporters and protégés of President Thieu—were accused of being involved in various forms of corruption. Father Thanh organized mass demonstrations in Saigon. Soon, the demonstrations spread throughout the country and President Thieu was compelled to make concessions. On November 1, 1974, the National Day (anniversary of the fall of the Diem's regime), Generals Toan and Nghi were removed from Corps Command and replaced by Maj. Gens Phan Van Phu and Nguyen Khoa Nam. Again, because I was still considered politically unreliable, I was not considered for command of one of these two army corps. (General Phu's promotion to the command of II Corps later proved to be a costly mistake. Phu was in poor health and could not sustain the stress of combat and long hours of flying. He openly complained to his staff during NVA's 1975 offensive that he had not wanted to be corps commander.) Almost 400 officers were discharged from the Armed Forces for corruption. Many ministers resigned and President Thieu proceeded to reorganize the government.

Although I agreed that corruption must be rooted out, I deplored the timing of the anti-corruption movement since social and political chaos in the rear would play into the hands of the enemy on the eve of their anticipated new offensive. What disturbed me more was that there were indications the corruption drive was supported or at least encouraged by U.S. officials in Viet Nam. Colonel Tuong, mayor of Danang, informed me, for example, that he had received a call from U.S. General Consulate officials in Danang advising him not to crack down on the upcoming anti-corruption demonstrations in the city. It was ironic because U.S. officials were partially responsible for the corruption practices in Viet Nam: their patronage system of buying obedience in exchange for favors had, in fact, nurtured and legitimated corruption. Now, in my opinion, these same U.S. officials were trying to use corruption and political instability to justify the U.S. disengagement from Viet Nam.

I watched these adverse political developments in Washington and Saigon with increasing alarm. I was particularly worried at the huge cutback in U.S. military assistance. One day, I expressed my concern to General Truong about the impact of the acute ammunition shortage on the outcome of the next war. Truong told me he was assured by a high authority in the Joint General Staff that we had reserve ammunition which was unaccounted for and which we could use in case of emergency. This was good to hear but I knew that tough times lay ahead.

Sure enough, encouraged by the Watergate scandal and the election of a new liberal, antiwar Congress, and an unprecedented increase in military aid from the USSR and China (It was estimated that this aid amounted to U.S. $1.7 billion in 1974 as compared to 700 million in 1973.), NVN increased their logistical build-up in the South during the second half of 1974. Our air reconnaissance sorties detected convoys of hundreds of Molotova trucks moving south, day and night, in the area northwest of Pleiku and southwest of Danang. Despite heavy losses inflicted by our airstrikes, these convoys kept moving. In the region northwest of Kontoum, VNAF armed reconnaissance detected a convoy of around 400 trucks and reportedly destroyed over 200. These figures could have been inflated but they gave an idea of the dramatic improvement in NVN's new logistical capabilities.

It was estimated that in MRI alone, during 1974, over 10,000 tons of supplies (mostly ammunition and food) were infiltrated every month. Our intelligence agencies reported that the Communists brought into South Viet Nam, from the moment the Paris Agreement went into effect until the end of 1974, a large quantity of heavy equipment consisting of 1,000 tanks of all types and more than 600 pieces of field artillery. The new weapons and military supplies included improved SA-7 rockets, T-54 tanks with launchable bridges, and 152-mm cannons towed by M-2 personnel carriers.

Air photos showed unusual activity in the city of Dong Ha just north of the DMZ. Dong Ha had become the main NVA logistical center where supplies were brought in from Hanoi by trucks moving down RN1, and by Navy and commercial ships through the strategic port of Cua Viet. Toward the end of 1974, air photos detected ammunition, matériel and other supplies stored in the open around Dong Ha. By that time, NVA did not bother to camouflage their supplies as the U.S. Congress, by prohibiting any military activity in the Indochinese Peninsula, had sent a clear signal to Hanoi that the U.S. wouldn't intervene in case of a new invasion.

On June 20, 1974, a navy patrol sighted a convoy of two steel-hulled boats and thirty wooden boats south of the port of Cua Viet. I sent a helicopter gunship to attack the enemy convoy, but after firing a few rounds, the helicopter's gun jammed. The convoy changed course and headed north toward Cua Viet, but one steel-hulled boat, still confused about its location possibly because of coastal fog, continued its course toward Hue. By that time, the Marine Division had been alerted. General Lan ordered the 1st Armored Brigade to attack the NVA transport ship which was sighted by the Marine Division thirty kilometers south of Cua Viet. One M-48 tank from the 17th Armored Cavalry Squadron fired one round of its 90-mm gun and sank the ship off the coast of Thon My Thuy Village, northeast of Hai Lang District Town. This instance where a ship was sunk on the open sea by a tank was probably unique in the annals of military history.

The Marines managed to salvage the ship, which bore the identification LCV 74. The Marines also recovered the bodies of the eight-man crew and part of a cargo consisting 82-mm mortar ammunition, 200 cases of Chinese canned pork, many Chinese rice bags, and 1,000 NVA uniforms. The boat's log revealed that the ship belonged to the 102nd Boat Company, 5th Naval Regiment. The 102nd Boat Company, stationed in Cua Viet, had eleven boats and two barges, seven of which routinely operated between North Viet Nam and Dong Ha.

While the situation in the Northern Theater remained relatively calm during the summer of 1974, NVA suddenly increased their activities southwest of Danang during the month of July. An infantry battalion and one Ranger battalion, which were to relieve the Ranger battalion at Nong Son FSB, were ambushed and overrun by elements of NVA's 711th Division. Nong Son was an important open air coal mine that had been closed because of the war. General Hinh, the 3rd Division Commander, sent a regimental task force to make a reconnaissance in force in the direction of Nong Son. It was stopped five kilometers south of the District of Duc Duc. On July 20, Nong Son fell to the enemy.

To cope with the worsening tactical situation in the Nong Son-Duc Duc area, General Truong decided to reinforce the 3rd Division with the 54th Regiment from the 1st Division. The 1st Division was one of the two ARVN heavy divisions with four regiments. The other was the 22nd Division in II Corps. However, even with only three regiments left, the 1st Division had to cover a sixty-kilometer front from the Song Bo approach to Hue to the northern slope of the Hai Van ridge. Therefore, at General Truong's direction, I had to pull the 15th Ranger Group attached to the Marine Division to constitute a reserve for the Northern Theater.

While the situation became a stalemate in the Duc Duc area, the enemy struck Thuong Duc in early August. NVA's attack on the district town of Thuong Duc, approximately fifty kilometers southwest of Danang, was indicative of what was in store for ARVN in MRI and, for that matter, for other military regions as well. Thoung Duc was located on a valley floor surrounded by high elevations which constituted the eastern slope of the Chaine Annamitique. Taking advantage of the newly built and repaired net of roads on our western flank, NVA moved their elite 304th Division from the DMZ to the valley of Ben Giang from where they attacked and overran the administrative seat of the district of Thuong Duc. The fall of Thuong Duc opened the way to the city of Danang itself.

As the 3rd Division was pinned down in the Duc Duc area, General Truong ordered the 3rd Airborne Brigade to Quang Nam to stop the advance of the enemy 304th Division toward the city of Danang. The Marine Division, minus the 15th Ranger Group, had to stretch out to cover the Airborne Division's positions west of RN1. Due to increased activities in the area west and south of Phu Bai Airport, I assigned the 15th Ranger Group to the 1st Division. As a result, I was without a reserve in the Northern Theater.

In the meantime, bloody combat took place on the peaks of the chains of mountains northeast of Thuong Duc. Although the 304th was stopped and beaten by the Airborne Division with heavy casualties during numerous hand combats, ARVN troops gave up attempts to recapture the district town of Thuong Duc. I was convinced that, had it not been for the Airborne Division, Danang would have already fallen in 1974.

The battle of Thuong Duc showed that NVA intended to take full advantage of the new system of roads and of their new strategic mobility to isolate and attack big cities from the rear. Communist strategy had not changed in 1974 and 1975, but the execution was made easier and more effective by the new road system. This strategy could be called a "strategy of indirect approach," a phrase coined by the famous British military strategist Liddell Hart. This strategy consisted of making a frontal attack with a relatively small force while executing a deep envelopment at the rear. It is safe to say that the collapse of South Viet Nam was nothing more than a series of successful envelopments. This was made easy, not only by the new road system built after the Paris Agreement, but also by the fact that South Viet Nam was a long stretch of territory with a very narrow width, at certain areas measuring less than one hundred kilometers from the mountains to the coastal line.

The enemy's new strategic mobility allowed them to strike any target at our flank and our rear while we were over-extended and lacked transportation means to deal with this new threat. It is significant to note that during 1972 in the Southern Theater of MRI, we had only one division with two regiments, while toward the end of 1974, three divisions were required to cope with the increasing pressure.

In the Northern Theater, NVA intensified their activities toward the fall of 1974. The enemy's stepped-up activities in the Truoi area were an illustration of the strategy of "indirect approach." Instead of crossing the Quang Tri River and attacking our troops on the demarcation line, the enemy chose to attack our rear and to disrupt our communication lines. The Truoi-Nui Da Bac area, south of Hue, was a very narrow corridor sandwiched between the mountains and the Dam Cau Hai Bay. If the enemy succeeded in capturing the high ground west of RN1, it would effectively cut off the Northern Theater from our logistical base of Danang and make the defense of Hue virtually impossible

The enemy also used the principle of indirect approach in small tactical operations in the Truoi area. The tactic consisted of infiltrating across the front line, then massing and attacking the battalion's CP from the rear. These CPs were often lightly defended and their fall usually resulted in the collapse of the battalion sector. Then, as the front line companies withdrew toward the rear to reassemble, they were ambushed and destroyed. In order to cope with this new tactic, we built a strong defensive position for the battalions' CPs or frequently changed their positions to prevent enemy reconnaissance. The executive battalion commander had to man an alternative CP to be able to take over the command of the battalion in case the main CP was overrun.

In August, NVA's 324B Division, which had taken a severe beating during earlier engagements, had been re-equipped and reorganized for new attacks south of Hue. The following report on NVA's offensives in the Truoi area and subsequent developments in 1975 is partially based on Colonel William E. Le Gro's own account.[68] As J2/DAO, Colonel Le Gro had at his disposition weekly summaries from DAO and J2/JGS, reports from DAO's regional office in Danang and from the U.S. General Consulate in Danang. The 271st and 812th Regiments, 324B Division, launched a coordinated attack on the Hill 350/Nui Mo Tau area on August 28. On Nui Mo Tau, the 2nd Battalion, 3rd Infantry, received over 600 artillery rounds but held the ground despite a furious assault from NVA's 803rd Regiment. However, an adjacent position held by the 129th RF Battalion was overrun. The other two battalions of the 3rd Infantry defending Nui

Bong, Hills 273, 224, and 350, bombarded by 1,300 rounds of artillery, were driven from their positions by NVA's 6th and 812th Regiments.

Thus, in one day, except for Nui Mo Tau, the 1st Division's gains during the summer campaign in the Truoi area were erased. NVA's 324B Division suffered heavy casualties but it now controlled the key high ground overlooking Phu Bai Airport and the strategic RN1. Heavy fighting throughout the foothills took place during the first weeks of September. The 1st and 2nd Battalions, 3rd Infantry, received the brunt of attacks conducted by NVA's 6th and 803rd Regiments. Although these two NVA regiments lost about 300 men and over 100 weapons, the 3rd Regiment was no longer combat effective due to casualties and losses of equipment.

In a diversionary effort to draw our troops from the Truoi area, NVA's 325th Division opened a new front in the Phong Dien sector north of Hue on September 21 by launching a strong attack on the 5th and 8th Marine and the 61st Ranger Battalions.The Marines held their ground despite intense enemy artillery bombardment. It was estimated that over 6,600 rounds of 130-mm field guns and heavy rockets hit our defensive positions. Our artillery responded in kind and exacted a heavy toll on the enemy. The 325th Division suffered heavy casualties in its failed offensive. In front of the Marines 8th Battalion alone, the enemy left over 240 bodies.

During the last week of September, however, NVA renewed their attacks in the Truoi area. NVA's 803rd Regiment took Nui Mo Tau. As a result, by the end of September, the 324B Division controlled all the strategic high ground west of Phu Bai from Nui Mo Tau to Nui Bong and Hill 350. It exploited its new successes by moving 85-mm field gun batteries of its 78th Artillery Regiment into forward positions to fire into Phu Bai Airport, forcing VNAF and commercial airlines to temporarily suspend operations to the only airport north of Hai Van Pass.

As the situation in Truoi became critical, I requested that the 54th Regiment be returned to the 1st Division. General Truong agreed. General Diem, the 1st Division Commander, used the 54th to relieve the 1st Regiment near Phu Bai. The 1st Regiment, the best regiment of the 1st Division, in turn, was ordered to replace the embattled 3rd Regiment in the Truoi area, and to conduct counter-offensive operations to regain the lost high ground beginning October 22. General Diem's plan consisted of conducting a diversionary assault on Hill 224 and Hill 350, with the main attack to be conducted by the 1st Regiment against NVA's 803rd Regiment on Nui Mo Tau. However, the attack was slowed by Typhoon Della which prevented air support. The 1st Regiment met strong resistance on Nui Mo Tau and made little progress. Its commander, Col. Vo Toan, a young and energetic officer, had been sent earlier to attend a six-month Command & General Staff Course in Dalat and the acting commander lacked the required leadership to motivate the troops in this crucial mission.

The situation stalemated on Nui Mo Tau with heavy casualties on both sides and General Diem decided to replace the 1st Regiment with the 54th Regiment.The 54th Infantry, reinforced with the 15th Ranger Group, had the mission of recapturing the strategic Nui Mo Tau. The 1st Regiment was given a few days rest and was ordered to take Nui Bong. By that time, the seriously depleted NVA's 803rd and 812th Regiments on Nui Mo Tau and Nui Bong had been replaced by the 6th and the 271st Regiments respectively. Despite heavy rains and difficulties with supplies and medical evacuations, the enemy offered strong resistance.

On December 1, Col. Vo Toan reassumed the command of the 1st Regiment and injected a new spirit into the attack on Nui Bong. On December 3, the 1st Reconnaissance Company and the 1st and 3d Battalions assaulted enemy positions fifty meters from the crest. They were driven back by strong enemy counterattacks and although the 1st Regiment had gained a foothold on the eastern slopes of Nui Bong, it failed to carry the crest.

The attack by the 54th Regiment on Nui Mo Tau was more successful. With good weather and effective air support, the 1st Battalion took one of the two crests of Nui Mo Tau on December 10 and captured the other the following day. To support the attack spearheaded by the 1st Battalion of the 54th Regiment, seventeen A-37 sorties were requested during the 9th and 10th of December. On the 10th, I directed airstrikes from my C&C helicopter. I had radio contact with the forward elements of the 54th Infantry and the A-

37 mission leader. I was glad that the mission leader that day was Captain Thanh, a promising officer and one of my cadets (Class 23) from the Military Academy. On that fateful day in December, Thanh was superb. He dropped bombs right at target. His skill and courage were instrumental in the recapture of Nui Mo Tau. A few days later, I flew to the 1st Air Division Headquarters in Danang to pin a gallantry cross on Thanh's uniform.[69]

The recapture of Nui Mo Tau disrupted enemy communication and resupply; it forced NVA's 78th Artillery Regiment to remove its batteries from its forward positions. As a result, VNAF and commercial airlines resumed operations at Phu Bai Airport on December 13.

During this time, I maintained contact with the Ormancys who, periodically, inquired about the progress of my discharge from the army. By the end of 1974, with increasing enemy activities, it became apparent that my leaving the army was out of the question. President Thieu would have a good reason to keep me in the army. Even if he had approved my resignation, I would have stayed because I considered it was my duty to serve my country at this crucial time of its history.

As 1974 drew to a close, I knew that our forces were stretched too thin and that we were without adequate reserves and means of transportation to cope with the future enemy plans that I knew were in the making.

Ironically, many students of Viet Nam spent their time searching for the causes of ARVN's debacle in 1975, but few realized that the seeds of that defeat were already apparent in 1974. Arnold R. Isaacs, who has done extensive research on the subject, compared the economic crisis in Viet Nam in 1974 to the Great Depression of the 1930s in the U.S.[70] According to Isaacs, unemployment was estimated at nearly one million people or one fifth of the work force. The inflation rate was sixty-five percent for 1973 and twenty-seven percent for 1974 and the wage increases of the average soldier or civil servant since 1972 were less than one-fourth of the increase in the cost of living. As a result, they were unable to support their families and satisfy the minimum necessities of food, clothing and housing. This had a devastating effect on troop morale. These economic difficulties, plus the lack of matériel and ammunition, along with the consequent increase in the rate of casualties, all contributed to the deteriorating performance of ARVN units on the battlefields.

According to Isaacs, ARVN lost 816 crew-served weapons and 19,340 individual weapons during 1974 compared to 384 and 16,897 respectively for 1972. Of thirteen infantry divisions, only seven were classified as combat-effective by U.S. military analysts. "As it awaited the more severe tests it knew would come in 1975," wrote Isaacs, "South Viet Nam's Army was a tired, dispirited and frightened force, lacking confidence in its leaders, its future, and itself." In my opinion, this was a fairly accurate description of ARVN's condition before the Communist spring offensive. Henry Kissinger, co-author of the Paris Agreement and, ironically, co-recipient of the Nobel Price with Hanoi's Le Duc Tho, confirmed this grim future for South Viet Nam and Cambodia. "After the summer of 1973," he wrote,

> I knew that Cambodia was doomed and that only a miracle could save South Viet Nam. North Viet Nam communications to us grew progressively insolent. There was no longer even the pretense of observing the Paris Agreement. And our legislative impotence added humiliation to irrelevance. We struggled to furnish what economic and military aid for South Viet Nam and Cambodia was obtainable from Congress. But the reasoning that had led to the legislated bombing halt also produced a systematic drop in aid levels. By the spring of 1975, Congress was considering a derisory "terminal grant" as if Saigon and Phnom Penh were the beneficiaries of some charity—when the accumulated strains led to their collapse and spared us that ultimate disgrace. In 1973, in my bones, I knew that the collapse was just a question of time.[71]

14

THE FALL OF
MILITARY REGION ONE

WHILE AWAITING A NEW NVA offensive in the two northern provinces of Military Region I, I followed with increasing concern the developments in other Military Regions. On January 1, 1975, NVA's 3rd and 7th Divisions, supported by T-54 tank units, launched a powerful attack on the provincial capital of Phuoc Long in MRIII, 115 kilometers north of Saigon. The Phuoc Long garrison consisted of 3,000 ARVN troops and about 1,000 RF and PF forces.

On January 5, 500 Rangers were heliborne to an area east of the city, but the Rangers were unable to link up with the besieged garrison. Although the fall of Phuoc Long would put the enemy at striking distance to the capital of South Viet Nam, President Thieu and the Joint General Staff decided not to inject an adequate force to save the garrison. A major concern at that time was that the rescuing forces might be trapped inside Phuoc Long and be destroyed by NVA's superior forces.

Phuoc Long, abandoned to its fate, fell to the enemy after a heroic, desperate fight. I was saddened by the news that Col. Nguyen Van Thanh, Phuoc Long province chief, and one of my best battalion commanders at the 9th Infantry Division, was killed with his troops. American inaction in face of this blatant violation of the Paris Agreement sent a clear signal to NVN that they had *carte blanche* to launch their spring offensive.

On March 10, 1975, NVA struck Ban Me Thuot in the Hauts Plateaux. The attack on this beautiful city again was a striking illustration of the enemy's strategy of indirect approach. Because the battle of Ban Me Thuot was the turning point in the Viet Nam War (it effectively marked the beginning of the end of South Viet Nam), it merits discussion in this chapter.

The Communists knew that they would pay a heavy price by attacking Pleiku, the seat of II Corps Headquarters. Instead, they moved their troops as if they were about to attack Pleiku; the 968th Division was positioned west of Pleiku and the 3rd Sao Vang (Yellow Star) Division blocked the An Khe area. The latter move effectively cut off RN19 linking Pleiku to the coastal city of Qui Nhon. They also cut off the road linking Pleiku to Ban Me Thuot with the 320th Division. On March 9, NVA's 10th Division attacked and overran the district town of Duc Lap, southwest of Ban Me Thuot. Then, on March 10, the 316th Division (called the Main Force Division of the West Hauts Plateaux Region), reinforced by Reserve Regiment 95-B, one sapper regiment, one artillery regiment and one armored regiment, launched a coordinated attack on the main objective, the city of Ban Me Thuot. At the time of the attack, Ban Me Thuot was defended by rear elements of ARVN's 23rd Division, consisting of the 53rd Regiment (occupying defensive position in Hoa Binh near Phuong Duc Airport), Ranger Groups 21, 24, and three RF groups.

The 23rd Division Headquarters fell on the 11th after an Air Force A-37, bombing enemy T-54 tanks, mistakenly dropped a bomb on the bunker of Col. Vu Quang, the division deputy commander, and destroyed the TOC's communication center. At the Hoa Binh base, one battalion of the 53rd Regiment resisted repeated assaults from three NVA regiments and destroyed many T-54 tanks. After six days of heroic defense, the battalion ran out of ammunition and the survivors had to disperse.

In his post-war memoir *Great Spring Victory*[72] NVA General Van Tien Dung commenting on the balance of forces in the Battle of Ban Me Thuot, wrote: "With regard to infantry, we have 5 while the enemy has only 1; with regard to tanks, we have 2, the enemy has 1; with regard to artillery, we have 2, the enemy has 1." This balance of forces allowed the enemy to strike at the targets of their choice to our rear.

Concurrently with their attack on Ban Me Thuot, on March 8, 1975, NVA launched a powerful attack in both Quang Tri and Thua

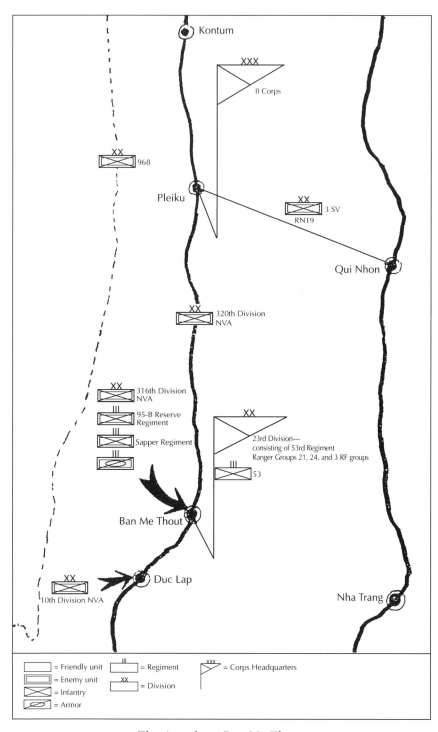

The Attack on Ban Me Thout

Thien Provinces. In Quang Tri, NVA's regular regiments and local Viet Cong battalions struck RF outposts in the foothills and infiltrated into the coastal lowlands. The 110th RF Battalion held its ground in the southwest sector of the province against strong enemy infantry assault. However, one Thua Thien RF company defending Hill 80 west of An Lo was attacked and overrun by NVA's 4th Infantry Regiment after an intensive 2,000-round artillery preparation. General Lan, the Marine Division commander, ordered the 147th Marine Brigade in An Lo to mount a counterattack the next day. The Marines killed more than 200 enemy, destroyed two tanks and captured many weapons.

At the same time in the lowlands of Quang Tri Province, one Marine battalion reinforced by RF units and supported by a tank company, destroyed two Viet Cong provincial battalions in Hai Lang District. In the coastal area of Phong Dien District, north of Hue, a coordinated attack by the 1st Company, 9th Tank Squadron, and one Marine company overran the forward command of the Viet Cong's Tri Thien MR, killing over one hundred Viet Cong including a high-ranking political commissar, and capturing twenty prisoners.

It is significant that during the Indochina War, Phong Dien District was a fortified Viet Minh stronghold. Bernard Fall, a French reporter at the time, in his famous book *La Rue Sans Joie* (Street Without Joy), described *Operation Camargue*, one of the most successful French military operations during the Indochina War in the same area. Later, during the Viet Nam War, Bernard Fall, now a naturalized American citizen and a researcher at Harvard University, was killed by a mine on the same "Street Without Joy" in Phong Dien while accompanying a U.S. Marine patrol.

By March 10, the Marine Division had regained all the lost ground southwest of Quang Tri and had eliminated intruding enemy units in the lowlands, but most of the Quang Tri population, estimated at 100,000, had moved to Hue and Danang to get out of the war zone. Watching the column of women, children, and older people streaming southward on RN1, I had a *sentiment du déjà vu* and was reminded of the carnage of the 1972 civilian exodus from the embattled city of Quang Tri. But this time, there was a difference: Danang, toward which they were heading, was also under heavy pressure and was far from being an ideal place to take refuge. In fact, two days after the offensive on Quang Tri and Thua Thien in the Northern Theater, NVA's 2nd Division launched a strong attack in Quang Tin province south of Danang. The hill districts of Tien Phuoc and Hau Duc fell on March 10 and Brigadier-General Tran Van Nhut, ARVN's 2nd Infantry Division commander, rushed in a relief column to defend the western approaches to the provincial city of Tam Ky.

Coincidental with the diversionary attack in the southwest sector of Quang Tri, the 324B Division, reinforced with two independent infantry regiments, again struck in the Truoi area. Supported by intense artillery preparation, the enemy launched a powerful attack on the chain of high ground that controlled the key Phu Bai logistical installations and airport. At the same time, three enemy provincial battalions infiltrated the lowlands of Quang Tri and Thua Thien. Their plan was to destroy the GVN administrative infrastructure and, in conjunction with the regular forces rushing from the mountains, to lead a general uprising of the population in the two northern provinces.

The 2nd Battalion, 1st Regiment, held its ground on Hill 121, but the 1st Battalion, 1st Infantry, was ejected from Hill 224. The 2nd Battalion, 54th Regiment, was forced to abandon its position on Hill 144, but counterattacked and recaptured its position on March 9. The elite Reconnaissance Company, 1st Infantry Division, surnamed the *Hac Bao* (Panther) Company, was driven out of Hill 50 southwest of Nui Bong after furious hand to hand combat.

To reinforce the defense line along the western chain of foothills, General Diem, commanding the 1st Division, dispatched the 15th Ranger Group to regain the lost positions. The 61st Ranger Battalion was ambushed on its way to the line of attack; it sustained moderate losses, but regrouped to join the 94th Ranger Battalion in a counterattack on March 10. The next day, a prisoner captured by the Rangers disclosed that NVA's 325th Division had moved south and was ready to join the 324B Division in the offensive in the Truoi area.

While General Diem was busy directing his troops to hold the defense line in the foothills, I took command of the operation to destroy NVA units which had intruded into the plains of the districts of Phu Thu and Vinh Loc, southeast of Hue. I constituted a task force consisting of the 8th Airborne Battalion, 2nd Airborne Brigade (the 2nd Airborne Brigade was scheduled to rejoin the rest of the Airborne Division in Danang at any moment), reinforced with two companies of the 1st Battalion, 54th Regiment, the 112th and 120th Thua Thien RF Battalions, and an APC troop from the 1st Armored Brigade. In two days, the task force succeeded in driving the enemy from nearly all populated areas in the coastal lowlands. It also eliminated two Viet Cong battalions. Among them was the crack K4A Battalion of the 5th Regional Regiment.

On March 12, I visited the 8th Airborne CP near a small pagoda on the southern outskirts of Hue, near the Hue Radio Station. While Lt. Col. Dao Thien Tuyen, the battalion commander, was briefing me, the Viet Cong fired a dozen 82-mm mortars near the pagoda. At the same time, heavy fighting erupted in the nearby village. A few minutes later, paratroopers brought in two prisoners in dirty maroon pajamas; they were possibly sixteen or seventeen years old. They were North Vietnamese soldiers assigned to a local Viet Cong company which had infiltrated into the Delta three days earlier. According to them, their mission was to enter a village and establish a "People's Tribunal" to try and execute all Popular Force (PF) soldiers as well as members of the Self Defense Force (SDF) and government cadres who resisted; to install a revolutionary administrative committee; to impress all PF and SDF into their ranks and then march to the district town and then to the city of Hue for the final liberation.

On March 16, a unit of the 54th Regiment ambushed a remnant of the K4 Battalion in the southeast outskirts of Hue, killing the battalion commander, his staff, and twenty men. Five prisoners taken by the 54th Infantry admitted that the population did not support them and only thirty-three men, mostly wounded, remained alive in the battalion.

It was evident that the Communists had misjudged the people's loyalty; in fact, they repeated the same mistake made during the 1968 Tet Offensive. Messages captured at the time conceded their costly defeats in battles for the control of the populated areas in the lowlands. The messages indicated that ARVN's determined and quick reaction and, more importantly, the population's loyalty to the government were the main causes of their defeats. Xuan Thieu, a NVN officer, in his memoir *North of Hai Van, 1975*, had the following to say regarding the battles which took place north of Hai Van Pass during March 1975:

> In certain areas, while engaging the enemy, we incurred heavy losses and this created a loss of confidence. One comrade shook his head and complained: "the plain is really difficult to swallow."
>
> I personally had the same feeling; when I heard that the units fighting in the plain had withdrawn to the mountains, I did not feel happy at all. I felt a little bit sorry, a little bit worried for the difficult and painful labor of cadres and soldiers. I was not really shaken, but there was something sad in my feelings.[73]

During this first round of NVA's offensive, Gen. Nguyen Bao Tri, my former boss at the 7th Infantry Division in My Tho and now director of the Training Directorate, was in Hue to inspect the Phu Bai Regional Training Center, which trained recruits for the units north of Hai Van Pass. We visited the RF units fighting in Phu Thu so he could report to the Joint General Staff about the intensity of the Viet Cong attacks in MRI. General Tri was impressed with both the performance of our territorials and the success of our operations in the lowlands.

During all that time, I ate and slept at I Corps Forward CP inside the Citadel; I did not even have time to talk to my family on the telephone in the evening, as I used to do in quieter times. My wife was very concerned about the situation in Hue. She called me every night and our children took these opportunities to talk to me. One night, Ngoc, my daughter, cried on the phone. She told me that her friends at school predicted that Hue would fall because the United States refused to resume air support. I reassured her that everything was under control, but I was painfully aware that my ability to hold Hue after the planned redeployment of the Airborne and the Marine Divisions outside of the Northern Theater was indeed questionable.

I was so preoccupied with the deterioration of the situation in the Truoi area and my inability to influence the outcome of the battle for the high grounds that I frequently had difficultiy sleeping at night.

Meanwhile, General Truong, in Danang, was facing a more serious problem: on March 12, he received orders from JGS to move the Airborne Division to Saigon, beginning March 17. Truong called General Vien, the Chairman of JGS, requesting him to reconsider, but he was told that the decision came directly from the President. General Vien informed Truong that the Airborne Division would participate in an offensive operation to retake Ban Me Thuot and that two battalions of the newly-created 468th Marine Brigade and a Ranger Group would be sent to Danang to replace the Airborne Division.

The next day, March 13, two days after the fall of Ban Me Thout, General Truong was instructed to meet with President Thieu in Saigon. According to General Truong, he was surprised at the absence of the other corps commanders and to learn that he was the only one President Thieu and Prime Minister Khiem wanted to see. He was stunned when President Thieu ordered the withdrawal of I Corps and the immediate abandonment of the two northern provinces of Quang Tri and Thua Thien. The Airborne Division was to be attached to II Corps before March 17 to help retake Ban Me Thuot. President Thieu also informed Truong that II Corps would start the withdrawal of its units north of Ban Me Thuot right after I Corps' withdrawal had been completed.

In Truong's view, the new orders were a departure from the old concept of "enclaves" which President Thieu had approved earlier and which was dubbed the "light at the top, heavy at the bottom" strategy by American military analysts. Frank Snepp, the CIA station chief in Saigon, reported in *Decent Interval*[74] that two weeks before the fall of Ban Me Thuot, President Thieu asked Prime Minister Tran Thien Khiem to study and draft a new plan of defense which called for a new demarcation line roughly linking Tay Ninh, Chon Thanh, Dalat, and Nha Trang with the defense of three bridgeheads or enclaves around Hue-Danang, Tam Ky-Chu Lai, and Quang Ngai in MRI.

This new defense plan was confirmed by General Truong who told me that during a meeting in early March with President Thieu in Saigon, the latter at one point spread his hand on the map and moved it back and forth in an arc linking roughly Ha Tien on the Gulf of Siam to the left with Nha Trang-Phan Rang area on the South China Sea to the right. *"Le futur Viet Nam, c'est ça!"* President Thieu said. In addition to this "heavy bottom," the new defense plan also called for the maintenance of three enclaves in MRI described as the "light top" of the defense system.

President Thieu's instructions to withdraw the troops from MRI and from the northern portion of MRII seemed to do away with the previously approved concept of enclaves. So, back in Danang, Truong called General Vien, chairman of the Joint General Staff, and strongly urged him to intervene with President Thieu to allow him to defend Hue, one of the enclaves in the previously approved defense system. President Thieu changed his mind and agreed to defend Hue.

The following is a reconstruction of the chronology of events leading to the abandonment of Hue, based upon my recollection, a 1982 interview of General Truong in *Doi* (*Life Magazine*), October 1982, and other documents made available since 1975.

On March 14, Truong flew to Hue and confirmed that Hue would be defended. He added, however, that a contingency withdrawal plan to Danang should also be considered. He informed me that the Marine Division, minus one brigade, was to move to Danang immediately to replace the Airborne Division; the latter was to be attached to II Corps in an effort to retake Ban Me Thuot. To compensate for the loss of the Marine Division, Truong gave me the 14th Ranger Group which was operating south of Danang. However, to shore up the defense of Danang, Truong directed me to move the 175-mm artillery battalion to Danang, along with one M-48 tank company. I told Truong of my concern about the military and psychological impact of the loss of the two elite Airborne and Marine Divisions on the Northern Theater. I requested Truong's help in keeping the portion of RN1 from Truoi to Danang open as the 1st Division was already extended to its limits. In my view, the defense of the Hue enclave or a contingent withdrawal of the troops from the Northern Theater depended on the availability of this crucial artery.

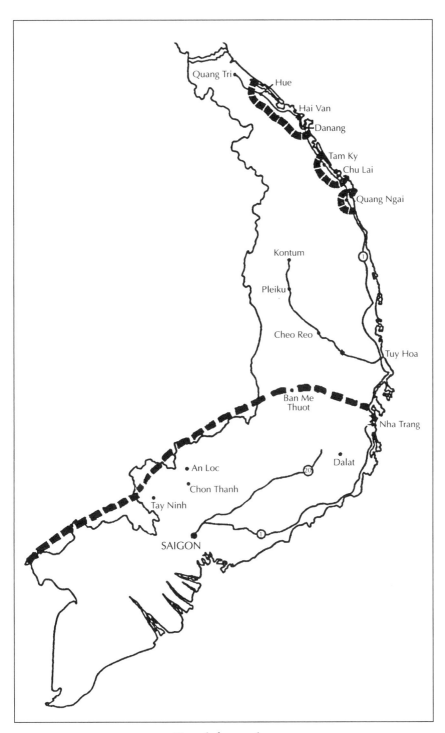

New defense plan

Although I did not tell Truong at the time, I simply did not believe in the concept of enclaves, given our reduced strength and limited airlift capability. To successfully defend the enclave of Hue, we should be able to protect the Phu Bai Airport and the Port of Tan My, which was questionable after the departure of the Airborne and the Marine Divisions. Even assuming that we were able to secure the airport and the seaport, we needed a huge airlift capability to supply, not only our troops, but the civilian population living inside the beachhead. It was all too clear to me that VNAF did not have the capacity to support the three planned enclaves in MRI, not to mention that Danang Airport, where the 1st Air Division was located, was already under the range of enemy missiles.

While the situation in MRI's two southern provinces of Quang Ngai and Quang Tin was rapidly deteriorating, the relief of the Marines in Quang Tri took place without incident. On March 17, the 14th Ranger Group, with a depleted effective force (less than 300 men per battalion), established its CP at Hai Lang, southwest of the city of Quang Tri, and sent its 77th, 78th, and 79th Battalions to replace the 369th Marine Brigade in the western sector of Quang Tri. The 258th Marine Brigade defending the eastern sector of Quang Tri was replaced by seven RF battalions under the command of two RF groups from Quang Tri Province. The shift of the units in Quang Tri was completed on March 17. The Marines' departure had a devastating effect on the courage and morale of the RF units and the civilian population.

Faced with the departure of the Marines, I reorganized the command structure in the Northern Theater as follows: Colonel Tri, deputy commander of the Marine Division, was responsible for the area north of Hue, and Brig. Gen. Nguyen Van Diem, commanding the 1st Division, was responsible for the area south of Hue. Colonel Tri, in addition to the 14th Ranger Group, seven RF battalions, an APC troop from the 17th Armored Squadron and the 147th Marine Brigade, had under his control the 51st Infantry Regiment, 1st Division, with two battalions. The 51st was defending the high ground southwest of the Marines. The 147th Brigade, with four Marine battalions, positioned at the strategic location of An Lo, controlled the vital Song Bo corridor.

In the southern sector, General Diem deployed the 3rd Regiment, with two battalions, on the high ground around the old FSB Birmingham, above the Huu Trach River. Southeast of the 3rd Regiment, the 54th Infantry, with two battalions, defended the Mo Tau area. The 1st Infantry, reinforced with one battalion of the 51st Infantry, one M-48 tank company and one APC troop, was assigned the sector from Nui Bong to the Truoi River. The 15th Ranger Group, reinforced with one battalion from the 3rd Infantry, was responsible for the defense of the high grounds south of Truoi.

The 258th Marine Brigade, pulled out from Quang Tri, was now under the control of the Marine Division, which had established its new headquarters at the Marble Mountains southeast of Danang. Two battalions of the 258th Brigade were to defend the northern slopes of the Hai Van Pass, which was guarded by the 914th RF Group.

Unknowingly, I had applied the "light at the top, heavy at the bottom" strategy in my new deployment of troops in the Northern Theater. I intentionally positioned five RF battalions and one under-strengthened Ranger Group to man the cease-fire line, hoping that NVA would not dare cross that line as it would constitute a too blatant violation of the Paris Agreement in the eyes of international public opinion. Subsequent events, however, proved me wrong.

At the request of General Truong, Prime Minister Khiem flew to Danang with some members of his cabinet on March 18 to study the problem of refugees who fled en masse to Danang from Quang Tri and Thua Thien. Prime Minister Khiem's mission was somewhat ambiguous as he had no clear direction from President Thieu with regard to national strategy. On the Hauts Plateaux, the tragic exodus from Pleiku had already begun. It was apparent that while President Thieu wanted to adjust the country's defense based on a new northern frontier extending roughly from Nha Trang, to Ban Me Thuot and Tay Ninh, he was not sure whether he should maintain an enclave in Danang, the second largest city of South Viet Nam. He was aware that, in order to hold a truncated Viet Nam with its northern border anchored around Ban Me Thuot, he needed to salvage the elite units now under attack in MRI. On the other hand, the abandonment of Danang would constitute a fatal blow to the

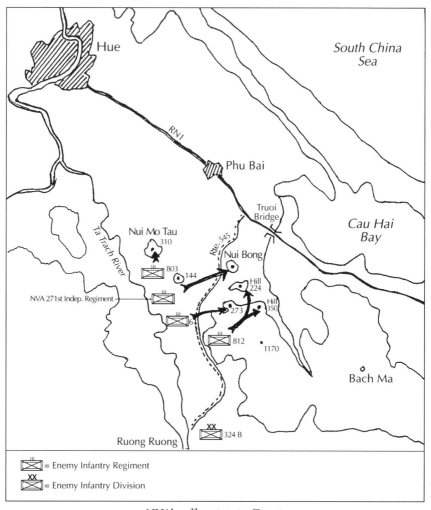

South China
Sea

Hue

RN1

Phu Bai

Cau Hai
Bay

Truoi
Bridge

Ta Trach River

Nui Mo Tau
310

Rte. 545

Nui Bong

803

144

Hill
224

NVA 271st Indep. Regiment

Hill
350

273

812

1170

Bach Ma

324 B

Ruong Ruong

= Enemy Infantry Regiment

= Enemy Infantry Division

NVA's offensive in Truoi

morale of the Armed Forces and the population. This was President Thieu's dilemma and his continuous vacillation between maintaining the Danang enclave and abandoning MRI altogether resulted in the ultimate destruction of MRI's fighting units and the subsequent collapse of the Republic.

Good leadership requires the ability to make hard decisions, to stick to these decisions, and to take appropriate and timely actions to implement them. In retrospect, President Thieu failed to provide leadership in a time of national crisis. He should have known by the summer of 1974, after the resignation of President Nixon, that he should not rely on the United States to come to his rescue in case of NVA's invasion. Consequently, actions should have been taken at that time to prepare for the orderly evacuation of MRI and MRII in order to defend the new line of demarcation. By the beginning of 1975, it was too late since our front line divisions were already heavily engaged with the enemy and their withdrawal under these conditions was indeed an invitation for disaster.

On March 13, President Thieu, overtaken by the calamitous events in MRII, seemed to be in favor of abandoning MRI. This explained his order to General Truong to proceed with the immediate evacuation of I Corps. Faced with Truong's apparent determination to hold MRI at all costs and his optimistic assessment of the situation in his region, President Thieu appeared to have changed his mind. He agreed in principle to hold the enclave of Danang and possibly the enclave of Hue as well.

There was, however, a colossal miscommunication between President Thieu and the I Corps Commander in that Truong's ability to defend the enclaves of Danang and Hue was based on his assumption that he was allowed to retain the Marine Division (General Truong had confided to his close associates that if he was forced to abandon Hue, his final defense of Danang would call for using the 1st, 3rd, and Marine Divisions on line and the 2nd Division in reserve.) In President Thieu's mind, however, Truong should be able to defend Danang with his three organic divisions. Also, it was President Thieu's understanding that both the Marine and the Airborne Divisions would revert to JGS as they were vital for the defense of MRIII and MRIV, the last bastions of the Republic. With regard to the defense of Hue, General Truong and I were gambling that NVA's forces would not cross the cease-fire line and that the 1st Division would be able to hold its line in the Truoi area.

In any event, during that fateful meeting on March 18 at Danang, where the five MRI province chiefs and the mayor of Danang were invited, the ambiance was outright pessimistic. Colonel Tuong, the mayor, reported that the morale of the population was very low and that many families had already left for Saigon. Colonel Pham Van Chung, Quang Nam Province Chief, told the prime minister that the morale of his territorials was still good, but that the people were very concerned about the departure of the paratroopers. According to Cols Dao Mong Xuan and Le Van Ngoc, Quang Tin and Quang Ngai province chiefs, the situation was critical, the RF and other territorial forces were deserting en masse, and as a result, these units were below half strength. Colonel Nguyen Huu Due, Thua Thien province chief, was the most optimistic among the province chiefs. He reported that although people had started to leave Hue in large numbers, the morale of his territorial forces was good and they would fight. Colonel Ky, Quang Tri province chief, presented the most pessimistic picture. Almost all civilians had left the province since the departure of the Marine Division. His territorial forces could not be expected to offer serious resistance in case NVA units attacked across the cease-fire line. Many civil servants had also left without authorization. Colonel Ky asked what disciplinary actions should be taken against these civil servants, and whether servicemen's dependents should be allowed to be evacuated. Prime Minister Khiem did not respond directly to the questions but he stated that he would send to Danang a governmental delegation to handle the problem of refugees from Quang Tri and Thua Thien Provinces.

After the meeting, General Khiem asked to talk privately to Truong and myself. We went to General Truong's office on the second floor of the main headquarters building. There, General Khiem disclosed that President Thieu intended to establish a new defense line along Hai Van Pass. Although General Khiem did not elaborate, this new presidential "intention" implied the abandonment of the two northern provinces. General Khiem made it clear to Truong that he would receive no additional troops and that the newly activated Marine Brigade would remain in Saigon to defend the capital.

The next day, March 19, Truong flew to Saigon to submit a defense plan calling for the defense of two enclaves around Hue-Danang and Chu Lai-Quang Ngai. President Thieu must have again changed his mind; he approved Truong's defense plan and the next day, March 20, Truong flew to Hue and told me that Hue would be defended. However, he instructed me to draw a contingency plan to evacuate the 1st Division and the 147th Marine Brigade to Danang.

When he returned to Danang that night, Truong received the following message from JGS:[75]

EXPRESS

HAND-DELIVERED MESSAGE No. 20/545H/3-1975 T20. 3/75S

From: JGS/G3
To: CG, I CORPS/MRI (Office of the CG)

Info: Office of the President
         Office of the General, Chairman of JGS/ ARVN

Text No. 9.428/F 341
Reference: Message No. 9.424/JGS/F342 on 20/145 11/3/1975 of JGS

Following the above-referenced message, JGS respectfully forwards to your Command the following instructions of the President of RVN.

First: Restricted Air Force and Navy means available can support only one enclave. Therefore, you should "mener"[76] delaying actions toward Hai Van Pass if situation warrants it.

Second: Acknowledge receipt of this instruction.

General Cao van Vien
Chairman, JGS/ARVN

What happened after Truong received the above message was not clear. I would guess, however, that he called Saigon again to pledge that he be allowed to defend Hue because I later learned that President Thieu would appear on television on March 22 to affirm his intention to defend the Imperial City.

On March 21, Truong must have had second thoughts about the advisability of defending Hue because on March 19, without warning, NVA's 308th Infantry Division (under the direct command of Hanoi's High Command), reinforced by armored elements, launched a frontal attack on Quang Tri RF battalions and forced them to withdraw to the My Chanh River. At the same time, two divisions, the 324th and the 325th, under the direct control of a newly formed NVA II Corps, launched a coordinated attack on the 1st Division sector in the Truoi area. Because of these new developments in the Northern Theater, General Truong called President Thieu and suggested that he postpone his television address until the situation around Hue became more clear. During that telephone conversation, President Thieu asked Truong about the wisdom of defending Hue. President Thieu, however, went ahead and recorded his video speech affirming the defense of Hue.

To understand NVA's new offensive in the two northern provinces, it is necessary to follow its reorganized command structure. After their defeats in the early March offensive, NVA divided the Quang Tri-Thua Thien area into two distinct fronts. The northern front, north of Hue, was put under the command of Tri Thien Military Region and the newly activated II Corps was responsible for the area south of Hue.These two command structures were placed under Hanoi's High Command, which also had direct control of NVA's 308th Division and supporting armored and artillery units attacking along the cease-fire line.

The same day General Truong talked to President Thieu, I flew to the northern front to make an assessment of the situation. I landed at the former Camp Evans and drove to My Chanh with Colonel Tri, the deputy Marine Division Commander, in charge of the defense of the northern sector. Colonel Tri had reinforced the RF units defending the south side of My Chanh River with two battalions of the 14th Ranger Group, whose effective had been dangerously depleted.

On the north side of the river, we could see NVA's T-54 tanks forti-
fying their positions in plain view of our RF units. They did not
even bother to camouflage their positions.

After My Chanh, I flew to the 1st Division Headquarters at Phu
Bai and was briefed by General Diem on the situation in his sector.
The strategic Nui Mo Tau was lost to the enemy. The 15th Ranger
Group defending the high ground south of the Truoi River was under heavy attack from elements of NVA's 325th Division, while the
1st Regiment north of Truoi was barely able to contain NVA's 324th
Division. While General Diem and I were considering our actions,
enemy 130-mm artillery shells started to fall on the 1st Division
complex followed by explosions. General Diem and I took shelter in
the bunker in a room adjacent to his office. I ordered my helicopter
to take off without me. Between two artillery salvos, I sneaked out
of Phu Bai in General Diem's jeep.

When I crossed the Truong Tien Bridge on the Perfume River, a
few 130-mm shells whistled by and exploded in the river. The po-
liceman who guarded the bridge did not even bother to salute me as
he was scurrying to seek shelter under the bridge. My CP inside the
Citadel was also under artillery fire. In fact, one artillery major was
killed when a 130-mm shell scored a direct hit on his jeep while he
was heading toward my CP.

Meanwhile, NVA divisions continued to tighten the ring around
Hue. On the northern front, NVA's forces stopped at My Chanh at
the boundary of Thua Thien Province to wait for resupplies. On the
morning of March 21, Tri Thien independent regiments, supported
by heavy artillery, attacked our positions from the Song Bo corridor to Phu Loc. Heavy 130-mm artillery fire fell on Hue. Assaults on
the Marine battalions in the Song Bo valley were repulsed with heavy
enemy losses. But in the southern sector of Phu Loc, the situation
was critical. Taking the brunt of the attacks by NVA's 324B and
325th Divisions, the 1st Division's line of defense along the western
foothills crumbled in certain areas. In the sector of the 1st Infantry
Regiment, just west of the Truoi River, NVA's 18th Regiment, 325th
Division, supported by the 98th Artillery Regiment, took Hill 350
and pressed on to Nui Bong. The latter changed hands three times,
but the 1st Infantry controlled it on March 22. In conjunction with

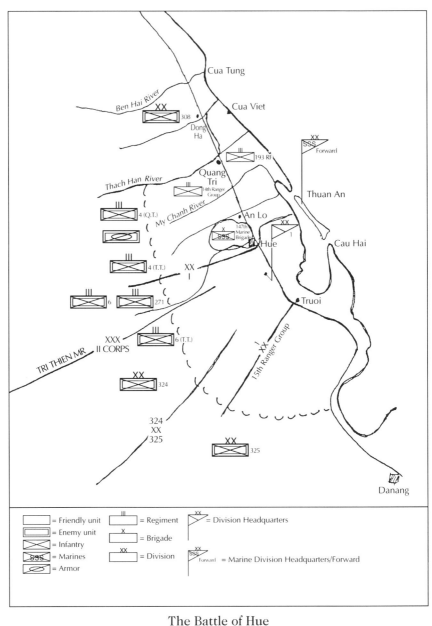

The Battle of Hue

the attack on Hill 350, NVA's 101st Regiment, 325th Division, launched a furious assault on the 60th Ranger Battalion, 15th Ranger Group, defending Hill 500 immediately west of RN1. The first assaults were repulsed by the Rangers, causing heavy losses to the enemy.

During the night of March 22, the enemy sent a sapper unit around Hill 500 to remove the mines on the eastern slope, then launched a powerful assault from that direction, taking the Rangers by surprise. Hill 500, which directly controlled RN1 at the most narrow defile in Phu Loc, was lost to the enemy, who began to conduct interdiction artillery fire on RN1.

Learning of the loss of Hill 500, I called General Truong and asked him to order the 248th Marine Brigade on Hai Van Pass to attack NVA's 325th Division units in Phu Loc to relieve the pressure on the 1st Division. General Truong said he would see what he could do to restore the control of RN1. After I talked to Truong, I called General Diem and ordered him to try to get in contact with the 258th Marine Brigade to his south and to help the Marines retake the strategic Hill 500 by conducting a diversionary attack along the western side of the Truoi River. After the recapture of Hill 500, the 15th Ranger Group should try to link up with the Marines to secure RN1.The counterattack, however, never materialized because by that time Truong had his hands full with the rapidly deteriorating situation in Quang Tin Province where the capital city of Tam Ky was under imminent threat of being overrun.

In the afternoon of March 22, Major Luyen, chief surgeon at Nguyen Tri Phuong Hospital, reported that he could not handle the increasing flow of wounded from the southern sector. Further, a few artillery shells had landed near the hospital and he was concerned about the security of his patients. I directed that he confiscate the Hue civilian hospital in downtown to transfer the most seriously wounded. I also directed my staff to request emergency medical evacuation to Duy Tan General Hospital in Danang. In the evening, I drove to Hue hospital and talked to soldiers of the 60th Ranger Battalion. They told me that they hurled grenades and fired point blank on the enemy human wave assaults from their positions on Hill 500, causing heavy casualties, but by the time they were attacked from behind, they ran out of ammunition and had to disperse. I told these brave men I was proud of them and that I would see to it that they be evacuated to Danang as soon as possible so that their families could be with them.

To the north, near Mo Tau Hill, the 54th Regiment succeeded in repulsing the attack by the 271st Independent Regiment and the 29th Regiment of the 304th Division, both under the control of NVA's 324B Division. A prisoner from the 271st disclosed that casualties in his regiment were very heavy and that the 9th Battalion was almost destroyed. NVA's attacks in the Truoi area continued on March 22 and a counterattack to recapture Hill 224 by the 1st Regiment failed.

In the afternoon of March 22, General Diem requested my permission to move his headquarters to Thua Thien Sector in Hue as Phu Bai was under enemy artillery range and could be attacked by enemy armored units breaking through the 1st Division line on the western foothills. I acquiesced to General Diem's request. I also told him to dissolve the Phu Bai Regional Center and use the trainees to replenish his units.

Although I had no authority to do that, I didn't have time to consult with JGS and didn't want the trainees to be drafted into NVA's forces. Col. Do Trong Thuan, commanding the training center, would be attached to my command until further notice.

On the morning of March 23, at General Truong's request, I flew to Danang to meet with him and his staff. This time, I had to fly along the coast to avoid enemy artillery and surface-to-air missile fire in the contested area south of Phu Bai airport. I did not understand the purpose of the meeting because Truong, again, told me to take necessary steps to defend Hue, and at the same time to make contingency plans to move the 1st Division and the 147th Marine Brigade to Danang. This time, however, I sensed that, due to the deterioration of the situation in Quang Ngai and Quang Tin Provinces, Truong seemed to be in favor of abandoning Hue and salvaging the troops north of Hai Van Pass for the defense of Danang. Nevertheless, I grew increasingly frustrated with this type of doubletalk; I realized that, even at this critical moment, Truong was still less than candid regarding President Thieu's instructions and his own strategy for the defense of MRI.

I told Truong that the evacuation of the 1st Division (The Marine 147th Brigade would be evacuated by sea) could only be executed under two conditions: 1) a pontoon bridge must be built on Cua Tu Hien Bay (which was fordable only during certain times of the year and only during low tide); and 2) Nui Vinh Phong, high ground immediately south of Cua Tu Hien, must be secured by a Marine unit which was to link up with the 1st Infantry Division. General Truong asked his staff whether these conditions could be met. The answer was affirmative, so I flew back to Tan My Naval Base, east of Hue, to meet with General Diem, Colonel Tri, and Colonel Due, Thua Thien province chief. (By that time, my headquarters inside the Citadel was under heavy artillery fire and enemy gunners were shooting at any incoming helicopters.)

I began the meeting by asking about the latest tactical situation. The situations highlighted were far from bright. In the northern sector, Quang Tri's 913rd RF Group had started to withdraw without authorization from the My Chanh line and even refused to stop at the next delaying position at An Lo, despite attempts from the 147th Marine Brigade to turn them back. This unauthorized withdrawal was motivated in part by the RF soldiers' concern about the safety of their families in Hue. Colonel Tri had reinforced the defense of the An Lo line with two battalions of the 14th Ranger Group.

In the southern front, NVA's 324B Division was pressing hard on the 1st Division in the Truoi-Nui Bong area while elements of the 325th Division were consolidating their positions in the Phu Loc defile and started to move into the plains of Phu Thu in an effort to cut the road linking Hue to the port of Tan My. The 1st Division's engineers had blown up the bridge on RN1 east of Loc Son to prevent NVA tanks from advancing toward Hue from Phu Loc.

I explained to my field commanders that we had to be prepared to evacuate Hue. My plan called for the evacuation of the 147th Marine Brigade by Navy LSTs along the coastline of Thuan An, south of Tan My, and the withdrawal of the 1st Division, the Rangers, and other Thua Thien local forces through the Cua Tu Hien on the Dam Cau Hai Bay. No tanks, trucks, or heavy equipment would participate in the evacuation. They should be destroyed or disabled. I then asked General Diem and Colonel Tri about the feasibility of this plan. Colonel Tri answered that it could be executed. General Diem stated that if the conditions I had mentioned to General Truong were fulfilled, he was sure he could move at least two regiments to Danang. General Diem's withdrawal plan called for the 51st Infantry to disengage first from its positions west of Hue, followed by the 54th Infantry in the Nui Mo Tau area, then the 3rd Infantry in the Son Hue Trach. The 1st Infantry in the Nui Bong would conduct delaying actions to protect the withdrawal of the division. General Diem added that the plan, to succeed, had to be executed the next day because after that Hue would be completely sealed off. I reminded General Diem and Colonel Tri to include in their plan such diversionary tactics as intensive artillery preparations for a feigned attack to camouflage their disengagement.

I then decided that General Diem and Colonel Hy, my chief of staff, should fly to Danang and submit the evacuation plan directly to General Truong. I asked them to stress to General Truong the necessity of building a pontoon bridge across the Cua Tu Hien and of securing the high ground to the south of Dam Cau Hai Bay. They took off at 5:00 pm. and when they came back at 7:00 PM., they informed me that, not only the plan had been approved, but it would be executed the next day.

I immediately called General Truong for confirmation. Since he was not in his office, I asked to speak with his deputy, Maj. Gen. Hoang Van Lac. General Lac told me that General Truong had a meeting with General Lan, the Marine Division commander, Commodore Thoai, MRI Navy commander, and the 10th Engineer Group commander after the departure of General Diem. General Lac also said that Thoai had assured General Truong that he would sink a naval ship in the middle of the Cua Tu Hien before 9:00 AM. the next day to permit the crossing of the 1st Division and that Lan had assured Truong that the high grounds south of Cua Tu Hien would be secured by two Marine companies.

Around 8:00 PM., I bid farewell to Monsignor Nguyen Kim Dien, Archbishop of Hue. Monsignor Dien was a native of My Tho. A quiet man and eloquent speaker, he was very respected by the people of Hue. Monsignor Dien had returned to Hue two days earlier from the Vatican where he had attended a seminar. The Phu Bai airport was under artillery fire and closed to civilian aircraft, so he had had to land at Danang and drive by car to Hue just one day before RN1 was cut off. Monsignor Dien received me in his living room, which was lit by a big candle because an artillery round had hit Hue's power plant the day before, so the city was completely without electricity.

Monsignor Dien was calm and dignified, but I sensed a feeling of sadness and resignation. He told me he was not surprised by the abandonment of Hue. He had received instructions to immediately rejoin his diocese and to stay with his people. He also said that according to reliable sources, the whole MRI and part of MRII would be abandoned to the Communists and that the new territory of South Viet Nam would comprise only MRIII and MRIV. He escorted me to the door and wished me good luck. It was totally dark outside. A few artillery shells exploded near the Citadel. As my car passed through the gates of the cathedral, I looked back and caught a glimpse of Monsignor Dien's forlorn silhouette in the middle of the door waving goodbye. I was deeply touched and confused, touched because I knew that this was the last time I would see him and confused because of the astonishing revelations made by this reputable man who had just returned from the Vatican.

During the closing days of the war, Viet Nam, indeed, was abuzz with rumors of secret agreements concerning the partition of South Viet Nam along certain lines. According to these rumors, MRI and MRII would be under the Provisional Revolutionary Government and would serve as a sort of buffer zone between North and South Viet Nam. I tended to disregard these rumors as unfounded speculations, but the new information coming from Monsignor Dien seemed to make sense since it coincided with the new border described by President Thieu to General Truong in March. In any event, these rumors were in part responsible for mass desertions in certain units as officers and soldiers asked themselves: "Why do we have to fight to defend Danang and Hue while it has been agreed that the new line of demarcation line would lie somewhere along Road 21 (Ban Me Thuot-Nha Trang)?"

On the morning of March 24, I Corps Forward staff boarded a Navy vessel for its trip to Danang. With my personal staff, I also boarded a small patrol boat for our journey south. I had considered flying to Hai Van and establishing a small CP there to follow the withdrawal of the 1st Division and the 147th Marine Brigade, but I chose to be with my staff. Further, being on a Navy ship, I would be able to follow more closely the naval operation to pick up the Marines on the beaches. In spite of heavy seas and shallow beaches, ninety percent of the Marines were able to board the LSTs during March 24 and March 25. The rest of the Marines joined the columns of the 1st Division and other infantry units in their march to Danang. The major problem, however, was that the pontoon bridge which was supposed to have been installed by the Navy and Corps Engineers on the Cua Tu Hien never got there. As a result, retreating forces had to commandeer local fishing boats to cross the bay.

A great number of 1st Division soldiers, in lieu of moving south, stayed behind to take care of their families in Hue. One of the biggest drawbacks in the Vietnamese Army, in fact, was the lack of its strategic mobility caused by the unresolved problem of servicemen's families. The soldiers fought to defend their villages, their cities, and their families and a great number of them would desert and stay behind rather than join their retreating units, even at the risk of being captured and killed by the enemy. To move the 1st Division south to defend Danang would require the prior evacuation of servicemen's families. This had not been done because there was no long-range planning and because of indecision and continous flip-flops at the highest echelons of the government and the Army. Further, the early evacuation of the families would have disclosed our plan to the enemy and would also have adversely affected the morale of the civilian population. As a result, ARVN was caught up in a dilemma which remained unresolved till the very end.

So, by the time General Truong stopped the sea movement of forces and equipment from Hue, on March 27 (after a Marine battalion of the 258th Brigade holding the Phu Gia Pass, fifteen kilometers north of Hai Van, came under attack), the 1st Division was able to gather only about 2,000 men in Danang. Like the 2nd and 3rd Divisions south of Hai Van Pass, which also registered heavy desertions within their ranks, the 1st Division, once considered the best in the Vietnamese Army, had ceased to be considered combat effective.

While the troops in the Northern Theater were abandoning the Imperial City and moving southward, the two southernmost provinces of MRI, Quang Tin and Quang Ngai, were under imminent threat of being overrun by superior NVA forces. On March 24, the day the 1st Division and the 147th Marine Brigade were disengaging from enemy units around Hue, NVA began the final assault on Tam Ky, the capital city of Quang Tin south of Danang, defended by Quang Tin's territorial forces, two battalions of the 5th Infantry, 2nd ARVN Division, to the southwest, and the 12th Ranger Group to the northwest. After intensive artillery preparation along the western line of defense, NVA's armored column broke through an RF battalion and the 3rd Battalion, 5th Regiment, and rolled to the center of the city. By afternoon, the city was lost.

After the fall of Quang Tin, General Truong ordered the evacuation of Quang Ngai Province. He instructed Gen. Tran Van Nhut, commanding the 2nd Division, to assemble his troops for the defense of the Chu Lai enclave between Quang Tin and Quang Ngai.

On March 25, while the evacuation of troops was under way, both north and south of Hai Van Pass, General Truong received the visit of a delegation from JGS headed by Lt. Gen. Le Nguyen Khang, Army inspector-general and the former commander of the Marine Division. General Khang carried orders to General Truong to release immediately the Marine Division for the defense of Saigon. Truong protested the order, explaining that he could not defend Danang without the Marines. Khang suggested that Truong give up Chu Lai and send the 2nd Division to Danang. Truong issued orders to move the 2nd Division to Danang by sea, but still insisted that he be allowed to retain the Marine Division.

In the afternoon of March 25, while General Truong and General Khang were discussing the fate of the Marine Division, Monsignor Pham Ngoc Chi, the archbishop of Danang, arrived at I Corps Headquarters and asked to see General Truong on an urgent matter. Truong asked me to receive Monsignor Chi in his office while he and Khang continued their discussion on the balcony on the north side of the building. By a strange coincidence, two days after

I saw Monsignor Dien in Hue, I was to see another archbishop before another city was to be abandoned.

Monsignor Chi started the conversation by asking bluntly what our intentions were regarding Danang. I was surprised by his question, but stated that as far as I knew we would fight and defend Danang. He then asked me to convey his request to General Truong to spare Danang. The defense of Danang would cause unnecessary destruction of the city and death to its citizen and a huge number of refugees. I told him I would convey his message to General Truong, but cautioned him against any unfounded expectation that the city would be abandoned by the military. Although he did not say it, I was certain that, like Monsignor Dien of Hue, he believed there was already an agreement to concede the whole MRI to the PRG and that it would be futile, even criminal, to continue to fight and sow destruction for a lost cause. If I was taken aback by his question, he was no less surprised and disappointed by my answer that Danang would be defended.

Monsignor Chi was right in that the defense of Danang would result in unavoidable carnage to the increasing flow of refugees streaming into Danang and the destruction of that beautiful city by the bay. By March 25, the situation was rapidly approaching chaos. A city of 300,000 people, Danang was suddenly overcrowded with 2 million refugees from Quang Tri, Hue, and Quang Tin. Soldiers deserted to take care of their families. Police desertions mounted and bands of armed stragglers roamed the streets. Shooting incidences between soldiers and police were reported. Food and water were running short and people panicked when they saw the evacuation of U.S. personnel and Vietnamese employees of the U.S. Consulate. Civilians and soldiers fought to board commercial and American ships to flee the city. The airport was invaded and military aircraft seized by panicking soldiers. Bands of hungry, thirsty children wandered aimlessly in the streets, demolishing everything that happened to fall into their hands. Danang, before its fall, was seized by the convulsion of collective hysteria.

In the midst of this chaos, my wife flew to Danang late in the afternoon of March 25 on a military aircraft; she had lost contact with me since the abandonment of Hue and she worried that I might be trapped inside the Citadel. She was relieved to hear that my staff and I had landed safely at Son Tra Naval Base the day she arrived in the embattled city. We stayed at Commodore Thoai's residence at the Naval Base. That evening, some of our friends from Hue, Dr. Nguyen khoa Nam-Anh and his wife, and Dr. Nguyen Van Vinh, requested help to flee the city. They could not believe that my wife would come to Danang at a time when people here would pay anything to escape.

Around midnight, Mr. Francis, the U.S. consul general in Danang, came to see Commodore Thoai to arrange for the evacuation of U.S. and Vietnamese personnel of the Consulate on a U.S. barge which was anchored on Danang Bay. To avoid chaos and the possibility of being commandeered by panicking soldiers, the barge would leave before daybreak. My wife called Lieutenant-Colonel Thanh, my chief of cabinet, who lived on Gia Long Street, and told him to find his way to Son Tra to be evacuated with his family. Commodore Thoai also agreed to allow our friends from Hue to board the U.S. barge a few minutes before its departure.

The next day, I flew my wife to the airport. She and the family of Brigadier General Khanh, commanding the 1st Air Division, boarded one of the last military flights out of Danang under heavy MP escort. That night, NVA started to fire artillery into the city and the airport.

As planned, the sealift of the 2nd Division began after dark on March 25. It was handled by a Naval Task Force consisting of new LSTs from Saigon and LSTs that had participated in the withdrawal of the Marines from Thua Thien. Soldiers from some units of the 2nd Division panicked and fought to get onto the ships causing temporary chaos to the first lifts. Order was reestablished and about 7,000 men from all units, regular as well as territorials, were transported to Danang. General Nhut, the division staff, and the embattled 4th and 6th Regiments were evacuated to the Ly Son Island, off Chu Lai to regroup and to await new orders.

Early in the morning of March 26, NVA fired fourteen long-range rockets into Danang Airbase, but the rockets missed their targets and hit a nearby refugee camp, killing mostly women and children. South and southwest of Danang, the 3rd Division barely held the districts of Dai Loc and Duc Duc against mounting NVA pressure. Certain units registered mass desertions as distraught officers returned and tried to send their families off to Saigon. The soldiers went back to Danang to be with their families and wait for new developments.

In the afternoon, Father Cong and Col. Ton That Khiem, the former Thua Thien province chief, came to see me. They were members of the ministerial delegation sent by Prime Minister Khiem to handle the refugee problem. However, they didn't have the resources to do the impossible task of feeding and housing almost 2 million refugees in the midst of the chaos of a city under siege. So, they came to say goodbye and to wish me good luck before they returned to Saigon.

As they were heading toward the door, I remembered I had a tael of gold (one ounce) I kept in my wallet to be used in case of emergency; now that I was going to be involved in the last-ditch fight to defend the enclave of Danang, I had no need for it. I called Father Cong back, handed him the tael of gold and asked him to give it to my wife in Saigon.

On the afternoon of the 27th, I flew to the 2nd Regiment, 3rd Division, in Cau Ba Ren, south of Danang, to get a firsthand assessment of the situation in the southern sector. As my helicopter landed in the courtyard of an abandoned elementary school, an elderly man rushed over and asked for a ride to Danang to escape the approaching Communists. He had to be removed by two MP's.

Lieutenant Colonel Tam, the regiment commander, reported that his regiment was under heavy pressure but said he still had the situation under control. I asked about troop morale. He said the soldiers were fighting well but some officers had left their units without permission and gone back to Danang.

I left the 2nd Regiment and flew to Dai Loc District Headquarters approximately fifteen miles southwest of Danang. As we approached the town, I noticed an unusual absence of activity within the district compound. I decided not to land, but instead circled the district while contacting the Corps TOC. I was told that radio contact had been lost and that the town might already be under enemy control. Later, I learned that the RFs left the district without a fight to go back to Danang. The same thing happened at the Danang ammunition depot where two RF companies simply disappeared. Back at Corps Headquarters, I was informed that the enemy had reached the outskirts of Danang west of the airport and scattered fighting was taking place not far from the 3rd Division Headquarters.

At 7:00 pm., I flew to Tien Sa Naval Base. As my helicopter settled down on the helipad in front of the Naval headquarters building, I heard big detonations in the direction of the airport. NVA artillery was firing at Danang airbase from the Col de Bay road southwest of Hai Van Pass. I went to Commodore Thoai's office and was surprised to see General Truong and General Lan, the Marine commander, having a meeting. General Truong was visibly exhausted; he smoked cigarette after cigarette. He nervously paced Commodore Thoai's office, his hand periodically touching the handle of his pistol. I watched him closely because I feared he might submit to the pressure and commit suicide. He told me the situation was very critical and that he was contemplating evacuating the Marine Division to Saigon by sea.

Around 9:00 PM., General Truong placed a call to Gen. Cao Van Vien, chief of JGS, and reported that the situation in Danang was such that it might fall at any time. Truong reported that two regiments of the 3rd Division were overrun and that the city was in a state of chaos. He requested that the Marine Division and remnants of the 1st and 3rd Divisions be evacuated.

General Vien suggested that Truong talk directly to the president. General Truong placed a call to the president, but President Thieu was not available. When he called back around 10:00 PM., Truong described the desperate situation in Danang. President Thieu asked him what he planned to do about it. General Truong answered that he would act according to the development of the situation. President Thieu hung up. A few minutes later, General Truong ordered the evacuation of the troops.

By that time, NVA artillery had shifted their fire to Tien Sa with deadly accuracy. We moved to the underground bunker behind Commodore Thoai's office. That was the bunker I had ordered built three years earlier in anticipation of the last-ditch battle I felt would be coming sooner or later. It was now in that bunker that General Truong, General Lan, General Hinh, Commodore Thoai, and I met under sporadic but deadly artillery fire to discuss the evacuation plan.

At 10:30 PM., General Truong asked me to fly to a Navy ship and establish an alternate CP to prepare for the evacuation of the Marine Division. The evacuation was to begin at 6:00 AM. the next day. I spotted Captain Son—the Navy Task Force Commander who came to Danang to help with the evacuation of troops at Hue and Chu Lai—standing near the bunker gates. I signaled him to follow me.

By that time, the chaos in Danang had spread to Tien Sa. The civilian population had invaded the Navy compound in the hope of boarding Navy ships and escaping the siege of Danang. As I walked out of the bunker, a Navy officer reported that base security personnel had just captured three NVA artillery forward observers with all their radio equipment among the civilian population. These artillery observers were adjusting their fire practically on their heads when they were arrested. No wonder their fire was so accurate. The mob was so angry at them that they took them to one of the piers and executed them on the spot.

While I was speaking with the Naval security team, artillery shells whistled above. A few rounds landed near the helipad, causing death and wounding many civilians. One round hit the Navy communication center and all direct communications with Saigon were disrupted. Nevertheless, the Naval Task Force off the coast of Danang still had direct communication with Naval Headquarters in Saigon, which re-transmitted to JGS and the president the latest developments of the evacuation operations.

I sent my aide-de-camp to look for my helicopter's pilots, who were taking refuge somewhere near the landing pad. He found Lieutenant Tam, the chief pilot. Lieutenant Tam was seeking protection against artillery fire under one of the piers near the landing pad. The other pilot was nowhere to be found. After ten minutes that seemed like an eternity, we took off while enemy artillery rounds exploded around us with deafening detonations. We headed for the sea flying in the dark looking for a LST to land on. I asked Captain Son to contact the LST crew by radio and requested that they signal their position. I then asked Lt. Tam if he had ever landed on a LST before. He said he had never even seen a LST in his life.

The tragic death of Gen. Phan Dinh Soan a few years earlier suddenly came to mind. General Soan and a U.S. Army colonel with a few other high-ranking officers were killed when the rotors of their helicopter hit one of the cables on the deck near the landing pad causing the helicopter to overturn and crash into the sea.

Now I was flying at night, in a dense fog, on the same path followed by General Soan, in an old helicopter piloted by one—not two—young, inexperienced officer trying to locate a tiny landing pad somewhere in the dark below. Finally, we saw a blinking light in the distance. I told Lieutenant Tam to watch the cables on the deck before landing. I don't know how he did it, but fifteen minutes later, Tam settled the helicopter on the helipad in the middle of a seemingly inextricable net of cables.

The next morning, Lieutenant Tam inspected the helicopter and discovered that the rotor blades were badly damaged from two 130-mm shell fragments. Generals Truong, Lan, Khanh, and Commodore Thoai were not as lucky. General Truong and General Lan's helicopters were damaged by enemy artillery fire and had to be abandoned. General Truong swam to open sea and was picked up by the crew of the destroyer HQ 404. Commodore Thoai was left behind and walked along the beach around the Son Tra Mountain and was later rescued by a small boat on the morning of the 28th. General Khanh, the 1st Air Division Commander, landed his helicopter near a small beach behind the Son Tra Mountain and swam to the sea. He was also picked up by HQ 404. General Diem, commanding the 1st Division, was not so lucky. He and some of his staff were killed when his helicopter was shot down somewhere south of Quang Ngai.

As soon as I landed on the LST, I transferred to the HQ 405 destroyer, which was equipped with good communication facilities, so I could coordinate the evacuation of the Marine Division. The Marine brigades were ordered to assemble on the north shore of Danang Bay, south of Hai Van Pass, where they were picked up by LSTs early on March 28. By the end of the day, about sixty perdent of the Marines were safely evacuated along with 1,000 soldiers from the 3rd Division. Several Marine stragglers mixed in with the local population and boarded civilian barges and commercial ships.

On the morning of the 28th, HQ 405 picked up Mr. Francis, the U.S. Consul General at Danang. Mr. Francis, who spoke excellent Vietnamese, was constantly at General Truong's side during the last few days. He was also present at the meeting the previous night at Tien Sa, but somehow they ended up on different ships. Around 11:00 AM., a message came from JGS stating that, according to presidential instructions, the order to defend Danang was still valid. General Truong on HQ 404 received a call from President Thieu directing him to recapture the city. By that time, however, the evacuation of the Marine Division was almost complete and NVA troops already occupied certain sectors of the city. To retake the city would require at least three fresh divisions supported by strong air and artillery support. We had one depleted division and no artillery or air support.

Scattered resistance from remnant ARVN units left behind lasted a few more days after the evacuation of I Corps. By night fall of March 30, the second largest city of South Viet Nam belonged to the enemy.

I was saddened by the fall of Danang. The collapse of MRI revealed to me the inability of our High Command to make hard decisions. Given our limited air and logistical support after the U.S. disengagement, it should have been obvious that the maintenance of enclaves in MRI was an unrealistic proposition. These enclaves would tie up three divisions and our strategic reserves, which were necessary for the defense of a truncated South Viet Nam as envisioned by President Thieu himself. On the other hand, the enemy could easily bypass these enclaves by moving their troops and logistical supplies through MRII and the Ho Chi Minh trail.

So, when I received the message to retake Danang, I thought that either Saigon was completely in the dark or the message was just for the historical record. In the Vietnamese Army, a man who did not want to take any responsibility was dubbed *che du*, a slang-phrase meaning "to cover himself with an umbrella." The message I received that morning was possibly an "umbrella" story.

15

THE LAST DAYS

THE NAVAL TASK FORCE, WHICH carried the Marine Division and the remnant units of I Corps, arrived in Cam Ranh on the morning of the 29th. Destroyer HQ 405, where I had boarded the night of March 27, was also part of the Naval Task Force. Commander Nguyen Dai Nhon, the captain of Destroyer HQ 404 transporting General Truong and one Marine brigade, received the order from JGS to leave the Marines at Cam Ranh and escort General Truong to Saigon. However, Truong refused to go to Saigon without the Marines. Finally, JGS relented and agreed to let General Truong and the Marines go back to Saigon together.

At Cam Ranh, I placed a call to General Tho at the military academy. I asked him whether he had received any instructions regarding the evacuation of the military academy. Tho said he had no instructions from Saigon. I suggested he call Prime Minister Khiem for instructions. In case he could not reach General Khiem, I suggested he evacuate the school because we needed to save our cadres if we were to reorganize our armed forces to defend a new truncated South Viet Nam. Dalat was too close to the newly defined border to be considered safe from enemy attack. The information from the Archbishops of Hue and Danang and the description of the new frontier as described by President Thieu, convinced me that there was some implicit agreement for a new partition of South Viet Nam; the graduates of the academy would be needed to lead the reorganized and reequipped units of our army.

Meanwhile, Lieutenant Tam, my pilot, had used tape to wrap the holes in the damaged helicopter rotor and on the 29th, my aide, Lieutenant Thang, and I boarded the helicopter for Saigon. We followed the coast of MRIII to avoid enemy anti-aircraft missiles. We refueled at Van Kiep Training Center west of Vung Tau. The commander of Van Kiep told me that he had received instructions to receive the remnants of the 3rd Division, which would be reorganized and reequipped at his training center. I called my wife in Saigon to let her know that I was safe. She was elated to learn that I was alive. After refueling, we took off and headed toward Saigon.

That evening, I had a joyful reunion with my family. The rejoicing, however, was short-lived as bad news from the battlefields kept coming in. The coastal cities of MRII fell one after another without a fight. Tuy Hoa, the seat of ARVN's 22nd Division, was now in enemy hands and the city of Nha Trang, the new seat of II Corps, was under heavy pressure after the 2nd Airborne Brigade, which was blocking NVA's advances on Road 21 linking Ban Me Thuot to Nha Trang, was driven from its position northwest of the city.

During the evening, I learned that General Tho had evacuated the military academy. Since some sections of the Saigon-Dalat road were already controlled by NVA, Tho decided to march his cadets to the coastal city of Binh Tuy; from there the cadets were trucked to the old U.S. logistical base of Long Thanh north of Saigon.

The day after I arrived in Saigon, I saw General Luong, the Airborne Division commander, at his headquarters near Tan Son Nhut Airport. I had high regard for General Luong's tactical skills. In return, he had always trusted me and was very outspoken when he talked to me. That day, Luong was upset regarding the piecemeal use of his division. All four brigades were assigned to different units and suffered heavy casualties and he was left in Saigon with his staff unable to save them from eventual destruction. He bitterly accused President Thieu of intentionally "scattering" the Airborne Division which he distrusted. He implied that a coup d'état was in the making to overthrow Thieu's regime and although he did not elaborate, I was under the impression that he was one of its key players.

I later discovered that, in addition to General Luong, other generals were very angry at the way the war was being conducted—

including the decision to withdraw from Pleiku and the subsequent collapse of II Corps—and they were convinced that, to save the country, President Thieu had to go. This was my impression when I visited Gen. Nguyen Bao Tri at the Training Directorate the following day. General Tri was a supporter of General Ky, who, according to rumor, was staging a comeback under the banner of a movement for national salvation. General Tri believed that the country could be saved but new leadership was necessary.

During the day, Col. Ton That Khiem came to return to my wife the tael of gold I had given to Father Cong at Danang on the 27th. Colonel Khiem explained that Father Cong gave the tael of gold to Khiem and asked him to return it to my wife. However, since the airport was closed the afternoon of the 27th due to NVA artillery fire, Father Cong and Colonel Khiem were stuck in Danang. The next day, Khiem boarded a commercial barge, but he was robbed of his gold during the trip to Saigon. So, he had had to replace the lost tael of gold with his own. He thanked me for saving his life because, had it not been for the tael of gold, armed bandits on the commercial barge would have executed him on the spot.[77]

While the fate of Nha Trang, the new site of II Corps Headquarters, hung by a thread, the situation in neighboring Cambodia was hopeless. Since August 1973, when the U.S. Congress had voted to approve the Case-Church Amendment, cutting all military assistance to the countries of the Indochinese Peninsula, the military situation in Cambodia had dramatically worsened. As a result of this cutback the U.S. plan to form and equip a 205,000-man army in Cambodia had to be canceled. While the United States had practically stopped all military assistance to the Lon Nol government, Hanoi stepped up its assistance to the Khmer Rouge units. Consequently, embattled government troops were unable to contain the Khmer Rouge offensive on Phnom Penh and on April 1, Marshal Lon Nol fled the capital. Cambodia was on the verge of collapse.

Meanwhile, efforts to form a three-party coalition government in Laos had failed. The Communist Pathet Lao seized power and evicted all Americans from the country.

In the midst of this bad news from Cambodia and Laos and the rumor of a possible coup d'état at home, I decided to escape the poisoned atmosphere of Saigon and to visit the former units of I Corps. I flew to Vung Tau to visit General Lan, the Marine Division commander, now in charge of the defense of this strategic seaport, to be appraised of combat effectiveness of this division after its withdrawal from MRI. General Lan received me in his new office on the ocean front. He appeared to have the situation in Vung Tau under control while his division was receiving new replacements in personnel and equipment.

The Marine Division at that time was possibly the most combat effective ARVN force, but, politically, it was not entirely trusted by President Thieu because the majority of officers and troops were northerners believed to be sympathetic to General Ky. President Thieu, therefore, preferred to keep it at a distance in lieu of moving it near Saigon. President Thieu's problem was that he needed the elite Airborne and Marine Divisions to defend the capital but he also feared that the officers of these units, unhappy about recent setbacks on the battlefields, would stage a coup to overthrow him.

The next day, I went to Cong Hoa General Hospital to visit General Truong. After his withdrawal from Danang, Truong, physically exhausted and understandably dispirited from the collapse of his command, was admitted to Cong Hoa for a check-up and rest. He face was pale and drawn. Normally a thin man, Truong looked almost emaciated. His sunken eyes had a bland glare and he apparently had not recovered from the agony of defeat; he appeared a mere shadow of himself. He had fallen so fast and so far that he seemed unable to cope with the traumatic experience of the last few days. To me, he was a pathetic figure, a victim of international political conjectures beyond his control.

As I offered my hand, Truong threw his arms around me. Then, without saying a word, he burst into tears. This was a battle-hardened soldier who had no fear on the battlefield. Unable to control myself, I felt tears in my own eyes. After he calmed down and regained composure, Truong asked me to go to Van Kiep Training Center, the new site for I Corps Headquarters and the 3rd Division, to supervise the reorganization of the units formerly under I Corps.

Nha Trang had just fallen and the 2nd Division, at least the remnants of it, was attached to III Corps; it was ordered to move to Phan Rang, south of Nha Trang, to help defend the Phan Rang Airport. After April 4, MR II was left only with the two coastal provinces of Ninh Thuan and Binh Thuan. JGS therefore decided to incorporate these two provinces into MR III. As a result, Gen. Nguyen Van Toan, III Corps commander, organized a III Corps Forward Command under Lt. Gen. Nguyen Vinh Nghi to direct a newly formed III Corps Task Force responsible for the defense of Phan Rang. The forces under General Nghi, in addition to the embattled and under-strengthened 2nd Division, consisted of the remnants of the 2nd Airborne Brigade, Ranger and RF units from the defunct II Corps, supported by the 6th Air Division stationed at Phan Rang.

For President Thieu, Phan Rang took on a special importance and he was committed to defending it at all cost. First, Phan Rang was his hometown where his parents and ancestors were buried and the loss of ancestors' graves and their desecration by the enemy would be considered a calamity of incalculable proportions. Second, Phan Rang was located on the new frontier of a partitioned Viet Nam and its capture by the enemy would be a fatal blow to President Thieu's new defense strategy.

While Phan Rang was located on the natural avenue of approach to Saigon via RN1 running along the coastline, the small town of Xuan Loc, approximately thirty miles northeast of Saigon, was the northern gate to the capital. Surrounded by rubber plantations located on gently rolling hills, Xuan Loc, the capital city of the Province of Long Khanh, was created by President Diem in 1957 to accommodate the northern refugees, mostly Mong, Thai, and Nung ethnic minorities, following the 1954 partition of Viet Nam under the Geneva Accords. After the fall of MRII, Xuan Loc took on an exceptionally strategic importance because it was located between RN1 and RN20, the two approaches to Saigon from the Center and the Hauts Plateaux. III Corps assigned the defense of Xuan Loc to ARVN's 18th Division reinforced with the one regiment from the 5th Division, the 81st Airborne Commando Group, and the 7th Ranger Group. Later, this divisional task force was reinforced with the 1st Airborne Brigade and elements of the Marine Division, which had just returned from MRI.

The day after my visit to General Truong at Cong Hoa Hospital, I drove to Van Kiep Center to gather the remnants of I Corps staff and Corps supporting units. While at Van Kiep, I learned that President Thieu had announced the formation of a new government under Mr. Nguyen Ba Can. I knew Can from when we were students at College of Phan Thanh Gian in Can Tho. Can was one class ahead of me. A graduate of the Institute of Administration in Saigon, Can occupied various governmental positions in the Delta. In 1960, after the abortive coup d'état against President Diem, my brother Tho—who went to Saigon with his armored regiment to rescue the Diem regime—was appointed province chief of Dinh Tuong and Can became Tho's administrative assistant. Subsequently, Can was elected Representative for the district of Dinh Tuong at the National Assembly. He was president of the National Assembly when President Thieu asked him to form a new government. I knew that Can was an astute politician, but I was concerned about his ability to lead the country in a time of crisis.

Mr. Francis, the former consulate general at Danang, came to Van Kiep in the afternoon. Mr. Francis asked me to support the new government. He also suggested that I take necessary steps to speed up the reorganization of the 3rd Division. This task turned out to be a monumental undertaking due to lack of personnel and materials. The most difficult equipment to replace were crew-served weapons and communication equipment. Even the M-16 rifle, the basic infantry weapon, was unavailable in the closing months of the war, so we had to scrounge supply depots and even take weapons from service units to give to infantry battalions that had suffered losses on the battlefields.

Pierre Darcourt, a noted French journalist, in the book *Viet Nam, Qu'as-tu fait de tes fils?*,[78] told the moving story of the death of the son of Mr. Tran Quoc Buu, the powerful chief of the *Confederation des Travailleurs* (C.V.T.), the equivalent of the American AFL-CIO. Because it was a vivid illustration of the tragic consequences of the shortage of ammunition and equipment during the closing days of the war, it is appropriate to quote the story at length:

"My son had chosen the army, not because he loved the war, but because we were at war. He fought well and has already earned many citations. We were very close. He wrote to me very often. A few months before his death, he was concerned . . . scared even. During the days of October, he wrote me a letter. I am going to read it to you. . ."

Tran Quoc Buu pulled out three sheets of paper, carefully folded, from his valet and started to read:

"Very dear Father. . .the situation deteriorates in my sector. Not because the population is receptive to the propaganda of the 'other side', but because we lacked the means with which to fight. The farmers, members of the Self-Defense Forces, do not have enough ammunition for their rifles and are forced to buy their grenades from the soldiers of the Regular Army, less engaged than them. The Regular Army does not avoid combat, but every time it engages the enemy, it incurs heavy losses because it is underequipped in materiel and weapons.

"To let you understand our situation, I have to give you some technical explanations. The communists use against us T-54 tanks and Russian 130-mm guns.The T-54 has a remarkable engine, is very mobile, rustic, heavily armored and equipped with: one 100-mm gun, two 30-mm and one 50-mm machine guns. It can cover 400 kilometers and carry 30 shells. In case of attack, we can use only for our defense the M-72 bazookas. This bazooka can be used only once (we throw it after usage) and is only effective at a range of one hundred meters. One thus has to attack the tanks on foot, at short distance and not miss it. It means entering the perimeter of absolute accuracy of their automatic weapons and to get killed...without being certain of destroying them. The approach is anyway practically impossible because the tanks are preceded or accompanied by infantry.

"The Russian 130-mm gun, although manufactured twenty years ago, is still a threatening weapon. Weighing eight tons, towed by a tractor on caterpillar, it can shoot up to a distance of 27 kilometers at a rate of six shells per minute. Only three 130-m. guns camouflaged in a forest, and one hour of bombardment, are needed to crush a district town with one thousand shells. No construction, no bunker (the shell can pierce a steel plate 27-mm thick) can resist this kind of destruction. The population flees and the troops get killed because we are equipped with 105-mm howitzers which have an inferior range. And the ammunition supply is limited ... three shells per gun, per day! While the enemy has an ample supply.

"To silence the communist guns, we are supposed to have an uncontested aerial superiority. It is true in theory, but completely false in practice. Since the gasoline crisis, our reconnaissance helicopters are allowed to fly only three hours per day. Furthermore, the communists, to neutralize them, have SA-7 missiles equipped with heat-seeking infrared heads, very manageable and accurate.

"Very dear Father, I know that you have many relations with the Americans. Your position as President of the C.V.T. will give weight to your words. You must explain to them the gravity of our situation. They must provide us sophisticated weapons. 'Tows' missiles mounted on motorized platforms and 'Cobra' helicopters, specially conceived to destroy tanks. They have them. Why do they refuse to give them to us? They have to provide the military and technical aid they had promised. I beg you, Father, to intervene with them. Otherwise, we will be crushed and defeated. We are not cowards. We have no fear to die. A condition to have a chance to survive ... or to resist usefully. Excuse me for imposing upon you this lengthy report. In my sector, the engagement and artillery fire multiply. In any event, I will hold my position and will not withdraw ... alive.

"My men follow me and trust me.

Your respectful and devout son."

Tran Quoc Buu slowly folds the letter, coughs to clear his voice and control his emotion, before continuing:

"The whole story of our defeat is summed up in these few lines. I found my son's letter after my return from a trip to Asia and Europe. When I read it, my son was dead three days before . . ."

The President of the C.V.T. accompanied me to the entrance, holding my hands for a long time, then adds, before leaving me:

"If you go to the front to see the soldiers, do not quote my conversation, Pierre. The men who will die for a cause they have found just and sacred do not have to know in advance that the cause was lost. It seems to me unnecessary and cruel to tell them so. I would not have told it to my son. . ."

As seen earlier, the 3rd Division faced the same problems of equipment shortage. It also had to cope with the shortage of personnel. General Hinh, the division commander, was allowed to receive the soldiers from the defunct 1st Division. In addition to the Division Staff, the 3rd Division had gathered over 1,000 soldiers who were assigned to the 2nd and 56th Regiments. The soldiers had started firing practice but their morale was very low. Despite General Hinh's tireless efforts to rebuild his outfit, it was obvious that the 3rd Division was not likely to be operational in time to effectively participate in the defense of the Phuoc Tuy-Vung Tau sector.

On April 10, while President Ford announced his proposal to Congress to provide South Viet Nam with a $722 million in military assistance and $250 million in humanitarian assistance, U.S. personnel were evacuating Phnom Penh. The next day, Cambodia belonged to the Khmer Rouge.

On April 15, Mr. Nguyen Ba Can presented his new cabinet. I was stunned to learn that Brig. Gen. Phan Hoa Hiep was the new minister for information. In 1972, Hiep, the dispirited 2nd Infantry Division commander, had called me in the middle of the night to submit his resignation following the Que Son disaster in which one of his regiment was overrun by NVA's 711th Division. I wondered how such an officer, who lacked the will to fight on the battlefield, could head an important ministry in time of national crisis.

Gen. Tran Van Don, the new deputy prime minister and minister of defense, stopped at Van Kiep the next day on his way to visit

III Corps Forward Command at Phan Rang. I briefed him on the status of reorganization of I Corps units. As we headed toward the helicopter pad, General Don disclosed the purpose of his visit. He came to ask me to serve as sub-minister of defense in the new government. Taken aback, I thanked him for his offer, but I declined, citing personal reasons. "Beside, even if I accepted your offer to serve in the new government," I added, as General Don boarded his helicopter, "I am sure President Thieu would reject my nomination." I detected an expression of disappointment and anger on the face of the new Minister of Defense as his helicopter lifted off and headed north.

After General Don's departure, I stood for a moment at the helipad and tried to make sense of what had just happened. I had never been close to General Don, although I had served under him as artillery commander at I Corps during the late 1960s, and briefly as G-3 at Army Command in 1963 before I went to the United States to attend the Command & General Staff College at Fort Leavenworth, Kansas. As commander of the 9th Division in the Delta, I did help him when he ran for a seat in congress in 1966. After the 1973 Paris Peace Agreement, as a member of the congressional armed forces committee, he often went to Hue to visit the troops. It was during one of these trips that he invited me to have dinner at the home of his friends, Mr. and Mrs.Ton That Ngoc. The Ngocs came from the royal family and were known for their impeccable hospitality and their exquisite traditional Hue cuisine.

My long professional association with General Don, I thought, may have been the reason he selected me to be his deputy at the ministry of defense under the new government. I was convinced, however, that I had made the right decision not to accept his offer, because I did not want to serve under a government I had no respect for, and also because I knew my nomination would have been rejected by President Thieu who still distrusted me.

General Truong arrived late in the morning at Van Kiep. He had recently been appointed assistant to General Vien, chief of JGS, and in that capacity he flew to Van Kiep to inspect the units under his former command. It was believed in military circles at the time that President Thieu dared not punish Truong for his abandonment of Danang because Truong had the protection of the Americans. (One of the first things General Weyand, the new U.S. Army chief of staff, had done when he arrived in Saigon a few days earlier was to pay a visit to Truong at Cong Hoa Hospital.) Further, Truong was considered one of Viet Nam's best generals and his punishment would have an adverse effect on troop morale. As a result, Truong was given the newly created and neutral position of assistant to the chief of JGS.

Truong must have known about General Don's intention to make me his deputy at the Ministry of Defense, because he asked me if I had accepted General Don's offer. He was visibly disappointed when I told him I had declined. As we walked to the headquarters building of the Van Kiep Center, Truong suggested I reconsider my decision. "As the Sub-Minister of Defense," said Truong, arguing his case, "I am sure you will be able to help us down here." I told Truong I had already made the decision and, for better or for worse, I was going to stick to it. Subsequent events proved that it was for worse, as that decision was to be the main cause of all my upcoming troubles.

On April 18, General Tho came to see me at Van Kiep. The senior class had just graduated and the military academy was temporarily deactivated due to enemy pressure in the area just north of Long Thanh. While at Van Kiep, we received the news that III Corps Forward's task force defending Phan Rang was overrun by NVA's superior forces supported by tanks and artillery. General Nhut, commanding the remnants of the 2nd Division, was rescued by a Navy ship, but Gen. Nguyen Vinh Nghi, commanding the Northern Front, and General Sang, the Air Division commander at Phan Rang, were reportedly captured by the enemy.

The fall of Phan Rang was a fatal blow to President Thieu's concept of a new South Viet Nam extending from Phan Rang to Ha Tien via Ban Me Thuot. It was also a fatal blow to his morale as ARVN units, before leaving the town, bulldozed and leveled the graves of his ancestors as the ultimate expression of hatred and anger. It is interesting to note that Phan Rang was once the capital of the old Cham Kingdom and many people believed that President Thieu himself was of Cham ancestry and that his destiny was to avenge the

Cham race whose culture and civilization have virtually disappeared due to forced assimilation under Vietnamese rule.

In the midst of these grim developments, Tho and I were hit by a different kind of calamity. In the afternoon of the day Phan Rang fell to the enemy, an MP detachment arrived at Van Kiep. The lieutenant colonel commanding the detachment said that he had received orders to escort both Tho and me to JGS and that we were to report to Gen. Dong Van Khuyen, JGS chief of staff, for further instructions.

First, I thought that we were arrested for suspected involvement in a pending coup d'état. This, however, was not to be the case. Back at JGS, instead of reporting to the JGS chief of staff, we were directed to a small building located near the main gates. That building was used as sleeping quarters for JGS guards. I learned that it had been hastily renovated to accommodate its new occupants. Around the building was a newly installed string of barbed wire fence. I was surprised to see that Gen. Phan Van Phu, the former II Corps commander, Gen. Pham Quoc Thuan, commandant of the NCO's Academy at Nha Trang and Gen. Nguyen Duc Khanh, commanding the 1st Air Division at Danang, were already present.

I was informed by these generals that we were under house arrest pending investigation concerning the "unauthorized" abandonment of our positions. General Khanh told me that Commodore Thoai, MRI Navy commander, and himself were instructed the day before to report in writing their activities before and during the evacuation of Danang. Commodore Thoai was authorized to go home but Khanh was detained for further investigation. To me, Khanh's detention appeared unfair because without infantry protection and under intense NVA artillery and missile fire, he had no choice but to evacuate his aircraft to save them from certain destruction.

After I talked to Khanh, I sent my aide home to inform my wife about my detention and to get clothing and other necessities. In the meantime, I tried to get more information from my other fellow detainees. I learned that General Don, the new minister of defense, had prepared a list of generals who had abandoned their post and that he had recommended to President Thieu that they be detained for investigation. As for me, I was personally accused of abandon-

ing Hue without authorization and for "inciting" Truong to evacuate Danang.

Of course, these accusations were untrue since Truong had personally ordered the evacuation of both of Hue and Danang and as
deputy corps commander, I had had to follow his orders. And now,
since Truong was untouchable, I had become a scapegoat. I was,
however, intrigued by the fact that only two days before, Don had
gone to Van Kiep to invite me to be his Sub-Minister of Defense. I
inferred from this that my rejection of his offer angered him and
pushed him to retaliate by including my name on his black list.[79]
One other possibility, which I found more plausible, was that President Thieu, increasingly concerned about a possible coup d'état,
was determined to neutralize politically unreliable generals by putting them under house arrest under the pretext of having withdrawn
without authorization. President Thieu in fact had personally ordered the evacuation of Hue, but he probably had me detained because I was considered dangerous to his regime.

I felt somewhat guilty for General Tho's detention because he
had heeded my suggestion to evacuate the military academy. I was
convinced, however, that I had given the right advice, since the
massacre of the cadets by better armed NVA regular divisions, supported by artillery and tanks, would constitute a loss of incalculable proportions at a time when we badly needed new cadres for
our Army. It should be noted that Tho was a strong supporter of
Prime Minister Tran Thien Khiem, whom Thieu knew was seeking
the presidency for himself and Tho's arrest may have had something to do with Thieu's suspicion in this regard.

The second night, General Truong came to our building and
spent the night with us. He came to share our hardship and to show
his solidarity and support. Unknown to me, there was a tumultuous
meeting early in the evening at JGS. I later learned that during the
meeting attended by both General Don and Vien, Truong brought
up the issue of our detention. "The punishment of Generals Thi
and Khanh and Commodore Thoai was not right," said Truong, "because they were my subordinates. They implemented my orders;
they were not guilty of anything. If you want to punish, you should
punish me instead."

According to Truong's own account (as related by *Doi Moi* Magazine, October 1982), his statement was followed by a frozen silence. General Vien looked at General Don, who had just returned from a mission in France. The new minister of defense and the chief of JGS looked at each other without uttering a single word. Afterward, Gen. Le Nguyen Khang, inspector-general of the Armed Forces, shouted angrily at General Don: "God damn it! the generals who are under house arrest are not guilty of anything!" Although he did not say it, he obviously implied that we were scapegoats for the mistakes made by higher-ups in the government.

The next morning, still unaware of the previous night's meeting at JGS, I called General Khang to inquire about the status of our investigation. I was taken aback by General Khang's outburst: "God damn it! Thi, don't worry, you have done nothing wrong! Those who make mistakes are the ones at the top." General Khang was at Danang the day before its fall and he knew too well that President Thieu's lack of decision and long-range planning were the main causes of the collapse of MRI. The fact that he freely aired his opinion at this point reflected the degree of frustration and anger within the Army and confirmed to me that the rumors of a coup plot had to be taken seriously.

Two days after we reported to JGS, we were transferred to a trailer park located in front of JGS's residential quarters, near the front gates. General Phu, the former II Corps commander, and I shared the same trailer. It was a single-wide trailer containing two bedrooms, a living room, a bath, and a kitchen area. General Phu was a thin man with a drawn face and sunken cheeks. He liked to spend most of the day outside, sitting on his feet, his hands crossing his bent knees *à la Viet Cong,* under a tree in the courtyard, smoking cigarette after cigarette. Phu, who had fought at Dien Bien Phu, was captured by the Viet Minh after the fall of the French *camp retranche,* and it was possible that he had picked up his captors' sitting habit in the Viet Minh POW camps. Were it not for the two stars on his fatigue uniform, one would think that he was a *can bo Viet Cong* (VC cadre).

The first day we moved to the JGS trailer park, I asked Phu about the details of the evacuation of Pleiku. Phu confirmed that at the meeting held at Cam Ranh on March 14, President Thieu ordered the immediate withdrawal from Pleiku and Kontum. As a consequence, the evacuation was executed without planning and in such haste that much heavy equipment was left behind including eighty aircraft. (Gen. Tran Van Minh, commanding the Vietnamese Air Force, later confirmed that he was not even informed of the evacuation plan.) Worse, the province chiefs and district chiefs were not informed of the decision to withdraw. At the Cam Ranh meeting, President Thieu commented that the RF and PF units were all Montagnards and they would be allowed to return to their homeland.

General Phu related that President Thieu specifically prohibited him from informing the American team in Pleiku about the planned evacuation. Col. Le Khac Ly, II Corps chief of staff, later reported that he decided to notify the U.S. advisory team at the last minute so they could flee the abandoned city. A close friend of General Phu disclosed to me that Phu wanted to court-martial Ly for disobeying his orders.

At the same meeting in Cam Ranh, it was decided, at General Vien's suggestion, that, to achieve tactical surprise, retreating units would withdraw along RN7, an old road that had been abandoned for many years. The troops practically had to cut a road through dense vegetation to head toward the coast. Many civilians who fled the Communists and joined the military columns were ambushed and killed by elements of NVA's 320th Division.

During a meeting of the National Security Committee, President Thieu called the evacuation a "success" and praised Phu for this "achievement." Later, after the collapse of MRII, Thieu accused Phu of cowardice and of having advised him poorly on the evacuation of Pleiku and Kontum. This was why Phu ended up sharing this trailer with me.

What General Phu did not disclose was that he was one of the people who had been selected to participate in a coalition government under a scheme drawn up by the French ambassador in Saigon, Jean Merillon. In the closing days of the war, the French were eager to step in to salvage what was left of South Viet Nam, their former colony. In his memoir published after the war, *Saigon et Moi*,

Merillon disclosed that during the month of April, French generals, most of them veterans of the Indochina War, arrived in Saigon in droves to provide advice to their Vietnamese counterparts. General Vanuxem, a close friend of President Thieu, was busy visiting the front lines and drawing up battle plans for President Thieu in a last effort to contain NVA's advance toward the capital. Famous paratroop commanders, such as retired Generals Gilles, Bigeard, Langlais, the heroes of Dien Bien Phu, also arrived in Saigon during that time to assess the tactical situation of South Viet Nam. They lost no time contacting French-trained Vietnamese generals to provide their advice regarding counter-offensive operations against NVA's units around Saigon.

General Phu, who had commanded an airborne company at Dien Bien Phu, was held in high esteem by the French generals who considered him suitable for the position of Minister of Defense under a coalition government between the three factions: the incumbent nationalist government, the third party opposition group, and the PRG. For them, General Phu, who had fought with them at Dien Bien Phu and who had endured with them harsh treatment by their Viet Minh captors, had nothing to do with the Pleiku debacle and the collapse of MRII. It was not surprising then that General Gilles, the former French paratroop commander in Indochina, asked Mr. Merillon to intervene with the Vietnamese government to release General Phu from house arrest so he could participate in the new government.

In his memoir, Mr. Merillon also disclosed that he had contacted Gen. Duong Van Minh and VC Gen. Tran Van Tra in an effort to seek a "neutral" solution to South Viet Nam. According to Mr. Merillon, China, eager to contain Russian influence and its Vietnamese surrogate in South East Asia, also would be favorable to such a solution. Chinese Prime Minister Chou En Lai had suggested to the French that a group consisting of Truong Nhu Tang, Nguyen Thi Binh, Dinh Ba Thi, and VC Generals Tran Van Tra and Le Quang Ba, be included in the coalition government to represent the pro-China bloc.

Mr. Merillon's plan called for the formation of a government of national concord and reconciliation composed of the following members:

Co-Presidents: Duong Van Minh, Tran Van Tra
Vice-Presidents: Vu Van Mau, Trinh Dinh Thao, Cao Van Bon
Minister of Defense: Phan Van Phu
Foreign Minister: Nguyen Thi Binh
Minister of Justice: Truong Nhu Tang
Interior Minister: Vu Quoc Thuc
Minister of Economy: Nguyen Van Hao
Minister of Commerce: Le Quang Uyen
Finance Minister: Tran Ngoc Lieng.

According to the above plan, if a minister belonged to the nationalist bloc, then his or her chief of cabinet should be a member of PRG, and vice versa.

Twenty-four hours after the announcement of the new government, France would ask European, Asian, and non-aligned countries to recognize it in order to pre-empt the takeover of Saigon by the Russian-backed NVA. In the meantime, to back up his bargaining position, Gen. Duong Van Minh would take steps to consolidate ARVN's remaining two army corps and to switch from conventional to guerrilla warfare, based on the recommendations of French generals.

With the formation of the new government of national reconciliation, General Minh would announce his readiness to establish diplomatic relations with China and other Communist countries, including Russia. China would seize this opportunity to send an ambassador to Saigon within twenty-four hours and would commit to the new government an initial financial aid of US$420 million, that was previously appropriated for Hanoi. France would transfer 300 million French francs previously appropriated for the old government of South Viet Nam to the new government to sustain the neutrality solution. In the meantime, France would request financial contributions from allied European countries to implement economic, cultural, and agricultural development, and humanitarian programs, estimated at US$290 million. The total of these contributions would equal U.S. prior financial assistance.

With regard to General Phu, it was unclear whether Mr. Merillon had intervened with Thieu's government in his favor. On the other hand, it was highly likely that President Thieu had been aware all

along of the French effort to form a government of national reconciliation to replace his own. Thus, even if Mr. Merillon had intervened for Phu's release, I doubt that Thieu would have acquiesced
to his request. The fact remained that Phu did not leave the detention center ahead of the rest of us.

Meanwhile, we were left alone in our trailer park. Although life
in the trailers was quite comfortable and our friends and families
were free to visit us, we became increasing nervous because, despite General Khang's assertion that we had not done anything
wrong, nothing had been done to secure our release. The reason for
that inaction probably was that General Don could not recommend
our release to President Thieu only a few days after he had recommended our detention. To do so would reveal his irresponsibility
and sloppy performance as the new minister of defense. The result
was that we were left languishing in our trailers, powerless in the
face of new military and political developments and uncertain of
our own future and the future of our families.

With the worsening of the military situation and the threat of a
pending attack on the capital, many high ranking officers had already sent their families to the United States with the assistance—
and even encouragement—of the Office of the U.S. Defense Attaché
in Saigon. From our trailers, we noticed the increasing number of
JGS officers who had fled just by watching the diminishing number
of lighted residences at night at the officers quarters across the street
from our trailer park.

The third day of our detention, General Khanh, the *tu vi* (astrology) expert, came to see me. He said that I was the only person
who could help secure our release. I asked him if he was joking. He
pulled out a sheet of paper from his pocket on which were inscribed
a rectangle with arrows and letters in black and red around the
rectangle.

"General, this is your *tu vi*, based on your birthday," Khanh
said with an intriguing seriousness. "Look at this *dai han* [a ten-
year span on the *tu vi*]," Khanh continued, pointing his finger at
the upper right hand side corner of my horoscope chart, "you have
here the star *dao hoa*, which indicates that you have the support of
women and that you can rely on them in case of distress. I have

looked at other generals' *tu vi*, but none has this star, especially during the current *dai han*. I therefore suggest that you contact the women who are in a position to save us in these critical hours."

Although I was aware of the considerable sway the wives of certain of our high ranking officials held on their husbands, I did not think it appropriate to ask for their help. Further, the only powerful woman I had ever met was Mme Khiem, the wife of the former prime minister. I met her during her trips to Hue to visit the servicemen's families or to make offerings at some pagodas. She was very nice to me. The first time I met her, she objected to my addressing her by *Ba* (Madame), but insisted instead that I call her *Chi* (Older Sister). In return, she called me *Chu* (a courteous and intimate expression when addressing a younger person). But now her husband was no longer prime minister and she was not in a position to assist.

Khanh, however, was persistent. He kept asking me to act for the sake of the group. I asked Khanh to place a call to Mme Vien, the powerful wife of the chief of JGS. I had never met Mme Vien before, but she was very charming on the phone. She spoke to me in French. She said she knew my brothers Tho and Thoi but she regretted she did not have the opportunity to know me personally, although she had heard about me. I explained to her, also in French, the purpose of my call. I informed her that General Khang had declared us innocent and asked her to intervene with her husband for our release from house arrest. She said she was sorry, but her husband had no authority regarding our case. Possibly as a consolation, she said she would send us a roasted pig for dinner and a military doctor to take care of our health.

Khanh was disappointed but he was not ready to give up. He sat still for a few minutes, searching his memories. Suddenly, he face lit up: "General, I know one person who could help us," Khanh said with a big smile. "Do you remember Mrs. Hong Nghe?" Mrs. Hong Nghe was the personal assistant to General Don when he was a congressman from the province of Quang Ngai in MRI. When General Don became minister of defense, he appointed her as his personal chief of cabinet. Mrs. Hong Nghe came from one of the great families of Hue. Her father was Viceroy of Quang Ngai and her mother was one of Emperor Thanh Thai's daughters. When she was young, the royal family had groomed her to become the future wife of Prince Bao Long, the eldest son of Emperor Bao Dai and the pretender to the throne of Annam. But this project somehow fell through and she ultimately married an army officer of modest origin.

Mrs. Hong Nghe occasionally accompanied General Don on his visits to Hue and Khanh often provided them with air transportation. During one of these visits, General Don organized a reception at the Ton That Ngoc's residence and I was invited. I remember that Mrs. Hong Nghe, because of her beauty and grace, was the center of attention that night. The following morning, at her request, I took her to the tomb of Emperor Gia Long, so she could pay respects to her distant ancestor.

I agreed with Khanh, so we called her at the Ministry of Defense. She said she was aware of our situation and appeared sympathetic to our plight. She came to the trailer park the next day and promised to work for our release. Before she departed, she said to me with a sad and mysterious expression on her face: "General, you would not have been in this situation, had you accepted General Don's offer."

Meanwhile, after the fall of Phan Rang, Xuan Loc, Bien Hoa, and Cu Chi became ARVN's last organized defense line against NVA's advance toward the capital. The strategic city of Bien Hoa fifteen miles north of Saigon was defended by a mechanized task force consisting of the 3rd Armored Brigade, the 33rd Ranger Group, the 2nd Marine Brigade and the newly-activated 4th Airborne Brigade. This formidable task force was under the command of Brig. Gen. Tran Quang Khoi, an able armor officer. The 25th Division under Brig. Gen. Ly Tong Ba, was responsible for the defense of the area around Cu Chi to the west. Since April 9, the young 18th Infantry Division under Brig. Gen. Le Minh Dao, reinforced with elements of the Marine and Airborne Divisions, had put up a heroic defense and repulsed many assaults from NVA's 6th, 7th, and 341st Divisions under the command of NVA's IV Corps. On the 19th, the Vietnamese Air Force, assisted by technicians from DAO, dropped one CBU (Cluster Bomb Unit) from a C-130 transport aircraft on an enemy concentration area east of Xuan Loc. The CBU is an awesome weapon. It produces a powerful downward pressure that kills any-thing in its field and causes people who survive the blast to suffo-cate in the post-explosion vacuum. The bomb wiped out a regiment of NVA's 341st Division. For an instant, NVA, thinking that the U.S. had resumed B-52 strikes in support of ARVN, momentarily stopped the offensive to reassess the situation.

It was the only bright note in the string of our successive de-feats and the Saigon press jumped on it to declare the success of our defense of Xuan Loc. For a while, Saigon was jubilant and the morale of the population shot up with the good news from the front.

Unfortunately, the bomb, while slowing down NVA's attack, did not stop it. On April 21, the 18th Division withdrew under heavy pressure to the new defense line Trang Bom-Long Thanh. NVA's Divisions 304, 308, 312, 320, 322, 325 and two divisions from NLF, supported by 300 tanks and 600 artillery guns of all calibers, were tightening the knot around the capital of South Viet Nam.

I was intrigued, however, when a high ranking VNAF officer later told me that, after the collapse of Saigon, approximately 1,000 CBUs fell into the hands of the Communists. I wondered what would have happened if these bombs had been allowed for use in support of ARVN troops in Phuoc Long and Ban Me Thuot?

On the evening of April 22, President Thieu finally went on TV to announce his resignation and the transfer of power to Vice Presi-dent Tran Van Huong. Rumor had it that President Thieu was so dismayed by the news of the desecration of his ancestors' graves in Phan Rang that he had wanted to resign since then. There might have been some truth to that theory because the violation of the sanctity of ancestors' graves was considered an ultimate calamity for the family and would bring disaster for its members. I remem-ber that when President Thieu's father died a few years earlier, he had hired a Chinese expert in geomancy to locate an ideal site for his father's grave which would assure him success and safety in his position. In this regard, the desecration of his father's grave must have been a fatal blow to his morale and may have been one the main causes of his decision to relinquish power.

After the war, Col. Nguyen Van Y, one of the most famous *tu vi* experts in Viet Nam, recounted the interesting meeting he had had with President Thieu the day before his resignation. Colonel Y was the Director of National Police under President Diem. He was put in jail after the coup d'état. Having nothing to do in prison, he started to study *tu vi* by devouring book after book dealing with this popular science.

Colonel Y recounted that President Thieu consulted him on his chances of becoming the first president of the Second Republic a few months before the 1967 presidential elections. At that time, Gen. Nguyen Cao Ky was considered the front runner because he had the backing of the Army and of the Americans. However, Colonel Y assured Thieu that he would clinch the presidency because he had very favorable stars during the current *dai han* while Ky's best star that had reached the *cu ngo* (zenith) on the astrology chart was obscured and, thus neutralized, by unfavorable clouds.

Sure enough, Thieu was elected president. But since that day, the new president had no contact with Y, until the eve of his resignation. One morning, as Y left his house to buy a newspaper, somebody grasped him from behind. He turned and recognized the man as a lieutenant colonel from the Presidential Palace.

"Big brother," said the officer, "if you escape and refuse to see the President, he will shoot me. Please, follow me to the Independence Palace. The President wants to speak with you." (Colonel Y had previously declined President Thieu's invitation.)

As he settled down on a chair in the reception area, the door swung open and President Thieu walked toward him and shook his hand. Following was the conversation between the two men as recounted by Colonel Y:

"Colonel Y," asked President Thieu, "how does my current *dai han* look at this time? Can I hang on to the presidency?"

Y shook his head and said, "Mr. President, your *dai han* has already expired. You cannot stay."

"What do you think about General Duong Van Minh's *tu vi*?" asked President Thieu. (Colonel Y had the *tu vi* of all army generals.)

"General Minh's *tu vi* is not good. He has no chance," Y answered.

"Then, how about General Khiem?" President Thieu asked, visibly worried.

"General Khiem's good *dai han* also has already expired, " Y said.

"My God!" exclaimed President Thieu in desperation, "this means the end of the Second Republic. The Viet Cong has won!"

This was a fatal blow to President Thieu's confidence, the straw that broke the camel's back. It was likely that Colonel Y's grim predictions prompted Thieu to relinquish power and flee. In his farewell address to the nation, President Thieu accused the U.S. of letting him down and of pulling the rug out from under him. He was right because the U.S. Congress had cut all military aid, but he did not want to admit that he was partially to blame for his own downfall. He did not want to look at the fact that the widespread corruption he had tolerated had provided powerful ammunition for the hostile Western media and U.S. antiwar movement in their demands for a U.S. pull-out from South Viet Nam.

In a final analysis, President Thieu's problems resided in the fact that he lacked popular support and had to rely entirely on the Army and American backing to govern his country. Further, he lacked integrity, charisma, and vision, which are necessary for a true leader to effectively inspire and lead his people through difficult times toward distant and loftier goals. Ho Chi Minh was a dictator and did not have to be concerned with his people's needs and aspirations. But this was acceptable and even expected in a communist regime. President Ngo Dinh Diem wanted to become a dictator, but this was not acceptable in a South Viet Nam just liberated from the French and partitioned from the Communist North. He was overthrown and killed. President Thieu did not know how to walk the fine line between dictatorship and democracy. He wanted to maintain strong discipline and curb political opposition, but under American pressure, he had to maintain a facade of democracy and respectability. So he switched unpredictably back and forth from one extreme to the other and finally fell victim to the weaknesses of both.

In fairness, President Thieu's job was not an easy one. He not only needed a certain discipline to fight the war, but he needed genuine political support to sustain the war effort and implement the pacification program. Mr. Kissinger—whom President Thieu disliked intensely for having pressured him to sign the Paris Peace

Agreement—recognized this dilemma. Kissinger marveled at the fact that President Thieu was expected to restructure his defense plan after the withdrawal of the American forces, win the war, and at the same time build democratic institutions in a war-ravaged country that had not known democracy in its history.[80]

It was analogous to asking a man to simultaneously draw a circle with one hand and a square with the other. The democratic leader would have no problem drawing two circles; likewise, the dictator would have no problem drawing two squares. But the leader of a developing country would be forced to draw two imperfect figures which, in the end, bear no resemblance to the circle or the square. This was the dilemma for most of the leaders in Third World countries. It was also President Thieu's dilemma.

On the morning of the 24th, two days after President Thieu's resignation, I received a call from Mrs. Hong Nghe. She wanted me to know that General Don, who had kept his job of defense minister in the Huong government, agreed in principle to set us free and that she was preparing the necessary paperwork. The next day, Mrs. Hong Nghe came to our trailer park to hand-deliver General Don's written order which released us from house arrest.

In his memoir, Mr. Merillon, the French Ambassador, related that Gen. Duong Van Minh repeatedly pressured him into letting him assume power right after President Thieu's resignation. It would appear that General Minh was fighting for the captain's chair on the Titanic, but in reality he was relying on his younger brother, Duong Van Nhut, a VC army major, to act as a go-between him and Hanoi in an effort to negotiate a cease-fire. He was probably hoping to form a puppet government of national coalition with Hanoi's blessing, similar to the Vichy government of Marshal Pétain in France in World War II. Mr. Merillon recounted also in his memoir that when he informed President Huong that General Minh was the person selected by the French to implement its neutrality policy in Viet Nam, President Huong was stunned. President Huong knew General Minh well (General Minh had been his pupil). He didn't think that Minh could be used in times of crisis.

Since the day I was free, I was in constant contact with my wife's nephew, Maj. To Ngoc Riep, who worked at the Capital Military District Headquarters, to keep abreast of the front line situation. On the 26th, the 3rd Division defending the Phuoc Tuy-Vung Tau sector, reported that two enemy columns reinforced with tanks launched a two-pronged attack on the district of Phuoc Tuy and the residence of the province chief after heavy artillery preparation. General Hinh, commanding the 3rd Division, immediately dispatched an airborne brigade to Phuoc Tuy. The paratroopers succeeded in breaking the enemy assault during the night and five enemy tanks were destroyed. At the same time, however, the 18th Division at Trang Bom was under heavy attack and NVA's artillery batteries were firing on Bien Hoa, the seat of III Corps.

On the 26th, Col. Huynh Thu Toan, commanding the Center for Renovation of Materials at Hanh Thong Tay on the northern outskirts of Saigon, came to see me. He wanted me to see Maj. Gen. Homer Smith, the U.S. Defense Attaché, to apply for the evacuation of my family to the United States under a program sponsored by DAO. General Smith had replaced Major General Murray who had resigned in frustration after unsuccessful attempts to obtain more money for the war effort. Before he retired, General Murray declared in a press conference in Honolulu the previous year: "The South Vietnamese were forced to substitute bodies, bone and blood for bullets. We set one standard for ourselves and another for the Vietnamese. It is not only sadistic, it is racist."[81]

Toan had been my classmate at the École Inter-Arms and his wife had been my classmate at College Phan Thanh Gian. She had come to see me at my trailer a few days earlier and informed me that she had devised a plan to use armored vehicles from Gia Dinh Province (the province chief was a friend of hers) to rescue me and Tho if NVA troops marched into Saigon. (General Khanh might be right about my horoscope's *dao hoa* star after all.) However, she and her children left Saigon on the 25th under the DAO program. DAO's mission was to oversee the military assistance program and General Smith, an expert in logistics, worked closely with his Vietnamese counterparts. He had a special program to evacuate the families of Vietnamese officers working in ARVN's logistics branch. As a result, Colonel Toan's family was one of the first to be evacuated by DAO. Before leaving, however, his wife insisted that he do everything in his power to help evacuate my family as well.

I called Tho and asked him to go with me to see General Smith at Tan Son Nhut. Toan, who had a close connection with DAO, accompanied us and served as our guide. General Smith was not available when we arrived, but his assistant agreed to put our families on the list of evacuees. He advised us that our families should be ready at a moment's notice.

The next day, Colonel Thoan, the 5th Division Deputy Commander, informed me that he saw my family was on the list of people scheduled to leave Saigon the following day, April 28. Colonel Thoan's wife and children had departed for Guam in the morning and he had taken them to DAO for departure processing.[82] While at DAO, he noticed that my family as well as General Tho's were to leave the next day. That night we assembled at Gen. Pham Quoc Thuan's home also located at Chi Hoa Officer residential quarters, so our families could be picked up at the same time. General Thuan was a former III Corps Commander in Bien Hoa and had been detained at JGS with Tho and me.

Around midnight, we received a call from DAO directing us to report to a pick-up point in the rear yard of a U.S. compound near Tan Son Nhut. Each person was allowed only a hand bag. My daughter Ngoc, who had broken her ankle the day before, had to walk with a cane and my wife carried belongings. As we were waiting for our families to be transported to the airport, my driver, Master Sergeant Phuoc, asked a U.S. officer in charge of the evacuation whether there was an additional place for my mother-in-law, who lived with her son, a VNAF lieutenant colonel, at the Tan Son Nhut Airbase. Knowing that the officer was a collector of communist weaponry, the ever-clever Phuoc pulled out a rare Chinese pistol and gave it to the officer who agreed to reserve an additional place. Phuoc drove to the airbase and brought my mother-in-law just in time to be picked up by a bus from the DAO office directly to the runway. My wife was elated.

My family left around noon. That night, Tho invited me to stay at his villa at the southwest section of the city. In the afternoon, a VNAF pilot who had defected to the enemy, took off with a F-5 jet from Nha Trang and dropped two bombs on Tan Son Nhut.

At 5:00 pm., President Huong resigned in favor of General Minh after a rubber-stamp Congress approved the transfer of power. Mr. Nguyen Van Huyen, an attorney, was appointed vice president; Professor Vu Van Mau became the new prime minister. Mr. Mau had been minister of foreign affairs under President Diem; he had resigned in protest when President Diem ordered raids on Buddhist pagodas in 1963. An ardent Buddhist and an early supporter of Gen. Duong Van Minh, Mr. Mau had become one of the leaders of the third party, which favored a coalition with the Communists. The new government was supposed to be a government of negotiation, but it was in reality a government of surrender. In his memoir, Mr. Merillon, in fact, blamed Gen. Duong Van Minh for the collapse of the French plan to restore peace to South Viet Nam by dealing directly with Hanoi from a weak position instead of cooperating with the PRG in an effort to preempt a take-over by NVN.

On the evening of the 28th, the first NVA missiles landed on the northwestern outskirts of Saigon. Tho and I climbed to the roof to watch the impacts of the missiles and estimate their points of departures. The missiles appeared to come from the direction of Cu Chi, which was defended by the 25th Division. Only later did we learn that the 25th, which had retreated to Hoc Mon ten miles northwest of Saigon, had been overrun, and that General Ba, the division commander, was captured by the VC with his bodyguard when he tried to escape.

With the fall of Cu Chi and Hoc Mon, the left wing of ARVN's last defensive line was ruptured. General Khoi's III Corps Mechanized Task Force was still holding Bien Hoa but the remnants of the 18th Division, repositioned at the old U.S. logistical base of Long Binh southeast of Bien Hoa, was under heavy attack.

On the morning of the 29th, I was informed that President Thieu and Gen. Cao Van Vien had already fled Saigon. President Thieu, who volunteered to put himself "at the disposition" of the new government, made it safely to Taiwan with former Prime Minister Tran Thien Khiem on an American airplane. His Special Assistant for Military and Security Affairs, Gen. Dang Van Quang, having the day before escaped arrest by Air Force officers acting under General Ky's orders, barely made it to the U.S. Embassy.   On the 29th,

Gen. Duong Van Minh appointed Lt. Gen. Vinh Loc, director of the National Defense College, as the new chief of JGS. Gen. Vinh Loc had actively participated under Big Minh in the overthrow of President Ngo Dinh Diem in 1963. Vinh Loc had fallen into disgrace with President Thieu, who had removed him from the command of II Corps after the 1968 Tet Offensive and put him at the helm of the newly created National Defense College.

Around noon, Mr. Vu Van Mau, the new prime minister, announced on the radio the liberation of all political prisoners and the reopening of all newspapers that had been closed by previous governments. More importantly, Mr. Mau asked the U.S. government to cease all involvement in Viet Nam's affairs and to close the DAO agency within twenty-four hours. I assumed that these were the conditions imposed by NVN and it was apparent that the Duong Van Minh government was a mere puppet of the Hanoi regime and was being used as a political instrument to take over the South without having to fight a costly street combat within the capital and against the still formidable ARVN IV Corps in the Mekong Delta.

At that point, Tho and I decided we could not serve such a government. I called General Khanh, the former Air Force commander in Danang, and asked for air transportation to leave Saigon. Khanh said Tan Son Nhut Airport was closed for air traffic and that he, too, was still trapped in downtown Saigon. In any event, he said he had no plan to leave the city. I suggested he reconsider. I also mentioned that the only way out this late was to board a Navy ship at the Naval Headquarters at Bach Dang. I called Lt. Comdr Van Trung Quan, who had married one of my cousins and who was working at the Naval Headquarters. I asked Quan whether the Navy was planning to leave or to stay in support of the Duong government. He was not sure but he suggested that we go to Bach Dang to await new developments.

As we drove past the U.S. Embassy on Thong Nhat Avenue near the Saigon Cathedral, U.S. Marine Chinook helicopters were picking up embassy personnel and Vietnamese evacuees on the rooftop of the embassy building; down below, U.S. Marine soldiers guarding the embassy compound were trying to control a panicking mob that was pushing toward the embassy gates in a desperate effort to escape.

When we arrived at Bach Dang, we saw that Gens Nguyen Bao Tri and Nguyen Duc Thang were already there with their families. General Khanh arrived in the afternoon. He had changed his mind. The new government appeared on the verge of capitulating to the enemy. Besides, his family had left Saigon two days earlier, and it was obvious that leaving would now make more sense to him. The irony was that he, an Air Force general, had to rely on the Navy for his escape, as he had relied on the Navy a month earlier to flee the hell of Danang.

While we were waiting for new military and political developments at Bach Dang Naval Headquarters, we were informed by Lieutenant Commander Quan that Gen. Duong Van Minh asked Admiral Chung Tan Cang to stay with his fleet so he could use the Navy as a bargaining tool in his negotiations with Hanoi. Late in the afternoon of the 29th, Admiral Cang sent Commodore Diep Quang Thuy, Navy Chief of Staff and one of my cousins, to the Independence Palace to meet with General Minh at the latter's request. General Minh told Thuy that the Navy should leave now. He also asked Thuy to take Col. Nguyen Hong Dai, his son-in-law, with him. It was the beginning of the end for his short-lived government and for the Republic of South Viet Nam.

That night, Quan led us and other generals onto the destroyer HQ1 anchored in front of the Naval Headquarters. Around 9:00 pm., Admiral Cang's fleet, under cover of darkness, sailed out of Saigon in the direction of the Port of Vung Tau, which was still held by the remnants of one Marine and one Airborne Brigade. Gen. Nguyen Duy Hinh, commanding the sector of Vung Tau, had already left with his staff early in the afternoon and the leaderless garrison was under threat of an imminent takeover by advancing NVA forces.

Our destroyer, however, reached Vung Tau without incident the following morning, April 30. We stopped near Con Son Island, 150 miles southwest of Vung Tau, to resupply and to wait for other Naval vessels which had departed Saigon and Can Tho that day. Commander Hung, commandant of Destroyer HQ1, asked all passengers to give him all the *dong* in their possession so he could use them to buy fish from the Con Son fishermen.

In the afternoon, the Navy radio relayed Gen. Duong Van Minh's surrender message to the Armed Forces. Unit commanders were instructed to stay in place, to depose their arms and be ready to surrender to the enemy.

Radio Saigon later announced that around 12:00 A.M., a tank from NVA's 203th Tank Brigade crashed through the gates of the Independence Palace. Bui Quang Thuan, the tank company commander, raced toward the palace balcony to raise the flag of PRG. Inside, Gen. Duong Van Minh and his entire cabinet awaited the arrival of the Communist delegation to discuss the transfer of power. He was insulted by a NVA colonel by the name of Bui Tin, assistant editor of the Army newspaper *Nhan Dan* (The People),[83] when Tin told General Minh that he accepted his surrender because he had no power to transfer. Minh was then rushed to Saigon's Radio Broadcasting station to broadcast his order of surrender to army units still fighting in various sectors of the capital and in the Mekong Delta.

We later learned from new evacuees that many generals and officers committed suicide after hearing Gen. Duong Van Minh's message in order to avoid the humiliation of surrendering. In the Delta, Gen. Nguyen Khoa Nam, IV Corps commander, and his deputy, Gen. Le Van Hung, the hero of An Loc in 1972, shot themselves to death after ordering their troops to disband. Gen. Tran Van Hai, commanding the 7th Division, and Gen. Le Nguyen Vy, commanding the 5th Division, also committed suicide.

I was saddened to learn that my fellow detainee at the JGS trailer compound, Gen. Phan Van Phu, also preferred to die rather than be captured by the enemy. He took poison on April 29 when he was informed of General Minh's imminent surrender. In his memoir, Mr. Merillon disclosed that he had telephoned General Phu early on the 29th at the French Hospital Grall—where Phu was recuperating—to ask him not to leave. Phu was among the key personnel in the French policy of neutrality for South Viet Nam and his presence in Saigon was considered essential for the success of this policy. Phu promised he would stay. He also assured Mr. Merillon that if Saigon fell to the enemy, he would die at the Hospital Grall. He had kept his promise.

On the morning of April 30, Gen. Nguyen Cao Ky, walking through the empty buildings of the General Headquarters in Tan Son Nhut, saw Gen. Ngo Quang Truong. Both boarded General Ky's helicopter, planning to head toward IV Corps in the Delta to continue the fight, but decided instead to fly to the U.S Seventh Fleet after hearing Gen. Duong Van Minh's message of surrender.

Mr. Merillon expressed his admiration for the heroic death of all Vietnamese generals who, according to Mr. Merillon, chose to apply Voltaire's phrase describing a general's honor: "To keep one's honor is not to lose so much." The reality was that, by choosing to die, these generals upheld the highest level of the Confucian concept of honor, which requires a general to die rather than surrender the fortress he was defending. In the nineteenth century, Phan Thanh Gian, a genuine Vietnamese hero, took poison after he failed to defend the Citadel of Vinh Long. He was later elevated to the status of a saint. Similarly, the Vietnamese generals who committed suicide in 1975, in my opinion, deserved the respect and admiration of the country because they upheld the purest tradition of the Confucian warrior.

Late in the afternoon, I learned that Gen. Vinh Loc, the new chief of JGS, had fled on a Navy barge after having earlier in the day broadcast an Order to the Armed Forces in which he accused the general officers who had fled the country of cowardice. He was unique in the annals of military history as a one-day chairman of the Joint Chiefs of Staff. As a matter of fact, everything was unique in the closing days of the Viet Nam War. For a period of one week, for instance, one witnessed the succession of three presidents: Nguyen Van Thieu, Tran Van Huong and Duong Van Minh.

A one-million-man army was annihilated in two months, five billion dollars of equipment was lost, a country betrayed by its ally and abandoned to its fate had collapsed and joined the ranks of other Communist countries. The bamboo curtain had fallen on the once rich and beautiful land of Viet Nam.

As darkness fell on Con Son Island, I left the upper deck of HQ1 and returned to the Officer Quarters below. Commander Hung was addressing the generals assembled in the reception room. "Gentlemen, we have been resupplied with fresh water and food and we are going to leave Viet Nam's territorial waters tonight," Hung said with a sad expression on his face. "Now, I would like you to tell me where you want to go." Then after a short pause, he added: "Australia or Subic Bay?"

There was a frozen silence in the room. For a moment, we looked at each other, confused and amazed. We did not know we still had a choice.

EPILOGUE

AS VIET NAM COMMEMORATES THE twenty-fifth anniversary of its reunification, the economy is in serious disarray, plagued by a huge bureaucracy, rampant corruption and money-losing state enterprises. On the greater geopolitical scheme, twenty-five years after the "Great Spring Victory," Viet Nam, ironically, will become the battlefield for a new Cold War against its one-time Communist comrade to the north.

A major obstacle to Viet Nam's economic development is that its aging Communist leaders, who honed their military skills during the war, lack the necessary economic experience and management skills to rebuild the country. In the view of Viet Nam watchers, the Communists may have won the war, but they have lost the peace. Further, the collapse of the former Soviet Union deprived them of a socio-ideological model and shattered their belief in the success of the socialist revolution.

A character in Duong Thu Huong's award-winning novel *Nhung Thien Dang Mu* (or *The Blind Paradises*) fittingly describes Viet Nam Communist rulers as "people who have spent almost their entire life designing a paradise on earth, but their limited experience has not allowed them to understand the nature of this paradise nor the road leading to it. . . ." The novel, by Viet Nam's best known post-war writer, was published in Hanoi in 1988, during the regime's period of cultural liberation.[84]

Today, after fourteen years of *Doi Moi* (or "renovation"), a mixture of free market capitalism and command economy, Viet Nam remains one of the poorest countries in the world, with a per capita income of US $350 and more like $60 in rural areas. (Even when their economies hit the bottom during the 1998 Asian economic crisis, Thailand and South Korea registered a per capita income seven and twenty-two times higher.) Other indicators point to an imminent economic downturn. Net foreign investments for 1999 decreased by thirty percent from the previous year. The budget deficit rose from 1.7 percent to five percent of GDP, the official unemployment rate stood at 4 million—not counting millions of part-time or unemployed farm workers.

In today's global economy, emerging nations need to provide an environment of fair competition and safe investment if they want to attract the foreign capital necessary for economic growth. This requires the institution of the rule of law, the eradication of corruption and bureaucracy and, most of all, the dissolution of government-subsidized state enterprises. In other words, in an age where innovation and pluralism have become interdependent, economic reform, to succeed, must be implemented concurrently with political reform. But for authoritarian regimes, political reform means the erosion of the government's grip on power and its ultimate demise.

In the face of this insoluble dilemma, Viet Nam's leaders have adopted a "wait and see" attitude, hoping that the problem somehow will go away. Meanwhile, anger over high taxes, rampant corruption, and a widening gap between the cities and rural areas have triggered protests and popular uprisings in some of the most impoverished provinces in the Red River Delta. A worsening economy will likely trigger further unrest and possible social upheaval.

On the geopolitical front, Viet Nam, sadly, is caught in the middle of a concerted U.S. effort to contain China, which has emerged as the new Asian threat. Despite the Western powers' professed commitment to active cooperation with Russia and "constructive engagement" with China, the post-World War II policy of "containment" remains a popular ploy. And Viet Nam has, once again, become a pawn in this global political chess game.

"History is an eternal recommencement," wrote a French historian. This is painfully true for Viet Nam. Containment, in fact, means establishing relations with surrounding countries and Viet Nam is not only China's neighbor but also its traditional enemy. (In 1979, Viet Nam engaged in a border war with China and subsequently had skirmishes with the Chinese Navy in the contested Spratly Islands in the South China Sea.) Thus, Viet Nam has regained its strategic value in U.S. eyes as a counter-balance to the ever-greater threat of Chinese expansionism.

If the unusually warm reception given to U.S. government officials in recent years is any indication, Viet Nam appears only too willing to accommodate its new role as the outpost for a new version of containment in which one Communist country is used as a shield against another. In essence, Viet Nam will become the battlefield for a new Cold War against its war-time Communist ally.

The dilemma for Viet Nam today is that it needs the presence of its former enemy on its soil to help counter its former ally's expansionism, knowing full well that the consequent influx of new ideas, technology and money will accelerate a democratization that could ultimately bring down its corrupt and unpopular regime.

Only by implementing genuine economic and democratic reform can Viet Nam resolve its political-economic dilemma and break the "eternal recommencement" of a history of wars and human tragedies, which has plagued it for so long.

NOTES

1. A small fish that abounds in certain parts of the Mekong Delta.

2. *"Vo cao dang, bat thanh phu phu."*

3. *"Trai khon tim vo cho Dong*
Gai khon tim chong giua chon ba quan."

4. After the war, the Viet Cong released Capt. Huynh Ba Xuan at the personal request of Mme de Lattre de Tassigny. Mme de Lattre subseqently sponsored Xuan and his family to France where he received the full military pension of a lieutenant colonel in the French Army.

5. There is a Vietnamese proverb: *"Phep vua thua le lang"* (Royal decrees are worth less than the village's customs).

6. "Dien Bien Phu is untakable."

7. De Castries was promoted to brigadier general the previous month. The French had to air drop his new two-star epaulettes into the camp retranche.

8. "And these heavy cannons rolling toward Austerlitz."

9. "The leaves which turned yellow in the trees which shiver. . . fall one by one on the shoulders of the statues."

10. *The Pentagon Papers* as published by *The New York Times* (New York: Bantam Books, 1971), 70.

11. Ly Tong Ba, *25 Nam Khoi Lua* (*25 Years of War*) (np: Huyen Su Printing & Graphics, 1995), 76.

12. Pierre Darcourt, *Viet Nam, Qu'as tu fait de tes fils?* (Paris: Edition Albatros), 83-85.

13. McClear, Michael, *The Ten Thousand Day War, Vietnam 1954-70* (New York: St. Martin's Press, 1981).

14. Frances FitzGerald, *Fire in the Lake* (Boston; Little, Brown & Co., 1972), 258.

15. In 1994, I met General Khanh in California. I asked him whether there is any truth to the rumor thar Taylor didn't like him. General Khanh confirmed that General Taylor disliked him because he came to the defense of the young generals who were admonished by Taylor for having caused political chaos in Saigon.

16. Robert S.McNamara, *In Retrospect: The Tragedy and Lessons of Vietnam* (New York: Time Books, 1995).

17. Arthur Schlesinger, *The Bitter Heritage: Vietnam and American Democracy: 1944-1966* (Boston: Houghton Mifflin, 1966).

18. Since then, the date of June 19 has been celebrated as Army Day.

19. Colonel Tuan later died in a Communist concentration camp after 1975.

20. "Panther" was the radio code for the 43ʳᵈ Ranger. "Sun" was the code normally used to indicate the officer in charge of the operation. "Child" was often used to indicate a subordinate unit.

21.After 1975, then-Colonel Hiep was sent to a Communist concentration camp for thirteen years. He came to the United States in 1994. I met him in Santa Ana in July 1994.

22. William Westmoreland, *A Soldier Reports* (Garden City, NJ: Doubleday, 1976), 410.

23. May 4, 1967, Memo on "Force Levels and Enemy Attrition" for Secretary McNamara.

24. Henry Brandon, *Anatomy of an Error* (Boston: Gambit, 1969). Henry Kissinger, *The White House Years* (Boston: Little, Brown, 1979).

25. FitzGerald, 263.

26. Sean Flynn was to disappear later in Cambodia while covering the war in that country.

27. In 1975, following the example of Chiang Kai-shek who escaped to Taiwan with his army, the government of South Viet Nam had, at one time, considered moving its seat to Phu Quoc to continue the fight.

28. Westmoreland, 242.

29. Henry Kissinger, *The White House Years*, 1469.

30. Edward Metzner, *More than a Soldier's War* (College Station: Texas A &M University Press, 1995), 193.

31. After 1975, General Manh and I became friends again and when he died in 1994 in San Jose, California, I was asked to give his eulogy.

32. Harvey Meyerson, *Vinh Long* (Boston: Houston Miffin Co., 1970).

33. Meyerson, 106.

34. Meyerson, 105.

35. *Newsweek*, 9 Oct. 67, p. 44.

36. Jeanne Kirkpatrick, *Dictatorship and Double-Standard* (New York: Simon & Schuster, 1982).

37. To my disbelief, Colonel Diep was later appointed chief of cabinet to the minister of the interior, who previously had served as Diep's civilian deputy province chief of Vinh Long.

38. Only after the Tet Offensive was ARVN equipped with the new M-16 rifles.

39. "Choose people with whom you trust your gold."

40. General Thanh died in 1971 when his C&C ran into a gunship while directing the invasion of Cambodia.

41. William M. Hammond, *Reporting Vietnam* (Lawrence: University Press of Kansas, 1998), 115.

42. Peter Braestrup, *Big Story* (Boulder, CO: Westview Press, 1977), 97, 98.

43. Marcus Raskin and Bernard Fall, *The Viet Nam Reader* (New York: Village Books, 1965), 376.

44. Letter from Col. Edward P. Metzner, USA (ret.), 25 May 1998.

45. The Psywar School created quite a scandal one day when, in presence of high-ranking Taiwanese officers, it staged a show in which the Vietnamese Army under General Tran Hung Dao, Viet Nam's most celebrated hero, soundly routed the Chinese Army.

46. *Leadership and Environment*, Military Review, U.S. Army Command & General Staff College, (Fort Leavenworth, Kansas, September 1972), 20.

47. After the war, it was revealed that Major Yet worked for the Viet Cong. His mission was to lead the commando team to my office, but he was killed by mistake by the commandos. He was cited posthumously for heroism by the Viet Cong after 1975.

48. Colonel Wyrough later resigned from the army and joined Ambassador Bunker's negotiation team on the Panama Canal.

49. *Military Academies and the Challenge of the Seventies*, Military Review, U.S. Command & General Staff College (Fort Leavenworth, Kansas, March 1972), 92-93.

50. FitzGerald, 369.

51. In his book, *It Doesn't Take a Hero* (New York: Bantam, 1994), General Schwarzkopf, the commander of Allied Forces in the Gulf War, and an advisor to Truong in Viet Nam, considered Truong one of the best tactical minds he had ever met.

52. After the war, it was reported that one soldier who served at the Military Academy was rewarded by the Viet Cong for having assassinated Colonel Su.

53. Hammond, 249.

54. Ibid.

55. Colonel Vy later became a general and commanded the 5th Division. Both Generals Vy and Hung committed suicide rather than surrender to the enemy in 1975.

56. General Vanuxem died shortly after the Viet Nam War and his daughter returned the flag of An Loc to the Vietnamese veterans in France.

57. Colonel Vang was later killed in a Communist concentration camp in North Viet Nam after 1975.

58. Arnold Isaacs, *Without Honor* (Baltimore: The John Hopkins University Press, 1983), 64.

59. William Le Gro, *Viet Nam from Cease-Fire to Capitulation* (U.S. Army Center of Military History, 1981), 128.

60. Henry Kissinger, *Years of Upheaval* (Boston; Little, Brown & Co., 1982), 32, 33.

61. Ibid., 330.

62. FitzGerald,

63. Under French rule, South Viet Nam, known as Cochinchine, was a French colony while North Viet Nam and Central Viet Nam had the status of French Protectorates.

64. Alfred McCoy, *Politics of Heroin: CIA Complicity in the Global Drug Trade* (New York: Harper & Row, 1991), 241.

65. Intelligence report from JGS.

66. Nguyen Khac Ngu, *Nhung Ngay Cuoi Cung Cua VNCH* (The Last Days of RVN) (Montreal: Nhom Nghien Cuu Su Dia, 1979), 168-69.

67. General Van Tien Dung, *Dai Chien Mua Xuan* (Great Spring victory), *People's Army Review*, (April & May 1975): 16.

68. Le Gro, *Viet Nam from Cease-Fire to Capitulation.*

69. Captain Thanh was killed during the evacuation of Danang. His A-37 jet fighter was hit by a NVA artillery shell on the runway during take-off.

70. Isaacs, 329.

71. Kissinger, *Years of Upheaval*, 370.

72. *People's Army Review* (April & May 1975).

73. Quoted by Nguyen Khac Ngu, 229.

74. Frank Snepp, *Decent Interval* (New York: Random House, 1977).

75. Nguyen Khac Ngu, 244.

76. In French in the original.

77. Colonel Khiem and Father Cong stayed behind after 1975 and were sent to a "re-education" camp for thirteen years.

78. Darcourt, 83-85.

79. General Don met me in California in 1985. He asked me to forget the past and to work for the future. In 1988, after I was elected chairman of the Leadership Committee of the Federation of Vietnamese Veterans, I offered General Don the post of vice chairman of the Committee.

80. Kissinger, *The White House Years*.

81. Snepp, 114.

82. Colonel Thoan rejoined his division after his family's departure. He was later sent to a re-education camp in North Viet Nam. He now lives in France.

83. Bui Tin defected to the West during a mission in Paris. He has since become a vitriolic critic of the Hanoi regime.

84. Duong Thu Huong, *Nhung Thien Dang Mu (Blind Paradise)* (Hanoi: np, 1988), 245.

GLOSSARY

APC	Armored Personnel Carrier
ARVN	Army of the Republic of Viet Nam
CBU	Cluster Bomb Unit
C&C	Command & Control
CP	Command Post
DAO	Defense Attache Office
DLO	Detachment of Liaison and Observation
DMZ	Demilitarized Zone
FLSVN	Front for the Liberation of South Viet Nam
FSB	Fire Support Base
FULRO	United Front for the Liberation of Oppressed People
GM	Groupement Mobile
GVN	Government of Viet Nam
ICCS	International Commission for Control and Supervision
JGS	Joint General Staff
KIA	Killed in Action
KK	Kampuchia Kraom (Free Kmer)
LSM	Landing Ship, Medium
LST	Landing Ship, Tank
LZ	Landing Zone
MAAG-V	Military Assistance and Advisory Group-Viet Nam
MAG-V	Military Assistance Command-Viet Nam
MIA	Missing in Action
MR	Military Region
NLA	National Liberation Army
NLF	National Liberation Front
NVA	North Vietnamese Army
NVN	North Viet Nam
PF	Popular Forces
POL	Petrolium, Oil, Lubricant

POW	Prisoner of War
PRG	Provisional Revolutionary Government
RF	Regional Forces
RN	Route Nationale
RVN	Republic of Viet Nam
SDF	Self Defense Force
TOC	Tactical Operation Center
VC	Viet Cong
VM	Viet Minh (Viet Nam Dong Minh Hoi or League of Vietnamese Alliance)
VNAF	Vietnamese Air Force
WIA	Wounded in Action

INDEX

I

J

K

N

W

X

Y

Z